Exploring Language
with Children

Exploring Language with Children

JOHN WARREN STEWIG

University of Wisconsin—Milwaukee

with chapters contributed by

Harlan and Ruth Hansen
and
Dorothy Huenecke

Charles E. Merrill Publishing Co.
A Bell & Howell Co.
Columbus, Ohio

Published by
Charles E. Merrill Publishing Co.
A Bell & Howell Co.
Columbus, Ohio

International Standard Book Number: 0–675–08885–2

Library of Congress Catalog Card Number: 73–85561

2   3   4   5   6   7   8   9   10—78   77   76   75

Printed in the United States of America

To Marge,
for helping me understand
the wisdom of Twain's maxim:

"The difference between the right
word and the almost right word is
the difference between lightning
and the lightning bug."

I can think of no better way to introduce this book on the teaching of the English language arts to children than to relate a classroom incident which seems to me to epitomize the spirit of this book. Serving as a language consultant in a school system, I was taken to visit a first-grade class in a small town on the Pacific Coast. When we entered the classroom a scene of pandemonium greeted us; chidren were standing on chairs, some were running about, many were shouting, and all were gazing upward. The center of their attention was a pigeon released to fly at will about the room. The excitement of the children was intense. The teacher allowed the action to continue for several minutes. Then on a signal to the owner of the pigeon, the bird was captured, returned to its cage; the children resumed their seats, and a reasonable degree of order prevailed.

When the teacher asked, "What did you see?" the raising and shaking of hands was furious. Everyone had seen memorable things and was bursting to relate them. One by one the children told the exciting things they had seen. With great wisdom the teacher permitted enough observations to be made while the interest was high, but not enough to dull the excitement. More than half the children had an opportunity to speak, while the others wildly signalled the desire to speak. Then the teacher said, "We all have such wonderful things to tell that I think we should share them and remember them by writing them down. How would you like to write a story about what you have seen?" Again the response was universal and avid. The children set to work, requiring no help from the teacher except for the spelling of words which she wrote on the chalk board.

After a time, a boy raised his hand and asked the question, "What do you call the color of the pigeon's neck? One minute it is pink, then it is blue, and then kind of mixed." The teacher replied, "You mean it is iridescent?" "Yes," said the boy, that's it. How do you spell it?" The teacher wrote "iridescent" on the chalk board. This boy and several other pupils observed in their stories that the neck of the pigeon was iridescent.

I was delighted to observe how readily these children, first graders with no more than six months of school experience, turned to writing. The slowest accomplished five or six lines of narration, equal in my experience to the work of many third graders. The fastest covered the front page with ten or eleven lines, and some turned the sheet over to continue on the back, a notable achievement for first graders in writing.

What had the teacher accomplished? She had first created a situation providing a novel and exciting experience. She terminated the experience while the interest and excitement were at their height. She encouraged oral response, and with subtle leadership, got the children to cover the range of the experience. Yet she terminated the speaking while the interest was still high, turning the children naturally and easily to writing. So motivated they wrote beyond normal expectation in both quantity and quality of statement.

The content and viewpoint of this book are in accord with the kind of teaching I have described above. Professor Stewig and his associates stress and restress the importance of active language use for children as early as possible in their home and school experience. They would applaud any teaching experience which aroused children to make a response into oral communication, and from oral communication to written communication. To promote these responses they would utilize every opportunity the classroom, the school, and the community can provide. They would awaken the imaginative responses of the children through literature, through classroom spontaneous drama, through the introduction of classroom visitors with a special experience to relate, and by means of brief or extended expeditions into the community itself. To teach language, then, this book recommends a procedure of experience with an aspect of life, resulting in an inward response of the child through interest and involvement, leading to response in words spoken naturally and to words written as an expected consequence. This procedure is not for small children alone; it is or ought to be continuous as children advance in language skill. Children in the upper grades need this important interlocking of experience and communication leading to responses in speaking and writing. Textbooks alone do not provide these experiences, yet in some classrooms in the upper grades no other source of language stimulation is offered beyond what the textbook provides.

The authors of this book not only endorse early, frequent, and active language use; they also stress the skills of listening. Today's children especially need this emphasis. They grow up in a setting of noise and confusion, often having to close their ears in self-defense. In many homes a constant blare of radio or televsion voices competes with the efforts of the occupants to communicate with each other. It is small wonder that many children do not listen at all, or only when extraordinary efforts are made to command their attention. Professor Stewig and his colleagues present much concrete help in this important but frequently ignored area of language experience.

In matters of grammar and usage, in earlier days too often the major content of language teaching, the spirit of this book is positive. For many years and by many teachers the presentation of the language arts to children was negative. They were instructed and drilled in what not to do when speaking or writing, but much less often encouraged to do any speaking or writing. The emphasis of this book is upon the doing, and of course learning while doing, but with a strongly positive position. While practically all speakers and writers need some correction in matters of word and phrase usage, the teaching of language skills to children should first induce communication and then apply to that communication such alterations as the nature of the content and the maturity of the writer or speaker would indicate. The communication comes first; after that is the time for emendation, conforming to expectation, and polishing.

In presenting grammar the authors are equally current and liberal. Grammar is presented as knowledge about the English language and its ways for the enrichment and understanding of the process of communication. Grammar is seen to be the description of language, not its guardian. Language makes the grammar. Understanding the grammar is a key to the development of powers of communication, but the grammar does not make the communication. The authors recognize that much of the natural grammar which directs English communication is already in the command of children when they enter the first grade.

School does not teach grammar; it brings the grammar already known to conscious use.

Artist teachers have written this book to assist in the production of artist teachers. Whatever minor faults may be found, the spirit and content of this book are highly commendable. The teacher who grasps the point of view and follows the specific recommendations to be found in it will be able to lead children to a competence in language beyond the ordinary, and in so doing will create users of English who admire, respect, and understand the nature of the language they use.

Robert C. Pooley

Professor Emeritus of English

The University of Wisconsin—Madison

The purpose of this book is to describe a wide variety of instructional strategies for involving children in exploring their language. The authors share a common view—that language is a vital and vibrant phenomenon, the study of which can be an exciting adventure. To the young child, the whole world is a fascinating encounter, and he studies it with an intensity at which adults marvel. The study of language, an integral and important part of the child's world, could be a similarly fascinating subject. The schools' pervading concern with acquiring proficiency in the outward forms of one type of language too frequently deadens a child's interest in language. To pique that interest, and the interest of his teacher, is the authors' purpose.

Chapter One describes how infants learn their language, and the proficiency children have developed by the time they reach school. The implications of this proficiency for school language programs are described. In Chapter Two, the author challenges us to think deeply about the purposes of an elementary language program, and the processes of planning such a program. She suggests learning objectives growing out of these processes which further the purpose of this book. In Chapter Three, the authors describe a language curriculum for early-childhood education which builds on and develops children's interest in language. The remaining chapters of the book deal with various specific facets of the language arts. The final chapter is concerned with a specific school population, the disadvantaged child.

The *Chapter Supplements* are a unique feature of the book. These are short reports written by undergraduate students preparing to be teachers. In these firsthand accounts, the writers describe ways in which they involved different groups of children in exploring language.

Two other features of this book are specifically designed to increase the teacher's interest in exploring language. At the end of each chapter Suggesstions for Further Study are included, which direct your language exploration to other areas related to the chapter. Sometimes these will direct you to materials which challenge the assertions made in this book. In addition, the majority of references in the book are annotated, in the hope that this will whet your appetite to explore by reading further.

Language: multiple, contradictory, always changing, a tool for thought, and reflective of the individual. These and many other things, but most of all—exciting. The child is immersed in language from the time his mother holds and comforts him with soothing sounds until he reaches school. For too many children, language then turns into something dull and frustrating. In the hope of keeping an interest in language alive, the authors have prepared this book, which encourages you to go exploring language with your children. Where will the exploration lead? No one but you and your children can know. Some directions have been suggested, but the possibilities are limited only by the limits of language itself.

John Warren Stewig

Contents

ONE   *Children and Language Learning*   *3*

TWO   *Curriculum in the Language Arts*   *29*

THREE   *Language in Early-Childhood Education*   *57*

FOUR   *Listening*   *87*

FIVE   *Oral Language*   *119*

SIX   *Spontaneous Drama*   *155*

   An Experience with Drama   *185*

SEVEN   *Writing with Children*   *193*

   An Integrated Language-Arts Unit   *227*

EIGHT   *Handwriting*   *239*

NINE   *Spelling*   *279*

   Individualized Spelling—It Can Be Done   *317*

TEN   *Learning about Language through Literature*   *325*

ELEVEN   *Vocabulary*   *353*

TWELVE   *Grammar and Usage*   *385*

THIRTEEN   *Language and the Disadvantaged*   *415*

   Index   *439*

*Exploring Language
with Children*

CHAPTER ONE

Children and
Language Learning

The doting mother leaning delightedly over the crib, cooing encouragement to her progeny is a common sight. Yet, as she does this, the mother may be unaware that her child is tremendously busy learning. From the moment of birth as the neonate bellows his protest, he is beginning one of the most impressive learning tasks attempted by man: the acquisition of language. From this noisy beginning until the child enters kindergarten, a prodigious feat is accomplished—the child learns his language.

In the beginning he lies in his crib and uses his tongue and lips to make a variety of sounds. Later, as a highly mobile and intensely curious preschooler he listens to and patterns after his peers. The child is learning the entire time: listening to sounds, making sounds, combining them in new and ingenious ways—always experimenting.

When he first begins experimenting, the young child makes a wide variety of sounds, many of which are unintelligible to listening adults. Gradually, those sounds which are not reinforced are dropped from the child's repertory of sounds, and speech becomes more understandable. Many developmental changes become apparent in the child as he grows. After this early experimentation, he begins to string sounds together into words. Still later, words on a string of thought are made into sentences, and so the child learns his language.

3

Though estimates vary among linguists and language scholars as to the age at which a child "knows" his language, agreement is general that the kindergarten child is in command of most of the language forms adult speakers use. One linguist has made the following contention:

> After the age of six there is relatively little in the grammar or syntax of the language that the average child needs to learn, except to achieve a school imposed standard of speech or writing to which he may not be accustomed in his home environment.[1]

This idea may sound a bit strange at first, for we know that the school devotes much instructional time to teaching children about their language. Why teach children about their language if they already know it?

To help answer this question we must make a distinction between two terms, *competency* and *knowledge*. Children do, indeed, have unconscious competency in *using* their language, i.e., the ability to produce appropriate linguistic forms in a given situation. This productive competency is usually attained by the age of six. They do not, however, have conscious knowledge of the structure, inner workings, and classification schemes describing their language. While children do come to school linguistically competent, conscious understanding of how the language functions is beyond them at this age. The authors of Chapter Three offer some specific suggestions about what aspects of language children are able to study consciously.

Children's Language and the Teacher

If the majority of this language learning goes on before a child enters school, of what concern is the process to teachers? Probably, if teachers at all grade levels knew more about this early language growth, language-arts programs in schools might be considerably different than they now are.

If teachers knew how much language children actually have and were aware of the linguistic sophistication possessed by the children

---

[1] John B. Carroll, "Language Development," in *Child Language, A Book of Readings,* eds. Aaron Bar-Adon and Weiner F. Leopold (Englewood Cliffs: Prentice-Hall, Inc., 1971), pp. 200–211. An extremely wide-ranging collection, ranging in date from 1927 to 1969, the book includes articles at many different difficulty levels, some exceedingly technical and some easy to read.

who sit in their classrooms, changes in teaching strategies could result. Today we still see large groups of children sitting mute listening to the teacher talk. Instead, small groups of children could be talking together as they enlarged their language patterns by verbalizing questions, opinions, thoughts, and doubts. Some specific instructional strategies related to this possibility are included in Chapter Three. Today, large numbers of children are frustrated by being unable to decipher those unintelligible marks in the beginning reading book. Instead, these children could be learning the joy of seeing their own fluent language springing into a new life in different form on paper. The authors of Chapter Three describe their ideas about reading and the young child. The author of Chapter Thirteen, in addition, describes her ideas about reading with the disadvantaged child.

The rest of this book will be concerned with identifying ways in which teachers can build on the language children speak. Each chapter, dealing with a different language art or skill, will assume that the most logical place to begin is with the competency the child already possesses. Specific instructional strategies and learning objectives suggested are designed to increase the child's basic competency. For now, it is enough to say that language programs could be considerably different than they are now if teachers fully understood the competency in language which children possess. Too often the school's enthusiasm for imparting knowledge about language overshadows the child's competency in using language.

How Is Language Learned?

Though interest in language is not new, the study of child language, particularly the means through which language is learned, constitutes an infant science.

As long ago as 1787 Tiedeman, a professor of philosophy at the University of Marburg, published the first significant studies of child language, a set of observations of children's speech patterns. Despite this early beginning, it is only within the last ten years that this tantalizing unanswered question has attracted many scholars' attention. In that decade, a wide variety of research studies were done which are beginning to provide answers to the question of how children learn language. Now, as a result of intensive investigations by a growing band of scholars, we know many interesting facts about children's learning of three major components of language: *phonology, mor-*

phology, and *syntax.*[2] Developmental stages have been identified, and acquisition procedures have been described; however, much work remains to be done. In the hope that this work may interest the teacher and encourage him to build on the competency children already have, some significant ideas about children's acquisition of language are examined here.

Developmental Stages

Study of the stages through which children pass in acquiring language has been done by several psychologists. As in the case of any listing of stages, the reader must keep in mind that the stages are relatively constant, though the rate may vary greatly. For example, the author of the following developmental sequence maintains that though phrases begin to appear between twenty-one and twenty-eight months, some normal children may not begin to speak in phrases until forty-eight months.

DEVELOPMENTAL STAGES IN CHILDREN'S LANGUAGE[3]

Age in Months	Nature of Language
4	coos and chuckles
6 to 9	babbles, produces such sounds as "ma" and "da"; reduplicates common sounds
12 to 18	small number of "words"; follows simple commands and responds to "no"
18 to 21	from about 20 words (at 18 mo.) to 200 words (at 21 mo.); understands simple commands; forms two-word phrases

[2] These three building blocks of language are explained more completely on pp. 388–91. Quite simply, *phonology* is the system of sounds in a language, *morphology* is the system of changes in word form, and *syntax* is the system of sentence structure. In addition to the treatment in this book, a very brief, though complete description, is included in William M. Austin, "The Suprasegmental Phonemes of English," in *Culture, Class and Language Variety,* ed. A. L. David (Urbana: National Council of Teachers of English, 1972), pp. 83–88.

[3] Adapted from Eric H. Lenneberg, "The Natural History of Language," in *The Genesis of Language,* eds. Frank L. Smith and George A. Miller (Cambridge, Mass.: MIT Press, 1966), p. 222.

Age in Months	Nature of Language
24 to 27	vocabulary of 300 to 400 words; two to three words in phrase, prepositions and pronouns
30 to 33	fastest increase in vocabulary, three- to four-word sentences; word order and grammatical agreement approximate language of surroundings
36 to 39	vocabulary of 1000 words or more; well-formed sentences using grammatical rules, though not all have been mastered; grammatical mistakes less common

Such identification of developmental stages tells us approximately *when* a child will be at a particular level of competency. Knowing when a child may be in a particular stage does not, however, give us any insight into *how* this happens. Several researchers have attempted to answer this question.

"He said his first word today . . .
Supersonic!"

The Mechanics of Acquisition

What processes does the young child use in acquiring language? Of what importance is his environment in aiding this acquisition? In this, as with many questions related to language there is no concensus about one correct answer.

One point of view which stresses the importance of biology is described by Eric Lenneberg, perhaps the best-known advocate of this theory.[4] Researchers who agree with him believe much of language acquisition is determined biologically and is not affected appreciably by the environment. Lenneberg has summarized the reasons for this belief. The importance of biological considerations is evidenced by:

1. the developmental schedule apparent in children. Both the onset and the order of developmental milestones are invariable.

2. the difficulty in suppressing language. The ability to learn language is so deeply rooted that children learn it, in spite of handicaps. Studies of children with several types of handicaps indicate that despite these, language is acquired.

3. the fact that language cannot be taught. Despite many efforts to teach language to animals, it appears that nonhuman forms of life cannot acquire true language.

4. the existence of language universals. Despite many superficial differences, all languages are based on the same organizing principles of semantics, syntax, and phonology.

Lenneberg's studies indicate that language is relatively independent of intelligence and that the basis for language capacity might well be transmitted genetically.

In summarizing, Lenneberg points out that children do, indeed, differ:

1. in their inclination to talk,

2. in their vocabulary, and

3. in what they have to say.

These factors may well be affected by environmental elements. The basic mastery of the linguistic system does not, however, differ greatly

---

[4] A brief explanation of this point of view is included in Eric H. Lenneberg, "A Biological Perspective of Language," in *New Directions in the Study of Language,* ed. Eric H. Lenneberg (Cambridge: The M.I.T. Press, 1964). This book includes papers by six other well-known language scholars.

from child to child, because of this innnate biological impulse to language.

In contrast, other researchers have investigated the role environment plays in language development. They have studied the differences between language development in middle-class children and those who are socially and economically disadvantaged. There are some quite apparent differences in verbal fluency between such groups of children. Interest in causes of such differences has led researchers to examine children's environments to find out which factors enhance language development. A complete summary of such research is beyond the scope of this chapter. However, a few studies will be described to give the reader an understanding of this point of view.

Brown and Bellugi examined the type of interaction which exists between mothers and preschool children, and their work increases our understanding of the role imitation plays in language learning.[5] The verbal interaction between mothers and their children from eighteen to thirty-six months of age was tape recorded. Then, the verbal interaction was analyzed to determine if mothers act in any predictable ways with their young children. As a result of the study, the researchers were able to describe quite completely some typical modes of behavior.

Much that happens between mother and child can be described as a process of *imitation* and *reduction*. That is, the mother says a sentence, and the child imitates it, in the process reducing some less important elements.

Mother's Sentence	*Child's Imitation*
1. "Fraser will be unhappy."	1. "Fraser unhappy."
2. "That's an old-time train."	2. "Old-time train."
3. It's not the same dog as Pepper."	3. "Dog Pepper."

It can be seen that the child preserves the word order or syntax of the mother's original sentence. He imitates, "Fraser unhappy," rather than "Unhappy Fraser." For the most part, the child retains the nouns, verbs, and adjectives in the mother's model. Word classes most frequently omitted are inflections, auxiliary verbs, articles, conjunctions, and prepositions. With this in mind, we can detect a strange similarity between these young children's sentences and abbreviated sentences adults use when sending telegrams. In both cases the high-information

---

[5] A more complete description of the experiment is included in Roger Brown and Ursula Bellugi, "Three Processes in the Child's Acquisition of Syntax," in *Language and Learning*, ed. Janet A. Emig et al. (New York: Harcourt Brace Jovanovich, 1966), pp. 3–24.

words are retained. Those words containing the biggest information loads, and, incidentally, receiving the heavier stress in the sentences, are imitated. Those words with low information value and which receive less stress are omitted.

Another process which occurs is that of *expansion*. Brown and Bellugi discovered that mothers frequently take a phrase, or idea fragment said by their child, and make it into a complete sentence, supplying what they assume are the missing words.

Child's Fragment	*Mother's Expansion*
1. "Mommy eggnog"	1. "Mommy had her eggnog."
2. "Sat wall"	2. "He sat on the wall."
3. "Pick glove"	3. "Pick the glove up."

An interesting parallel exists between this process and the previous one. In both, the syntactical arrangement is maintained, though in this case the mother adds auxiliaries, prepositions, verb forms, and articles.

Much of the verbal interaction between mothers and children can be seen, as a result of this study, to be cyclical. The mother says a sentence and the child repeats it, while reducing the number of elements included. The child says an idea fragment and the mother expands it, adding necessary elements. The process is apparently an important one in the language acquisition of children, though some conflicting evidence exists (See C. Cazden entry in the Bibliography).

The process described probably has implications for the language learning of culturally disadvantaged children, who frequently grow up in homes where an adult model may not be present. The study points to the crucial nature of the mother model, or some verbally trained substitute (if the mother must work). Since the process occurs as early as eighteen months and occurs with frequency, it is important that children be provided with such a language model. Probably preschool programs for three- and four-year-old children are too late because the most crucial language learning may well take place before then.

Another pair of researchers has explored mother-child relationships, examining the differences between middle-class and lower-class mothers. While Brown and Bellugi limited their study to verbal behavior, this study examined nonverbal behavior. Such behavior forms a significant part of early communication as much that transpires between mother and child is nonverbal. Schmidt and Hore examined three areas of communication:[6]

---

[6] Wilfred H. Schmidt and Terence Hore, "Some Nonverbal Aspects of Communication between Mother and Preschool Child," *Child Development* 41 (September 1970): 889–96.

1. body contact,
2. body closeness, and
3. glancing behaviors.

These communication elements are obviously more difficult to study than verbal behavior because of their transitory nature. Therefore, mothers and children were videotaped. Precise procedures for tabulating the incidence of each type of behavior were devised. It was found that lower-class mothers made more use of body contact, while middle-class mothers, whose language was more complex, made more use of glancing behaviors. The authors point out that such differences in mothers' behaviors may well influence the language behavior of the children.

Another researcher, while not denying the importance of a model in children's acquisition of language, points out that simple modeling may not adequately describe the process. Klima sees the process, even among the very young, as a sophisticated one in which the child uses data to form generalizations. Klima feels that, surrounded by innumerable examples of language, the child studies these and then makes deductions about the system. He says:

> In a sense, the child is like a linguist, making and rejecting hypotheses about the language . . . after ten years, the child knows all the principles of the English language. The child obviously poses the right questions and in the right order.[7]

Another writer whose description of the process agrees with Klima, but whose terminology to describe it differs slightly, is James Britton. He talks of language *improvisation*—the child takes forms he hears and makes variations on them as he searches for regularities in English. Britton says:

> It would seem to be nearer the truth to say that they imitate people's methods of going about saying things than to say that they imitate the things said.[8]

---

[7] Edward S. Klima, "Knowing Language and Getting to Know It," in *Language and Language Behavior*, ed. Eric M. Zale (New York: Appleton-Century-Crofts, 1968), p. 34.

[8] Britton, James N., *Language and Learning* (Coral Gables, Florida: University of Miami Press, 1970) p. 42. The quote is from the chapter "Learning to Speak," pp. 33–96. The summaries of Piaget's and Vygotsky's studies of children's language in this eminently readable book are a fine introduction to more complex works.

Children and the Phonology of English

The sound system, or phonology, of English forms the backbone of language. It is the first acquired and most pervasive of language forms. The child begins using his vocal apparatus at the moment of birth and continues talking as an adult much more than he uses any other type of communication.

It is commonly assumed that the child's cry at birth is his first sound. Interestingly, there is evidence to show that as early as the fifth month after conception, the foetus emits noises.[9] By the fourth month after birth, it is easy to distinguish comfort and discomfort sound in the child's cooing. A long process, the learning of categories of speech sounds, has begun.

Though estimates vary about how many different significant speech sounds exist in English, there is agreement that different categories of sounds are readily distinguishable. An early and continuing job for the child is to begin the process of acquiring these different categories. At first, a child makes only the unrestricted, open sounds similar to adult vowel sounds. Sound is at this point one large, indistinguishable category. Gradually, consonants are perceived as different from vowel sounds, resulting in two classes. These two classes are divided and redivided as the infant perceives and makes different categories of sounds.

The learning of the sound system is characterized by much experimentation. As the child lies in his crib, he babbles sounds—some remotely resembling English, others bizarre combinations to be eliminated from his "sound vocabulary" later as he senses the adults around him do not use them. It has been pointed out that at this age such experimentation with sounds is almost a full-time occupation. This babbling serves three purposes:

1. It is enjoyable and provides the equivalent of play for the young child.

2. It provides practice in the skill of making sounds.

3. It provides a stream of sounds from which parents select those they wish to retain. Those are reinforced while others atrophy because they are ignored.[10]

---

[9] Andrew Wilkinson, *The Foundations of Language* (London: Oxford University Press, 1971). The author, in clear, easily readable style summarizes many ideas about language acquisition. The chapters on oral language and reading will be of interest to the teacher.

[10] Adapted from Wilkinson, *The Foundations of Language*.

Not only does the child produce sounds, but he is developing his listening skills by hearing and responding to speech. It has been determined that as early as four to five months the child can distinguish between male and female voices.[11]

As he listens, the young child hears his parents use pitch, stress, and juncture to communicate meaning. Even before he understands the basic meanings of the words used, the child begins to understand these suprasegmental signals. Evidence exists which indicates that children pick up the "feeling-tone" transmitted by parents' speech before individual word meanings are learned.

Children and Word Forms in English

Children begin by producing sounds; these gradually are combined to make word-like forms. Often these one-word utterances, called *holophrases*, stand for a thought, more complete than the single word form would seem to indicate. Holophrases merge into short phrases, often two words in length, in a *telegraphic* stage. This in turn leads into more fully developed sentences.

At what point in this development do children perceive words as separate entities, apart from the stream of speech in which they are embedded? While a child may indeed understand the import of a sentence because of accompanying suprasegmental "messages," at what point does he begin to understand separate words? This question has intrigued researchers for some time. Several studies have been done in an attempt to find an answer.

One study used sixty-six children of 4½ to 5 years of age as subjects. Children were asked to separate a phrase into word units and then to reverse the units. The idea behind the procedure was that if children could perform the task, they were demonstrating knowledge of words as independent units. Though the evidence was not interpreted as completely conclusive, the researcher found enough children experiencing difficulty with the task to conclude that apparently children perceive in larger units than words and have difficulty in determining a word as a discrete unit.[12]

---

[11] E. L. Kaplan, *The Role of Intonation in the Acquisition of Language* (Ithica, New York: Cornell University, Ph.D. dissertation, 1969). (Available from University Microfilms, Inc., Ann Arbor, Michigan.) Kaplan also refers to research by A. R. Moffitt which reports that by five months, infants can distinguish between phonemes (the sounds) of English.

[12] Janellen Huttenlocher, "Children's Language: Word-Phrase Relationship," in *Child Language, A Book of Readings*, eds. Aaron Bar-Adon and Weiner F. Leopold (Englewood Cliffs: Prentice-Hall, 1971), pp. 319–21.

This lack of ability in understanding words as separate units is seen by some writers as causing difficulty in learning once children reach school. Bereiter and Engelmann, authors of a highly structured language program for culturally disadvantaged children, postulate that such children speak, not in distinct words, but rather in whole phrases or sentences which function like giant words. These phrases, the authors maintain, cannot be taken apart by the child and recombined and transformed in different ways. Yet, the child must be able to use language in this way in order to compete in school. To develop this ability in children, the authors have created a highly controversial program, for which they claim notable results.[13]

Another question, concerned not with the meaning of words but rather with their form, has intrigued researchers. How early do children learn to use the variety of word forms which are obligatory in English?

Morphology, or the study of word forms is a fascinating aspect of English.[14] Before we become adults, we must master such regular verb forms as *play* and *played* in addition to such irregular ones as *sing* and *sung*. Verbs are not the only morphological changes speakers of English must know. Nouns also inflect, or change form. Sometimes we add an /s/ to make a plural (boot, boots), sometimes we make internal changes (foot, feet), and at other times we do nothing (deer, deer). In addition, adjectives, adverbs, and pronouns demand form changes. Confusing to say the least!

When do children learn these rather elaborate procedures? Teachers often assume they "teach" children something about this aspect of English. In reality this is another feature of language which is largely learned by children before they enter school.

An early study examined this facet of English. Berko devised a test to determine if children could control the morphological aspects of English.[15] She was interested in finding out if children internalized the

---

[13] See C. Bereiter and S. Engelmann, *Teaching Disadvantaged Children in the Preschool* (Englewood Cliffs: Prentice-Hall, 1966). For a briefer explanation and defense of the approach, see Jean Osborn, "Teaching a Teaching Language to Disadvantaged Children," in *Language Remediation for the Disadvantaged Preschool Child*, ed. M. A. Brottman. Monographs of the Society for Research in Child Development, Serial #124, Vol. 33, No. 8, 1968, pp. 36–48. For a critical comment, see Suggestions for Further Study, page 21, Item #3.

[14] For a fuller explanation of this term, see page 390.

[15] Though her research has been replicated several times, Berko's original study remains of the most interest. See: Jean Berko, "The Child's Learning of English Morphology," *Word* 14 (1958): 150–77. A further aspect of the study is her investigation of children's understanding of compound words. These results indicated that children often have private and unshared meanings for these words, which interfere with communication because of their extremely personal nature.

morphological system and could generalize new cases, rather than if they could demonstrate rote memory of real words. For this reason she used made-up, or nonsense words, to illustrate the four most common aspects of English morphology:

1. plural and possessives of the noun,
2. third person singular of the verb,
3. progressive and past tense, and
4. comparative and superlative forms of the adjective.

Line drawings to illustrate each question were also prepared and were shown to the children as they responded to the test items. The items required that the children respond using correct form. To indicate their knowledge of pluralization of nouns, for example, children were shown a picture of an imaginary animal and were told: "This is a _____ (made-up word)." Then they were shown a picture of two such imaginary animals and asked how they would finish the sentence: "Now there are two _____."

Berko used the test with four to seven-year-old children and found that they had little difficulty in performing the tasks. She discovered, in contrast to findings in other tests of language ability, that in her test no significant differences existed between boys and girls. The children demonstrated that they had internalized the system of English morphology. She concludes: "there can be no doubt that children of this age range operate with clearly delimited morphological rules."[16]

Children and the Grammar of English

Grammar is a term ordinarily used to encompass all the structural elements of English. In this section we shall use it in a more limited way, however, to refer to a child's understanding of word function and syntactic relationships.

We, as adults, speak using all the available word classes, arranging them in elaborate patterns difficult to analyze. It was contended earlier that children, perhaps as early as six years of age, also use all these form classes and a wide variety of syntactic patterns. Do children start to use these elaborate structures as they begin to speak?

There is some evidence that in traveling toward a fully developed adult grammar of English, children move through a simpler system of

---

[16] Berko, "The Child's Learning of English Morphology," p. 171.

their own. Studies of children's language indicate that before such classes as noun, verb, adjective, adverb, and others are mastered, an intermediate step is necessary. This is commonly called the *pivot and open class grammar stage.*

As early as eighteen months, the two-word phrases which children make can be divided into two groups. The larger of these two groups includes *open* words which can be said by themselves or can appear with pivot words. Such words as *boy, sock, mommy, other, yellow,* and *lettuce* are included in this group. The second, smaller group is made up of *pivot* words which must always appear with an open word. Such words as *allgone, byebye, off, fall, pretty, a, dirty, this,* and *here* are included in this group.

Though certain words often appear in either the pivot or open class, such classification is not universal. When a word is a pivot word for a particular child, it is always a pivot word for that child, though the same word might be an open word for a different child.

The fascinating aspect of this pivot-open grammar idea is that, though completely untaught, it appears to be a universal phenomenon. Studies of German, Russian, Finnish and Samoan children, for example, reveal the presence of such a two-part pivot and open grammar in those languages. Although the terminology and descriptions vary,[17] researchers of children's language concur in the existence of this preliminary grammar form.

Contrast in English is apparent as early as this pivot and open-grammar stage and continues to be an important element in the language. Adult English grammar is full of contrasts, for instance, the difference between mass and count nouns, between affirmative and negative constructions, and between indirect and direct objects. How much of this do children know, and at what age? Recent studies indicate the previous question must be refined to specify what we mean when using the word "know," for one can know in different ways.

Lovel examined 180 children from ages two through eight, on ten grammatical concepts including the three mentioned in the previous paragraph.[18] He found there were significant differences in the children's abilities to perform three tasks. The children were asked to:

---

[17] Braine, for example, calls the categories pivot and X-words, using the latter term to describe the "residual" class into which all words other than pivot words go. See Martin D. S. Braine, "The Ontogeny of English Phrase Structure: The First Phrase," in *Child Language, A Book of Readings,* eds. Aaron Bar-Adon and Weiner F. Leopold (Englewood Cliffs: Prentice Hall, Inc., 1971), pp. 279–89.

[18] K. Lovel, "Some Recent Studies in Cognitive and Language Development," *Merrill-Palmer Quarterly* 14 (April 1968): 123–38.

1. *imitate* what the researcher did,
2. *comprehend* what the researcher asked, and
3. *produce* the contrast for which the researcher asked.

In all cases, the following relationship was found:

$$I > C > P$$

That is, ability to imitate (I) was greater than the ability to comprehend (C), which was greather than the ability to produce (P). Apparently, the ability to imitate is perfected first, with the ability to produce being perfected last.[19]

That children are intrepid in trying to produce language and are not content with simple imitation is evident. We have all heard a child try a sentence which was certainly intelligible, but not grammatically correct. Children frequently use such sentences as:

"Where I can put them?"
"Where I should put it?"
"What he can ride in?"

These are proof of the fact that though imitation, as described earlier, is important, it is not the only process a child undertakes. It is apparent that these sentences are not formed through simple patterning processes, as no adult would say them. Rather, it indicates that the child is attempting to produce sentences of his own. His understanding of grammatical complexities is limited; therefore, his sentences approximate adult forms, but do not quite succeed.[20]

The Language of Older Children

As children grow older their speech becomes more intelligible, and adults have a tendency to focus on their meaning, rather than on forms. Nursery school or kindergarten teachers often focus on *what* a child says, rather than on how he says it. In so doing, however, some de-

---

[19] Lenneberg in "The Natural History of Language" says comprehension usually precedes production by a few months, though in some cases this may be delayed much longer than that.

[20] For a more complete explanation of this, and of the growth in ability to form *WH* questions, see: Ursula Bellugi, "Linguistic Mechanisms Underlying Child Speech," in *Language and Language Behavior*, ed. Eric M. Zale (New York: Appleton-Century-Crofts, 1968), pp. 36–50.

velopmental phenomena as interesting as those found in earlier language acquisition may be missed.

A study of children's language done by the eminent Swiss psychologist Piaget resulted in his formulation of a theory of child language.[21] Rather than dealing with acquisition of basic grammatical forms, this theory is concerned with describing the child's ability to shape sentences for an audience. In this construct, formulated after observing children in school classes, all language is seen as belonging to one of two categories. Piaget believes all children pass through two stages, the *egocentric* stage and the *socialized* stage.

In the *egocentric* stage the child is unconcerned about whether or not he has a listener. He makes no attempt to determine the view or interest of the hearer. There are three types or categories of egocentric speech:

1. *repetition,* in which the child repeats sounds for the sensual pleasure of talking, including words which make no sense.
2. *monologue,* in which he talks as though he is thinking aloud and no attempt is made to address anyone.
3. *dual or collective monologue,* in which an outsider is always present, though in serving as a stimulus to talk, he is expected to neither attend nor respond. In such a situation the child is talking aloud in the presence of others, but ignores their indifference or responses.

The last category is very familiar to nursery school and kindergarten teachers. It is manifested, for example, when a group of children are painting at a table. The physical presence of the group stimulates children to talk. The child may describe what he is doing: "Now I'm painting the house's roof. See the green—it's dark. Now the brown chimney, way up at the top." Such talking may go on for an extended time, but no response is expected from the group.

In the second large category, *socialized* speech, the child is in some way responding, reacting, or interacting with other speakers. There are five types of socialized speech, including:

4. *adapted information,* in which the child exchanges his thoughts with others and is able to adopt the point of view of the listener.
5. *criticism,* including all remarks made about the work or be-

---

[21] Jean Piaget, *The Language and Thought of the Child* (Cleveland: The World Publishing Company, Meridian Books, 1965). The chapter on children's questions sheds light on a subject until now inadequately studied.

havior of others. In such cases, the language of the child is specifically directed to a given audience.

6. *commands, requests, and threats,* in which a definite interaction is apparent between one child and another.
7. *questions,* including most of those asked among peers, which require an answer.
8. *answers,* to real questions (with interrogation marks) and to commands.

Piaget is quick to acknowledge that, as with all classification systems, his is open to the criticism of arbitrariness. Nonetheless, its value to teachers and future teachers is obvious: it provides us with a way of thinking about children's language and of organizating our observations. (See Suggestions for Further Study, p. 21.)

At what point does a child pass from one stage to another? It is apparent in this, as in other developmental descriptions, that children take varying lengths of time to pass through the stages. A linguistically advanced child may enter the socialized stage long before one who has less language ability. In addition, the transition from one stage to another is not always permanent. That is, a child whose speech has been primarily socialized for some period of time may revert to the egocentric stage as a security measure. When a family breaks up in divorce or perhaps with the arrival of a threatening new baby, the child who has been using socialized speech may revert to egocentric speech until the problem has been dealt with.

One conclusion related to these stages may seem surprising to teachers of young children. Piaget has stated that *monologue,* one of the types of egocentric language, plays an important part in the language of children between the ages of 6 and 7. Further, he feels that egocentric language may account for nearly half of the total spontaneous speech of the child at the age of 6½. Is such the case with American children's language patterns today? This remains an interesting question which could be researched.

Another researcher concerned with child language is Lewis. He, too, has commented upon the phenomenon labeled by Piaget *dual monologue,* the speech carried on as the child does something. The activity may be painting a picture, building a block city, or pushing a truck around the floor. Often, speech is a concomitant part of the action. He says:

this self-addressed speech is more than an accompaniment to action
. . . it is part of the action, which is thus both non-linguistic and

linguistic. The words are a means by which a child is helped to direct his attention, to regulate what he is doing, to "think aloud."[22]

This phenomenon is also described by Luria, a respected Russian psychologist, who called it *planning speech*.[23] Though the terminology is different, it refers to the same thing. Luria says this speech is used by the child to anticipate his actions and to block out distractions as he carries out his plans.

Researchers and writers on this topic agree that, though this type of speech may become less frequent as children grow older, it does not completely disappear. Many times as adults we find ourselves verbalizing, despite the fact that we are alone. Such "talking-to-one's self" is common, but usually ignored. Yet, it is the counterpart of this early speech form.

Summary

Such a brief sketch of language acquisition can do little beyond illustrating some major areas in which a child grows as he makes what has been called a miraculous journey from the crib to kindergarten. Many of these language processes are still being explored; many of the questions remain unanswered. For the teacher, the implication of this chapter is that language acquisition is crucial. The child, at whatever age he comes to you, is an active producer of language. Though there may be some rough edges, some forms not yet controlled, in general he has a capacity for langauge which we must respect. The language curriculum you offer him must be more concerned with building on what he already possesses than with having him analyze someone else's sentences. That curriculum must help him gain an increasing sense of power in saying what he wants to say in original, innovative ways. In that way only can he come both to a sense of delight in using language and a sense of wonder in learning more about his language. The remainder of this book will attempt to identify many ways in which you

---

[22] M. M. Lewis, *Language and the Child* (The Mere, Bucks, England: National Foundation for Educational Research, 1969), pp. 32–33. You will find Part III, "In the Classroom," contains many valuable suggestions, as well as offering insights into British ideas about language education.

[23] This type of speech has a counterpart called *narrative speech*, which is used for recounting the past. Both are described in A. R. Luria and F. I. Yudovich, *Speech and the Development of Mental Processes in the Child* (London: Stapees Press, 1959).

can explore language with children to gain that sense of delight and wonder for your children and yourself.

Suggestions for Further Study

1. Read the book by Piaget, some details of which are summarized in this chapter (pages 18–19). What aspects of the research lead you to accept or reject parts of his theory about child language? What features of the research are similar to the Brown and Bellugi study?

2. Observe in a preschool or kindergarten situation for a short period of time. Record all the speech of at least two children. Attempt to analyze it in relation to Piaget's two categories. Do the children you observed use more egocentric language than the subjects in his study, or less? Are there some sociological factors about life in the United States today which might affect how much of each type of language children use?

3. Two favorable references to the work of Bereiter and Engelmann were included in this chapter, see page 14. In contrast, see the article by Sarah Moskovitz, "Some Assumptions Underlying the Bereiter Approach," *Young Children*, October 1968, pp. 24–31. She cites the danger of accepting a rigorous-appearing approach without examining its theoretical or empirical underpinnings. Which of these references seems to make the most convincing case?

4. The contention was made in the chapter that by the time they enter school, children use all the major sentence types. After reading about these sentence types (several sources are suggested in the chapter on grammar), observe the speech of some young children. Do those in your sample really make use of all the types?

5. Some writers believe the inability to deal with words as discrete units impedes the school progress of disadvantaged children. Bereiter and Englemann, mentioned in this chapter, are among them. Make a comparison between their statement about this issue and the work of Basil Bernstein, a British linguist, who has written about the same problem in British speech. How are the two positions similar or different?

6. The Berko study offers insights into children's language competency. Take some of the items from her test and use them with a group of nursery school or kindergarten children. What similarities or differences do you find between the children you test and the results she reported?

7. Analyze several lessons in an elementary language-arts series, at a grade level of your choice. What percentage of lessons seem designed to build on the child's language competency? What percentage attempt to increase his knowledge about language? Compare your results with those of other students. Are the percentages different at different grade levels?

Bibliography

Amsfeld, Moshe, and Tucker, G. Richard. "English Pluralization Rules of Six-Year-Old Children." *Child Development* 38 (1967): 1202–17.

This is one of several studies based on Berko's work, but in this study the researchers tested both production and recognition of forms. Their research leads to the conclusion that children are in control, but *not* in complete control, of this aspect of language by the age of six. Children deduced plural forms from the singular model, and singular forms from a plural model. The subjects did better on the first than on the second task.

Bolles, Edmund Blair. "The Innate Grammar of Baby Talk." *Saturday Review* 55 (March 18, 1972): 53–55.

The writer, a former Peace Corps worker in Tanzania, offers some interesting informal observations about language acquisition. Though his comments are highly derivative of more complex works by Chomsky, the interpretation of this material in light of linguistic patterns in Tanzania is engaging.

Cazden, C. "Environmental Assistance to the Child's Acquisition of Grammar." Ph.D. dissertation, Harvard University, 1965.

This study raises questions about the importance of the expansion process, particularly in light of results attained by *expatiation*, a process of reinforcing through sentences related to what the child said, but not expanding as such. Comparing three groups of black children assumed to be linguistically deprived, Cazden found the expatiation group more advanced at the end of the treatment period.

Chomsky, Noam. "Language and the Mind." *Psychology Today* 1, no. 9 (February 1968): 48–51.

An eminent linguist describes acquisition of language as the process of theory construction. Chomsky feels the child discovers theories of language using only small amounts of data, at a time when he is not capable of complex intellectual achievements in many other domains. It is his contention that this complex theory building is relatively independent of intelligence and experience. The child is able to select hypotheses and confirm or deny his choices with the limited amount of evidence available.

Dale, Philip S. *Language Development*. Hinsdale, Ill.: The Dryden Press, Inc., 1972.

The author's easy-to-follow style and clear explanations of complex theories make this a fine introduction. The book conveys Dale's enthusiasm for his topic and should develop similar enthusiasm in his readers. Most of the chapters conclude with at least one related reading, presenting another point of view, in addition to extensive reading and reference lists.

Ervin-Tripp, Susan. "Language Development." In *Review of Child Development Research*, edited by L. W. and M. L. Hoffman. New York: Russell Sage Foundation, 1966.

The chapter contains a complete consideration of very early language development, including studies pointing out that differences in the effects of stimulation and reward are not apparent until after the first three months. She acknowledges that there is no known relation between the sounds made in the prelinguistic period and real speech.

The section of the chapter on phonological development is easier to understand than is usual in material of this nature. The explanation of the way in which learning is a sequence of progressively finer discriminations of sound differences is helpful. The sections on syntactic and morphological development point out clearly that the age at which control of the language is accomplished varies with different languages.

The chapter closes with a section on the functions of language, including comments on the idea that speech is an accompaniment to action. The material included on style variations evident in different situations has implications for classroom teachers. A glossary and bibliography are included.

Lavatelli, Celia Stendler. *Language Training in Early Childhood Education*. Champaign, Ill.: ERIC Clearinghouse in Early Childhood Education, 1971.

A valuable summary of language development research is included in Chapter 1 (pp. 3–48), by Donald Moore. Chapter 2 (pp. 49–59) contains a useful explanation of the difference between deep and surface structure. The child's understanding of the transformation process is explained and suggestions for how to teach this idea are included. The third section of the book contains a chapter by Bellugi-Klima, a respected linguist, describing a test for eliciting what children know about language.

McNeill, David. "The Development of Language." In *Charmichael's Manual of Child Psychology*, Vol. 1, edited by Paul H. Mussen. New York: John Wiley and Sons, Inc., 1970.

This is probably the most complete summary source available. Despite the exhaustive treatment, the author does refer readers to the earlier summary by McCarthy (in the second edition, 1954) for coverage of earlier research.

The chapter opens with consideration of telegraphic and holophrastic speech, pivot and open class, and other early grammatical classes, with an extensive recapitulation of significant research.

A description of the language acquisition device as formulated by Chomsky is a helpful inclusion. The way in which language is processed through this, as hypotheses are generated regarding the regularities underlying speech, is also described.

The role of parental speech is examined, with particular attention to how this speech is filtered through the child's developing system of rules. Other topics considered include negation and question transformations, and the minimal information available on semantics.

The chapter does require a fairly sophisticated understanding of linguistics, or a willingness to "dig-out" the sometimes abstruse points being explained. This is despite the author's admirably lucid writing style.

The chapter closes with an extensive Linguistic Appendix (p. 1138) and an equally complete bibliography, both of which will help a student with a continuing interest in the topic.

MacGinitie, Walter M. "Language and Development." In *Encyclopedia of Educational Research*, edited by Robert L. Ebel. New York: The Macmillan Co., 1969, pp. 686–99.

The author surveys and summarizes all of the significant research in this area; the result is a valuable introduction to a complex field. His reservation about accepting without question research which has been done is important. Much of this research has been done with unusually bright children (often the investigator's own children) in somewhat atypical situations (alone with adults in a problem-solving context). Because of this, results must be interpreted cautiously. While all children may indeed go through the stages described, the ages at which this happens with more typical children may be different.

Mecham, Merlin J. *Audiolinguistic Skills in Children*. St. Louis, Mo.: Warren H. Green, Inc., 1969.

The discussion of differences between production and comprehension abilities is clear and points out the important role imitation plays in the acquisition of phonology. There are particularly helpful suggestions on language tests, and on the role of the teacher who has a language-delayed child in her classroom (Chapter 5, pp. 44–65).

Osser, Harry et al. "The Young Child's Ability to Imitate and Comprehend Speech." *Child Development* 40, no. 4 (December 1969): 1063–76.

Subjects used were four- and five-year-old middle-class whites and lower-class Negroes, who responded to production and recognition tasks. Data were analyzed taking into account the major nonstandard English dialect differences as outlined by Loban. Despite this compensation, the LCN group made more errors on both measures than did the MCW. The researchers concluded that decoding an unfamiliar dialect penalized the LCN group. There were substantial differences in both groups between imitation (production) abilities and recognition abilities.

Rodd, Linda J., and Braine, Martin D. S. "Children's Imitations of Syntactic Constructions as a Measure of Linguistic Competence." *Journal of Verbal Learning and Verbal Behavior* 10 (August 1971): 430–43.

This article reports research typical of much investigation in this area: intensive experimentation with small groups of subjects concerning complex grammatical questions. In this study, researchers used male and female subjects, ages twenty-one to twenty-eight months, to clarify the relationships existing between production and imitation abilities of children. The study confirms the observation that children do not simply echo the adult models heard, but rather assimilate and reorganize the model utterance.

Slobin, Dan I. *Psycholinguistics*. Chicago: Scott, Foresman and Co., 1971. An easily readable introductory paperback, this presents especially valuable information about grammatical models in understandable terms. The sections on transformations, and on phonological acquisition are also of interest.

CHAPTER TWO

Curriculum in the Language Arts

by Dorothy Huenecke

The language arts occupy an important place in elementary school programs. The term *language arts* includes the primary communication skills of reading, spelling, and speaking as well as such unifying skills as creative writing, drama, and interpretive listening. How these skills can be integrated into a harmonious entity, forming the basis for the majority of human learning, is a major curriculum concern. For the classroom teacher wrestling with the problem of a desirable interrelationship among the language arts *and* the relation of language skills to other skills, numerous questions are perturbing. Typical questions are:

> What language skills are really important for learners at any particular stage of development?
>
> How can the broad outlines of what is important be specified in detail?
>
> Which instructional resources can best contribute to the attainment of my purposes?
>
> How can I teach spelling to learners who aren't really interested?
>
> How much should I stress reading?

29

Do I have to teach drama?

How should I use the graded language-arts series?

General answers to such questions as these can be sought through the study of a rational approach to curriculum development. As these questions exemplify, curriculum development is a process involving decisions about: What? When? For whom? How? Prior to concern with these questions, however, comes the most fundamental question: *Why?* The field of curriculum points to ways of dealing with this question also. To this end, a discussion of the rational approach to curriculum development is presented.

Rational Curriculum Development

In a rational approach to curriculum, consistency is the hallmark. Consistency is required in the curriculum decisions made at various levels of responsibility. The basic level is society or the community which a school serves. Following directly from the societal level is the institutional level, comprised of such school personnel as superintendents and principals. One of the major responsibilities at this level is the management of the schools in ways consistent with the community's value orientation. The next level of decision making, the instructional level, consists primarily of teachers. Among the major responsibilities of the teacher is the identification of purpose, the design of methods to attain purpose, and the evaluation of progress toward the desired purpose, all of which need to be in harmony with the community's expectations. Figure 1 presents a model based on Goodlad and Richter to illustrate this relationship.[1]

A closer examination of these levels can emphasize the need for consistency. The *societal level* is represented by such agencies as school boards and the local, state, and federal government. These agencies might determine general aims to be pursued, but they are not usually concerned with specific proposals for attaining these aims. A typical product from this level of decision making is a statement of goals for a school system, prepared by the local board of education.

The *institutional level* involves decisions made by central office and supervisory personnel, administrators, or curriculum committees. These

---

[1] John I. Goodlad and Maurice N. Richter, Jr., *Development of a Conceptual System for Dealing with Problems of Curriculum and Instruction,* Cooperative Research Project No. 454, United States Office of Education (Los Angeles, University of California and Institute for Development of Educational Activities, 1966).

Levels of Decision Making   *Areas of Decision Making*

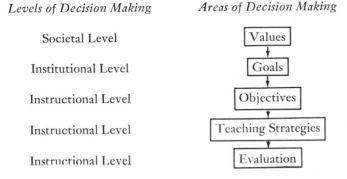

Societal Level

Institutional Level

Instructional Level

Instructional Level

Instructional Level

Figure 1— *A Conception of the Curriculum Decision-Making Process*

decisions are made for types of learners rather than for specific children. Decisions might be made regarding the type of experience an eight year old might find stimulating or the organization of the language-arts content. A typical product from such a group is a curriculum guide.

At the institutional level, knowledge about learning theory, philosophical concepts, contemporary society, and subject matter can be used in the decision-making process, but information about individual learners in specific situations is unavailable. Decisions are made for hypothetical learners who are prototypes of individuals.

The *instructional level* involves decisions made by a teacher or team of teachers who have direct responsibility for specific children. Curriculum decisions at this level include those relating to specific objectives and the feasibility of a particular activity for a specific group of learners. In this case, information about individuals is an important source of data.

Instructional-Level Decisions. It is at the instructional level that teaching occurs and that the learners can be found. This is undoubtedly the level of decision making of most interest to the readers of this book. To examine it in greater detail, four classic questions having great relevance for the teacher should be studied:

1. What educational purposes should the school seek to attain?
2. What educational experiences can be provided that are likely to attain these purposes?
3. How can these educational experiences be effectively organized?

4. How can we determine whether these purposes are being attained?[2]

To put it another way, the identification of direction or purpose is the essential first decision required of the teacher. His purposes should be consistent with those of the institution. Following this, the development and organization of educational experiences or learning activities is needed. Last, evaluation is necessary to determine whether the specified purposes have been attained. This process is illustrated in a model from Duncan and Frymier shown in Figure 2.[3]

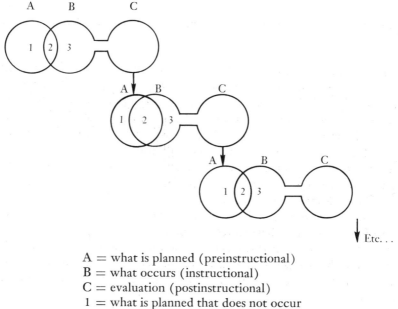

A = what is planned (preinstructional)
B = what occurs (instructional)
C = evaluation (postinstructional)
1 = what is planned that does not occur
2 = what occurs that has been planned
3 = what occurs that has not been planned

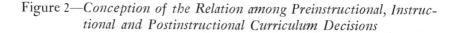

Figure 2—*Conception of the Relation among Preinstructional, Instructional and Postinstructional Curriculum Decisions*

[2] Ralph W. Tyler, *Basic Principles of Curriculum and Instruction* (Chicago: University of Chicago Press, 1950).

[3] James K. Duncan and Jack R. Frymier, "Explorations in the Systematic Study of Curriculum," *Curriculum Theory Development: Work in Progress, Theory into Practice*, vol. 6 (Columbus, Ohio: College of Education, The Ohio State University, 1967).

If A and B are congruent, everything which has been planned occurs in the teaching situation and everything that occurs in the teaching situation has been planned. In actuality, this rarely happens. More frequently, much of what has been planned occurs, but much unanticipated instruction also occurs.[4] One of the major reasons for considering the above four questions is to reduce (not necessarily eliminate) the inefficiency and ineffectiveness which result when there is little consistency between preinstructional and instructional decisions.

The instructional level of curriculum decision making forms the focus of this book. More precisely, much of the rest of this book is devoted to learning activities or teaching strategies in the language arts.

But how does the teacher decide which strategies are appropriate for him in *his* situation with *his* students? Clearly, there are vast numbers of teaching strategies and resources, but teachers operate with limited time facilities and resources. In order to resolve what may be a source of conflict, teachers should reach decisions about strategies with conscious knowledge of their own values and goals.

Although the classroom teacher is influenced by societal values and institutional goals, he needs to examine his own values and goals to deal rationally with the curriculum decisions that bombard him. Teacher's personal values and goals need to be congruent and/or complementary to the society and institution being served if the teacher is to remain happy and mentally healthy in his teaching situation. It is no small wonder that rationality is to be desired under conditions such as these! Figure 3 illustrates the dilemma.

In the sections that follow, values, goals, objectives, teaching strategies, and evaluation techniques will be examined.

Values

In today's ever-changing, fluid society it is unwise to generalize about group values, expectations, or mores since many of these may be ethereal. Shifts in societal values have been hypothesized by many writers.[5] The value shifts they have suggested, particularly in relation to such topics as work, sex, money, and family structure, may have a vital impact on what society expects from education.

---

[4] Dorothy M. Huenecke, "The Relation of Teacher Expectations to Curriculum Guide Implementation" (Ph.D. diss., University of Wisconsin, 1969).

[5] See chapter bibliography entries Mead, Packard, Reich, Toffler, and Whyte.

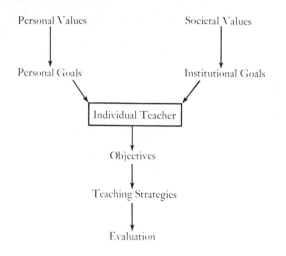

Figure 3—*The Curriculum Decision Dilemma at the Instructional Level*

It is very difficult to determine contemporary values or hypothe-size future direction. A major problem in assessing societal values is that they can best be viewed historically. It is virtually impossible to determine current mores or values, particularly if they differ from those that have become conventional.

For the classroom teacher, local community values and expecta-tions may have more relevance than those of the larger society. In a country as vast as the United States, including virtually every type of geography, topography and climate, populated by people from every walk of life, having within its borders members from many religious and ethnic groups, the views of the local subculture may be far more influential than those of the larger society. Assessment of these views and how they contribute to an educational environment is a necessary pre-requisite for rational curriculum development.

Personal Values.   As indicated in Figure 3, evaluation of one's own personal values is needed also. Attitudes, beliefs, and values are terms often used interchangeably in discussing the "feeling" dimension of humans. In actuality, the difference among these terms is probably one of degree rather than kind. *Attitudes* are fairly transient responses to certain situations; *beliefs* are somewhat more stable and deep-seated. *Values* refer to the deepest and most meaningful human feelings; they affect not only one's thoughts, but his actions as well.

Seven criteria a feeling must meet in order to be classified as a value are suggested in the book *Values and Teaching*.[6] The criteria include:

choosing
1. freely
2. from alternatives
3. after thoughtful consideration of the consequences of each alternative

prizing
4. cherishing, being happy with the choice
5. willing to affirm the choice publicly

acting
6. doing something with the choice
7. repeatedly, in some pattern of life.

Three major criteria are stressed. First, values must be chosen, not imposed. Second the person holding a particular value must be proud of it. Third, feelings classified as values must be manifested in behavior; if a feeling is not supported in action, it is not a value.

A rationale for much human behavior can be found in the individual's values though identifying these is not easy. Introspection may yield the identification of several feelings that meet the valuing criteria. In addition, *Values and Teaching* describes numerous strategies that can be utilized in the value-clarification process. This book is an excellent resource for teachers who want to examine values with their students, but it is also useful in suggesting procedures to be used in examining one's own values.

In the investigation of personal values, it is important to keep in mind that *no area of human concern is irrelevant in dealing with values in relation to education.* Although values concerning individual worth, work, and intelligence have an obvious relation to the classroom behavior of the teacher, any affective area has relevance in the interaction among human beings, especially in schools. In *Values and Teaching* ten areas are identified that are particularly fertile for yielding data about values:

1. money
2. friendship
3. love and sex

---

[6] Louis E. Raths, Merrill Harmin, and Sidney B. Simon, *Values and Teaching* (Columbus, Ohio: Charles E. Merrill Publishing Co., 1966).

4. religion and morals
5. leisure
6. politics and social organization
7. work
8. family
9. maturity
10. character traits

If a person can become increasingly aware of his feelings in relation to such topics as these, he will increase his self-knowledge. For teachers, this awareness may aid in identifying what is important for education. Clarification of such ideas results in the establishment of educational goals.

Educational Goals

Educational goals are broad statements that generally identify desirable ends of education. Goals are long range; it may be intended, for example, that goals be attained by the end of twelve years of schooling.

Innumerable sets of goals have been developed. Virtually every school district has a list which they have either developed or adapted from another source. Although most of these sets of goals are very similar, it is, nonetheless, crucial for teachers to examine carefully what has been outlined as important by their school district. As a result, curriculum decisions at the instructional level can be congruent and/or complementary with those made at the institutional and societal levels.

State Department Goals. Another source for goal statements is state departments of education. In the state of Georgia, for example, the Georgia Board of Education developed a set of goals appropriate for "children and youth—to live successfully in the Georgia and United States of 1985 and beyond." To accomplish this, four tasks were undertaken:

1. The examination of the social, economic and political life of Georgia.

2. The projection of the probable social, economic, and political life in Georgia through 1988.

3. The identification of goals for education; the knowledge, skills, and values that will enable the citizen of Georgia to live successfully in the future.

4. The projection of the type of education system necessary to achieve the desired goals.

As a result, a list of seventy-seven goals was developed. Some which might appropriately be the concern of the language arts are included below:

1. The Individual and Himself
   The individual possesses the ability to read, speak, write and listen.
2. The Individual and Others
   The individual possesses the ability to understand and cope with dissent.
3. The Individual and his Physical Environment
   The individual possesses an appreciation of the beauty of nature.
4. The Individual at Work
   The individual possesses pride in workmanship and accomplishment.
5. The Individual at Leisure
   The individual uses as a listener, participant, and/or observer one or more of the arts or crafts in recreational and leisure time activity.[7]

National Sources of Goals. Educational goals may be developed by the federal government through such activities as the White House Conference on Education. National education organizations also formulate goals to reflect the thinking of their members. Statements of goals or purpose may be obtained from such organizations as the International Reading Association, the National Council of Teachers of English, and the Association for Supervision and Curriculum Development.

Goals from these sources may be widely publicized and discussed, but there tends to be less follow-through on them than on district-wide or state goals. In general, the farther removed the source of goals at the institutional level from the situation where they are to be implemented, the less likely they are to be translated into objectives, at the instructional level.

Teacher Goals. Regardless of the source of goals, the teacher needs to define for himself what *he* believes are the important outcomes of a long-term educational experience. Generally, the major task is not identifying worthwhile goals but ordering priorities among them.

---

[7] Division of Planning, Research, and Evaluation, *Goals for Education in Georgia* (Atlanta, Georgia: Georgia Department of Education, 1970).

Examining basic feelings and values may expedite this perplexing task. Whether goals are formulated by individuals or institutions, however, several common elements are generally considered:

1. The nature and concept of the society in which these goals will operate.
2. An image of the type of person education is striving to create.
3. The structure and amount of knowledge available at any particular time.[8]

As the goals cited in this section evidence, goals are statements identifying such broad behaviors they offer only *macroscopic* direction for the teacher. To be practical in terms of everyday use, goals need to be refined into objectives that provide *microscopic* direction. Translation of goals into detailed objectives takes place on the instructional level of decision making as described in the following sections.

Instructional Objectives—One Approach

Instructional objectives are statements of intent for specific learner behavior. They vary from goals in that they are more specific—so much so they can realistically be attained in thirty minutes to an hour of instruction.

Decisions pertaining to instructional objectives require much teacher time and consideration. In specifying objectives, teachers have access to many aids: textbooks, curriculum guides, programmed materials. Regardless of the expertise of those who prepared these materials, however, one essential component is lacking—only the professional teacher in the situation has access to the specific learners. Knowledge of students' needs, interests, and abilities is crucial at the instructional level.

Mager Objectives. A widely used format for stating objectives is based on *Preparing Instructional Objectives* by Robert Mager.[9] Essentially, three components are required:

1. the conditions under which an identified behavior is to occur
2. a readily observable behavior
3. the criteria of acceptable performance

---

[8] Lowell Keith, Paul Black, and Sidney Tiedt, *Contemporary Curriculum in the Elementary School* (New York: Harper and Row, Publishers, 1968).

[9] Robert F. Mager, *Preparing Instructional Objectives* (Palo Alto: Fearon Publishers, 1962).

The first phrase in these objectives is a description of the conditions under which the behavior should occur. The conditional phrase identifies the situation in which the learner is to demonstrate his attainment of the behavior. Examples of conditional statements include: "Given a human skeleton . . .," "After viewing the film 'The Five Chinese Brothers' . . .," and "After the class has agreed on a title for the picture. . . ."

The second phrase identifies the desired learner behavior. Using Mager's format, it is imperative that the behavior be observable. The following behavioral terms are useful in stating this type of objective:

write	perform	dissect
recite	verbalize	assemble
list	arrange	reproduce
construct	circle	complete
rephrase	pantomime	underline

The last phrase describes minimal acceptable performance. If the established criterion is not achieved, the objective has not been attained. Criterion performances most often are described in quantifiable terms; the concept of percentages is useful in this regard.

It should be clear that these are highly structured statements requiring a high degree of specificity. This fact contributes significantly to the *usefulness* of these objectives as well as to their *uselessness*. That is, these statements should be used only when a precise, predictable outcome is desired, for instance, in such areas as punctuation, spelling, and pantomime. The following objectives serve as examples:

1. Given a paragraph with no punctuation at the end of sentences, the student should be able to place a period, an exclamation point, or a question mark correctly in thirteen of the fifteen sentences.
2. When presented with the words orally, the student should be able to write his spelling words with 100 percent accuracy.
3. When given a slip of paper with a description of a common activity written on it, the student should be able to pantomime the activity so that the other students can correctly identify what he is pantomiming within one minute.

This type of objective has questionable value when individuality of response is desired. Mager objectives should be used in situations where an accurate outcome is possible. They are appropriate *only* in convergent situations where correct information is obtainable. In situations where a large number of answers exist or where accurate information is unobtainable, this type of objective is unsuitable.

Instructional Objectives—Another Way

A second widely used format for stating objectives is based on the taxonomies of educational objectives which classify human behavior into three realms: cognitive, affective, and psychomotor.[10] In contrast to the Mager-type objective, when the cognitive and affective taxonomies are utilized, behaviors are identified that are *not* readily observable. Nonobservable intellectual and emotional behaviors from the taxonomies are specified for which behavioral indicators must be identified when evaluation is made.

Further, the conditions under which the behavior is to occur and the criterion performance are not identified. Thus, use of the taxonomies results in an objective statement that specifies only the behavior and the content to which it is to be applied. Examples of this type of objective and a discussion of the taxonomies follow. Further examples of this type of objective are found in Chapter Three.

Cognitive Taxonomy. The cognitive taxonomy lists six major categories of cognitive or intellectual behavior, which are sequential and cumulative. They represent a hierarchy of behavior; each behavior prepares for the next while including all those that precede it in the classification. Objectives based on the cognitive taxonomy can be employed in virtually any area of the language arts. Even for such skills as penmanship which basically requires muscular coordination, knowledge is required. The major cognitive levels, examples of behavior at each level, and sample objectives are presented below:[11]

1.0 KNOWLEDGE

Knowledge involves recalling such things as specifics, methods, processes, or structure. It is concerned with bringing to mind appropriate material. Little, if any, alteration of the material is required.

Objectives stated at this level could employ such behavioral terms as:
a. define
b. recall
c. recognize

---

[10] See chapter bibliography entries Bloom, Krathwohl, and Simpson.

[11] Benjamin S. Bloom, ed., *Taxonomy of Educational Objectives, Handbook I: Cognitive Domain* (New York: David McKay, Inc., 1956).

Sample objectives:
The student should recognize capital letters in cursive writing. The student should recall the definitions of the following terms: transformational grammar, syntax, word class.

2.0 COMPREHENSION

This level involves understanding the literal message of an idea, including the ability to translate, interpret, and extrapolate.

Objectives stated at this level could employ such behavioral terms as:
a. translate (verbalize mathematical symbols, etc.)
b. draw inference
c. generalize
d. summarize
e. draw conclusions
f. predict

Sample objectives:
The student should generalize about the writing style of E. B. White.
The student should translate his reading story into a play.

3.0 APPLICATION

Application involves the ability to use abstractions in concrete situations. The abstractions could be general ideas, rules, methods, principles, or theories which need to be remembered and applied.

Objectives stated at this level could use the term:
a. apply

Sample objectives:
The student should apply his knowledge of short vowel sounds as found in the consonant-vowel-consonant pattern in figuring out new words that follow that pattern.
The student should apply his knowledge of suffixes to make the following words plural: . . . .

4.0 ANALYSIS

This level involves breakdown of material into constituent parts so the relation among parts is clear. Such analyses will illuminate the basis and organization of the material.

Objectives stated at this level could employ such behavioral terms as:
a. classify
b. identify elements
c. detect (fallacies, causal relations, etc.)

Sample objectives:

The student should classify the following words as to their word class: . . . .

The student should identify the common elements in "The Three Little Pigs," "Snow White and the Seven Dwarfs," and "Little Red Riding Hood."

5.0 SYNTHESIS

Synthesis involves the putting together of elements and parts of a whole. This process combines elements to form a structure that is new to the learner.

Objectives stated at this level could employ such behavioral terms as:

a. design
b. integrate
c. propose
d. formulate
e. create

Sample objectives:

The student should create an original story using the format of a fairy tale.

The student should integrate at least two propaganda techniques into an original TV commercial.

6.0 EVALUATION

This level involves making judgments in terms of *internal* evidence (organization, consistency, etc.) or in terms of *external evidence* with reference to standards of criteria.

Objectives stated at this level could employ such behavioral terms as:

a. distinguish
b. assess

Sample objectives:

The student should evaluate the effectiveness of the use of metaphors in a poem of his choice containing at least three metaphors.

The student should evaluate a TV commercial using criteria which he establishes.

Affective Taxonomy.   The same general assumptions forming the basis of the cognitive taxonomy also apply to the *affective taxonomy.* That is, levels presented below are sequential and cumulative.

The following levels comprise the affective taxonomy:[12]

---

[12] David Krathwohl, et al., *Taxonomy of Educational Objectives, Handbook II: Affective Domain* (New York: David McKay, Inc., 1964).

1.0 RECEIVING

At this level the learner is sensitized to the existence of certain phenomena and stimuli. The learner is willing to receive these stimuli while remaining neutral or in a state of suspended judgment.

Objectives stated at this level could employ such behavioral terms as:
a. aware of
b. conscious of
c. sensitive to

Sample objectives:
The student should be aware that poetry can be written in many forms.
The student should be sensitive to the fact that there are many interpretations of Robert Frost's poetry.

2.0 RESPONDING

Responding involves doing something with or about the phenomena.

Objectives stated at this level could employ such behavioral terms as:
a. obeys
b. accepts
c. enjoys
d. participates
e. is interested in
f. appreciates
g. rejects

Sample objectives:
The student should participate willingly in a spelling game.
The student should enjoy reading.

3.0 VALUING

At this level the learner displays a particular behavior consistently in appropriate situations.

Objectives stated at this level could employ such behavior terms as:
a. desires
b. is committed to
c. is devoted to
d. values

Sample objectives:
The student should value the right of everyone to express his opinions.

The student should be committed to taking care of the books in his room.

4.0 ORGANIZATION OF VALUES

As more and more values are internalized, situations arise where more than one value is relevant. At this level, the learner is continuously involved in organizing his values into a hierarchy or harmonious relationship.

5.0 CHARACTERIZATION BY A VALUE OR VALUE COMPLEX

At this level of internalization, the values that have been previously organized control the behavior of the learner to the extent that he is described or characterized according to these values. He acts according to these values without conscious thought. A total philosophy or world view is developed. This level takes a long time to achieve and is changed only by a traumatic experience.

Instructional objectives based on the first three levels of the affective taxonomy can be used for any area of the language arts. Levels four and five are not appropriate when considering instructional objectives because they involve long-range behaviors. Because objectives are statements of purpose that can realistically be attained after one or a few sessions, the more advanced affective behaviors cannot realistically be attained under these conditions. Instead these levels are better described in statements of goals which identify long-range outcomes.

Psychomotor Domain.   The third area of human behavior is the *psychomotor domain*, which includes the motor skills or those requiring muscular coordination.

Objectives using psychomotor behaviors apply most obviously to the following language areas: penmanship, articulation, enunciation, and the decoding dimension of reading. The major levels, behavioral terms within each level, and sample objectives are listed below.[13]

1.0 PERCEPTION

This level is parallel to the first level of the affective taxonomy. It refers to the process of becoming aware. Which sense or combination of senses form the avenue of awareness is important in this domain. Behavioral terms that can be used include:
a. hears
b. sees

---

[13] Elizabeth Simpson, "The Classification of Educational Objectives, Psychomotor Domain," *Illinois Teacher of Home Economics* 10 (Winter 1966–67): 110–44.

c. feels (touches)

d. smells

e. tastes

Sample objectives

The student is visually aware of the difference between "B" and "D."

The student hears the difference in format between free verse and conventional poetry.

2.0 SET

A set involves preparatory readiness or adjustment for a particular kind of action or experience. A set can be *mental*, requiring prerequisite knowledge; *physical*, requiring appropriate anatomical adjustment; or *emotional*, requiring a willingness to respond. In addition to terms from the first level of the cognitive taxonomy and the second level of the affective taxonomy, the following may be used:

a. assumes the position

Sample objectives:

The student should position his paper correctly before beginning the penmanship lesson.

The student should locate his reading story after the page number is identified.

3.0 GUIDED RESPONSE

This level involves the overt behavioral performance of the learner under the guidance of the instructor. This behavior may be the result of imitation or trial and error. The following behavioral terms can be used at this level:

a. imitates

b. follows along as demonstrated

c. discovers

Sample objectives:

The student should imitate the figures "D" and "B" on his paper as the teacher demonstrates them on the blackboard.

The student should imitate the sounds the teacher makes.

4.0 MECHANISM

At this level, a particular learned response has become habitual so it is part of the learner; the learner has developed confidence and skill in this behavior. Any behavioral terms indicating a single action can be used at this level.

Sample objectives:

The student says his spelling word before spelling it aloud.

The student projects his voice clearly when participating in creative dramatics.

5.0 COMPLEX OVERT RESPONSE

At this level, a complex motor act can be performed with a high degree of skill. Appropriate behavioral terms are those that signify complex actions performed skillfully.

Sample objectives:

The student should be able to set up the puppet stage by himself.

The student should be able to choose appropriate tapes and use the tape recorder correctly at the listening station.

Three Taxonomies.   In many instances a simple lesson will incorporate objectives from all three domains, as illustrated in the following lesson for a primary group:

The learner should recognize new words in his reading story. (Cognitive taxonomy)

The learner should be able to pronounce the new words. (Psychomotor taxonomy)

The learner should be interested in reading his new story. (Affective taxonomy)

Contrasts and Cautions

There are several distinct differences between the objectives based on Mager and those based on the taxonomies. Mager's objectives require three components: a statement of behavior and content, the condition under which the behavior is to occur, and the minimal acceptable performance. The taxonomic objectives consist of only the first of those components. This is not to say that when taxonomic objectives are utilized, consideration is not given to learning conditions and evaluation. These factors merely are not included in the statement of purpose itself. Thus, when taxonomic objectives are used, in addition to the objective itself, explicit attention must be given to the teaching environment designed to provide for the attainment of the objective. Mager's conditional phrase identifies conditions allowing for the attainment of the specified behavior. A separate statement is needed for this purpose with taxonomic objectives.

A similar situation exists with regard to evaluation. Mager's third phrase describes the minimal acceptable performance of the objective. When taxonomic objectives are utilized, identification of an evaluation technique for assessing performance needs to be detailed apart from the objective.

Another contrast between the two types of objectives concerns the behavior. In Mager's approach to objectives, the behavior must be readily observable. This is not true for the cognitive and affective taxonomies. With both types of objectives, however, inferences are made about unobservable behavior. With the Magerian format, the inference is made that "listing" or "reciting orally" is an indication of certain cognitive processes. If this were not the case, there would be little value in the listing or reciting. With objectives based on the cognitive taxonomy, the intellectual process is identified and the overt behavior that gives evidence of this behavior is inferred. "Reciting out loud" may be inferred as evidence of "recalls," so indeed may "lists." One of the strengths of taxonomic objectives is that they allow for a variety of ways in which an intellectual or affective behavior can be expressed. Many examples of this variety of expression are included in the following chapter dealing with language learning in young children.

A third difference between the two types of objectives relates to the number of learners for whom the objectives can appropriately be designed. In general, taxonomic objectives can be formulated for a larger number of students than can Mager-type objectives which eliminate the appropriateness of one objective for many students because of their high degree of specificity. Any given taxonomic objective can apply to many students for several reasons. *First,* because there are a variety of ways in which a particular cognitive or affective objective can be expressed, many students can be accommodated within one objective. Thus, if "summarize" is the desired behavior, some students can summarize orally, others can summarize in paragraph form, and others, by outlining. All three situations can provide evidence of the learner's ability to summarize. A *second* reason taxonomic objectives can be applied to many students is that no criterion needs to be established. This means different degrees of accuracy and different amounts of work can be accepted from learners who possess different needs and abilities. Because Mager-type objectives are so specific, any one objective can be applied only to a small group.

Cautions.   Several cautions regarding objectives need to be voiced. Objectives have been discussed as statements of purpose for learner behavior that the teacher formulates apart from the learner. This need not be the case. In many instances, it is highly desirable that the students for whom the objectives are intended be included in the formulation process.

Objectives detail purpose and give direction to instruction. When an objective is developed, it is assumed that the learners for whom it is intended have not achieved the behavior specified. *At no time* should an objective be formulated under the following conditions: 1) it is reasonably impossible for the student to attain the objective, 2) the student can already perform what is specified in the objective. In both cases, a teacher abrogates his responsibility if he violates these conditions.

Finally, the whole area of instructional objectives needs to be kept in proper perspective. *Objectives are a means to an end, not an end in themselves.* If the practice of writing objectives becomes ritualized to the extent that concern for the quantity of objectives or their format takes precedence over the content and quality of the objectives, the purpose of objectives is lost.

Teaching Strategies

Teaching strategies, educational experiences, and learning activities are generally synonymous terms referring to activities designed for students for the purpose of attaining specified behaviors. Here, again, consistency is of the utmost importance. Teaching strategies should be planned that seem likely to encourage desired learner behavior as specified in objectives.

Although it is impossible to predict that a given type of learning will result from a given teaching strategy, thoughtful analysis reveals that some strategies are more apt to promote certain behaviors than are other strategies. Clear definition of objectives is essential for such an analysis.

When objectives specify intellectual behavior, analyses based on the cognitive taxonomy can yield useful data. Overgeneralization is hazardous, but, in most cases when learning at the knowledge level is sought, lectures, discussions, or reading assignments can be appropriately incorporated into teaching strategies for the attainment of knowledge. These strategies are invariably content oriented and often teacher centered. When higher-level cognitive behaviors are sought, less teacher-centeredness is desirable.

A parallel can be drawn for behaviors classified at the higher affective and psychomotor levels. Thus, as you proceed through the levels, more and more individual interpretation is required. Strategies that encourage independence and freedom are most likely to encourage the attainment of these behaviors.

No specific strategies are discussed in this chapter because in the chapters that follow a wide variety of teaching strategies are presented. As the reader incorporates many strategies into his repertoire of teaching behaviors, it is hoped that he will be aided in the selection of which strategies to employ under which conditions, by the curriculum principles presented in this chapter.

Evaluation

Evaluation of students' abilities and progress presents some of the most perplexing problems encountered in teaching. Questions of reliability, validity, and objectivity plague the teacher. Far too often the term evaluation conjures up images of standardized and teacher-made tests. This is truly unfortunate as evaluation involves judgment that can be made based on evidence from many sources, not just test results.

When the model for rational curriculum decision making, illustrated on page 31, is employed, one major aspect of the evaluation of instruction stands out above all others: *evaluation must always be done in relation to objectives.* Judgment of achievement should be made only in relation to what has previously and thoughtfully been defined as desirable achievement.

Evaluation of Mager-Type Objectives. If the Mager-type objective format is used, questions of evaluation are encountered from the beginning. Decisions about identification of criterion performance and methods for evaluating behavior are made as the desirable behavior is identified.

As cited earlier, this type of objective is most useful for specifying skills. Evaluation thus becomes a relatively simple matter because deciding whether a student can read a particular story orally, for example, is accomplished by obvious means.

A major consideration with Magerian objectives is the criterion performance. Generally, 100 percent accuracy is too much to realistically expect for all the students for whom the objective is intended. On the other hand, if the expectation of the criterion performance is lower than 85 percent, it is questionable whether the objective is appropriate. Another objective for which greater accuracy can be realistically expected might be better. The establishment of uniform minimal performances tends to limit Mager objectives to small groups of students.

Evaluation of Cognitive Objectives. Movement through the levels of the cognitive taxonomy takes one from generally convergent to generally divergent situations. For this reason, evaluation of the lower levels is often easier to obtain than of the higher levels. This is because solutions requiring convergent thinking involve data that can usually be verified or authenticated.

For example, in either oral or written form, students can be readily evaluated for the following behaviors:

> ability to recognize the initial consonant sound of /d/ (knowledge).
>
> ability to recognize iambic pentameter (knowledge).
>
> ability to recall the main characters of the story (knowledge).

Less congruent but still relatively easy behaviors to evaluate include:

> ability to translate what is happening in a picture into words (comprehension).
>
> ability to summarize the peculiar features of fairy tales (comprehension).

Evaluation becomes more difficult in a divergent situation as the possibilities for being correct increase. Thus, when students are to assess a poem using a given set of criteria, personal interpretation and application of the criteria can result in as many different yet "correct" assessments as there are students.

Evaluation of Affective Objectives. It is with the *affective taxonomy*, however, that the greatest problems of evaluation occur. It is impossible to assume at the stage of identifying affective behaviors how the manifestation of that behavior may appear in the student. The way an individual might express his attitudes or appreciations is indeed uncertain. For example, an intent gaze might be an indication of enthusiasm by a generally passive child, but it could indicate boredom on the part of another. Evaluation in the affective realm is further complicated by the fact that attitudes which have no opportunity to be expressed in the school may be possessed by a student. It would be foolish to assume under these conditions that the attitudes are lacking.

It is in the affective realm that many of the joys of teaching occur. When an apathetic child becomes enthused over a picture, a song, a field trip, his teacher can know a very special satisfaction. When a child shyly hands his teacher a poem he wrote the night before, hours of hard work are suddenly rewarded. Surely such behaviors are to be cherished whenever they occur, even if their achievement cannot be readily systematized or assessed.

Few would deny the importance of student interest or involvement. Thus, the necessity for identifying affective behaviors in objectives seems apparent even in the face of many difficulties to be found in attempting to evaluate them.

Summary

Decisions about *what* to teach and *how* to teach are among the most pressing in education. At various levels of decision making, these decisions should be faced. At the *societal* level of responsibility, the value orientation or mores of the community influence decisions about what should be taught in a general way. At the *institutional* level, the tasks of school administrators include more specific designation of content as well as some consideration of instruction, the manner in which content is presented.

It is at the *instructional* level of decision making where teachers operate. One of their major responsibilities is to specify content and desirable student behaviors. They also need to organize content and, based on knowledge about their specific students, determine which instructional strategies are most likely to attain the specified behaviors.

As the reader progresses through this book, he may become increasingly aware of the many possibilities available to him as a teacher. As he faces decisions about purpose, content, learner behavior, and teaching strategies, he should attempt to act consistently with societal and institutional expectations. Further, each decision he makes needs also to be consistent with his other decisions. Hopefully, the ideas presented in this chapter can be of aid to the teacher in reaching thoughtful, consistent decisions.

Suggestions for Further Exploration

1. Determine whether the following curriculum decisions should most appropriately be made at the societal, institutional, or instructional level:
    a. Should students be allowed to read controversial books?
    b. What should the sixth-grade students do in spelling on Wednesday?
    c. What language-arts textbook series should be ordered for the school?
    d. How should creative writing be evaluated?

2. Choose such an area of language arts as creative writing. Formulate at least six questions that a teacher must deal with in this area at the instructional level.

3. Following is an example of an educational goal: "The student should be able to express himself with ease." Formulate five instructional objectives for it.

4. For one month, collect newspaper and magazine articles that deal with purposes or goals for education. Categorize and analyze them.

5. Locate the teacher's manual for an elementary language-arts textbook. Categorize the objectives according to the three taxonomies and the level within each category. Can you draw any conclusions from your classification?

6. Read *Classroom Questions: What Kinds* by Norris Sanders for a presentation of the types of questions to ask to elicit thinking at the various cognitive levels. Develop questions in a language-arts area at each level.

7. Read *On Writing Behavioral Objectives for English* edited by Maxwell and Tovatt (Champaign: National Council of Teachers of English, 1970). The chapter entitled "On Hunting and Fishing and Behaviorism" by Robert F. Hogan (pp. 125–29) is particularly well written. As a result of reading this and comparing it with what is presented in this chapter, determine for yourself which approach detailed in the above book presents the more convincing case about objectives.

Bibliography

Bloom, Benjamin S., ed. *Taxonomy of Educational Objectives. Handbook I: Cognitive Domain.* New York: David McKay, Inc., 1956.

Division of Planning, Research, and Evaluation, *Goals for Education in Georgia.* Atlanta, Georgia: Georgia Department of Education, 1970.

Duncan, James K., and Frymier, Jack R. "Explorations in the Systematic Study of Curriculum." *Curriculum Theory Development: Work in Progress, Theory Into Practice,* vol. 6. Columbus, Ohio: College of Education, The Ohio State University, 1967.

Goodlad, John I., and Richter, Maurice N., Jr. *Development of a Conceptual System for Dealing with Problems of Curriculum and Instruction.* Cooperative Research Project No. 454. United States Office of Education, University of California, Los Angeles, and Institute for Development of Educational Activities, 1966.

Huenecke, Dorothy M. "The Relation of Teacher Expectations to Curriculum Guide Implementation." Ph.D. dissertation, University of Wisconsin, 1969.

Keith, Lowell, Blake, Paul, and Tiedt, Sidney. *Contemporary Curriculum in the Elementary School.* New York: Harper and Row, Publishers, 1968.

Krathwohl, David R., Bloom, Benjamin S., and Masia, Bertram B. *Taxonomy of Educational Objectives. Handbook II: Affective Domain.* New York: David McKay, Inc., 1964.

Mager, Robert F. *Preparing Instructional Objectives.* Palo Alto: Fearon Publishers, 1962.

Mead, Margaret. *Culture and Commitment: A Study of the Generation Gap.* Garden City, New York: Natural History Press, 1970.

Packard, Vance O. *The Pyramid Climbers.* New York: McGraw-Hill Book Company, Inc., 1962.

Raths, Louis E., Harmin, Merrill, and Simon, Sidney B. *Values and Teaching.* Columbus, Ohio: Charles E. Merrill Publishing Co., 1966.

Reich, Charles A. *The Greening of America.* New York: Random House, 1970.

Sanders, Norris M. *Classroom Questions: What Kinds?* New York: Harper and Row, Publishers, 1966.

Simpson, Elizabeth J. "The Classification of Educational Objectives, Psychomotor Domain," *Illinois Teacher of Home Economics* 10 (Winter, 1966–67): 110–44.

Toffler, Alvin. *Future Shock.* New York: Random House, 1970.

Tyler, Ralph W. *Basic Principles of Curriculum and Instruction.* Chicago: University of Chicago Press, 1950.

Whyte, William H. *The Organization Man.* New York: Simon and Schuster, 1956.

Author's Comment

In the preceding chapter Dr. Huenecke has given us a strong framework within which to consider curriculum planning in the language arts. She has challenged us to think deeply about what should be taught, to whom, and how. As she points out, the most crucial question—*why* something should be taught—is the most difficult to cope with. The four questions she has raised on pages 31–32 are crucial for every teacher.

In the following section, we are presented with a point of view about language learning in early-childhood education. The Hansens, experienced early childhood educators, describe their approach to language learning. In describing the approach, they address themselves to the important issues raised by Dr. Huenecke. They detail their answers to her questions, and discuss taxonomic objectives for early language learning.

CHAPTER THREE

Language in
Early-Childhood Education

by Harlan S. and Ruth M. Hansen

By its sounds, symbols, and signs, language has made it possible for man to be a distinctive creature. Language is characteristically human and plays a leading role in most human activity. Because language is vital to becoming a civilized person, adults must provide young children opportunities to acquire language early and then direct them in its use.

Language builds more easily and efficiently when there is a need to communicate and to learn new words to communicate more effectively. The earlier a child confronts this need to communicate, the sooner he is able to internalize his perceptions and store them in his memory. From this language reservoir, he can bring forth new combinations of words as he experiences new things, ideas, and situations in his environment.

The purpose of this chapter is threefold: 1) to examine the functions of language, 2) to suggest basic principles upon which classroom teachers can develop language experiences, and 3) to suggest sample practical techniques involving children in the effective use of language. These functions, principles, and techniques must represent a realistic bridge between what is happening inside and outside of the classroom.

If this is accomplished, the language learned will enable young children to better understand, interpret, and integrate into their environments.

The Function of Language

Early-childhood education encompasses programs from birth through the primary grades, or, in terms of language, from the child's first newborn cry to a more sophisticated and highly solidified language pattern. To understand our professional roles in guiding the early acquisition of language, we need to review the basic functions of language.

Language Identifies Wants and Needs.   This function of language is basic to human communication. All humans, from birth, have needs requiring satisfaction. Initially, a gesture, a grunt, or a cry may make known one's desires. But as his desires and needs become more complex, or more refined, the child has no alternative but to learn and use that language which will insure prompt and full gratification.

Language Facilitates the Acquisition and Exchange of Information and Ideas.   Without language one would have a limited understanding and awareness of life. Language determines one's picture of reality and gives meaning to experience. The fact that no one person can understand or experience all that the world has to offer demands an exchange of information and ideas. This exchange broadens one's understanding of personal experiences and makes him aware of events not yet experienced.

Language Is a Means of Expressing Feelings and Emotions.   Language is rarely neutral, even in the exchange of information and ideas. Language which conveys a host of affective sensations provides therapeutic release as well as a vehicle to hurt, to humor, to hate, to hail, to convince, to excuse, to taunt, or to love. The greater the language facility, the greater the chance for emotional release and the more directly one's feelings, via language, hit their mark. Teachers need to encourage children to release their feelings, thus enabling children to build appropriate language for this function. Feelings are basic to human nature. To suppress them in the name of classroom control retards the development of the language that serves the function of expressing emotions.

Language Is a Means of Self-Identification.   The need for self-understanding is continual throughout life. Each person strives to find out, or attempts to run from finding out, who he is and what his limits and potentials are. Language is tied directly to self-identification in two ways. Initially, it is the language of others which helps build or break a child's self-esteem. Words such as *good, bad; right, wrong; do, don't; can, can't; should, shouldn't;* continually remind him early in life of the kind of person he is perceived as being. It also continually reminds him of the kind of person someone else would have him become. However, as he gains inner dependence, it is a person's ability to understand, explain, defend, and justify himself to himself which produces the climate for self-acceptance and worthwhile change. Language facilitates this continual introspection and seeking of inner security as well as enables one to seek external help.

Language Is a Means of Social Interaction.   Men are social beings —forced by circumstances and specialization into contact with others. Man works with others for a livelihood and seeks others for companionship. How well he can communicate his ideas and interests will determine how successful he will be in both endeavors. Language not only aids in communicating with others, it enables one to better understand and accept one's fellowmen in order to work and relax in closer harmony.

In addition, language denotes the man. It is one of the initial measures people use in accepting and rejecting others—not only in the quality of the thought, but in the skills of expression.

Language Is a Basis for Reflective Thinking.   Language need not be vocal. Many more thoughts and ideas churn internally than ever see the vocal light of day. People constantly reflect on the multitude of situations and problems encountered in all phases of their daily lives. One's ability to put these thoughts into proper perspective allows for a more organized vocalization of them. Such ability also assists in mentally settling minds and putting reflections in some order. The reflective-thinking process is enhanced or hindered by the language brought to the task.

Language Is a Basis for Extended Thinking.   Creativity must operate from a foundation of some sort, we do not create from a void.[1] How well one is able to put together new language combinations is dependent on the number and quality of words available to him. We often expect

---

[1] Helpful suggestions for the teacher are included in Paul F. Torrance's *Encouraging Creativity in the Classroom* (Dubuque: William C. Brown, 1970), a book characterized by a wealth of practical illustrations drawn from actual classrooms.

creative language from children without giving consideration to the need for providing a rich foundation of varied language experiences. These experiences provide the basis for the expansion to new and imaginative language.

Language Is Adaptable to Alternate Forms of Communication. Although oral language was mainly dealt with in the previous discussion of language functions, oral expression is but one of a variety of methods of communicating. Gesture, graphic and mechanical code systems intermix to form the multiple communication systems used by humans. Our ability to understand, interpret, and respond to the varied forms rests on our awareness of these alternative forms of communication, as well as on a common language base in which to translate them.

Hopefully, this brief consideration of the functions of language has illustrated the broad spectrum that "language" embraces and will give direction in the evaluation and selection of early-childhood language programs.

Language Approaches

Children come to initial education programs with random language acquired through experiences in the home and community. There is a need to systematize experiences so all children develop a broad language base. But at the same time, the unique dialects and idiolects found within the children, their families, and community need to be given their rightful role. The teacher of young children needs to identify an approach to language development which will assist him in providing optional language experiences. A short discussion of the presently available alternatives should assist in making decisions regarding the advantages of each approach, and aid the reader in determining which is best for his situation. As Dr. Huenecke pointed out on page 29, making decisions of what to teach, to whom, and how, are difficult ones to make. It is hoped that this consideration of alternatives will make such decisions easier for the teacher of young children.

The Language Kit Approach. The language kit, of which the *Peabody Language Development Kit* (Level P—3 to 5 years mental age) is perhaps the best known, provides a total language program.[2]

---

[2] By Lloyd M. Dunn and James O. Smith. Available from American Guidance Service, Inc., Circle Pines, Minnesota, 55014.

The Peabody Kit provides language-development activities to fill a forty-minute period each day throughout the school year. The program functions independently of other content areas and features a systematic segmental approach to language development.

In the absence of a better plan, this kit offers an organized approach to developing language. However, because children come to initial education programs with various language needs, the sequential aspect of the program may be inappropriate for some who are beyond or behind that particular lesson on that particular day. In addition, it may be that, while the skill is appropriate, the content included in the lesson has little relation to what is happening in the children's environment and, therefore, has little relevance for them.

Perhaps the best use for such programs as these is as supplemental work for individual children with special language disabilities.[3]

The Language Arts Text-Series Approach. Textbook language series have traditionally been introduced at the beginning of third grade. Although a few new series are including grades one and two, preschool and kindergarten teachers have nothing available presently. However, the continued emphasis early-childhood education is receiving will no doubt prompt publishers to explore the development of programs for the very young. The extension of this subject-matter approach into the early years continues to segment learning and often fails to integrate language into the total learning environment.

The Reading-Program Approach. In the absence of a language-arts textbook, a reading program often doubles as the language program.[4] New vocabulary is represented by the words in the stories and usage parallels the sentence structure of the stories. This represents a very narrow approach. Language acquisition and use justify their own existence; language development need not be subservient to other content areas. Rather, increased language development should heighten a child's contributions to other parts of the curriculum.

---

[3] An extended section on research using the kits with such children is included in the *Manual* of the *P.L.D.K.*, pp. xviii–xxii.

[4] Many articles have appeared about both sides of this issue. Arthur M. Enzmann, "A Look at Early Reading," *The Reading Teacher* 24 (April 1971): 616–20, is among those who have pointed out that the more important question is *how* such early instruction is given. Other sources include Christine LaConte, "Reading in Kindergarten," *The Reading Teacher* 23 (November 1969): 116–20, and the comprehensive summary available in Delores Durkin, "When Should Children Begin to Read?" in *Innovation and Change in Reading Instruction* (Chicago: The 67th Yearbook of the National Society for the Study of Education, Part II, 1968), pp. 30–71.

The Total-Program Approach.   This approach, having great potential for effective language development, is described in detail following.

The Program as a Basis for Language Development

The total-education program, which includes the classroom as well as community environment, provides the most legitimate and meaningful basis for language development.[5]

The following discussion deals with the need for establishing a classroom climate that will stimulate children to learn. It *describes* language techniques rather than *prescribes* them because it is felt that the most effective language development results when a child responds to his environment rather than to a kit of language activities and lessons. The key to language development is providing a stimulating and enriching environment which generates new language patterns.

Any approach to educating young children must rest upon some basic assumptions—or keystones. These provide the rationale for selecting appropriate content, materials, and activities in which children are to be involved. Without the identification of these keystones, programs may eventually accomplish worthwhile outcomes but in the manner of someone driving to an unknown point without the benefit of a map or concise directions. This is a luxury one may indulge in while on a vacation, but in the elementary school curriculum, time is of the essence! In order to expose young children to the world around them in the limited time available, professionals need to systematize their approaches, even though such approaches can be individualized and open ended.

The following keystones provide a model for teachers of young children to examine, digest, and compare with their existing or emerging set of basic assumptions. Basic assumptions are similar to the values you were urged to examine in Chapter Two. These assumptions or values need not be absolute; yet, they should be given consideration in establishing early-childhood programs which will maximize the language potential of each child. As you read the following, think about the values you hold. How do your values concerning early-childhood

---

[5] For a more complete description see: D. C. and M. A. Davis; H. S. and R. M. Hansen, *PLAYWAY: An Interest Center Approach to Initial Education* (New York: Winston Press, A Division of Holt, Rinehart and Winston, 1973), including expanded treatment of learning environments, interest centers, play centers, unit topics, and scheduling.

language education compare or contrast with those presented in this chapter?

Keystones

Keystone 1. The early years provide the initial direction intelligence, achievement, and attitude patterns will take in later years, and, therefore, early programs need to address themselves to long-range goals rather than to shortsighted yearly goals.

Benjamin Bloom's review of studies relating the impact of the early environment on later growth patterns concluded that by age nine at least 50 percent of the general intelligence achievement and attitude patterns measured by age eighteen have been developed.[6] Because many researchers suggest that scores on standardized intelligence tests and achievement measures directly correlate with verbal acuity, the early development of language is crucial. And because the early identification of attitudinal patterns is now receiving greater focus, we must concentrate more on helping children acquire the language facility needed to internalize, interpret, and articulate their feelings. Further evidence suggests that it is questionable whether any amount of remediation at a later date can compensate for a void of enriching experiences in the early environment.

Keystone 2. A concept of differential treatment makes it possible for the scope of the total environment, in and out of school, to be introduced into the early-childhood learning environment. *Treatment,* in the simplest sense, refers to the degree of depth and scope afforded a certain concept by the activities and materials employed in its consideration.[7] Three types of treatment have been found to be appropriate in discussing educational situations.

Skill Treatment given to an idea or an activity implies an overlearned, habitual reaction or conditioning on the child's part. When the child is skilled in certain areas, he has mastered the feat. At the early-childhood level, there are few areas where children have the ability to become skilled—mainly, in the operational acts of listening, following directions and persisting; and in the manipulative acts of cutting, past-

---

[6] Benjamin Bloom, *Stability and Change in Human Characteristics* (New York: John Wiley & Sons, 1964).

[7] For an expanded discussion of treatment see D. C. Davis, *Patterns of Primary Education* (New York: Harper & Row, Publishers, 1965).

ing, folding, tearing, and marking. Children need to develop the appropriate language to accompany skill development in these areas.

Foundational treatment sets the stage for a later development. It requires a minimal group understanding to assure that children are ready for further exploration and involvement. Ideas and experiences treated foundationally result in specific vocabulary which a child utilizes orally and mentally for further verbalizing.

Basic readiness areas of reading, writing, and communication systems fall under foundational treatment. Because these areas are important to the child's later progress in school and in life, and because they demand a mental and verbal understanding to some normative level, the development and use of accurate and appropriate language is vital.

Finally, *impressional treatment* intends only to systematically make children aware of materials, topics, and experiences. There is no attempt to define or fix this affective learning because at this age children are unable to draw upon a storehouse of experiences and vocabulary in articulating their innermost thoughts. Early-childhood education programs need to broaden a child's horizons during these critical years by exposing him to a wide variety of enriching experiences. Hopefully, when the child encounters these materials and topics later in school or life, he will be better prepared to understand them.

The performing arts provide the most logical avenue for impressional treatment. To insist on a foundational or skilled treatment in this area would fail to allow each child to accept, reject, change his mind —and would fail to provide the early opportunity to initiate a basic self-value system.

In these days of accountability many educators, politicians, and parents may reject the notion of impressional treatment. Not measuring objectively every area of the curriculum upsets the cost accounting procedure deemed so necessary by some. Yet, the school's job is broader than just "opening up" heads and stuffing in "things." Feelings and appreciations need to be nurtured gently and slowly so that each child has the opportunity to identify his own likes and dislikes, independently of what his mentors deem "good" or "bad," "worthy" or "unworthy."

The use and development of language during impressional treatment becomes highly individual—and may remain internal and seemingly dormant until the vagueness begins to clear and form a more well-defined pattern. Teachers of young children must not become frustrated because of previous teacher-training practices which placed a heavy emphasis on verbalizing the content of the curriculum. Rather, they should keep sight of the eventual outcomes of effective impressional treatment—a child whose language will reflect the enthusiasm and excitement derived from being immersed in an interest he selected.

Keystone 3. A stated curriculum is necessary to identify the content of the program, and a stated or implied vocabulary is necessary for meaningful involvement.

There are many ways of stating—or not stating—a curriculum. Some people feel a curriculum should emerge from children's interests, fixing experiences and related language as they randomly emerge.[8] To others, it is crucial to identify those process skills that are important for understanding and that apply to many situations. Learning and vocabulary are built, in addition, around such concepts as *over, under; large, small; high, low; in, out; behind, in front of;* and so forth. Others would plan and have available a variety of curricular areas in which children could become involved if they so chose. Another approach identifies and applies crucial unit topics but leaves actual learning and application for more appropriate spontaneous small-group and individual situations. And finally, there is a strong move to bring the content of grades into the early years with sequential subject-matter blocks of time and with children generally progressing in groups at the same rate and by the same method. In each case, the curriculum planner is attempting to answer the questions raised in Chapter Two, though the resulting curricula are very different from one another.

The approach utilizing the systematic unfolding of a unit topic is identified here as having the optimal potential for laying group foundations while allowing for individual application. A unit lays the vocabulary for a topic, establishes a way of thinking about the topic, and stimulates ways of observing and identifying in the broader environment. All children are involved in this unfolding while being at various levels of understanding and application. The open-ended quality of the unit allows each child to apply this knowledge in meaningful and spontaneous, not contrived, experiences throughout the unit and school year. This procedure allows him to progress at his own rate through his own set of learning styles from the previously laid foundations. Each following unit adds more potential for individual application. This is the type of flexible expectation described by the author of Chapter Two when she identified the advantages of taxonomic

---

[8] A clear statement of this belief is included in G. Sowards and M. Scobey, *The Changing Curriculum and the Elementary Teacher* (Belmont, Calif.: Wadsworth Publishing Co., Inc., 1968), pp. 31–35.

objectives in planning a curriculum. Some appropriate unit topics encouraging this individual response will be discussed in the section on learning environments.

The important point to remember is that if language comes from the curriculum, what a child "gets out" of the curriculum in terms of language and vocabulary development will be in proportion to the thought and planning a teacher has "put in."

"Doing your own thing" may be important. Yet, in the early years a child's "thing" may be a random, fleeting thing to which adults put too much meaning. To be gently nudged "up and beyond" their present interest, ability, and language level in areas of cognitive, motor, and affective development will allow children to develop more interests and to become more personally involved as growing young adults.

Keystone 4. A one-to-one correspondence must exist between the in- and out-of-school environment to make classroom learnings and related language have immediate value to the rest of the child's world. To that end, *resource persons, field exploration,* and *artifacts* must be extensively utilized.

The major point to be noted is that no one teacher and no one classroom can hold all the knowledge, expertise, and experience necessary to satisfy the changing needs and goals of our educational programs. Why not, then, tap the community for available sites, skills, and related tangibles to provide a bridge between the classroom and the community? In so doing, we will be fulfilling the often discussed, but seldom realized, goal of "education for life and life for education."

Resource persons can make important contributions to education. They leave valuable impressions, add otherwise unavailable expertise and skill, and provide children with a realization of the various roles of adults in society, hopefully giving them a future glimpse of vocational aspiration and leisure-time interests. They also expose children to other language models, bringing into the classroom the dialect and idiolect patterns of the community.

The primary function of *field exploration* is to make children actively aware of and involved in curriculum content at its source. They are able to *experience* what is being taught in the classroom and develop and use the vocabulary in its natural situation.

Artifacts provide in-class tangibles representing various aspects of the environment when on-site visits are not possible or are unnecessary. The purpose of these tangibles is to make children aware of and help them understand the role of the artifacts in the environment. By viewing and becoming acquainted with the use of these tangibles, the child fixes the vocabularly associated with them in his language pattern. He is, consequently, able to examine and verbalize many more aspects of a situation than he could with intangible substitutes. Tangibles provide insights into size, shape, texture, weight, density, color shades, and natural phenomenon, as well as the specific purpose under study.

Frequently, parents or other guests visit the classroom to explain and demonstrate the use of artifacts or tangibles.[9] For example, during a unit on cutting and pasting, parents may be asked to send cutting and adhesive materials from home. Items ranging from nail clippers to lawn clippers and from homemade paste to carpet tape are included in the collection. As the children explore and become involved with this display, they use the vocabulary associated with the items and begin to understand the role the materials play in their home and community environment.

As the child explores scales, rules, measuring cups and other tangibles provided during a number unit, he begins to realize how numbers are used in everyday life and he is motivated to learn them.

The authors investigated the use of the speaker-phone in an elementary school as an alternative to field trips and resource people.[10] The speaker-phone has an external receiver and speaker allowing classes of children to speak with or hear a distant resource person. Using this medium necessitated advance planning with the speaker and advance identification of appropriate questions to initiate the discussions. It was found to be a very effective substitute for going on field trips or bringing in resource people. The upper grades talked to a newspaper publisher regarding editorial policy, a bank president regarding interest rates, and political figures regarding conservation and pollution. The kindergarten group was even more active; they made arrangements for their own field trip by calling the bus and the museum, asked a lumberman to help explain ways to keep their block structure from falling, called the city manager on Earth Day to see what jobs they could perform, and discovered the multiplicity of words when they called a television director to inquire about the special words he uses in his job. These experiences called for planning ahead and for utilizing vocabulary in real-life situations. As a result, they had a far

---

[9] A parent questionnaire, sent out early in the year, often reveals that many parents can serve as resource people. A sample questionnaire is included as Appendix 2 of this chapter.

[10] This device is called by different names, including Conference Telephone, but all variations work in essentially the same fashion.

greater impact on the students than the contrived "language period" customary in many classrooms.

Teachers need to be aware of the available community resources. Sending questionnaires to parents and community members, talking with parents at conference times, writing parents letters discussing topics under study and suggesting parental contributions (See Appendix 1) are only a few of the methods a teacher should employ. The task of finding people, places, and things to enrich a topic or activity demands persistence and hard work, but the rewards in learning and related language development make it worthwhile.

Keystone 5. The identification of eight learning environments goes beyond present subject-matter concerns and involves both the long- and short-range goals of early-childhood education. These learning environments highlight the major areas to be emphasized in the total program. Whether they be designated by a systematic Unit Topic, a loosely organized series of activities, or an isolated experience, evidence of each needs to be present if we are to fulfill our goal of providing a total-education experience for each child. The eight learning environments are 1) play, 2) physical fitness, 3) contemporary living, 4) basic tools, 5) performing arts, 6) social thinking, 7) service, and 8) scientific thinking.

Learning Environments

Although keystones provide a theoretical basis for curriculum planning and give direction for more specific ways of creating enriching experiences, the eight learning environments take teachers directly into the classroom and involve them more specifically in their work with children. An examination of each learning environment will provide the basis for some practical applications.

Play. Play needs to come back into favor in education programs.[11] Whether one calls it individual directed activities, free time, or liberty play, it still means the same thing. It allows children some time during each day to freely explore and interact with their environment. It is unrelated to any subject-matter field and should have few rules.

The important thing in play programs is to make available ample stimuli so that a group of children can make worthy selections. This

---

[11] For a more extensive treatment of the values of play, see R. E. Herron and B. Sutton-Smith, *Child's Play* (New York: John Wiley & Sons, Inc., 1971).

choice allows children to identify their own interest and regulate their own involvement. The teacher moves throughout the room as a guide, stimulator, helper, and challenger.

Play obviously encourages language. Too often in group situations, some children are not ready to talk at a particular time, are too shy to talk at a particular time, or are not called upon even at the particular time they *are* ready. The interest generated in free selection and the Playway approach to learning results in a natural spontaneous language development.

Equipment needs to be selected which involves children in the following forms of play and their related language use:

1. Intellectual Play—books, number and science devices, maps, historical collections
2. Therapeutic Play[12]—clay, sand, water, punching bags, workbench
3. Sensory Play—easels, paint, paper, old magazines, collage materials
4. Aesthetic Play—musical instruments and books, records, art books and prints
5. Physical Play—balance beam, ball, jump ropes, tricycles, climbing ropes
6. Miniature Play—dolls, dress-up clothes, street signs, flowers and vases, items to reproduce life-like situations

The first five play purposes are self-explanatory. Miniature play, however, requires a brief discussion. Miniature play has as its major goal the development and use of language. It is termed "miniature" because it sets up in the classroom miniature reproductions of life-like situations and allows children to play the roles they see around them.

The traditional miniature play center is the housekeeping corner. Too often, however, this corner outlives its usefulness because it remains a permanent part of the classroom and ceases to stimulate language. The insightful teacher will change the center to incorporate other miniature situations: shoe shop, hat shop, flower shop, beauty shop, travel bureau, first-grade corner, fix-it shop, handicapped corner, and others that restimulate children to discussion and problem solving.

An example of the language use stimulated by miniature play is the following conversation overheard one day in the "flower shop." One

---

[12] An engrossing account of the use of therapeutic play in treating an emotionally disturbed child is included in Virginia M. Axline's *Dibs—In Search of Self* (New York: Ballantine Press, 1969).

child, who was being the florist, "I'm really worried, Room 102 ordered a dozen and one-half roses and I don't know how many that is. What should I do?" From another child, who was being the florist's assistant came the answer, "All I know is you'll need a lot of Styrofoam for that big of an arrangement."

Physical Fitness. The physical play material mentioned under the previous learning environment was for individual self-selected purposes. In addition, there should be a short, daily, carefully planned physical-education period devoted to the development of all children's physical efficiency.[13]

The children need to be instructed orally and by demonstration that physical education includes elements of balance, coordination, strength, relaxation, endurance, body flexibility and projection. As activities are introduced, the children should be made aware of the reasons for the activities, for example, "This heel click will help your flexibility" or "Chinese Get Up is excellent for developing your strength." This procedure provides cognitive understanding and vocabulary development. Marc, a new child in the kindergarten program was struggling with the "rocking chair," an exercise most of his classmates had mastered. Mike was overheard saying to him, "I know it's hard to do but keep trying 'cuz it's good for endurance and strength."

Contemporary Living. This learning environment focuses on the here and now, not just because children are a part of it but because they need to examine it and put it in some perspective. Children's verbal input includes far more than many adults imagine. As children sit at the dinner table, they hear conversation about such things as unemployment, taxes, jobs, money, autos, government, neighbors, community situations, and the like. We need to help children find their places as they become intellectually and verbally involved with the contemporary scene. Techniques for stimulating language in the contemporary-living learning environment are described below.

The *calendar* can be effectively utilized to stimulate language, providing it is a calendar which highlights children's birthdays, field trips, resource persons' visits, and community, state and national events. Animated discussions result as the children use a linear calendar to keep track of upcoming events as well as solve number problems that arise.

---

[13] For another teacher's statement of the value of physical activity in relation to language, see Leona M. Foerster's "As They Move They Learn," *Instructor* (March 1972): 59.

"Four kids are absent today, let's figure out how many are here today," or "It's been ten days since the minister showed us the gestures he uses with deaf people and I can still remember how they sing 'Glory, Glory, Hallelujah' with their hands."

A *news bulletin board* highlights pictures and stories from our daily life. Encouraging young children to bring in these items will result in a few contributions, but encouraging parents to assist their children in browsing through the paper for interesting items will be of greater benefit. Newspaper and magazine publishers spend millions of dollars each year to find unique human interest pictures which give a different slant on a subject, set up a problem situation, or distort reality through optical illusion. These provide tremendous discussion stimuli. News stories which highlight special events or children in the news also furnish a meaningful discussion base and supply the added bonus of exposing children to the world around them.

Yet, it is amazing how schools will spend untold dollars for commercial pictures and other language-stimulating devices, overlooking the newspapers and national picture magazines which can provide classrooms with more than sufficient material while keeping students abreast of contemporary life. A teacher was asked to review some commercial educational materials developed to stimulate language. She used it several days with her kindergarten children with disappointing results. The next day she brought to her class a newspaper picture of the huge outdoor sculpture by Picasso which graces an open square in Chicago. What a lively discussion ensued as the children tried to describe what they thought it was!

Conversation, Reporting, and Discussion is a three-part technique which substitutes for the traditional "show and tell," "bring and brag," or "pump and prime," and signifies a new approach to this part of the daily program with greater results in language development. The authors recently made a survey of "show and tell" practices described by teachers attending several different early-education workshops. Among the restrictions listed by teachers were: boys on Tuesdays, girls on Thursdays; bring only one item; must say at least three things about it; must speak in full sentences; must speak out loud; must bring unit item on Monday, news items on Tuesday, personal item on Wednesday. . . . The teachers who set up these restrictions gave "language development" as their purpose of "show and tell!" Apparently, however, they are developing language only on certain days and around certain topics! What about the rest of the day? There is no need to accomplish everything during this period, and it is especially impossible under such arbitrary conditions.

Furthermore, the fifth rock that is brought in, the new shoes, the lost teeth build little new vocabulary and need not be made a part of group sharing. These items may be of great importance, but there are other ways to recognize them, thus eliminating the risk of children grabbing the last thing they see as they leave the house just to have something to "show and tell."

Conversation suggests the need for the teacher to talk with each child as he enters the room. During this informal conversation, the teacher can suggest that Jon put the fifth rock he has brought to school on the observation table for his classmates to see, can help Tammy find a comfortable place for the doll she has brought for the third consecutive day, and can exclaim over Brad's lost tooth. In essence, these children do have "show and tell" but not at the expense of the total class's time. This conversation time is also beneficial in uncovering personal information important to know in dealing with the child, such as a fight in the family, extreme marital problems, or a pending death. Too often this information needlessly ends up being shared with the other children.

Reporting gives those children with items to share the opportunity to explain them to their classmates. Children might report on a news item, something for the observation table, or an artifact relating to a Unit Topic. These items will result in increased language and information development. As an example, during the number unit, Stephie brought her father's abacus. She reported what it was, demonstrated how it was used, explained that her father got it while visiting the Orient, and showed the children the Orient on the globe.

Discussion, which may be teacher or child initiated, emerges from a need for a common situation. It could, for example, relate to a news article on the President's trip, a "dangerous stranger" in the neighborhood, fire-prevention week, famous people's birthdays, or a behavior problem within the group. It provides another opportunity for children to use language and new vocabulary in responding to the topic under consideration.

Basic Tools. The basic tools learning environment includes what has been traditionally called the "three Rs" with additional emphasis on the language arts. The major areas under study in this environment are:

Oral language—what, how, and when it is used
Nonverbal language—everyday and special gestures

Five basic written code systems—graphic (picture) writing, word
    writing, idea writing, ABC writing, and electronetic writing[14]
Scribbles—the developmental phases of writing
Numbers—an idea code system of thinking or recording
Measurement—a standard way of looking at something
Tools for writing—sticks, pencils, pens, magic markers, crayons
Manipulative acts—cutting, pasting, folding, tearing, marking
Operational acts—listening, following directions, persisting

This basic tools learning environment is too broad to be given
adequate coverage in this chapter. It might be of value, however, to
highlight one sequence of several Unit Topics related to this environment, which can unfold language to children in a logical and historical
manner.

A Unit Topic on "Gestures" can involve children in nonverbal
communication, including spontaneous everyday gestures, occupational
gestures, or interpretive dance and movement gestures. Showing a film
without sound and having children interpret the story as well as in-
viting guests who use gestures in their occupations adds relevance to
this topic.

A Unit Topic on "Talk" exposes children to the many dialects
and idiolects in our culture. Children realize that, while people say
the same things, they say them differently. Presenting to children a
tape recording of many Mother Goose rhymes spoken in various dialects reinforces this notion.

A Unit Topic on "Folktales-Storytelling" introduces children to
the oral base of language by explaining the many versions of folktales.
Children create their own versions as they perpetuate this folkway of
communication. One kindergarten class heard several versions of "The
Runaway." In Russian the story is about a bun: in Norwegian, a pancake; in Scottish, a bannock; and in the United States, a gingerbread
boy.[15] After listening to these variations, the children created their
own version. In their story, a huge MacDonald hamburger rolled out

---

14 Electronetic writing is a term used to include recording ideas on film,
filmstrip, record, audiotape, videotape, and computers.

15 Almost any tale is available in several versions. In doing this one with
children, you might consult: Ruth Sawyer, *Journey Cake, Ho!* (New York: Viking
Press, 1953), "The Wee Bannock" in *More English Fairy Tales*, ed. Joseph Jacobs
(New York: Schocken Books, 1922), "The Pancake," in *Time for Fairy Tales Old
and New*, ed. May Hill Arbuthnot (Chicago: Scott, Foresman and Co., 1952), or
Tasha Tudor, *The Tasha Tudor Book of Fairy Tales* (New York: Platt and
Monk Publishers, 1969).

of the drive-in, bragged that it couldn't be caught, was chased by the cook, policeman, children, dogs, and cats. Finally it rolled into the kindergarten, where it was caught and devoured by the children.

Yet another Unit Topic, on "Mother Goose," represents a basic core of literature for the very young, originating from Charles Perrault's collection of folktales published originally in 1967. This unit examines the legends of Mother Goose origins, acquaints children with Father Goose, exposes them to an in-depth collection of Mother Goose literature, and points out the mother-father love function that literature offers.

"Book" is another Unit Topic which exposes children to the full range of this concept. Children examine why books came into being, their history, how they are made, their physical properties, where they can be obtained, as well as authorship and illustrations. Having children collect a wide variety of books, make their own books, visit with author or illustrator guests, and examine artifacts of early book forms will give children firsthand experience with the topic. Hopefully, this early involvement with books will put meaning into the decoding skills of the reading program as children look beyond to the excitement books hold in store.

Finally, a Unit Topic on "Five Basic Written Code Systems" involves children in the examination of graphic writing, word writing, idea writing, alphabet writing, and special writing such as shorthand and mechanical systems. Children communicate in all five writing codes, realizing the circumstances under which each does a more effective job.

These six Unit Topics provide scores of activities for language development. The teacher must be cautioned, however, that young children are not involved in these topics at a skilled level. The *foundational* and often *impressional* treatment of these topics give children an initial awareness of language. Hopefully, this awareness will stimulate a greater involvement in the skills as children see them as a means to a greater end.

The important job for teachers of young children is to know the content of these topics, to involve children in the vocabulary of each area, and to provide tangible resource persons, field exploration, and problem-solving situations so the vocabulary becomes fixed through proper and appropriate use. There are many sources available describing the content in each of these basic tool areas.

Performing Arts. This impressionally treated area lends itself to many classroom guests, as children are exposed to the world of expression through dance and movement, music, art, literature, folkcraft, and industrial arts.

Guests who play musical instruments, paint, sculpt, sew, carve wood, create imaginative settings, or form industrial products provide language in the descriptions of their skills as well as in the vocabulary attached to the related equipment.

An "Artist of the Month" or "Composer of the Month" can elicit children's personal reactions to many artists and their works while building language as the children relate these reactions to their own value system.

Materials available during play will allow children to select avenues of expression in a performing arts interest area. Records and tapes of all varieties of music and literary forms should be available. Comparing the various illustrations of a common story lets children respond to literature in a different way. In addition, the teacher may present the same story in different ways: orally, in book form, on film, and in record format. Following such a variety of presentations, a discussion of which form brought the book alive for each child requires that language beyond just the words or pictures of the story be used in making judgments.

Treated impressionally, the performing arts allows children to use language gained from contact with artifacts and artists to build a personal value structure. In so doing, it also exposes children to the language of line, form, texture, subject, mood, color, character, beat, shape, materials, and media which are the foundation of the performing arts areas.

Social Thinking. Social thinking involves children in activities which challenge them to look at themselves and their relationship with others. The *process* of social thinking is far more important than the *facts* of social situations, places, and events. The term *self-concept* is often used to describe the emphasis at the initial education level. However, while the concentration is on "self" it must include the broader aspect of self, namely, relationships with other beings.

Activities which involve children in the social thinking process include:

a. Self-description activities—Young children are egocentric, yet seldom have a full conception of their external appearance. Mirrors— full-length, three-way, magnifying, and others—need to be employed to highlight all physical features. A child, listening to his own voice on a tape recorder becomes aware of how he sounds to others. Using cameras to record classroom activities encourages children to use language in describing situations which have been photographed. A camera taken on field trips retrieves the on-site impressions for in-depth follow-up discussions.

   b. Self-esteem activities—Children need opportunities to talk about their capabilities, limitations, interests, wishes, and long-range goals. This introspection encourages recognition of their own uniqueness as well as a feeling of self-worth. A parent reported the following incident several months after her kindergarten child had been involved in a "Who Am I" unit:

> Tracy had fallen and cut a deep gash in her forehead. While it was in the healing stage, her father in a joking manner called her "scarface." Holding back tears his daughter retorted, "It doesn't matter what I look like on the outside. The important thing is what I'm like inside!"

   c. Activities related to family—Family pictures help children see common features within the family while highlighting individual differences. And discussing or assuming family roles demonstrates the need for family interdependence.

   d. Activities related to people—Children need to be exposed, in person or through graphics, to diverse people. Exposing children to people with varied characteristics sensitizes children to these differences while making them aware of many similarities. If it is true that attitudes are formed at a very early age, teachers must expose children to situations that allow them to see each person's worth beyond the too-easily formed surface biases.

   Implied in all of these activities is the need for refining one's relationships with others so that each child can effectively function in a world of people and yet retain his unique individuality. Because language forms the major element in his contact with others, its continual development and refinement is crucial to the social process.

   Service. The other aspect of social thinking is thinking about someone else. This should receive systematic handling. Too frequently, service is given little attention in educational programs, yet we expect children to automatically grow up being concerned for others. There are many opportunities for service projects which enable children to use language to convey their feelings and emotions. These projects include sending cards and messages to shut-ins or to senior citizens in care centers, writing group or individual expressions of sympathy after a local or national tragedy, and telephoning a sick classmate or teacher.

Scientific Thinking. Scientific thinking involves children in the processes of observing, questioning, predicting, recording, classifying, checking, and generalizing. As in social thinking the emphasis is on the process, not on the product.

Children need to intellectually, tactilely, and verbally explore a host of natural and sensory phenomena. Supplying appropriate equipment such as microscopes, magnifying glasses, and dissecting or probing tools adds to the experience.

To build scientific vocabulary along with the thinking processes which employ this vocabulary will provide children with many spontaneous opportunities throughout the year to apply this knowledge. Even though adults tire of the young child's asking the question "why" over and over again, they should not turn him off by ignoring such questions. Instead, turn these questions into opportunities for children to seek their own answers. In so doing, the "whys" will slowly be replaced by self-sustained active inquiry. And new language will grow with each new discovery.

The preceding discussion of keystones and learning environments is intended merely to whet the appetite for further exploration. An entire year's educational program cannot be spelled out in a few pages. However, it is hoped that this discussion will form the basic framework from which teachers can derive language objectives and activities that are appropriate and relevant to their particular classroom of children.

Oliver Wendell Holmes said that "Language is a temple in which the soul of those who speak it is enshrined."[16] Teachers of the very young need to assist children in reflecting more than just words. Rather, they must nurture language which allows effective expression of the inner depths of each child's heart and mind. Only then can language truly be considered an art!

A tacit assumption in this chapter has been that most children will come to the classroom with "normally" developed language skills. The program described is essentially a *developmental* one, designed to provide a rich array of experiences to further extend a child's competency in and enthusiasm for language. Realistically, however, the teacher must be aware that, even at this early stage, some children will manifest language problems needing *remedial* attention.

---

[16] David Kin, ed., *Dictionary of American Maxims* (New York: Crown Publishers, Inc., 1955).

Diagnosing Early Language Deficiencies

The major task of teachers of young children in the area of language deficiencies is to be aware of potential problems and to seek professional assistance immediately. Some language deficiencies which are left unattended for several years solidify into deep-rooted patterns which become increasingly difficult, if not impossible, to redirect as time goes by.

Teacher-education institutions give little or no education in the remediation of language deficiencies, except to specialists. Most classroom teachers are, therefore, unqualified to handle the language problems of their students. A rule of thumb to follow is to call for professional assistance on all suspected language problems.

Many school systems make the services of psychometrists, psychologists, or speech clinicians or therapists available. Let the professional decide if testing is necessary and suggest classroom techniques which will aid in overcoming the identified problem.

Of what language problems should a teacher be aware? Following is a sample list:

> Problems for referral to a speech clinician—irregular syntax; lack of plurals, possessives, and connectives; not including all sounds, especially s's and th's which are not acoustically intense; garbled speech and the lack of articulation; and pronounced speech defects.
>
> Problems for referral to a psychologist—a child who never talks; immature language patterns (baby talk, two- or three-word sentences); a child's continued third person referral to himself; tangential association (responding with speech thought unrelated to topic); not understanding words; and not following directions.

In some cases, several professionals may need to work together to diagnose and suggest remedies for the problem. And some problems, especially in the area of suspected mental retardation, are difficult to diagnose at this early age because professionals need to hear speech patterns which often the child has not yet acquired, to help identify a more deep-rooted problem.

If testing is required, there are several language tests available.[17] The *Illinois Test of Psycholinguistic Ability* is representative of a

---

[17] Complete information about the following and other tests can be found in *The Sixth Mental Measurements Yearbook*, ed., Oscar Kristen Buros (Highland Park, N.J.: The Gryphon Press, 1965). Information about possible uses, appropriate populations, validity and reliability, prices and sources are included.

comprehensive language test measuring two levels of speech organization: meaningful and automatic-sequential. At the meaningful level, three abilities are tested—decoding (Do fish swim?), encoding (Show me what you do with this. [hammer]), and associating (Soup is hot, ice cream is _____). "Here is an apple, here are two _____" is an example of automatic-sequential. The age span of the ITPA is 2.5 to 9 years of age.

The *Peabody Picture Vocabulary Test* is representative of tests of understood vocabulary. Word comprehension or understood vocabulary is measured by having a child point to pictures, one of which represents the word given. The age span of the Peabody Test is 2.5 to 18 years of age.

The *Templin-Darley Screening and Diagnostic Tests of Articulation* are representative of tests to measure articulation levels of children 3 to 8 years of age. A representative example of a language deficiency test is the *Slingerland Language Disability Test* for children of 5 to 14 years of age. Finally, the *Englemen Concept Inventory* is a sample of tests of concept development for children ages 4 to 7 years.

Early diagnosis and professional help are essential! Certain language problems of young children, if not treated early, may result in fixed lifetime language deficiencies. The teacher plays a crucial role in diagnosing language problems in time for professional assistance to redirect them into positive language patterns.

Summary

This chapter has dealt mainly with creating an enriched classroom environment to stimulate vocabulary and language use. While some practical ideas are included, the objective is to identify the content areas in which children need conceptual learning and to identify related language facilities for these content areas. It is hoped that the sample ideas will spark teachers to create many more.

A brief discussion of the basic functions of language was included to review the varied ways language is used. Another brief discussion of language-program approaches emphasized the need for evaluating and selecting approaches which will produce the most comprehensive results.

The approach identified in this chapter as having the most potential for language development is the "total-program approach." The total-program approach identifies basic keystones upon which the content rests and provides the major learning environments from which concepts and language are derived. The learning environments of play, contemporary living, physical fitness, basic tools, performing arts, scientific thinking, social thinking, and service provide this learning and language foundation.

The need for remediation of language problems at a time when they can be more easily overcome was stressed and it was suggested that teachers become familiar with diagnostic tools and refer children to specialists, when necessary.

The role of the teacher in early language development is crucial. He must identify content crucial to the needs of children. He must gather resources which allow children to approach the content from many avenues. And, through the classroom environment, he must constantly challenge children to acquire and use language as they meet new situations and solve new problems.

In providing the climate that offers a broad range of language experiences and in guiding each child's exploration of this environment, the teacher of young children will help insure that each child in his care has the opportunity to reach his full language potential.

Suggestions for Further Exploration

1. Review the available language-arts series which includes materials for preschool and kindergarten levels. Analyze the content to determine how effectively the approach relates the children's language development to their environmental language needs.
2. Keystones of an early-childhood-education program were suggested in the chapter. Identify basic assumptions of keystones *you* deem essential for an effective early-childhood-education program. How do your keystones compare with those suggested in the chapter?
3. Learning environments serve to identify the major focuses of a program and the language needed to articulate each focus. Are the suggested eight learning environments all inclusive? Develop your own set of learning environments and compare with those suggested.
4. Talk with several preschool and kindergarten teachers. Have them describe their approach to language development. Compare their approaches with the language-program approaches reviewed earlier in the chapter.
5. The chapter includes some sample classroom activities within each learning environment. What other ideas for classroom activities or play tangibles did the described activities generate in you? List several of these new ideas for each learning environment.

6. Select one content area within the learning environments. Search the community for available artifacts, resource persons, and field exploration sites related to that topic.
7. Secure a camera (instamatic-type cameras use film cartridges and do not require settings). Take slide pictures of people in the community who use gestures in their occupations. Consider referees, music conductors, policemen and firemen, airport ground crew, and others.

Appendix 1

Sample Parent Letter

Date

Dear Parents:

In the next few weeks children in our class will be exploring "Who Am I?" and "Names." The objectives of these units will be to establish foundational recognition of individual's names, differences between people, specific word recognition of names, self-image roles, and family contributions to each child.

Enjoy listening and conversing with your child about names, your child's self-image, and his individual behavior. Please provide needed information about interesting and unusual family names. If you have kept a family record or family photo album, permit these to be shown by your child in our self-expression center. Whenever you can, supply interesting family experiences concerning family names. Tell these to your child.

A special project, *Who's Who in the Kindergarten*, will be undertaken. Information for this project will need to be supplied by you, the parents. Could you find time to write a brief outline about your child, including entire name, nickname, reason for selection of name, birth weight, and little tidbits about your child's unique personality?

Once I had a child in class who discovered her middle name was *Eden*. This is the exact way she reported this information to her classmates, "My middle name is Eden, and Eden means beautiful, and . . . and . . . and when my daddy first saw me he thought I was the most beautiful thing he had ever seen."

These letters to you from school will be sent quite regularly. Each letter will be mailed through your child as a special postman or postmaid. Consider them as special delivery messages with tender loving thoughts on how we all can make school experiences very important.

Sincerely yours,

Ruth Hansen
Peter Hobart School

Part 1

This first paragraph of these home-school letters sets the specific information about Unit Topics and related school events.

Part 2

This part gives parents ideas and suggestions to do at home concerning the unit focus. Specific artifacts and resources which they may supply for adequate treatment of the curriculum are described. Requests for artifacts should be completely on a voluntary basis because many parents have a multitude of home tasks to do. Encourage only relevant materials to be provided, using the objectives of each unit as guides.

Part 3

This paragraph relates a true-to-life school experience illustrating how this unit has been experienced by other children in past instruction.

Part 4

A sentence or two adding a personal communication between teacher and parent-family is effective. The teacher adds those footnotes such as Artist of the Month, needs for empty cans for easel painting, and other learning materials that parents willingly supply upon request for each unit and special event in the curriculum.

Part 5

The closing lines remain professional. These letters to parents will vary in style because of each writer's personal pattern. It will be well to consider this form of communication as a blend between personal friendly letter writing and professional business communications. As you vary your style and personal form, keep in mind that it is best these letters not become overly personal nor overly professional in either *style* or *form*.

Appendix 2

Community Resource Questionnaire

Name _____

Address _____

Phone_____(home) _____(office, if appropriate)

    Listed below are several classifications in which parents and other interested community members can assist in expanding classroom study. Resource persons, field exploration, and artifacts provide firsthand experience with topics. This enables children to bridge the classroom environment with the home and broader community environments. Please respond in those areas of your interest and expertise.

1. Hobbies _____

2. Collections _____

3. Play musical instrument _____

4. Travel—where _____

    slides _____

    pictures _____

    artifacts _____

Occupation _____
    Would a visit to your place of work be worthwhile and possible?

    Would you be willing to visit the classroom to discuss or demonstrate? _____yes _____no?

    What days are best for you? _____

    What times are best for you? _____

    Would you need transportation? _____

    Would you be available for a classroom telephone call, if appropriate? _____yes _____no

Bibliography

Davis, D. C. and M. A., and Hansen, H. S. and R. M. *Playways, An Initial Learning Program.* New York: Winston Press, 1973.

Included in this program are twenty-five crucial early-childhood learning units and descriptions of learning environments, interest centers, and play centers.

Ginsburg, Herbert. *The Myth of the Deprived Child.* Englewood Cliffs, N.J.: Prentice-Hall, 1972.

The author discusses use and abuse of IQ scores and other measures with deprived children. He concludes that poor children's language is not generally deficient in important respects and that many enjoy a rich verbal culture.

Herron, R. E., and Sutton-Smith, B., *Child's Play.* New York: John Wiley & Sons, 1971.

Current research on play is described. Reports on the value of play in cognitive learning and the review of Piaget's concept of play are noteworthy.

Landreth, Catherine. *Early Childhood, Behavior and Learning.* New York: Alfred A. Knopf, 1969.

For a comprehensive overview of the early years development in all areas, this book provides research to support child development as well as overviews of various approaches in studying children.

Leeper, Sarah et al. *Good Schools for Young Children.* New York: The Macmillan Co., 1969.

This guide for working with three-, four-, and five-year-old children discusses language-arts activities and other content areas.

Michaelis, S. U. et al. *New Designs for the Elementary School Curriculum.* New York: McGraw-Hill Book Company, 1967.

This text gives a comprehensive overview for becoming familiar with skills in all subject-matter areas. These skills then need to be translated into appropriate content and activities.

Munro, Margaret. *The Psychology and Education of the Young American.* New York: Elseview Publishing Company, 1969.

This excellent foundation book has a chapter on the nature of language dealing with language acquisition and use. It also discusses language deprivation and language disorder.

Todd, Vivian and Heffernan, Helen. *The Years Before School: Guiding Preschool Children.* New York: The Macmillan Co.

This preschool methods text has a good section on language development as well as suggestions for the entire curriculum program.

CHAPTER FOUR

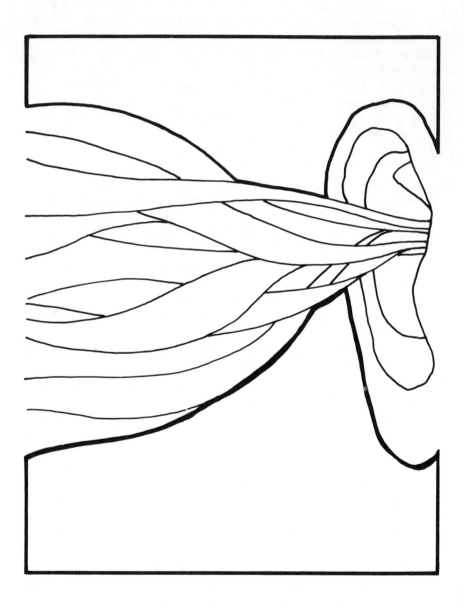

Listening

Almost from the moment a newborn child is laid in his crib, he is intently at work taking in information through our most-used receptive channel—the ears. Though this first listening is crude compared to the sophisticated, inferential listening adults do, it is a beginning. As the child grows, his listening processes develop as he senses, sorts, and begins to act upon the aural signals he receives.

By the time a child goes to school, he has listened for uncounted hours, largely on his own initiative. As with speech, most children receive little direct instruction in the home about how to listen. Despite the fact that most listening habits are assimilated unconsciously rather than taught, the child has learned the necessity of listening to learn. In this as in other areas, however, there are marked differences in how much the child has learned.

In some homes, children are encouraged to listen. Parents are around who listen and respond to what the child says. Dinner time is an occasion for talking and listening. The groundwork is laid, albeit unconsciously, for the idea that listening is a courtesy paid to the speaker. Duker has pointed out, "Generally it is agreed that parents

87

who listen to their children tend to be the best teachers of good listening habits." [1]

In other homes, little or no premium is put on listening. Frequently, children from culturally disadvantaged homes have poorly developed listening skills.[2] Their families are often fragmented because of instability and seldom gather for leisure exchange of talk. If the home environment is crowded with young children, it is usually permeated with noise. Apparently children from such surroundings often "tune-out" the noise, and, consequently, their listening skills develop slowly.

A Distinction in Terms

Before proceeding, a distinction must be made between two terms, *hearing* and *listening*. Though these are often used interchangeably, they refer, in fact, to two distinctly different abilities. *Hearing* refers to the physical reception of the sound waves through the ear. *Listening* refers to both the process of hearing and of responding as the listener reacts to the physical stimuli or uses the information he has heard. There are many classifications of listening, called either types or levels. The number of these and accompanying terminology varies with each writer. Which classification system is used makes little difference. The important thing to remember is that while most children with whom you will work can hear, few will be good listeners. This is the point at which your responsibility as a teacher of listening is apparent.

The Child as Listener in School

As any kindergarten teacher can tell you, there is a wide difference in listening ability among children. This difference remains apparent at all grade levels, though the spread seems to widen as children grow older. Whom can the teacher expect to be a good listener?

---

[1] Sam Duker, "Listening," in *Encyclopedia of Educational Research*, ed. Robert L. Ebel (New York: The Macmillan Co., 1969), pp. 747–51. An overview of the most significant recent research, this article provides a starting point for readers interested in knowing the major concerns in many areas of education.

[2] Such children do less well on listening tests, even after instruction. See Arlene K. Feltman, "The Effect of Reinforcement on Listening Skills of the Culturally Deprived" (Master's thesis, The Ohio State University, 1967). Though the groups designated as "deprived" responded favorably to tangible rewards, their group scores were lower than those of "average" groups.

Before any child can be an effective listener, he must be able to hear adequately. A continuing job of every teacher is to be alert for signs of children with hearing problems. One estimate is that between 5 and 10 percent of all children may be hearing impaired.[3]

Especially at the beginning of a school year, as the teacher begins working with a new group, one of his tasks is to determine if any of the children in the room have hearing problems. This is important at any grade level, for hearing problems develop at varying times. A child's loss may not have been detected by previous teachers, especially if it only recently became apparent. Detecting hearing problems is not a simple task, as different children may:

a. have trouble hearing different types of sounds,
b. hear with different efficiency at different times, due to such physical conditions as being overly tired, and
c. manifest their hearing problem in different ways.

The teacher looks for signs which indicate that rather than being an inattentive listener, the child may have a hearing impairment which needs referral to a specialist. For example, the child may:

1. have trouble hearing /th/ words, which contain the softest sound in the language.

2. have a problem hearing consonant sounds, as they are softer than are the vowel sounds in words.

3. have trouble understanding long sentences. Children with hearing problems can usually cope only with short sentences.[4]

4. have problems in voice production, including:
   a. abnormal pitch, intensity or quality of the voice,
   b. unusual speech rhythm, or
   c. articulation errors which are persistent.[5]

5. have trouble making a distinction between different phonemes.

---

[3] Harry A. Greene and Walter T. Petty, *Developing Language Skills in the Elementary Schools* (Boston: Allyn and Bacon, 1971).

[4] Ideas are adapted from material presented in Charles Van Riper, *Speech Correction* (Englewood Cliffs, N.J.: Prentice-Hall, 1963).

[5] Ideas are adapted from material presented in Lee Edward Travis, ed., *Handbook of Speech Pathology* (New York: Appleton-Century-Crofts, 1957).

6. have memory-span problems and cannot remember sequences. For example, the sequence activity, suggested on page 100, would prove difficult to children with hearing problems.

7. gesture frequently to make his ideas or wants known.

If such signs are evident, the teacher refers the child to the speech-and-hearing therapist employed by the school system or suggests to the parents the need to take the child to a doctor for hearing tests. The teacher makes such recommendations, even though some children he suspects of having hearing problems may simply be poor listeners. One writer has reported:

> According to some ear specialists, it may be that more than half of proclaimed deafness is nothing more than inattention.[6]

If hearing tests reveal no pathological problem with the child's hearing, the teacher must help the child to listen attentively. Those children whose listening skills are underdeveloped are a major focus of this chapter.[7]

Even among children whose hearing is adjudged "normal," there is a wide range of difference in listening ability. What types of children may the teacher expect to listen well?

The child who is intelligent is apt to be a good listener.[8] Though the exact nature of this relationship is uncertain, several researchers have found a significant relationship between listening skills and general intelligence. The child who is a good reader is also apt to be a more skilled listener than other children.[9] As both are receptive language skills, it is logical to posit such a relationship, which is in fact borne out by research studies. Sex differences are evidently not as apparent in this language skill as in some others. After six weeks of instruction

---

[6] Sara W. Lundsteen, *Listening–Its Impact on Reading and the Other Language Arts* (Urbana, Ill.: National Council of Teachers of English, 1971), p. 28.

[7] For those children whose hearing is impaired, special attention, beyond the training of the teacher, is required. For a teacher with such a child in the room, the following may be of help and may serve as a reference to recommend to the parents: Jacqueline Keaster and Gloria Hoverstein, *Suggestions to the Parents of Pre-School Children with Hearing Impairment* (Rochester, Minnesota: The American Academy of Ophthalmology and Otolaryngology, 1968). An inexpensive pamphlet which covers many areas of concern, this work suggests ideas for games and exercises parents can do with their hearing-impaired children.

[8] Duker, *Encyclopedia of Educational Research*, p. 749.

[9] One of several studies documenting this idea is by Charles T. Brown, "Three Studies on the Listening of Children," *Speech Monographs* 32 (June 1965): 129–38.

in a sequential listening program, Hollow found no significant differences in listening ability between boys and girls in her 200-child sample.[10]

Listening Demands

People frequently react to comments about the necessity of improving listening skills by wondering why this is a concern: Since everyone listens, why worry about it? One valid reason for helping children improve their listening skills is that we listen a large part of our lives, both in school and as adults.

A study done in schools indicates the important role listening plays in the lives of children. The researcher, Wilt, who studied 568 children in sixteen classrooms, investigated the amount of time spent in each of the language arts.[11] In addition, she studied the relation between what *actually* happened in the classroom and what teachers *thought* happened in their classrooms. She discovered that children spend an average of more than 2½ hours listening during a 5-hour school day. Especially interesting is the fact that this amount was more than twice the amount estimated by teachers. Though the Wilt study is by now an older one, it has not been replicated on a large scale. What are conditions like in schools in the 1970s? It is safe to assume that children still spend a good part of their school lives listening.

A smaller study investigated the amount of time devoted to the various language arts in the classrooms of 266 teachers.[12] The results indicated that the order of priority was:

    1st—reading
    2nd—writing
    3rd—speaking
    4th—listening

[10] Sister Mary Kevin Hollow, "An Experimental Study of Listening Comprehension at the Intermediate Grade Level (Ph.D. dissertation, Fordham University, 1955). Contrary evidence is presented in Larry L. Barker, *Listening Behavior* (Englewood Cliffs: Prentice-Hall, 1971), p. 45. Barker's discussion of fifteen factors which affect listening is a valuable reference.

[11] Miriam E. Wilt, "A Study of Teacher Awareness of Listening as a Factor in Elementary Education," *Journal of Educational Research* 43 (April 1950): 626–36.

[12] A. Van Wingerden, "A Study of Direct, Planned Listening Instruction in Four Counties in the State of Washington" (Ph.D. dissertation, Washington State University, 1965). It can be argued, of course, that a study so limited geographically can have few implications for the entire country. The study does raise questions about what conditions are; one would hope a nationwide study could be undertaken soon.

Apparently, though much time has elapsed since the Wilt findings became available, little change has occurred in the teaching patterns in elementary schools. Listening instruction remains on the bottom of the list; children still spend much time in an activity for which they receive little instruction. Of the respondents, 52.9 percent reported that there was "little" direct planned listening instruction in their program. A survey made by Brown revealed that less than 1 percent of the total content of elementary language-arts textbooks is devoted to listening instruction. Because this is the case, teachers too seldom know how to teach listening.[13] One of the concerns of this chapter will be to point out some ways in which teachers can work to improve listening skills.

Children listen much of the time they are in school; is the same true of adult life? An early study pointed out clearly the importance of listening in the lives of adults.[14] Rankin discovered that 68 percent of his subjects' waking hours were spent in some form of communication. The types and percentages were:

1. listening, 45 percent of the total
2. speaking, 30 percent of the total
3. reading, 16 percent of the total
4. writing, 9 percent of the total

If such a study were replicated today, what would be the results? Because of the increase of such passive entertainment as television, the percentage of time spent in listening has probably increased. We do not know for sure, but it is apparent that to function well both in school and the adult world, the child needs well-developed listening skills: such skills are increasingly called into use in other important areas. A study by the University of Michigan Research Center indicates that 58 percent of the public's political information is gathered from newspapers and magazines.[15] With the brevity and (some say) the bias of electronic media, it is apparent that critical listening is of utmost importance to our society.

---

[13] Kenneth L. Brown, "Speech and Listening in Language-Arts Textbooks," *Elementary English* 44 (April and May 1967): 336–41 and 461–65.

[14] Paul T. Rankin, "The Importance of Listening Ability," *English Journal* 17 (October 1928): 623–30. Though it was done with a small sample, several more recent studies done with larger samples have replicated his results, indicating the validity of Rankin's pioneer work in this area. See Donald E. Bird, "Are You Listening?" *Office Executive* 40 (April 1955): 18–19, or Lila R. Breiter, "Research in Listening and Its Importance to Literature" (Master's thesis, Brooklyn College, 1957).

[15] Reported in "The Art of Listening," in *Listening: Readings,* compiled by Sam Duker (Metuchen, N.J.: The Scarecrow Press, 1971), Vol. 2, p. 151.

Yet another reason for stressing the importance of listening is that much content is lost after listening occurs. It has been estimated that only one week after listening to an oral presentation, the average listener has forgotten 25 percent of what he has heard. After a month's interval, fully 50 percent of what was retained has been lost. Not only do we need to listen often, but we also lose much of what we have heard.

Listening: A Problem

In addition to demands for listening on both children and adults and evidence that wide differences in listening ability exist, some features of the act of listening create problems. One of these is the nature of the listening process. Mention was made earlier of the fact that children who are good readers will often be good listeners. This is logical because both are receptive skills. There is a fundamental difference between the two, however, The listener usually cannot control either the rate of presentation or the number of repetitions. In reading, the child can control both. If something makes no sense, he can reread, and then reread again, pausing to consult a dictionary to determine the meaning of a crucial word. Such luxury is not the listener's prerogative. The ephemeral words are spoken at a rate he does not choose, and it is often impossible to hear the same thing over again. It is true that tape recordings or records allow the child to control the number of repetitions. However, in more usual situations when he is listening to a person speak, the listener must "catch it on the wing."[16]

The converse problem, of the speaker going too slowly so the listener loses interest, has also been noted by several authorities. Common estimates are that we can listen comfortably at rates from six to ten times faster than a speaker can speak.[17] This discrepancy has been investigated by researchers who have demonstrated that in test conditions subjects can listen at rates up to 450 words per minute.[18] Such studies make use of mechanically compressed speech, eliminating the problem of high pitch which usually results when records or tapes are played at too fast a speed. Though the ability to listen and comprehend

---

[16] Paul S. Anderson, *Language Skills in Elementary Education* (New York: The Macmillan Company, 1972), p. 70. This point and many helpful suggestions for listening activities make the book a valuable one for teachers. The section on the teacher's voice quality (pp. 83–84) is well worth reading.

[17] Anderson, *Language Skills in Elementary Education*, p. 70.

[18] See for example, David B. Orr et al., "Trainability of Listening Comprehension of Speeded Discourse," *Journal of Educational Psychology* 56 (1965): 148–56.

compressed speech has been well established, no use of this information has been made at the elementary level at this time.

Is Improvement Possible?

Given that children listen with varying effectiveness but that many demands to listen are placed on *all* children, one question occurs. Does direct instruction in how to listen result in improved listening ability? According to the evidence presented by Brown, apparently authors of elementary materials for children don't believe so because they devote little attention to improvement of this skill.

In spite of this neglect of listening, several research studies indicate listening is a teachable skill. These are summarized by Duker in a book useful to teachers.[19] Duker surveyed a wide range of materials and concluded that considerable agreement exists among researchers: the skill of listening can be taught, and the results of such teaching can be measured.

A recent study by Childers is representative of those demonstrating the value of teaching listening skills.[20] Using a large group of children (N = 111) including a wide variety of intelligence levels, Childers tested listening ability before and after a series of lessons designed to increase listening skills. Children in all the groups improved their listening skills significantly.

It is apparent that listening is a necessary skill which can be improved through direct instruction. Many teachers want to help their children do this. The question remains: How does one go about this task? There are basically two approaches to listening instruction:

a. use of a commercial program, or
b. creation of a program by the classroom teacher.

Commercial Programs

A distinguishing feature of most commercial programs is their highly sequential, organized nature. Such programs identify a specific

---

[19] Sam Duker, *Listening Bibliography*, 2nd ed. (Metuchen, N.J.: The Scarecrow Press, Inc., 1968). This unique resource compiles annotations for 1332 articles and studies about listening.

[20] Perry R. Childers, "Listening Ability Is a Modifiable Skill," *Journal of Experimental Education* 38 (Summer 1970): 1–3.

set of listening subskills to be improved, often specify procedures for teacher and pupil, and typically make provision for evaluation of how well the skill is learned.

Teacher-Made Programs

Commercial programs provide a solution to the problem of a teacher with too many subjects to prepare in too short a time. In a real sense, however, no such program meets the specific needs of the children in a particular classroom as effectively as can one created especially by the teacher in that situation.

A major advantage of a teacher-made program is its *flexibility*. As he senses children's listening problems, the teacher can alter and adapt the sequence of experiences in response to the needs of the particular group. Sample listening experiences are included in this chapter. These should not be followed prescriptively but may suggest some ideas to try, once you determine the listening needs of your children. Hopefully, the sequence will encourage you to think about other experiences you can plan for your group.

Setting the Stage

Whether in preparation for a listening lesson or in the context of listening for directions in a subject-matter-related lesson, it is crucial that the teacher set the stage for careful listening. Much inattentive listening occurs because the speaker proceeds without preparing the listeners adequately.

Before beginning, the teacher should make sure to compensate for any physical distractions. This suggestion seems self-evident; in actuality children are often required to listen in less than ideal conditions. Lundsteen comments that:

> it is not uncommon for children to be expected to listen far beyond the time of their likely attention span with lawn mowers going or children playing outside the window, with noise-amplifying flooring, sweltering weather (unairconditioned), or over-heating— every imaginable kind of inhibition to attention.[21]

---

[21] Lundsteen, *Listening—Its Impact on Reading . . .* , p. 28.

As a teacher you need to be aware that children have grown accustomed to shutting out sounds. Ecologists express growing concern about noise pollution; children are among others shutting out the high-level noises pervading our atmosphere. This is not surprising, when we consider that overall loudness of environmental noise is doubling every ten years. Quiet eludes us: in addition to loud noises, we are constantly bombarded by the ubiquitous mechanized music which fills the spaces in restaurants, elevators, and waiting rooms. That is among the less offensive; many noises in our environments approach deafening level.

Even in school children *must* tune out. The task of finishing an assignment while other children, perhaps no more than fifteen feet away, are reading orally is not an easy one. Since children have learned to ignore sound, when you are planning a lesson in which they must listen, you will need to set the stage carefully so that they can listen.

In addition to setting the stage, it is important that teachers set the *expectation* of listening attentively. Frequently, children ask over and over again to have simple directions repeated. When the teacher acquiesces, the result is less efficient listening habits. It is crucial that teachers establish in children's minds that directions and instructions will be given once, and once *only*. Naturally this cannot be done precipitately: some warning must be given and practice in listening attentively must be provided.

The teacher can easily talk with the children, perhaps pointing out that he has had to repeat instructions several times and alerting children to the fact he does not intend to continue doing so. The teacher should systematically reduce the number of times he repeats directions until he says all of them only once. This encourages careful listening to all instructions.

Children also need to be prepared by being informed about the *purpose for listening.* Some brief introduction, perhaps stating the nature of the instructions and why the children are to listen, will help establish the purpose for listening. The teacher does not entreat children to listen "Because listening is important," but rather "Because when I have finished giving the directions there are three activities you are to do." This procedure puts listening into a very practical framework: the child begins to realize that unless he listens, he will be unable to accomplish the task.

What to do with the child who does not listen, even though directions are repeated only once? The remedy is to maintain the policy, telling the child he can find out from some other child what the instructions were. The bother of being interrupted by a child who has not listened soon annoys others who have, and they are not slow to let the nonlistener know they don't want to listen for him.

Probably one of the most significant things a teacher does to encourage good listening habits is to be a good listener himself. It is unreasonable in children's eyes, as in those of an adult, to ask others to do something we ourselves don't do. Yet too often teachers, preoccupied in many tasks, ignore the child when he speaks or reads. A student teacher once personified such preoccupation in a negative way. While a child was reading orally during reading groups, she got up from her chair, walked halfway across the room, wrote an additional direction she had forgotten on the chalkboard, walked back and sat down in the reading circle. You can imagine the child's feeling! Not only does this reinforce in the child's mind that what he does is not important, it further reinforces the idea that listening is not important to the teacher.

While it is true for any group of children, it is probably especially true for children from culturally different backgrounds that the teacher must listen attentively if he wishes to establish good listening habits. Many of these children grow up in crowded living conditions where the air is filled with the sounds of many people and the intrusive noise of the television set. The quieter atmosphere of the classroom where the teacher, an adult model, listens to him, may in fact be the only place he enjoys an adult listening ear.

A factor teachers of culturally different children must keep in mind is that evidence of listening varies from culture to culture. Hall comments that members of a culture manipulate such things as posture and eye contact differently, though often teachers of different cultural groups may be unaware of this. Information about such differences in European cultures has existed for some time. Other groups' evidences of listening have not been widely studied. Hall warns that teachers of Mexican-American, Puerto Rican, and Negro children must be aware that ways of showing one is listening may vary with these cultures.

> Basically the informal rule for black culture goes somewhat as follows: if you are in the same room with another person, or in a context where he has ready access to you there are times when there is no need to go through the motions of showing him you are listening because that is automatically implied.[22]

---

[22] Edward T. Hall, "Listening Behavior: Some Cultural Differences," *Phi Delta Kappan* 50 (March 1969): 379–80.

The sensitive teacher of such children will do his best to learn what these culturally induced manifestations are in order to facilitate learning.

A Sequence of Skills

Earlier it was pointed out that there are two basic approaches to teaching or refining listening skills. One approach is for the teacher to develop a listening program for his children. What follows is a sequence of listening skills which may be used to develop a listening program, though it is not intended that any class would necessarily follow the sequence completely, or in this exact order. The teacher, working closely with a group over an extended period of time, can easily determine if the children are profiting from a particular segment of the sequence and can either condense, expand, or eliminate it.

Listening to Natural Sounds. It is beneficial to begin a sequence of listening experiences by having children stop everything they are doing, and simply listen to all the sounds they can hear around them. The group can then discuss the sounds they heard, perhaps listing them on the chalkboard. Having children listen for the variety of sounds they hear on the way to school is a helpful activity. To make this more complex, have children think about what conditions might affect sounds (time of year, of day, atmospheric conditions). Children can become very sophisticated listeners as a result of such activities. One day when we were doing this activity, I was surprised to find a child in my fifth-grade class could correctly identify, not only that it was a sports car which had been started outside our window, but also what *kind* of a car it was—very well-developed listening skills, indeed. Such experiences as these make children *aware* of the variety of sounds which surround us and sensitize them to information we can gather through our sense of hearing.

Listening to Created Sounds. Children enjoy contributing objects to a "Listening Box." Several objects hidden from sight in a cardboard box can be used to make sounds which the children are asked to identify. One begins simply, perhaps with a scissors, and moves to more complex sounds. Eventually children can tell the difference between the sound made when a metal lid is opened (for instance, the kind on a band-aid box) and the sound made when a plastic lid is opened (for instance, on a refrigerator storage box).[23] To begin the activity, the teacher should provide the box with objects in it, but quickly the children take over, and they enjoy bringing a variety of objects to put in the "Sound Box." Such an activity can sensitize children to rather minimal differences in sounds which are similar, as they enjoy being "sound detectives."

Listening to Voices. A simple game can be made of having children listen to voices in an effort to determine who was speaking. The teacher instructs the children to close their eyes. Then he walks quietly around the room, stopping to tap one person on the shoulder. After returning to the front of the room, the teacher has the child say three or four sentences, and the other children guess who said them. It is a simple game, but it does encourage careful listening, particularly as the only clue the children have is an aural one.

Developing Words to Describe. In doing the preceding and other listening activities, the teacher is working to develop a vocabulary which describes sounds the children have heard. This is slow to develop; some of the less specific words come first. "It was a loud sound," or "It was a soft sound." On the other hand, children can be led to see that we can describe several aspects of sound:

> its *pitch*—the highness or lowness of the sound. Comparisons can be made, and when listening to three sounds, words like higher, highest or lower, lowest can be encouraged.
>
> its *timbre*. Children should be encouraged to describe the quality of the sound—it is a soft sound, a harsh sound, a raspy, or buzzy, or singy sound.[24]
>
> its *duration*. All sounds can be characterized as constant or intermittent, and children can be asked to describe the nature of this aspect of the sound. If it is intermittent, can the pattern of sound

---

[23] It is often wise to have children listen to sounds from similar but slightly different sources. Listening to many different kinds of clocks, for example, sensitizes children to minute differences in sounds. See the lesson "A Story about Clocks," in *This Is Music for Today*, Teacher's Edition, eds. William R. Sur et al. (Boston: Allyn and Bacon, 1971), Grade 1, pp. 178–80. You might have children make a collection of clocks in the classroom to use as the basis for a sound-discrimination lesson.

[24] These terms may sound rather imprecise, but the point is to encourage the child to put into words the sense impression he has taken in through his ears. For the teacher to insist on the one word which seems most appropriate to him would be to defeat the purpose of the exercise.

and silence be described in words? Many listening activities of this nature can be planned with the music teacher, who will be happy to suggest experiences in which children listen to various musical instruments. If you have no music teacher, consult any of the elementary music series looking especially at the listening sections provided.[25]

Listening for Sequence. It is simple to encourage attentive listening in quasi-game situations by having children listen to sequences and then tell or write what they have heard. Kindergarten children can listen to simple sequences made by rhythm instruments and then tell what they heard. The teacher might play a sequence: bell, then drum; bell, drum, drum; or drum, drum, bell. This can be done first in the open and later behind a small screen to focus the attention on listening.[26] The sequences can become more involved as children's ability increases.

With older children, you may read a string of numbers: 2, 7, 11, 4, 9. Begin with a short string and gradually increase it, being sure to vary odd and even numbers. Read the sequence evenly at first, and then try patterning with the voice: 2, 1, / 4, 3, 4, / 7, 9; or 3, 2, 1, / 2, 5, / 7. Encourage children to discuss such questions as: "Which way is easier to remember—when the numbers are read evenly, or in a patterned sequence?" Children find that the challenge of listening and remembering the sequence is an enjoyable experience, and attentive listening is encouraged.

Try sequencing with a simple series of directions, which you read while children listen and then respond. When you begin, three directions may be enough; see how far you can extend this. A sample series might include:

"Write your:
   a. middle name,
   b. our classroom number, and
   c. the name of the street you live on."

---

[25] See for example, William R. Sur et al., *This is Music for Today* (Boston: Allyn and Bacon, 1971). The unit "Adventures in Sound," Book 3, pp. 52–71 (Teacher's Edition) plus accompanying record provide a sequence of listening activities designed to increase children's sensitivity to sound differences.

[26] This and other suggestions are included in Naomi K. Zigmond and Regina Circi, *Auditory Learning* (San Rafael, Calif.: Dimensions Publishing Company, 1968). See especially the chapter on listening activities for primary-grade children.

With older children who have had more practice, such a sequence might include:

"Write your:
    a. age,
    b. the number of years you've lived here,
    c. your mother's first name,
    d. the sum of 7 x 9,
    e. your favorite food,
    f. your middle name, and
    g. your shoe size."

Listening to Anticipate. The ability to anticipate is closely linked to the ability to extract meaning while listening. A child may learn to anticipate when presented with a piece of poetry in which some of the words are left out. The purpose is to encourage children to use whatever clues they can garner in trying to guess what the missing word might be.

For example, the teacher might read the following poem, and leave out the italicized words. Children are then encouraged to offer their suggestions about what word might logically fit into the blank, based on what they have heard until then.

Cat

by Mary Britton Miller

The black cat yawns,
Opens her *jaws*
Stretches her legs,
And shows her *claws*.

Then she gets up
And stands on four
Long still *legs*
and yawns some more.

She shows her sharp teeth,
She stretches her lip,
Her slice of a tongue
Turns up at the *tip*.

Lifting herself
on her delicate toes
She arches her *back*
As high as it goes.

> She lets herself down
> With particular care,
> And pads away
> With her *tail* in the air.[27]

It is unnecessary to insist that children give the one word the poet chose. There is often more than one answer possible; the teacher encourages children to discuss the reasons they think their answer is most likely. In addition to listening for missing words, children can also listen for missing phrases. In using the following poem, for example, children need to listen attentively to gather information about the pattern of the poem, so they can anticipate what will come next. They are to fill in the italicized lines.

The Mysterious Cat

by Vachel Lindsay

> I saw a proud, mysterious cat,
> I saw a proud, mysterious cat,
> Too proud to catch a mouse or rat—
> Mew, mew, mew.

> But catnip she would eat and purr,
> *But catnip she would eat and purr,*
> And goldfish she did much prefer—
> *Mew, mew, mew.*

> I saw a cat—'twas but a dream,
> *I saw a cat—'twas but a dream,*
> Who scorned the slave that brought her cream—
> *Mew, mew, mew.*

> Unless the slave were dressed in style,
> *Unless the slave were dressed in style,*
> And knelt before her all the while—
> Mew, mew, mew.

> Did you ever hear of a thing like that?
> Did you ever hear of a thing like that?
> Did you ever hear of a thing like that?
> Oh, what a proud mysterious cat.

---

[27] From Mary Britton Miller, *Menagerie*, first ed. (New York: The Macmillan Co., 1928).

This is also available in Isabel J. Peterson, selector, *The First Book of Poetry* (New York: Franklin Watts, 1954), p. 3. Though the illustrations by Elgin are nondescript, the book offers a particularly fine collection of animal poems. The section called "Just for Fun" will also appeal to children.

Oh, what a proud mysterious cat.
Oh, what a proud mysterious cat.
Mew . . . Mew . . . Mew.[28]

Listening to Determine Meaning. There are times when the teacher prepares children for something they will listen to by discussing the meaning of unfamiliar words in advance. At other times, he encourages children to listen carefully to determine meaning from context. He might read the following:

Mary and Tom were walking home in the rain. They came to a big puddle on the sidewalk, and he splashed in the middle. Mary was very indignant. She made a face at Tom and ran home ahead of him.

You could ask the children to tell which of the following they think is correct.

a. Mary was wet.
b. Mary was confused.
c. Mary was tired.
d. Mary was angry.

Often the meaning may not be entirely clear. In the above example, it is apparent that Mary could be either (a) or (d). The purpose when beginning such exercises is not to pin down one specific meaning, but rather to encourage children to think about what they have heard, to discuss the evidence on which they have based their answer, and to determine which is the most likely possibility. The materials to motivate such listening and discussion can be made up by the teacher, or they can be drawn from literature.

The teacher might read one of Lionni's stories about a timid mouse named Theodore, who gained confidence in a devious way. The teacher

---

[28] Reprinted with permission of The Macmillan Co. from *Collected Poems* by Vachel Lindsay. Copyright 1914 by The Macmillan Co., renewed 1942 by Elizabeth C. Lindsay.

This is also available in William Cole, selector, *I Went to the Animal Fair* (Cleveland: The World Publishing Co., 1958), p. 12. The book includes such old favorites as "The Owl and the Pussy Cat," and also poems about unusual animals: badgers, lizards and woodchucks. The delicate black line drawing by Colette Rosselli add a winsome charm to the book.

could then engage children in a discussion about some of the words used. For example, he might read the following section:

> "Quirp!" said the mushroom.
> "What does it mean?" asked Theodore's friends, dumbfounded.
> "It means," said Theodore, "that the mouse should be venerated above all other animals."
> The news of Theodore's discovery spread quickly.
> His friends made him a crown.
> Animals came from far away with garlands of flowers.
> Wherever he went he was carried on the turtle's back on a cushion of flowers.
> And wherever he went he was venerated above all other animals.[29]

Rather than trying to pose some specific alternatives, as in the example on page 103, the teacher might simply ask children to tell what they think the word *venerate* means, based on what they have heard. To aid in vocabulary development, he might, after this initial informal listening exercise, have a few children look up the word in a dictionary to find other aspects of the definition.

Critical Listening. A more sophisticated kind of listening requires that children listen critically, in order to answer questions posed about the material. There are many times a shared listening experience may naturally culminate in some discussion questions. In this case, as in the case of a written question the child is to answer, the teacher's goal is to move beyond mere factual questions to ones requiring more involved thinking processes.

After children have listened to the following passage, they might be asked the simple recall questions below, so the teacher can determine how accurately they have listened.

> The cockroach belongs to an insect order that includes the grasshopper, the praying mantis, the cricket, the katydid, and the walking stick. The name of the order is Orthoptera, which means "Straight Wings." Most of these insects have two pairs of wings; the back pair folds like a fan under the long, straight front wings.[30]

---

[29] Leo Lionni, *Theodore and the Talking Mushroom* (New York: Pantheon Books, 1971).

[30] Joanna Cole, *Cockroaches* (New York: William Morrow and Co., 1971), p. 11.

Questions:

1. What are some other members of the group to which the cockroach belongs?
2. What does their scientific name mean?
3. How many wings do most of these insects have?

Beyond such basic, factual questions, however, it is the goal of the teacher to ask more involved questions, requiring critical listening. The Bloom Taxonomy was explained at length in Chapter Two, to which the reader is referred for a review. Sample questions, arranged from Level One to Level Six are included here to illustrate how such questions can be used in stimulating critical listening. The following material might be read to children:

> Sand Paintings, believed to have magical healing powers, are made by the Navajo, the largest of all Indian nations. The sand painters are Navajo medicine men, also called singers. They chant ceremonial songs as they create traditional designs from memory. The paintings are made by carefully dropping dry pigments, powdered stone and charcoal on a bed of clean sand.[31]

After children have listened to the paragraph, they might be asked the following questions:

Level One: What is the largest of the Indian nations?

Level Two: Would it be usual to find people other than the medicine men making the paintings?

Level Three: What might the medicine man's reaction be to a suggestion that new designs be used?

Level Four: Given what you know about the art, what can you assume about the relation between materials used and tradition?

Level Five: Could you assume the role of a Navajo, and tell a friend of your job as a sand painter?

Level Six: How could you tell if sand paintings were effective in accomplishing their purposes?

---

[31] Shirley Glubok, *The Art of the Southwest Indians* (New York: The Macmillan Co., 1971), p. 15.

Activities of this sort can lead to more sophisticated thought about what was presented, as children develop the ability to ask themselves such questions as:

1. What is the reliability of the source? Is the material drawn from books or people who are qualified in the area of their presentatation?

2. What is the relevance of the argument? Good listeners try to determine what helps make the point and what is simply extraneous.[32]

3. Is the speaker using language emotively to cloud my thinking, so I won't remember the actual facts which are presented?[33]

The above materials are factual, but at times the teacher uses literature when attempting to encourage critical listening. The ability to draw inferences, to extend or extrapolate ideas beyond the basic material in a story is a mature skill which develops slowly. As he discusses a story the class has shared orally, the teacher is motivating children to use what they have heard to answer higher-level questions the answers for which were not given in the story.

The teacher might use the disarmingly original story of the bat,[34] unlike his brothers, who has aspirations to write poetry. He encounters an audience for his writing in a neighboring mockingbird. After reading the entire story for the children, the teacher might ask such questions as the following:

How do you think the bat might react if he encountered somebody in trouble on his nightly flights? What evidence do you have in the story about the nature of his personality?

Do you think the mockingbird was genuinely interested in the bat's poems? What clues do you have? At what points in the story

---

[32] This distinction can be made with television commercials. Worthwhile listening lessons can be planned involving children in listening at home in the evening, and then discussing in class the next day what they observed. This author noted such an example recently in a commercial for a washing machine, the advantage of which was its smooth enamel washing drum, perfect for permanent press clothes. In reality, all washers feature such drums.

[33] This material is adapted from Anderson, *Language Skills in Elementary Education*, p. 76.

[34] Randall Jarrell, *The Bat Poet* (New York: The Macmillan Co., 1964). Written by a gifted American poet who also wrote fine prose, this small book recounting the adventures of the bat is illustrated with line drawings by Maurice Sendak.

is there a difference between what he says and what he does? Would he have reacted differently if the poems hadn't been as well-written?

Teachers Evaluate Themselves

In this, as in other curricular areas, the teacher is—like it or not—a model for children to emulate. This is fine if he is also an attentive and appreciative listener. If such is not the case, he may unconsciously be fostering poor listening habits among the children. Because listening habits, like much habituated behavior, often remain unexamined, a checklist for teachers is included here. The teacher is encouraged to confront questions in two areas:

How effective am I as a planner?

1. Do I realize children have difficulty listening attentively for long periods of time? Can I plan my sequence of learning activities with variety so that listening is a pleasant and not overly lengthy task?

2. Do I plan my presentation carefully so children listen to one thing at a time? Are my instructions planned with clarity so children can easily understand them?

3. Are my explanations, carefully given throughout, clear and concise? Have I planned more than one way to say something, so if children do not understand the first time, I am prepared with an alternative?

4. Do I plan some times during the day when an individual may come to me and share something orally? Do I work to establish a rapport which encourages such oral sharing and listening?

How effective am I as a presenter?

1. Do I encourage good listening by limiting the amount of talking I do?[35]

---

[35] Studies of the amount of talking teachers do yield the conclusion that ⅔ of the time it is the teacher who is talking. A study indicated that teachers ask eight questions for every question asked by a child. See Stephen M. Corey, "The Teachers Out-Talk the Pupils," in *Listening: Readings,* complier Sam Duker (New York: The Scarecrow Press, Inc., 1966). Teachers have found it possible to change their behavior in this area. See: Karen Drury Norris, "Shut Up, Teacher," *Today's Education* 60 (November 1971): 46.

2. Do I use changes in pitch, tempo, and volume of my speaking? Can I manipulate these paralinguistic elements to hold the children's attention? Do I also consciously use kinesics to add richness to my speech?

3. Do I give children time to think when I ask a question? Can I endure some "empty spaces" while children cope with the verbal problem I have presented? Or does silence threaten me, so that I have to fill it up with talk?

4. Do I wait to get the attention of all the children before I begin to speak? Have I eye contact with the majority of the listeners before I begin?

5. Do I remember to give some positive response to each speaker without needlessly summarizing or paraphrasing what he has said?[36]

6. Do I make sure that when only one child has difficulty understanding, I clarify for him later, rather than interrupting the train of thought of all the children while I explain?

7. Is my speech free of repeated expressions or phrases which are unnecessary or offensive? Two which are common among teachers are "you know . . ." and "Listen . . . ."

8. Do I listen attentively to children when they talk, and express my interest and appreciation in what they say?

The above is not to suggest that the teacher's major job is that of presenter or dispenser of information. Such was the case fifty years ago; ideas about the teacher's role are changing quickly. Nonetheless, there are times a teacher does present information, and such presentation ought to be as effective as possible. Thinking about the above questions may help the teacher increase his effectiveness.

Children Evaluate Themselves

It is often helpful to involve children in evaluating listening habits. Discussions about what group members think constitutes a good listener can begin at the kindergarten level, and children can draw up lists which may be posted in the classroom and reviewed periodically.

---

[36] This point and several other suggestions are included in Guy Wagner, "Teaching Listening," included in a series of leaflets entitled *Education* (Indianapolis: Bobbs-Merrill Co., 1967); this is a resource of much usefulness.

In first grade, for example, such a list is often quite simple. One drawn up cooperatively by a first-grade class and their teacher resulted in these rules.

A Good Listener

Am I a good listener? If so, I:

1. Look at the person who is talking to me.

2. Don't talk until it is question time.

3. Think about what the person is saying.

4. Keep my hands and feet quiet.

It is readily apparent to an adult, of course, that such criteria do not necessarily ensure attentive listening. It is very possible to be listening attentively while not looking at a speaker. However, at this level, when we are trying to build listening habits, it is more *likely* that good listening will occur if the child listener maintains eye contact with the speaker.

As children become older, the list of points included on the chart can become more sophisticated. A fifth-grade class drew up the following list.

Things a Good Listener Does

Do you think you are a good listener? If you are, you do these things:

1. Prepare to listen physically and mentally.

2. Anticipate the plan or organization of the talk. Listen for cues the speaker gives.

3. Listen for a summary. If the speaker doesn't give one, try to make one yourself.

4. Take brief notes on information talks.

5. Think of questions to ask the speaker. What else do you want to know?

6. Think about how the things the speaker said are alike or unlike what you already know.

Standardized Listening Tests

The teacher evaluates his own listening skills and encourages children to evaluate theirs, but at times he may wish for some more methodical means of evaluating children's growth in listening. Some commercial listening programs provide for evaluation. If the teacher has evolved a teacher-made program, he will also need to evolve a means of evaluating its effectiveness. Is this enough? Some teachers may not feel so, and, as a result, search for a standardized test in listening. Such tests are widely available in other skill areas; the selection is abundant in reading, for example. There is little available to a teacher interested in assessing listening, however.

One possibility open to teachers is to use the listening section from the *Sequential Tests of Educational Progress* (Princeton, New Jersey: Cooperative Test Division, Educational Testing Service). The test attempts to measure three factors:

a. *comprehension*, identifying main ideas, remembering significant details, and sequence of ideas.
b. *interpretation*, understanding the implications of main ideas, details, and the interrelationships between ideas.
c. *evaluation*, judging the validity of ideas, the organization of materials, and recognizing the intent of the speaker.

The classroom teacher administers the test; children respond to multiple-choice questions. One problem inherent in the testing is that there may be considerable variation from classroom to classroom, depending on how effective the teacher is in administering the test. The rate and mode of presentation may affect the reliability of the test.[37] Another limitation of the test is that the longest time it requires children to listen is five minutes; children are often involved in listening for longer periods than that, even in an elementary classroom. As a result of these factors, there is some doubt as to whether the test really tests listening.[38]

---

[37] One writer has suggested this limitation could be overcome by having the materials presented by a trained reader on tapes. See Andrew Wilkinson, "Listening and the Discriminative Response," in *Claremont Reading Conference 33rd Yearbook*, ed. Malcolm P. Douglass (Claremont, 1969).

[38] Reservations about the test have been expressed by Charles M. Kelly, "An Investigation of the Construct Validity of Two Commercially Published Listening Tests," *Speech Monographs* 42 (June 1965): 139–43. On the other hand, both the reviews, by Lindquist and Lorge, in *Mental Measurement Yearbook*, 5th edition, by Oskar Kristen Buros (Highland Park, New York: Gryphon Press, 1959), are favorable.

The teacher must use it with caution and interpret the results with care, but since it is virtually the only such test available at this time, it is important for teachers to be aware of it.

The teacher combines both informal in-class observation of pupil listening behavior and more formal test responses. He does this because he realizes that some children do better in one situation than in another. Lundsteen reminds us that:

> it is likely that in testing situations some of the "best" listeners may have high mental ability and are normally relatively inattentive under nontest circumstances; and some others simply do poorly in a test environment.[39]

Summary

Listening could be called the most elusive of the language skills; many demands are made, and yet too few children leave the elementary school as efficient listeners. Reasons for this were suggested in this chapter and ideas about improving the skill were given. To write and read about an aural skill can be frustrating, but I have done so in the hope that you will translate these ideas into a vital listening program in your classroom.

Suggestions for Further Exploration

1. Select a story or piece of informational writing of interest to you; practice reading it until you are satisfied with the results. Obtain a tape recorder and make a tape of your reading. Wait a week or so, then listen critically to the recording. Is it the kind of reading to which children would listen with interest? If not, what aspects of your presentation need work?

2. If you have access to a group of children, plan a short lesson and give it, recording it either on audiotape or videotape. The advantage of videotape is that it allows you to monitor your use of kinesics. Review the recording. Does the presentation encourage attentive listening, or are there elements you think need further work?

3. Electronic music, piped into most public places, is so all-pervasive we seldom notice it. Yet, in some ways it can be looked upon as noise

---

[39] Lundsteen, *Listening—Its Impact on Reading* . . . , p. 65.

pollution. Check your phone book to see if there is a supplier of such sound in your community. Call and arrange an interview with one of the staff. What rationale is given for such music? Can the people who provide this service also provide a documentation about its value? On what basis do they justify this service to those who consider using it?

4. Much concern has been expressed recently about noise pollution. You might be interested in reading about this problem. See Karl D. Kryter, *The Effects of Noise on Man* (New York: Academic Press, 1970); William Burns, *Noise and Man* (Philadelphia: Lippincott, 1969); or Theodore Berland, *The Fight for Quiet* (Englewood Cliffs: Prentice-Hall, 1970).

5. Is the average classroom a quiet place in which to listen and work? Observe in several classrooms and note what the sources of noise pollution are. Think up some ways these sources could be controlled, if not eliminated.

6. The Montessori approach is based on education of the senses including listening. You may find it of interest to read about the work of this pioneer educator. Of special note is her approach to developing listening skills, described in *The Montessori Method* (Cambridge, Mass.: Robert Bently,1964), pp. 203–6, 209–14.

Bibliography

Bednarz, Barbara. "Project Sound Makes It." *Elementary English* 48 (January 1971): 86–89.

The author points out that listening to sound is related to creative writing, and she includes a list of thirty-one musical selections which can be used as starters to elicit writing from children.

Bryant, John E. "Listening Centers: A Sound Investment in Education?" *Journal of Learning Disabilities* 3 (March 1970): 156–59.

Most articles describing listening centers as a means to individualization of listening instruction are favorable—this raises some questions about the idea.

Campbell, E. "Teaching Listening: A Case Example." *Audiovisual Instruction* 13 (November 1968): 1003.

The article describes a program for inner-city children which centered on poor listening habits of children including: tuning out, doing other things instead of listening, not thinking critically, and listening to words instead of ideas. This language program was designed to increase the listening skills, encourage maintaining attention, and develop an appreciation of the children's culture.

Farrell, Muriel, and Shirley H. Flint. "Are They Listening?" *Childhood Education* 43 (May 1967): 528–29.

The article stresses the importance of listening with a purpose. Several musical games are described which are to teach discrimination between pitches, timbres, tone qualities, tempo changes, and differences in rhythm.

Funk, Hal D., and DeWayne Triplett. *Language Arts in the Elementary School: Readings.* Philadelphia: J. B. Lippincott Co., 1972, pp. 259–84.

Especially notable for the recency of the materials included, this paperback volume brings together four important nomothetic articles suggesting to the teacher what he should do about listening.

Hamachek, Don E. "How to Get Your Child to Listen to You." and "How to Listen to Your Child." *Todays Education* 60 (April 1971): 33–48.

An excellent resource for the teacher—as it will cause him to reexamine his listening behavior—and for him to recommend to parents. Written in easily readable, concise fashion, both articles have a practical emphasis.

Herman, Wayne L. "The Use of Language Arts in Social Studies Lessons." *American Educational Research Journal* 4 (March 1967): 117–24.

During the six-week unit topic, the author had three judges record what went on in fourteen randomly selected fifth-grade classrooms. Results showed that in these social studies classes, children were engaged in listening and speaking 78.8 percent of the time, and were reading only 13 percent of the time. Children who were slow learners were called on a significantly smaller number of times than were bright children.

Kelly, Charles M. "Listening: Complex of Activities—and a Unitary Skill?" *Speech Monographs* 34 (November 1967): 455–66.

The author contends, in contrast with the statement in this chapter, that listening tests really tell us very little of value. He offers a wide-ranging critique of the literature and concludes by stating such a complex skill cannot be adequately assessed by the relatively crude measures now available.

Lundsteen, Sara W. "Critical Listening and Thinking: A Recommended Goal for Future Research." *Journal of Research and Development in Education* 3 (Fall 1969): 119–33.

The author points out that research and writing in this area is confused and confusing. The lack of agreed-upon definitions is partly the cause; she bases her work on Russell's definition. The article reviews the significant research, including that of Kellogg, Saadeh and Reddin, and contains a review of her extensive research. She identifies the need for teachers to develop their own critical listening skills so they can help children improve this skill.

Lundsteen, Sara W. "Language Arts in the Elementary School." in *Teaching for Creative Endeavor*, ed. W. B. Michael. Bloomington: Indiana University Press, 1968.

By a writer long known for her concern about and insights into listening skills, this section advocates a creative problem-solving approach to teaching listening. Many activities are described, and the author includes some brief notes about what research says to the teacher.

Mial, Dorothy J., and Stanley Jacobson. "Accent on Listening." *Todays Education* 57 (October 1968): 67–69.

The authors stress the importance of listening for *content* (facts and figures), *feeling* (how what the speaker is talking about affects him), and for *process* (what the speaker is trying to accomplish). Several games and techniques are included which are to improve students' skills in doing this.

Reddin, Estoy. "Listening Instruction, Reading and Critical Thinking." *The Reading Teacher* 21 no. 7 (April 1968): 654–58.

The researcher administered the Gates Reading Test and the New Critical Thinking Test before and after a sequence of eighteen listening lessons given to 381 intermediate grade children. The listening instruction did not result in significant increases in reading scores. Only for the sixth-grade groups did the instruction result in significantly increased critical thinking scores.

Russell, D. H., and Elizabeth F. *Listening Aids Through the Grades*. New York: Bureau of Publications, Teachers College, Columbia University, 1959.

Though by now an older reference, this still contains the most comprehensive collection of listening activities in existence. Over 100 activities are listed, divided into primary and intermediate grades, and into levels of listening skill. The introduction is of interest because of its analysis of the similarities and differences between reading and listening.

Books for Children

Borten, Helen. *Do You Hear What I Hear?* New York: Abelard-Schuman, 1960.

Borten's evocative prose, richly laden with unusual similes, is here turned to description of a wide variety of sounds. From the sound of a daisy's petal falling to the roar of trucks, she leads a reader to an appreciation of the wealth of information and sensuous delight our ears afford us.

Branley, Franklyn M. *High Sounds, Low Sounds*. New York: Thomas Y. Crowell Co., 1967.

When doing a listening unit, it is often possible to interest children in the science of sound. Branley's book does an admirable job of making complex matters simple. The experiments he suggests will intrigue children. The illustrations, done in Galdone's usual relaxed style, are a valued and integral part of the book.

Brown, Margaret Wise. *The Summer Noisy Book*. New York: Harper and Row, Publishers, 1951.

This is the story of little Muffin, an appealing pooch of indeterminate origin, and the sounds he hears both on his way to the country and while he is there. The story, to involve children, gives the sound and then asks children to guess what makes that sound. The cheerful pictures in full color by Leonard Weisgard are a happy addition to the story. This is from a series of books: see *The City Noisy Book, The Country Noisy Book, The Indoor Noisy Book,* and *The Quiet Noisy Book*.

Elkin, Benjamin. *The Loudest Noise in the World*. New York: Viking Press, 1954.

Prince Hulla-Baloo who lives in Hub Bub, the noisiest city in the world, has a doting father. The prince wants the loudest noise in the world for his sixth birthday present. This requires elaborate arrangements involving millions of people. Unfortunately, the plan goes awry, but the resulting present is the most beautiful one in the Prince's whole life.

Guilfoile, Elizabeth. *Nobody Listens to Andrew.* Chicago: Follett Publishing Co., 1957.

> The charming misadventures of Andrew, who tries valiantly to tell everyone his important message. All are too busy to listen, until he finally bellows out the news about the bear under his bed. The response such news causes completes the slim book.

Johnson, LaVerne. *Night Noises.* New York: Parents Magazine Press, 1968.

> Especially appealing to very young children, this slender tale recounts the adventures of a little boy upstairs in bed, who plays a game of listening to noises and trying to identify what they are. Particularly good for fostering basic auditory perception.

O'Neill, Mary L. *What Is That Sound?* New York: Atheneum, 1966.

> From the crash of the first poem to the thump of the last, the author's writing resounds with vibrant noise. She explores the unusual: wail, bleat, riffle, and twang. More common sounds are reshaped by the poet's unique vision into a fresh experience.

Showers, Paul. *The Listening Walk.* New York: Thomas Y. Crowell Co., 1961.

> A little boy, his pipe-puffing father, and their old dog go on a walk around the city. Sometimes the noises are soft: the sound of the dog's toenails on the sidewalk; sometimes they are loud: the boom of a jet. Always they are fascinating to the little boy, who uses his ears to sense the city in an unusual way. The pictures by Aliki, though limited in color, are fresh.

Shulevitz, Uri. *Oh What a Noise.* New York: The Macmillan Co., 1971.

> Through a surrealistic setting the nameless little boy who is the hero wanders from bedroom to bathroom to brush his teeth. On the way he encounters a noisy menagerie including cats, whales, parrots, monkeys, donkeys, lions and giants. The noise accumulates until its cacophony is deafening. All subsides gradually, as he returns sleepily to his bed.

Slepian, Jan, and Seidler, Ann. *The Junior Listen-Hear Program.* Chicago: Follett Publishing Co., 1967.

> This set of five picture books, boxed together, develops listening and auditory-discrimination skills. *The Silly Listening Book* develops gross listening. *An Ear Is to Hear* is for discriminative listening, *Bendemolena* is for listening to vocal play, *The Hungry Thing* is for listening to rhymes, and *Ding-Dong, Bing-Bong* develops discriminative listening to word pairs. The humorous tone of all the books is delightfully abetted by the charming illustrations of Richard Martin. *The Teacher's Source Book* is included in the package. Another series, the *Listen-Hear Books,* for older children, deals with particular sounds which may present difficulties to children.

Spier, Peter. *Gobble, Growl, Grunt*. New York: Doubleday & Co., 1971.

In an eye-catching succession of brilliantly colored pages, the illustrator has portrayed over 600 animals and the sounds each makes. Valuable both for the visual stimulation it offers, and for the familiarity it encourages with a wide diversity of sounds.

Tresselt, Alvin. *Wake Up, City!* New York: Lothrop, Lee and Shepard, 1957.

This is a sensitive evocation of the city just before dawn; as the sky brightens a variety of noises begin and increase in number and intensity. Children will enjoy making the sounds to go along with the narrative. The sketchy pictures in limited color by Duvoisin provide a variety of views. See also: *Wake Up, Farm*, by the same author-illustrator team.

CHAPTER FIVE

Oral Language

Developing the Art of Oral Language

This chapter focuses on enriching the basic skills in oral language which most children bring to school. It is generally agreed that most children are in command of the basic structure of their language before they come to school.[1] While there still are, at that time, some significant gaps in the skills which children possess, basic linguistic competency is for many children essentially established.[2] Our task therefore, if we are

---

[1] This fact has been established and accepted by many linguists. A comprehensive statement of young children's language acquisition is by Vera P. John and Sarah Moskovitz, entitled "Language Acquisition and Development in Early Childhood," in *Linguistics in School Programs*, The Sixty-ninth Yearbook of the National Society for the Study of Education, Part II (Chicago: The University of Chicago Press, 1970), pp. 167–215. Though difficult reading, this volume provides a wealth of information for the persistent reader. A section on the contribution linguistics makes to school programs will help teachers interested in learning how to use linguistic understandings.

[2] Carol Chomsky, *The Acquisition of Syntax in Children from Two to Ten* (Cambridge, Massachusetts: The M.I.T. Press, 1969). The author studied four different structures in the language of children over five years old and discovered that these are acquired in identifiable stages but that none were mastered by school age.

dealing with a group which has this competency, is to provide an array of experiences which will allow children to move beyond such basic competency to a more masterful fluency. The teacher provides experiences which will challenge children to extend, enrich, and elaborate the language patterns they already command.

The Primacy of Oral Language

An examination of some common facts about oral language which are too often overlooked will reveal the reason why linguists have for some time identified oral language as *the* language. This form, and not the written form which must be viewed as a symbolization removed from the actual language, merits our attention for several reasons:

1. Oral language is the most commonly used mode of expression. Studies have indicated that as adults we use oral communication more frequently than written language.[3]
2. Oral language is the first form which a child learns and, for many children, remains the mode in which he feels most secure.
3. Oral language is the form all peoples develop. Of the 2,796 languages in the world, all have an oral form, even though only about 153 have developed a written form.[4]

Oral Language in the Curriculum

Though it is apparent that children need to go beyond basic language skills to develop oral fluency, it is only recently that elementary school language-arts curricula have begun to shed their emphasis on written language and reflect the importance of the oral form. It is still,

---

[3] It is interesting that this was established some time ago and still remains true. In a study done in 1929, Paul T. Rankin reported that subjects spoke almost three times as much as they wrote. ("Listening Ability," Proceedings of the Ohio State Education Conference, pp. 172–83.) More recently a study by Ralph G. Nichols, "Do We Know How to Listen?" *The Speech Teacher* 10 (March 1961): 118–24, established that every seven out of ten minutes we are conscious, we are communicating verbally.

[4] In Mario Pei's *The Story of Language* (New York: Mentor Books, 1965), the author discusses in readable fashion many aspects of the 2,796 languages we speak. You will find the chapters on dialect and on place names of much help in stimulating children's interest. Information about the number of written languages is from the *New York Times Encyclopedia Almanac,* 1970.

unfortunately, true that neither elementary textbooks nor curriculum guides give the teacher enough encouragement for working on this aspect of language.

Brown did a study which examined the content and emphases in elementary language-arts series textbooks and concluded that although editors and writers:

> state explicitly and imply that oral communication should be stressed. . . . Nevertheless, actual emphasis in the books does not support this.[5]

Brown studied fourteen different language-arts series and as a result of this research concluded that "it is apparent that writing and grammar are emphasized more than speaking and listening."[6] This emphasis is in spite of numerous studies, to be discussed in the chapter on grammar, which point to the inefficiency of conscious teaching of grammar as a means of improving language fluency.

The study by Brown is an older one, but it has not been replicated. In newer language-arts materials, revised content and emphases are placing greater priority on oral language activities but written language activities still predominate. Another pervading influence on what is taught is the curriculum guide, and a recent examination of these found that "there is rarely any evidence of a deliberate sequence designed to develop oral skills."[7] More recent than Brown's study, Davidson's analysis reinforces our suspicion that the teacher interested in developing oral fluency in a sequential and structured way apparently receives little and rather intermittent support from both curriculum guides and language texts.

Probably one reason for the minimal emphasis on oral language is that, to date, little has been done with identifying the separate components of oral fluency. Little is available in organized fashion related to the following questions:

1. What specific oral competencies should children have as a result of contact with the oral fluency strand in a language-arts curriculum?

---

[5] Kenneth L. Brown, "Speech and Listening in Language-Arts Textbooks," *Elementary English* 44 (April 1967): 336–41.

[6] Brown, p. 341.

[7] Dorothy Davidson, "Trends in Curriculum Guides," *Elementary English* 45 (November 1968): 891–97.

2. What are the most efficient ways of developing the desired competencies? What experiences, contacts, problems, and challenges should children encounter in order to develop oral fluency?

3. What kinds of measurement and evaluation of oral fluency are appropriate? How could we measure the specific competencies to determine if our program is effective?

Walter Loban, in a fresh and direct article written especially for classroom teachers, has commented on the problem of evaluation in oral language.

> Developing adequate means of evaluating growth in oral skills will be especially essential, for until anything is evaluated it is unlikely to receive much emphasis in the total teaching scheme. "Give me the power to evaluate and I will control the curriculum," is a memorable saying. The boundaries of the curriculum inevitably shrink to whatever is evaluated, and at the present time oral proficiency is scarcely evaluated at all.[8]

Though Loban's article was written some time ago, a search of the literature about oral language reveals that even now attention to this vital area is minimal.

There seem to be at least two reasons for this evaluation problem. The *first* is the complexity of the oral message, and the *second* is its transitory nature. Any oral message is made up of a wide range of subcomponents: the basic oral sounds, the paralinguistic elements, and such little recognized components as gesture and kinesics. Thus, analyzing oral communication for evaluative purposes is a much more complex task than analyzing written communication. *Second,* the transitory nature of oral communication militates against effective evaluation. Once a message is frozen in writing it can be considered at leisure, re-examined, and pondered. Unless one had audiotape equipment, and indeed, preferably videotape equipment for preserving those nonverbal aspects of language, evaluation is almost impossible. Once something is said, it is lost. Until teachers can find the time and have use of facilities to tape students' oral comunication so this data can be analyzed later, effective evaluation in the oral area will be limited.

---

[8] Walter Loban, "Oral Language Proficiency Affects Reading and Writing," *The Instructor* (March 1966): 97ff. This brief article, filled with practical suggestions, emphasizes building classroom activities on the research in the area. The suggestions about sentence manipulation and about children hearing a variety of adult readers as models will be helpful.

Where to Begin: Informal Conversation

The kindergarten teacher's role in oral language is primarily one of encouraging the child's spontaneous oral language while helping to increase his fluency in using words to say what he wants to say. Most of the children with whom the kindergarten teacher works will be anxious to talk: with the teacher, with other children, and in small-group situations. Thus, the most important thing a kindergarten teacher does to increase oral fluency is to demonstrate interest in what children want to share with him.

The teacher does this in several ways. His listening ear must be available to the children as frequently as they need it. If he is elbow deep in mixing fingerpaints it is absolutely crucial that the teacher suggest to the child another (and more appropriate!) time for him to share what he wants to say. Thus the teacher says something like: "I can't talk with you right now, Bobby, or the paint will dry out, but come and sit by me when we have milk and I can listen then." It's admittedly true, in fact almost inevitable, that by milk time which may be only ten minutes away, the child will have forgotten what he wanted to say. True, but unimportant. What *is* important is that the teacher has established in the child's mind that what he has to say is significant, even if something prevents the teacher from listening at the exact moment the child has something to share.

Another way the kindergarten teacher demonstrates to children the importance of oral language is by the informal oral conversation groups which he forms and encourages. He will often draw two to six children together; perhaps to observe something, to reflect upon someone's idea, to share part of a book, or to help solve a problem. His purpose in these groups is to provide a milieu in which children may learn the delight of and, incidentally, some of the informal rules which govern small-group conversation/discussion.

The majority of kindergarten teachers seem imbued with the desire to facilitate the type of informal conversation and discussion considered here. The same is not, unfortunately, true of teachers of other grades. What are the values of informal conversation groups, and why should all teachers encourage them?

The values which accrue from such informal conversations are many. Frequently, a strengthening of the *self-concept* can occur as the child learns to interact with a group of peers. The child learns to cope with situations verbally, instead of withdrawing or having a tantrum, which may have sufficed at home. Another value is that development of *language learnings* may occur as the child finds out, for example, that though his idea may be clear to him it may not be clear to the listeners.

Conceptual learnings are another value of these informal conversation groups, for instance, when one child talks about a topic another child has never encountered, discusses an unfamiliar aspect of a familiar topic, or when another way of viewing a topic is suggested.

Any and all of these learnings can and do occur without the teacher being in the group. While it is true that, if there, he can help expand and relate any of the learnings which are occurring, he is not the crucial element in the group. As Lindberg says so well, there are many talkers in any elementary classroom, and the teacher who learns to regard himself as *one*, but not even the most important one, will have gained the freedom to allow children to learn on their own.[9]

There is no reason to assume that, once children leave kindergarten, these same values are not available from small-group conversations, but it is rare indeed to see any time specifically provided for such activities above kindergarten level. This interesting dichotomy between what we see as valid learning in kindergartens and do not accept in other grades is well worth thoughtful examination.

More Formal Conversations: Share and Tell

Share and Tell, humorously called "Bring and Lie" by Lucy of *Peanuts* fame, is one of the most abused of widely recommended practices in the elementary school. It is probably no exaggeration to claim that in most classrooms it is a complete waste of time.

Yet, this is unfortunate for the activity has much potential and the language learning it can offer to young children is wide ranging and long lasting. Surely when a teacher works on this skill, he is helping children develop an ability of much utility in adult life. For whether it is mother chatting with glee over a new dress found on sale or father with scarcely concealed pride showing off his new fishing lure, we all as adults engage in variations of this technique in sharing with our peers something which delights us.

Why then, is the elementary share-and-tell period almost universally such a listless preoccupation, frequently enforcing wandering

---

[9] Lucille Lindberg, "Oral Language or Else," *Elementary English* 42 (November 1965): 760–61. This article opens with a clear statement of the ways in which reading and writing are enhanced by the development of oral language competencies. It is of help to a teacher interested in developing speaking fluency because of the specific suggestions it offers.

attention upon something of interest to neither the possessor nor the listener? The answers to this question lie primarily in the techniques employed by the teacher.

To be of maximum effectiveness, the teacher should use the following techniques:

1. He gives undivided attention to what is going on. While the temptation may be great to balance the attendance register or to enter information on health records, the teacher always gives each sharer his full attention. This is because, at first, this activity is *informal*, but it is also *directed*. It is not free and spontaneous, though these are qualities the teacher is trying to develop. Such qualities are learned, and the teacher has to guide the discussion: by making appropriate comments, by asking leading questions, perhaps even by holding part of the article for the child. The first point to remember is that the teacher is an *active*, not a passive participant. As children develop the skill of taking part, the teacher's role becomes less. By the time the practice has served its purpose, eliciting a free flow of discussion centered on a topic, the teacher will be involved in only the most minimal way.

2. He develops the ability to ask intelligent, probing questions. Not such questions as: "Who gave you the fire truck, Tom?" Or, "When did you get the doll, Anne?" These elicit one- or few-words replies and do not help the teacher in expanding oral fluency. Rather, he asks such questions as:

   a. What else can you tell us about the doll, Anne?
   b. Have you seen any other toys today that look like Bobby's steam shovel? How are they like one another?
   c. Does the story Becky told remind you of anything which happened to you?
   d. What do you suppose you might have done if the same thing had happened while you were at the parade?

   Such questions are not easy to ask, but skill in this area can be developed. The teacher interested in such questioning skills is able to refer to several helpful sources. The best known of these is the *Taxonomy of Educational Objectives* developed by Bloom.[10] While it is not devoted specifically to questioning

---

[10] B. S. Bloom, ed., *Taxonomy of Educational Objectives: Handbook I: Cognitive Domain* (New York: David McKay Co., 1956). The brief summary contained in the book's appendix provides a good introduction to this book.

techniques, but to thought processes on six different cognitive levels, it is of much help when studied and reflected upon.

The Importance of Questions

It might seem at first that anyone intending to teach should be able to ask stimulating, open-ended questions. Research has demonstrated quite conclusively that such is not the case. The ability is neither native nor easy to develop. Research done on classroom questions in general,[11] on questions asked in reading classes in particular,[12] and, surprisingly enough, even questions asked in art classes,[13] indicates that many teachers need to improve the open-endedness of the questions they ask.

Developing Describing Competencies

Describing is one competency which can be expanded and enlarged as the teacher helps children toward oral fluency. Describing, only one of several components of fluency, is considered at length here to show how many different activities can lead to the goal of fluency.

Describing People. Children enjoy the opportunity to observe and then use words to create oral descriptions. While such activities may culminate in written activities for older children, younger children delight in and learn from describing people orally. For the primary child this is essentially a two-step procedure. First, the teacher works on

---

[11] Meredith D. Gall, "The Use of Questions in Teaching," *Review of Educational Research* 40 (December 1970): 707–21. Gall examines studies, dating to the early 1900s, which have examined such aspects of questioning as types teachers ask, amount of questions asked, schemes for categorizing questions and changing teachers' abilities to ask questions, and children's questions. It is a comprehensive survey, including a helpful chart summarizing eight of the most recent classification systems.

[12] Frank J. Guzak, "Teacher Questioning and Reading," *The Reading Teacher* 21 no. 3 (December 1967): 227–34. Guzak used classrooms at the second, fourth- and sixth-grade levels, tape recorded the reading groups, and then analyzed the types of questions asked, using the Bloom categories. He concluded that 56.9 percent of all questions asked were at the recall level and commented on "the trivial nature of teachers' literal questions."

[13] Robert D. Clements, "Art Teachers' Classroom Questioning," *Art Education* (April 1965): 16–19. One might expect teachers emphasizing creativity would ask open-ended questions. This survey, using a sample of elementary through college art teachers, found most of the questions to be low cognitive-level ones.

simple describing. He may tell children to secretly pick a friend they would like to describe and observe that friend in spare moments throughout the morning. In the afternoon, each child can give an oral description, and the others can guess the identity of the child being described.

When beginning the activity, the teacher may simply have the children observe randomly, and he then accepts and encourages all reporting. Later, when the children have developed some facility in this process, he may work with the group to help them categorize or organize the descriptors they have been using, as an aid to further improvement. The question: "What kinds of things about the person have we been including in our descriptions?" results in a list which, when posted in the room, will help children develop this skill.

A slightly more involved task is that of *comparing.* The child can choose two "subjects" to observe, and then by noting the likenesses and differences between the two, attempt to create for his listeners an oral impression of both children.

Describing Objects. Children can be challenged to give an oral description of objects, which presents a different sort of challenge than does describing people. The teacher may have a large cardboard box with objects in it and allow a child to describe one of them for the rest of the children, who can guess what the object is.

It's important to remember that, even though this can be a delightful game for children, the main purpose of the activity is *not* the guessing but rather the developing of describing competencies. Therefore, at some time after the children have enjoyed playing the "game," the teacher draws from them a list of elements which should be included in a good description. Such a list would include many aspects of the subject. After initiating this activity with objects he has selected, the teacher encourages more participation by stimulating children to bring objects for the "Describing Box."

In addition, at some time while working with this activity, the teacher helps children to understand that descriptions can be made in at least two different ways. One of these is *finite,* the other is *comparative.* Sample statements are included on page 128 to indicate how various elements might be described in both ways.

Describing Pictures. Pictures represent one type of object which can be described, but because they are more visually complex than most other objects, they deserve special attention as motivation in developing describing skills fluency.

TYPES OF DESCRIPTIONS

Finite	Comparative
A. *Size*	
"The object is about six inches long."	"The object is about as long as a water glass is tall."
B. *Color*	
"It's blue with a lot of black mixed in it."	"It's the color of the sky just before a thunderstorm."
C. *Texture*	
"It's made of lots of small peaks arranged close together in a regular pattern."	"It's like a rough kind of sandpaper."

Almost any kind of picture can be used to stimulate describing skills. One easy way to begin this activity with children has been described in an article which establishes the rationale for this oral language experience and includes a list of materials to use with children.[14] The procedure is a simple one. The teacher selects a poem, folktale, or fairy tale which is well-known, and then locates illustrations of it by several different artists. Children are shown the pictures and are encouraged to move through a three-step procedure: first simple *describing*, then *comparing* two illustrations, and finally *valuing*. This last term needs some clarification; it means here a statement of preference. The teacher is developing the fluency which enables the child to say: "I like this picture because . . . ." It is often as adults that we make statements beginning: "I like . . . ." But it is only rarely that we move to the more sophisticated statement which includes a fluent reason for this preference.

Observing and Describing Language.   One important aspect of a language program ought to be the study of language itself, an entity worthy of consideration. As a scientist might study animal or plant forms in his laboratory, so linguists utilize scientific techniques of observation and hypothesis to study language. To do this it is essential to secure a "chunk" of material to study.

One easy way to study language is to arrange for a tape exchange with a group of children in another part of the country. A student

---

[14] John Warren Stewig, "The Owl, The Pussycat, and Oral Language," *Elementary English* 50, no. 2 (February 1973): 325–30.

teacher with whom I worked recently evolved a very successful unit with a group of fifth-grade children. She contacted a teacher in another state and the classes prepared tapes about their cities as a social studies project. For over a week these children were involved in gathering material, sifting sources, collaborating in writing, and practicing reading their writing before recording their program about the city. The project entailed a wide variety of written and oral language skills.

Beyond the social study learning, however, the student teacher was able to develop some interesting study of language. After the social studies content had served its purpose, the student teacher had the children focus on language by having them listen *just* to the sounds on the tape, ignoring the content. This task proved a bit difficult, perhaps because the children were not used to studying oral language, and so they listened to the tape several times. As they did this, the student teacher had the children identify specific speech items they could discern which were different from their own. After they had listed these items on the chalkboard they categorized the items. The speech on the tape revealed differences in the three major classifications or building blocks of language:

1. morphology—there were specific word forms which were different
2. syntax   —there were some sentence constructions which were different
3. phonology —there were many pronunciation or sound differences which were apparent

The children enjoyed discussing these differences and learned from the experience. Some of the learnings were general, i.e., speech can be studied. Some of the learnings were quite specific. After some questioning by the teacher, children realized that it was in the vowel phonemes that the greatest differences occurred between the other children's speech and their own. As a result of this project, these children experienced working in the way linguists work: collecting data in the form of recorded speech and analyzing that data to see what patterns occur. Certainly all of this took place on a very simple level compared with the work of professional linguists. Yet such a project must be regarded as both a significant and somewhat unusual language experience for children. It transcended the usual mundane experiences with workbook pages and gave children insights into the vital force of language.

Children Create Beauty with their Voices

In an era when more time is spent in passive consumption of electronic media and less on the arts created by the individual, a suggestion to provide time for children to explore and extend the range, power, and expressiveness of their voices is apt to go unheeded. Yet, it is indeed true that children can create beauty with their voices, if they are helped to see how to do this.[15] The aim of this section is to make some very specific suggestions about how teachers can help children achieve great satisfaction from the expressive qualities of their voices. In the chapter on creative dramatics, mention is made of some of this expressiveness as related to body movement and physical involvement; here the emphasis is on voice alone.

Oral Reading

The teacher reads to children each day for a variety of purposes, including the important one of sharing with children a wide spectrum of literature they might not otherwise encounter. A second equally important purpose is to provide a model of an adult as reader in order that children may see this activity as pleasant, both to listener and reader.

The teacher reads every day, and reads widely, both from literature for children and also from literature written by children. Even five minutes a day can result in a vast quantity of literature being shared during the course of one year. For example, if you were to read just one poem a day for an entire school year, your children would encounter about 180 poems, which is more than most children encounter in their entire elementary school career. If you were to read prose for just five minutes per day, being able to share on an average five or six pages of prose each day—imagine how many books children could encounter in a year! Neither of these plans would be good as described, for a program of reading must be carefully chosen to include a variety of forms. The figures are included simply to make the point that vast quantities of literature, of whatever form, can be shared with children if the teacher will simply discipline himself to do this on a regular basis.

---

[15] For another statement by this author of the need to help children explore the expressive range of their voices, see "Teaching the Language Arts," in *The Elementary School*, ed. Frost (Boston: Houghton Mifflin, 1969), pp. 364–82. The section provides a good introduction to the language arts.

The Teacher as a Model for Oral Reading

As with storytelling, the purpose of oral reading in the classroom is not only as a pleasurable activity for children in a passive role. It extends to involving children in reading to the group. This does not mean reading around the circle in reading class, but rather, more expressive creation which occurs when the child has chosen something he likes so much that he wants to share it with others.

In order to make this sharing more effective, the teacher does several things:

1. He brings to conscious level what children have assimilated unconsciously about effective oral reading. Through discussion, the teacher can draw from children some things an effective oral reader does. These may be simply discussed, or they can be formalized in a chart which can be posted in the room. In either case, children might identify some of the following:

   a. The reader establishes eye contact with his listeners before beginning.
   b. He tells something interesting about the selection (perhaps why he likes it) before he begins.
   c. He has practiced enough so he can read fluently without excessive dependence on the book. The book is a reminder, or a cue-card, not a crutch.
   d. He uses his voice effectively to catch and hold interest. With younger children this point may be identified very simply: "His voice told us when he ended a sentence." With older children, it will be discussed in more sophisticated fashion: "He stressed the important words," or "He used the pauses effectively."

   The teacher will not necessarily discuss oral reading techniques with the group as a whole; not all children will be ready to begin oral reading at the same time. The teacher may work with a small group of children, but post the chart where everyone can see it. This will stimulate other children's interest, and soon many will want to prepare something to read to the class.

2. He helps children select something to read, keeping in mind:

   a. the child's reading ability, and
   b. what has been read in class recently.

The teacher is trying to ensure as pleasant an experience as possible for all the children in the room. Thus, if he finds that the child has chosen something too difficult, he will suggest that the child try something closer to his reading level. Similarly, if several children have read a particular form of literature until those listening begin to show signs of boredom, the teacher may suggest the child choose a different form.

3. He provides time for children to practice, because like many of the oral arts, oral reading requires practice. A child needs time alone to practice what he has chosen: to manipulate pitch, stress, and juncture in a variety of ways. He needs to experiment, using his voice in a variety of sentence contours, in order to bring life to the lifeless word.

4. The teacher provides time for the child to evaluate his own work before reading to the group. This can be done in at least two different ways. The teacher may make available to the child one of the inexpensive and easily operated cassette tape recorders. This, plus a small space, will result in some helpful evaluation of the reading. Children find listening to themselves as revealing as do adults; the child is sure to find different ways to read the material as a result of his use of the tape recorder.

   Another way to ensure that evaluation takes place is to let children prepare a reading and encourage them to work in pairs or small groups of three or four, to practice the reading before giving it for a larger audience. The important thing is that a child have time to practice the reading and get some reaction to it from other children.

5. The teacher helps a child evaluate his performance by asking questions. Before the child reads for a group, the teacher will find time to listen to him read the selection. After doing this, the teacher helps him consider and evaluate his own work. The teacher might ask such questions as:

   a. Where do you feel you read especially well? What things about your reading in this section (or sections) are particularly good?

   b. Where do you have trouble getting the reading to turn out the way you want it to? What things make trouble for you there?

   Oral reading leads naturally into storytelling, for the line between the two, especially when the reader is particularly skilled, is fine.

Storytelling

The ultimate purpose in the teacher sharing stories orally with his children is the same purpose as that of oral reading. In both activities the teacher is trying to establish in children's minds that these oral activities are worth the time and concern of an adult. His final goal is to motivate children so they will want to assume responsibility for the activity. To achieve this goal the teacher provides a model, and in the case of storytelling this involves learning and telling stories to his children.

Selecting a Story to Tell. The first step is to choose a story which you like—one which captures your imagination. Read through several stories, and then set the project aside. After a while, one or two of them will come back to you—you should probably learn one of these.

Preparing the Story. There are three basic steps in preparing the story. The first of these is to divide the story into *units of action*. As you read any story you will notice that most seem to divide into an easily definable series of actions, or episodes. These can be summarized in brief note form, and then the sequence of units of actions or episodes can be learned. This procedure, for most people, will prove to be a more efficient way of learning the story than simply trying to begin at the beginning and memorize to the end.

The story used here as an example is a delightful old Ukrainian folktale, summarized in units of action below. This should illustrate the procedure which can be applied to almost all stories.

THE CAT AND CHANTICLEER[16]

Unit One

This unit builds on the "stage-setting" you will do prior to telling the story, describing how the two animals live happily together in a house near the woods. In this unit the cat leaves the house to search for food, after warning Chanticleer to ignore the fox should she come lurking around.

---

[16] From Marie Halun Bloch, trans., *Ukrainian Folk Tales* (New York: Coward-McCann, 1964), p. 11.

Unit Two

The fox comes, calls to Chanticleer who forgets the cat's warning and reveals his presence. The fox breaks into the house through a window, grabs Chanticleer and runs off.

Unit Three

The cat hears Chanticleer's cries and after running to catch the fox, beats her and returns to the house with Chanticleer. The cat fixes the window, repeats the instructions and leaves again.

Unit Four

The fox returns and pleads to be let in. Chanticleer remains silent, but the second time the fox begs to be let in, Chanticleer forgets. The fox breaks the window, snatches Chanticleer and races home.

Unit Five

Chanticleer calls for help. The cat doesn't hear, and Chanticleer calls again. This time the cat hears, rescues his friend and returns home. Again he fixes the window, admonishes Chanticleer, and goes off to hunt.

Unit Six

Repeat of Unit Four.

Unit Seven

Chanticleer calls for help as he is carried home by the fox, but his cries reach the cat too late: the fox is safely inside her house when the cat dashes up.

Unit Eight

After pondering the problem, the cat returns home, dresses as a kobzar (similar to a gypsy) and returns to the fox's house with a oandura (like a guitar) and a sack.

Unit Nine

The fox and her family are inside when the cat arrives. The cat sings a pretty song and one of the daughters is lured outside to listen. The cat clubs her, puts her in his sack, and goes back to his singing. This procedure is repeated until all the children are captured.

Unit Ten

The cat sings again. This time the mother fox stamps angrily out to see what is keeping her children. She, too, is captured. Chanticleer is freed and the cat and Chanticleer live happily ever after.

Exact Wording. The second task is to identify those sections which do need to be memorized verbatim. This may include some words, some repeated phrases, or perhaps some larger sections. In this story, we need to use the word *chanticleer*, rather than substituting the more familiar word rooster, to retain the character of the story. We need to retain the phrase; "Chanticleer, cousin dear, let me in!" sung by the fox, because it forms a refrain throughout the story, as he tries to trick Chanticleer into letting him into the house.

A discerning storyteller also learns verbatim certain repeated sections in any story because the repetition encourages children to join in as the teller recites the lines. In this story, the pitiful cry of Chanticleer is repeated four times, and is probably best memorized and repeated identically each time.

> Pussy dear! Brother dear!
> The fox is taking me
> Beyond the green woodlands,
> Over the yellow sands,
> Beyond the rapid waters,
> Over the lofty mountains!
> Pussy dear! Brother dear!
>   Set me free!

Finally, the whole verse which the cat sings when trying to capture the fox family should be retained.

> Oh, tili-lich-ki
> The fox has three daughters
> And a son, Philipiko.
> Oh, tili-lich-ki
> Do come out and listen
> to my pretty singing.[17]

We retain all of these elements as they are in the story because to eliminate them is to destroy some of the essence of the story. Many folk- and fairy tales will include elements like this, but they will not be difficult to learn.

Learning the Story. The task of memorizing a story in its entirety is indeed formidable, especially today when demands for more "prac-

---

[17] Reprinted by permission of Coward, McCann & Geoghegan, Inc., from *Ukrainian Folk Tales* translated by Marie Halun Bloch. Copyright © 1964 by Marie Halun Bloch.

tical" activities press upon us all. The delightful things about story-telling is that few stories need to be memorized, though many may have short sections, as identified above, which will be learned exactly. Despite these sections, most stories are more interesting to listener and teller alike if the teller learns the essence of the story and allows it to unfold in a slightly different way each time he tells it.

Once the units of action are identified, these can be learned in an easy, conversational tone, using any words which come easily to you. It is simple enough to learn the units of action. Write them on index cards and carry them around with you. Then each time you have a few minutes, you can review the action and the sequence. Reread the cards, perhaps while you are waiting: for a red light, for the checkout line at the grocery, for an appointment with the doctor, for the elevator to arrive. Using a procedure like this, I find it usually takes me about three or four days to learn such a story as the one summarized above.

Gestures. An additional way to enhance the story is to use simple gestures when they seem appropriate. Some authors recommend subordination of gestures because of their feeling storytelling must not become drama. Despite this opinion, judicious use of some gestures can enhance a story. In the story used as an example here, while saying the line "over the lofty mountains," it seems logical to outline the mountains with one's hand, especially when telling the story to very young children in order to help focus their attention. While such gestures must not obscure the story, or become intrusive, certainly each individual can use good judgment in this matter. Arbuthnot reminds us that gestures can enhance a presentation, but that they must be geared to the age group. She summarizes: "But they [gestures] probably should diminish to the vanishing point with older children."[18]

Music. An additional way to enhance the telling of stories is to create simple tunes for songs which the characters sing. Songs occur with frequency in children's literature.[19] In "The Cat and Chanticleer" story, for example, desiring to hold children's attention, I made up the simple tune in Figure 4 to accompany the song the cat sings when luring the foxes onto the porch.

---

[18] May Hill Arbuthnot, *Children and Books*, 4th ed. (Chicago: Scott, Foresman & Co., 1972).

[19] A brief survey of folk- and fairy-tale literature reveals that many of these tales include songs. You might enjoy making up simple tunes for any of the following songs. (1) There are several different songs included in "The Widow's

Oh, ti-li lich-ki, The fox has three daugh-ters

and a son Phi- li-pi-ko. Oh, ti-li- lich-ki,

Do come out and li-sten to my pre-tty singing.

Figure 4

Simple tunes like this are easy to create and serve two purposes. *First*, they capture children's attention and provide for active involvement in the story. Even very young children enjoy singing along with the storyteller. In this story, the song is sung five times, and in a group of four year olds with whom I recently worked, the children who could not really learn the melody during the first telling of the story, nonetheless enjoyed singing some of the words.

Second, such songs reinforce in children's minds that creating or composing music, as composing in other art forms, is a logical school activity. As the teacher, you can teach these songs to the children

Lazy Daughter," in *Favorite Fairy Tales Told in Ireland*, ed., Virginia Haviland (Boston: Little, Brown and Co., 1961). (2) The song in the Brothers Grimm *Rumpelstiltskin* (New York: Harcourt Brace Jovanovich, 1967) with pictures by Jacqueline Ayer. The pictures by Ayer, done in a subdued but not sombre pallette, are particularly evocative of a different time and place in history. (3) The doleful song in "The Cauld Lad of Hilton" is in marked contrast to the more usual cheerful songs in *Fairy Tales from the British Isles*, ed. Anabel Williams-Ellis (New York: Frederick Warne and Co., 1960). (4) The awful creature in "Ruddy-my-Beard" sings a menacing song. Included in *Tales from the Welsh Hills*, ed. Ellen Pugh (New York: Dodd, Mead and Co., 1968). (5) The mocking monkey sings in "Born a Monkey, Live a Monkey" included in *West Indian Folk Tales*, ed. Philip Sherlock (New York: Henry Z. Walck, Inc., 1966). (6) Finally, for a more ambitious project, and one which will probably need the aid of your music teacher, try setting to music the carol which occurs in Kenneth Grahame's *The Wind in the Willows* (New York: Charles Scribner's Sons. 1960).

before you tell the story, either by simply singing the song without accompaniment, or by playing the melody on an autoharp or other instruments. The final goal is not the teacher as performer, but rather the child as composer of simple tunes.

Recent emphases in music education have included the composing of music, as opposed to the more conventional singing activities.[20] Children enjoy making up melodies, and when a melody composed by a group of children can be utilized in a storytelling session, it provides an additional impetus to create.

The Teacher as Storytelling Model. While storytelling is a pleasant activity which serves the useful purpose of exposing children to a wealth of literature they might not otherwise encounter, regular storytelling serves another purpose. Children see the teacher as a storyteller and this demonstrates for them that storytelling is an acceptable and pleasurable activity for adults. Especially in the early primary grades when children try to emulate the teacher, this practice helps establish storytelling as a legitimate activity in the minds of children.

Children as Storytellers. The teacher's goal is to encourage children to begin telling their own stories. As the kindergarten teacher encourages children to talk during share-and-tell periods, he is encouraging spontaneous oral composition. He lets children tell short stories, and often they will be only two to six sentences in length at the beginning, to lay the groundwork for more formal storytelling activities later.

In addition to encouraging children to make up their stories, the teacher may want to use particular materials to motivate stories. An interesting way to do this is to use any of the several tradebooks which have pictures but no printed story line. Those by Mercer Mayer are particularly helpful in eliciting stories from children.[21] The teacher shares the book with his group, asking questions and drawing comments from the children as they look at the book together. Later, he may have the children create a group story, dictating it to him orally as he writes it down. Or he may have children who want to share their own oral story on an individual basis.

---

[20] John Paynter and Peter Aston, *Sound and Silence* (Cambridge: The University Press, 1970), pp. 1–8. The introduction to this series of exercises, designed to expand the student's sense of what music is, provides a literate and challenging statement of interest to the general classroom teacher.

[21] Mercer Mayer, *A Boy, a Dog, and a Frog* (New York: Dial Press, 1967) and *Frog, Where Are You?* (New York: Dial Press, 1969).

What-If Questions. Another effective way to elicit stories from children is to pose "What-If" questions for the class.[22] The teacher can present one of these questions, either early in a day or the week, and then provide time later for children to tell their story in answer to the question. The goal in making up "What-if Questions" is to provide an open-ended structure. This procedure might seem to be a contradiction of creativity. Such is not the case. The fact that a question *is* posed does add some structure to the storytelling, but the open-ended nature of the questions encourages the child's creativity.

Recently a group of college juniors, preparing to work with children, created the following "What-if Questions," all of which proved effective in eliciting good stories from the children with whom they were used.

What-If?

a. What if when you stepped outside your house all the other people in the world had disappeared?

b. What if everything that you touched melted?

c. What if you could be anything in your mother's kitchen?

d. What if when you touched anything it spoke to you?

e. What if you went to bed one night and the sun didn't come up the next morning?

Children's Stories. Included below are some samples of stories told by the children with whom this set of "what-if" questions was used.

a. I'd cry, and I would run around yelling and screaming. I would be scared, because I would think that what got them would get me, too. So I would run back into my house and hide in the clothes hamper. I would keep on screaming.

Sue, Grade Two

b. One night I was in bed, and a monster was also in it. He stuck a claw into my head, and then he disappeared. I was bleeding! As I got up I touched my dresser and it melted. Then I knew I had a curse on me.

---

[22] This type of question is also recommended by F. Paul Torrance and R. F. Meyers, *Creative Learning and Teaching* (New York: Dodd, Mead and Co., 1970), pp. 212–14. The book contains many helpful ideas on motivating creativity, acquiring the skills of creative learning, teaching children to question, and providing a responsive environment.

Everything I touched would melt. In my class I went to the teacher and touched him. He melted. All the kids said, "How did you do that?" I told them all about it. I went to my desk and touched it, and it melted. Then it was time to go home. I touched the school and it melted. And that was the end of the school and of my curse.

Bob, Grade Five

c. I would be a refrigerator, and this is what I would do. It was supper time, and mother got the plates, and the forks, spoons and knives out. She made hamburgers and french fries. Then she sat cokes on the table. She was going to the refrigerator.
She opened the door and went to get the catsup, but I didn't want her to have it. I held onto it. She pulled and pulled and pulled. She said, "Let me have it." So I let her have it. I told the catsup to take off his lid. So he did, and red catsup went all over her head.

Debby, Grade Five

d. Once there was a little doll and I wanted to talk to her. One day she said she wet her diapers. I was so surprised that I fainted. Then she said I think I have to dump a pail of water on her face. Then I woke up and I saw her with a pail of water in her hand. I was about to say don't dump the water on me but she did. I was so mad I said I'll get you sometime. But she said shame, shame, on you. And she said are you going to change my diapers. And I said yes. And we lived happily ever after.

Marcie, Grade Three

e. One day I got out of bed. The sun had not come up. It was 10:00 A.M., so I thought I would visit the man in the sun. I put on my coat, shoes and other clothes. I went out with a flashlight because it was so dark. I talked to the man in the sun. He was asleep, so I waked him up. Then the sun began to shine.

Nancy, Grade Three

The teacher can also encourage children to create their own "what-if questions," once they understand the procedure. Children delight in making up this type of question. The following were among those made up by a fifth-grade class:

1. What if you woke up one morning and you were very bold?
2. What if you were a clock without a face?

3. What if you were a watermelon without seeds?

4. What would you do if you woke up and were bald?

Choral Speaking

Whether it's called choral speaking or choral reading is unimportant. What is crucial is that children encounter the joys of interpreting poetry orally in a group. In this section the two terms will be used interchangeably. Both terms refer to children, either in unison or divided into some sort of grouping, saying together a piece of poetry they enjoy.

A rich diet of poetry as part of the teacher's oral-reading program is undoubtedly one of the best ways to establish interest in, and to continue developing enthusiasm for, the art of choral speaking.

The kindergarten teacher, as he reads many poems to the children, will discover them repeating with him some of the words, or perhaps even a phrase or two. The teacher should encourage this, but participation at this level remains simple. Some groups may enjoy saying simple rhymes together, perhaps some from Mother Goose.[23] If this seems appropriate the teacher helps them learn to say a poem orally, but formal work in choral speaking is more logically a concern of the primary and intermediate grades.

Arbuthnot has pointed out that children may be divided into many types of groupings for choral reading: unison, refrain and chorus, dialogue or antiphonal, line-a-child, or solo voices with choirs.[24] Any teacher with a good poetry anthology will find poems which are

---

[23] There are innumerable versions of the Mother Goose verses. One of especial interest to the teacher is William and Ceil Baring-Gould's *The Annotated Mother Goose* (New York: Clarkson N. Potter, Inc., 1962). It offers both a plentitude of details concerning the verses and some charming black and white illustrations by early illustrators. More accessible for children is the version by Brian Wildsmith (New York: Franklin Watts, Inc., 1964). The sensuous color and bold design qualities make this a sophisticated treatment to delight the eye. In marked contrast is Tasha Tudor's version (New York: Henry Z. Walck, Inc., 1944). This will enchant children for whom Tudor's introspective and intimate view seems just right to interpret the verses.

[24] Arbuthnot, *Children and Books*, pp. 220–51. This is an excellent reference for any teacher to know. The book, in addition to providing an interesting history of choral speaking as an art, also gives innumerable suggestions for specific poems which can be used. Many of these are already "scored" or divided into sections for use by a choral speaking group.

of use, but some are suggested here in case you have never tried locating poetry for this purpose. For *unison* reading you might like to try: "Indian Summer" with any age child.[25] For *refrain and chorus,* the repeated line, "Lawd, lawd, lawd" in "Grey Goose," can be especially effective.[26] For *dialogue* or *antiphonal,* try using the delightful "The Blind Men and the Elephant."[27] For *line-a-child,* the poem entitled "Two Friends" is particularly appropriate.[28] The poem "Introduction" is an especially good one to use for *solo voice with choir.*[29] Have the choir read the descriptive material and one child read the dialogue.

Scoring the Poem. As a composer decides which instrument will play a specific part in a musical score, so the teacher will need to decide—at least at the beginning—which children will say what lines.

It is important to specify that the teacher will do this as children *begin,* for it will soon become apparent that children will have ideas about how the poem should be divided. The teacher encourages these ideas and takes the time necessary to try out the variety of ways children suggest.

A group of fourth-grade children recently evolved the following way of dividing this poem as the way they liked best after experimenting with several different ways of saying it.[30]

---

[25] Mary Downie and Barbara Robertson, *The Wind Has Wings* (New York: Henry Z. Walck, 1968), p. 92. The collection serves as an introduction to the work of many Canadian poets.

[26] You will enjoy sharing other poems by Dunning et al., *Reflections on a Gift of Watermelon Pickle . . .,* (New York: Lothrop, Lee and Shepard Co., 1967), p. 122.

[27] The collection by Arna Bontemps, *Hold Fast to Dreams* (Chicago: Follett Publishing Company, 1969), p. 73, purposefully integrates the old and the new in poetry and is wide-ranging in both topic and style.

[28] This is taken from the collection of Stephen Dunning et al., *Some Haystacks Don't Even Have Needles* (Chicago: Scott, Foresman & Co., 1969), p. 59. The book is an exciting one both visually and because of the fresh images presented in the poems.

[29] Herbert Read, *This Way, Delight* (New York: Pantheon, 1956), p. 38. Don't miss "In Just-Spring" by E.E.Cummings, one of many delights in this collection.

[30] From the book *Picture Rhymes from Foreign Lands* by Rose Fyleman. Copyright 1935, Renewal, © 1963 by Rose Fyleman. Reprinted by permission of J. B. Lippincott Co.
  Also in May Hill Arbuthnot, *The Arbuthnot Anthology of Children's Literature* (Chicago: Scott, Foresman & Co., 1971), p. 152.

The Goblin

by Rose Fyleman

| Group 1 | Groups 1 & 2 | Groups 1, 2, & 3 |

A goblin lives in our house, in our house, in our house,
A goblin lives in our house all the year around. (*All children*)

Bob   He bumps
Jane   And he jumps
Mary And he thumps
Ted   And he stumps.
Tim   He knocks
Al   And he rocks
Liz   And he rattles at the locks.

| Group 1 | Groups 1 & 2 | Groups 1, 2, & 3 |

A goblin lives in our house, in our house, in our house,
A goblin lives in our house all the year around. (*All children*)

Marking the Poem. Teacher and children alike may find it helpful to go through the poem and mark it, so they will remember *how* they want to read it, once a favorite way is agreed upon.

A group of fifth graders with whom I worked enjoyed the following poem, so we marked it in order to remember how we wanted to say the poem. We worked out the following very rudimentary system of marking:

/ = a slight pause

// = a complete stop

⌣ = a continuation of the voice so that the thought is continued to the next line

∧ = a heavy stress on the word

∨ = a lighter stress on the word

A goblin lives in our house,/in our house,/in our house,/
A goblin lives in our house all the year around.//
He bumps ⌣
And he jumps ⌣
And he thumps ⌣
And he stumps.//

He knocks ⌣
And he rocks ⌣
And he rattles at the locks.//
A goblin lives in our house,/in our house,/in our house,/
A goblin lives in our house all the year around.//

To begin, children will need to stick closely to the poem to gain expressive ability in this art. As the teacher senses his children are developing the skill to read or speak chorally, he may encourage the children to add sounds to enrich the poem.

Creating Verbal Obbligatos.   Many poems which can be used for choral speaking lend themselves to the creation of verbal *obbligatos.* The term obbligato, borrowed from music, means a persistent background motif. Usually this refers to a repeated theme played by an instrument against the major melody in a piece of music.

In the case of choral reading, it means having some children in your group repeat at patterned intervals words or sounds appropriate to heighten the mood of the poem or evoke the image more clearly.

For example, in "Trains" part of the children may repeat the words clickety-clack in some rhythm they have created as the rest of the children say the poem.[31] The teacher may want to have one group of children with high voices repeat the clickety-clack in one rhythm while another group with lower-pitched voices repeats the same words at a different rhythm. This provides a background while the third group says the poem.

Similarly, interesting results can be obtained by having children with different voice pitches laugh at different times as background to the poem, "Laughing Song."[32] Another poem which lends itself readily to the enhancement of an obbligato is "The Cat's Tea Party." [33] Experimenting with mew, meow, and other cat sounds done in different pitches and different rhythms can result in a very rich obbligato background for the poem.

A more involved background is necessary for "Three Little Puffins," which mentions panting, puffing, chewing, and chuffing—all in

---

[31] James S. Tippett, "Trains" in Arbuthnot, *The Arbuthnot Anthology* . . . , p. 86.

[32] William S. Blake, "Laughing Song," in Arbuthnot, *The Arbuthnot Anthology* . . . , p. 117.

[33] Frederick E. Weatherly, "The Cat's Tea Party," in Arbuthnot, *The Arbuthnot Anthology* . . . , p. 119.

one poem![34] Children enter with enthusiasm into the planning of this intriguing collection of sounds as they vary rhythm and pitch to create an obbligato which may surpass the poem in interest.

Finally, no teacher interested in doing choral speaking with children will want to miss the delightful challenge in "Jabberwocky."[35] There are all manner of beasts: toves, mome raths, borogroves, jubjub birds, in addition to the fearsome Jabberwocky. Children have been able to create fantastic obbligatos of much complexity as they imagine sounds in rhythm for each of the animals included.

What children are creating in this activity is a sound experience in which the emphasis is on using a piece of poetry as a departure point for a complete creative expression. Certainly the same careful attention must be given to the basic reading of the poem as in simple choral speaking, but beyond that children are free to create as imaginative a group of sounds as they can.

Mention should be made of the valuable uses a tape recorder can serve. As children create their obbligatos, they get wrapped up in the excitement of creation and performance, so a recorder is necessary. The teacher captures the sounds on tape so, after the children have done the poem in one way, they may listen to it, reflect upon it, and discuss it. As they do this, new ideas for different ways to do the piece will occur to them. Perhaps someone will suggest adding something, another person will suggest deleting something; yet another may feel altering some part of the total poetry experience would help. As the children reshape, rework, listen and reshape again, the piece moves from its first tentative beginnings to a finished choral sound experience, alive as only children's imagination can bring something to life.

Combining Forms: A Poetry Experience

One of the most challenging of oral-language experiences for children is that of putting together sounds or music and the spoken word in a poetry tape.

---

[34] Eleanor Farjeon, "Three Little Puffins," in Arbuthnot, *The Arbuthnot Anthology* . . . , p. 125.

[35] Louis Untermeyer, selector, *The Golden Treasury of Poetry* (New York: The Golden Press, 1959), pp. 208–9. The introductions to each poem are helpful to the teacher and the Joan Anglund illustrations will appeal to children. The section on "Good Things Come in Small Packages" (limericks and epitaphs) is particularly delightful.

The project, clearly described in a short article,[36] involves children in selecting a poem and preparing it as a finished product. The steps in the procedure are as follows:

1. The child selects a poem he likes.

2. He plans the sound or music background for it. The background might include sounds as in the poem by Fyleman discussed above. If he is using music, the goal is to get some piece which intensifies the mood of the poem. The thing to be avoided is the type of ubiquitous sounds which surround us in restaurants and elevators everywhere today.

3. The child records his sounds or music. Children can do this by taking a cassette to the sound, if it is one not present in the classroom. He might want a ticking clock, perhaps for use in "The Gingham Dog and the Callico Cat."[37] If he uses records for background, he can dub the sound on the cassette tape.

4. The child practices his poem, varying the three paralinguistic elements of pitch, stress, and juncture, until he achieves an interpretation which satisfies him.

5. He makes the final tape, using either another cassette recorder or a reel recorder. As he plays the background on one tape, the child reads the poem aloud and the two are recorded on the other tape.

The procedure is a simple one and easily within the capabilities of intermediate grade children. You will need to demonstrate the procedure first and then supervise the actual recording with the children. Practice in reading the poems and in recording the background sounds can be done on an independent basis as the children have time. In addition to recordings of music, the teacher may want to explore the possibility of obtaining some sound effects records. There are many

---

[36] Barbara S. Thuet, "The Music of Poetry," *The Instructor* (April 1971): 83, The classroom teacher who wrote the article provides detailed information about how her children did this project using cassette recorders and poems they chose.

[37] Eugene Field, *Poems of Childhood* (New York: Charles Scribner's Sons, 1904), p. 117. Despite the publication date, the book is still in print and will be of interest to the teacher who knows the reputation of the illustrator, Maxfield Parrish. Many of the poems speak of objects and events unfamiliar to today's children, but "The Duel" is engrossing and useful for this purpose.

of these available.[38] The cost is no more than that of regular records, and a few would be a good addition to the school library collection.

As the poems most frequently will be short poems, several can be put on one tape. Children can, if the recorder available is equipped with earphones, go and listen to the poems when they have free time. Intermediate grade children are also delighted to have an opportunity to present their finished poetry tapes for younger children; a session spent sharing the poems with younger children is rewarding to both groups.

Suggestions for Further Exploration

1. The statement made in the chapter that oral language is *the* language is an oversimplification indicating that it is a more basic or fundamental form than is the written language. Record some speech, and then transcribe it into writing. What elements of the speech cannot be transcribed? What can we communicate in writing that we cannot communicate in speech?

2. *Describing* was one oral language component considered at length in this chapter. There are other components of oral language, e.g., fluency—the ability to string thoughts together in coherent fashion. Try to identify some other components and make up activities to develop these in children.

3. Read Esther Edwards' "Kindergarten Is Too Late," *The Saturday Review of Literature* 51 (June 15 1968): 68–70+. The article points to the need for early education, especially in language skills. Try to develop a rationale to convince a school superintendent of the need for a four-year-old language-centered program. Role play your presentation of this to another student who is the superintendent who is opposed.

4. Read Jane Goodsell's "Telling Time," *The NEA Journal* 49 (November 1960): 27–28. Though the article is an old one, Goodsell considers with tongue-in-cheek humor the problem of making sharing time worthwhile. After reading this, visit some elementary

---

[38] Consulting the current issue of Schwan Record Catalogue (issued monthly) will give you a current list of such records. Some which have proved especially useful are: *Sound Patterns* (Folkways 6130), *The Sounds of London* (Folkways, FD 5901), *The Storm* (Audiophile Records), *Japan: Its Sounds and People* (Capital ST 10230) and *The World of Man* (Folkways FC 7431).

classrooms during sharing period. How many of the periods implement her ideas? In what ways could these sessions be made more
effective?

5. The importance of oral reading and of asking other than recall
   questions was stressed in the chapter. Remembering that it is *not*
   always important to discuss what you have read with your children,
   select a book you would enjoy reading. Plan several questions related to the book which would require children to operate on levels
   other than recall.

6. Much use is made of poetry in doing choral reading with children,
   though there is some indication that what children like may be
   different than what teachers like. See, Richard C. Nelson, "Children's Poetry Preferences," *Elementary English* (March 1966):
   247–52. Select six poems you think would be appropriate for choral
   speaking and identify the reasons you think each of these would be
   appropriate.

7. Though a storyteller communicates primarily through the effective
   use of his voice, he may communicate much through the accompanying gestures he uses. Select a story and follow the steps outlined in the chapter for learning it. Then, tell the story to a small
   group of children, recording your telling. A second time tell the
   story to a different group, having someone record you on videotape.
   Compare the two recordings. What different things about your
   effectiveness as a storyteller can you learn from each recording?

8. Try to make up ten "What-if" questions as described in the chapter.
   Use them with a group of children to motivate some oral storytelling. Either transcribe or record what they say. In analyzing the
   results, try to determine which of the questions elicited the most
   interesting stories. Can you determine the reasons why some were
   effective, and some were not?

Bibliography

Bamman, Henry A, et al. *Oral Interpretation of Children's Literature.* Dubuque: William C. Brown, Inc., 1964.

In brief compass (119 pages) and with few chapters (5) the authors have managed to deal concretely and sympathetically with a wide range of oral activities too frequently ignored. Many examples drawn from the elementary classroom clarify the author's directions. The chapter on oral reading, and the one on choral speaking are particularly useful. The only disadvantage, which should not deter the reader, is the unimaginative format. The book is better than it looks.

Blake, James Neal, *Speech Education Activities for Children.* Springfield, Illinois: Charles C. Thomas, Publisher, 1970.

Though Chapter Seven, specifically related to speech disorders, may not be of interest to the classroom teacher, the rest of this small book will be. The contents range from oral reading to debate, and attention is given to dramatic activities and storytelling. The lists of references following the chapters augment the brief treatment given each topic.

Colwell, Eileen, *A Storyteller's Choice.* New York: Henry Z. Walck, 1965.

The teacher will find any of the twenty stories in this collection of unusual interest to children. But the book's strength is the concluding material: a section on the author's ideas about the art and one on specific notes for each story. In the latter, Colwell indicates approximate telling time, difficulty level for the teller, appropriate audience age; in addition background on the stories and suggestions to improve the telling of each is provided.

Henry, Mable Wright, ed. *Creative Experiences in Oral Language.* Champaign: National Council of Teachers of English, 1967.

The book contains chapters on a variety of topics contributed by several specialists, including a preface by the editor. The section on creative dramatics is the strongest and most extensive, but the chapters on choric interpretation and storytelling will be of help. The scoring of poems will prove a useful guide to teachers who have not done choral speaking.

Hunter, Madeline. "The Elements of Effective Communication." *Childhood Education* 46 (December 1969): 158–61.

The author identifies four elements in communication: the message, encoding, transmission, and decoding. She stresses the help which awareness of these can be to the teacher, both in developing his own communication skills and also those of the children. The importance of language in sharpening perception is noted, and a useful section on nonverbal clues for the decoder is included.

Petty, Walter T. *Research in Oral Language*. Champaign: National Conference on Research in English, 1967.

A very useful compilation of articles which appeared originally in *Elementary English*, this volume serves as a summary of research in several aspects of oral language. The teacher wanting to know about oral language and social/personal development, the effects of environment, listening skills, and evaluation will find much recent information. Each article summarizes many other pieces of research which are less accessible to the teacher than is this volume.

Possien, Wilma. *They All Need to Talk*. New York: Appleton-Century-Crofts, 1969.

The author deals with the entire range of oral activities, from more structured reporting, to more free drama activities. The book is rich in specific examples drawn from actual classroom experiences, and the varied uses of children's literature is another strength. The paperback format makes it a practical source-book for teachers.

Rich, Dorothy. "Spurring Language Creativity in Young Children." *Young Children* 23 (January 1968): 175–77.

The article emphasizes preschool through primary grade language learning and offers many ideas for stimulating oral language. Much emphasis is placed on active involvement. The relationship between language and observation, memory and sensory experiences is explored, with suggestions for activities. The use of pictures for stimulating storytelling is described.

Sanders, Norris M. *Classroom Questions—What Kinds?* New York: Harper and Row, Publishers, 1966.

The author's comprehensive yet readable treatment of this problem should be of immediate practical use to most teachers. He establishes the need for a classification system of more questions based on that by Bloom on objectives, and then proceeds to devote a chapter to each of his levels: memory, translation, interpretation, application, analysis, synthesis, and evaluation. Though most of the examples are drawn from social studies, the perceptive language-arts teacher will find much of value in this small paperback.

Sawyer, Ruth. *The Way of the Storyteller*. New York: The Viking Press, 1962.

The book has two equally useful parts: one on storytelling as an art, and the other including stories adapted for telling. Rather than an organized look at techniques, the book is an intimate reminiscence about a long, successful career by a master storyteller. It is intensely engrossing, though the practical-minded may object to its lack of specific directives. Ms. Sawyer's charm lies in her ability to beguile: a few words and then twenty pages later the reader becomes aware of being swept along in delight.

Scott, Louise Binder. *Learning Language Skills*. Manchester, Missouri: Webster Publishing, McGraw-Hill, 1971.

Another of the new, sequentially organized programs designed to develop oral language fluency in young children, this one offers a set of four different levels, for children ranging in age from four to eight. As do the other programs, this one focuses attention on listening, making sound discriminations, using sentence patterns, noticing likenesses and differences, classifying, telling stories, and reasoning. As with some other programs, components of each set may be purchased separately.

Seymour, Dorothy Z. "A Fresh Look at 'Show and Tell.'" *Young Children* 23 (May 1968): 270–71.

Ms. Seymour advocates teaching children the difference between information which belongs in offhand conversations and that which can contribute to the learning of other children. She offers quite specific suggestions for dealing both with the shy and the aggressive child. Perhaps the most interesting point the author makes is the need for organization of the sharing period; this was long thought to be unnecessary. She points out how to establish standards for sharing and for listening.

Shedlock, Marie L. *The Art of the Story-Teller*. New York: Dover Publications, 1951.

This version of a now classic work merits attention, as much for its legible and attractive format as for its content. Though the book was written many years ago, both the section explaining Shedlock's ideas and the section of stories adapted for telling are unique. The chapter on artifices (techniques) for capturing and holding interest is valuable, as is the chapter on questions asked by teachers. Two chapters on elements to avoid and seek in selection of material are primarily of historic interest. The many stories included will enrich the storytelling program.

Skull, J., and A. Wilkinson. "The Construction of an Oral Composition Quality Scale." *British Journal of Educational Psychology* 39 (November 1969): 272–77.

The only available evaluation scales in this area are old (Hosic, 1925, Beverley, 1925, Harring, 1928, Netzer, 1939); all were troubled with the problem of recording the speech. This attempt, which admittedly deals only with standard English, is for fifteen-sixteen year olds. Sample talks of short duration were given without notes, which children had a week to prepare on tape. Ten were selected as representative of the widest range of ability. Forty assessors who ranked the tapes in order of competence were used. The amount of agreement between the assessors suggests that teachers could use this scale by comparing their own students' recorded tapes with the sample tapes.

Tooze, Ruth. *Storytelling*. Englewood Cliffs: Prentice-Hall, 1959.

The author opens with an interesting chapter on the history of storytelling, and then moves to the qualities of the storyteller. The emphasis on developing the senses, and the need for a wide command of words is well stated. In the chapter on techniques for telling stories, the exercises for improving voice quality are unique and worthy of the teacher's attention. Section Two, the longest in the book, presents a collection of stories adapted for telling. The bibliography, a fine one, includes brief descriptions of many of the stories listed.

CHAPTER SIX

Spontaneous Drama

Why Is Drama A Language Art?

This chapter states that spontaneous dramatics is one of the language arts; more accurately, dramatics *should be* part of the language-arts program. To understand this difference, one must examine the nature of language-arts programs in the elementary school.

A curious aspect of these programs is that their emphasis is somewhat out of touch with the way adults use language. Linguists have long pointed out the primacy of oral language, that is, the importance of speech. They call attention to the fact that most adults use language orally. This is true whether they are a college methods professor leading a discussion or an automobile mechanic discussing with his service manager the reason for performing a particular repair. For most of us, we use, *most* of the time, whatever oral proficiency we have developed. A look at elementary language-arts programs reveals that this is not generally true of these programs.

Language-arts programs have become codified; it is not impossible to predict what a typical program might be like. The teacher will most often be using one of the nationally distributed hardback basic language texts by a major publisher. Frequently, he will also be using a spelling book, while somewhat less frequently, he will be giving either cursory or compulsive attention to one of the many handwriting series. In many language-arts programs, written work is the most pervasive element. In all the proliferating splendidness of the basic materials, there is little emphasis on oral arts—listening and speaking.

Several writers have commented on the need to develop sequential programs in listening,[1] oral language,[2] and dramatics,[3] but little has been accomplished in these areas. It is these areas, and the related speech skills so crucial to most adult speakers, that are most frequently ignored in elementary language-arts programs. Further, while it is true that some children do get rather limited experiences in oral language (during the show-and-tell period for example), regular dramatic experiences are almost never a regular part of the language-arts program.

Because language is primarily a spoken art, language programs which do not give children chances to talk are inadequate. The addition of dramatics to the language-arts curriculum can provide necessary opportunities for development of language. Specific language skills which drama develops are discussed later in this chapter.

This does not mean that dramatics develops *only* language abilities, for there are many benefits derived when it is included in the school curriculum. These also will be discussed at length later.

Definition

We have been talking about drama in the elementary school, but it is possible that the exact nature of the process being recommended is unclear.

We are thinking about spontaneous, or improvised drama as opposed to formal play making. Improvisation is the informal, though not unplanned, response on the part of a child to some material, motivation, or stimulus. This response can be oral, or physical—through bodily movement. The main characteristic of the responses is that they

---

[1] G. Wesley Sowards and Mary Margaret Scohey, *The Changing Curriculum and the Elementary Teacher* (Belmont: Wadsworth Publishing Co., 1968), pp. 129–35.

[2] Wilma M. Possien, *They All Need to Talk* (New York: Appleton-Century-Crofts, 1969). The author has examined fully, giving many classroom examples, the variety of oral activities which are possible in the elementary school.

[3] Ann Shaw, "A Taxonomy of Objectives in Creative Dramatics" (Ph.D. dissertation, Columbia University, 1968). The first attempt, made quite convincingly, to apply the procedure of writing behavioral objectives to creative dramatics. People in the arts, generally, view this approach with skepticism. It will be interesting to see how this attempt is accepted by creative dramatics leaders.

are improvised. This type of experience is basically made up of the following components:

Component #1: The Material

This is motivation of some nature and usually appeals to the senses of the child.

A. The teacher may use a poem or part of a story to motivate children. In using prose selections, the leader is always aware of the need to condense and simplify, for most of these selections are too long to be used in their original form. The leader pares the story down to the "bare-bones" of the plot, to bring it to manageable length for playing.

B. The teacher may use a visual stimulus of some nature. Teacher-leaders have used reproductions of paintings, a photograph (any from Leavitt's book, as the one below, would be useful),[4] or perhaps an object (a mask borrowed from a historical society, or a piece of African sculpture might be useful).

This photograph could be used as a visual stimulus for dramatization.

---

[4] Hart Day Leavitt and David A. Sohn, *Stop, Look and Write!* (New York: Bantam Books, 1964).

C. He may use the sense of touch, for example, by having children interpret in movement the surface textures of a piece of wood, corduroy, glass, corrugated cardboard or tweed.

D. The sense of smell may be used when the teacher has children pantomime their reactions to odors. Actual odors are preferable to imagined ones, and children easily create impromptu scenes built around a character's reaction to olfactory stimulation.

E. Even the sense of taste, a seldom utilized avenue of learning in schools, may be used to evoke a drama response among children. Taking such a simple taste as that of a lemon, for example, the teacher can give children an opportunity to react.

These then are the sources of material to which the leader turns in preparing matter for spontaneous dramatics. What does he *do* with these basic sources, however?

Component #2: The Discussion-Questioning Segment

After exposing the child to the motivation, and indeed sometimes *as* this is going on, the discussion occurs—spontaneous, unplanned, but directed by the leader through his questioning.

He may use such questions as the following (keyed to the examples given in the preceding material).

A. Do you have any clues in the story as to what the characters are like? How could this story have ended differently?

B. What are some words we could use to describe the main character? What might have happened before the picture was taken? What might happen now? What could happen next?

C. What does the surface of the material feel like? Is it regular? If not, do the irregularities form a predictable pattern? By using your body in recurring up-and-down movements, could you represent the contrast between the two levels of the corduroy?

D. Giving the children paper cups filled with such unfamiliar spices as cumin, savory and chervil, the teacher lets children smell these and express their thoughts about them. What do they smell like? Where might you encounter an odor like this? What types of people could be there? What would they be doing?

E. In working with the taste stimulus suggested, in this case, of a lemon, the teacher might explore with children such questions as:

> Who is tasting this? Where are they? Are they alone? Why? What happened prior to this to lead the person to want to taste the lemon? Was it simple curiosity—or was something more involved? What happens after they taste the lemon? What kind of

action could it lead into? Are there things which could happen as a result of this action?

It should be remembered that these are simply sample questions, not designed to be followed prescriptively by a teacher interested in emulating what is described here, but rather only as *examples*.

Similarly, there is no *one* right answer to a question. Though this chapter is full of questions, there are no answers provided. This is because the teacher's primary concern is to elicit many responses of much variety, to get at the diversity of ideas available when working with children.

Component #3: The Actual Playing of an Idea

This component varies greatly, depending upon the age of the children, the amount of experience they have had with drama and their leader has had in directing it, the point the lesson happens in the sequence of drama experiences, and the creativity of the children.

Sometimes children will respond with movement, either representative or abstract.[5] At other times they will pantomime and convey with gestures and facial expressions a thought or idea. At still other times, children will be moved to add dialogue to their playing, to supplement the more basic bodily communication.

The above variations are not to be thought of as stages, for, if they are progressive at all, it is only in a very rough way. Though it does appear that dialogue is among the last of the dramatic elements to appear, groups and individuals will make use of one or several of these possibilities at different times, depending both upon the type of motivation and their response to it at a particular moment.

Component #4: Evaluation

There are basically two types of evaluation which occur in creative drama: *concurrent* and *terminal*.

Concurrent evaluation is of two types, teacher evaluation and group evaluation. As the teacher observes children working, he notes which children are successful in capturing an idea and conveying it, and he further encourages the group by positive commenting. He may make such general comments as: "My, I see so many cats and they *are* being very different," or "I can really feel the lightness in your bodies

---

[5] Teachers find *Movement in Time and Space* (16 mm, b&w film, available from Time-Life Films, New York) provides an enlightening introduction to the ways in which movement activities can lead to drama.

as you move—it comes across well." He may make such specific comments as: "What an effective frog Billy is being," or "Mary's bird is flying so well."

Group evaluation occurs when the teacher senses a need to consolidate something particularly effective, when he wants to help the group shift direction, or when he simply feels the children need a change of pace. He draws the children together, usually in close physical proximity to him to encourage their participation in this transitory quiet period, and they briefly share their reactions to what has been going on. Sometimes the teacher starts the discussion with a very specific question: "What could we do with our legs to make them seem more like a horse?" At other times he asks more general questions, for example: "Did you like what you were doing?" This phase of the session is short, rarely more than a few minutes in length, but it both helps children return to thinking more analytically about what they have been doing and helps change directions or make a transition to related but different activities.

Terminal evaluation occurs at the end of each session. On paper this looks like a logical and fairly easy thing to accomplish—in actual practice, it is not.

The leader may find it takes him quite a while to arrive at the ability of leading this evaluation session which should be a summing up of what has been accomplished and of what remains to be accomplished. Children and leader together discuss what they did which was particularly effective, what was honestly attempted but did not turn out to be effective, and what skills, ideas, thoughts and feelings remain to be worked on at the next session.

It must be emphasized that this is not the teacher evaluating the children, but the teacher and children evaluating *together* how the session went.

Terms

In previous sections, terms have been used which may have been unfamiliar to you; some attention to these is necessary. The most common title for what this chapter is about is *creative dramatics*, but this term—though widely used—is avoided here. There are two reasons for this:

1. First, "creative" has been misapplied to such a variety of different phenomena that it is almost impossible to establish a

clear, denotative meaning for it. People bring a variety of reactions to the term, including some negative ones; therefore, it is not used here.

2. Second, drama should *always* be creative, so as an adjective the word creative is redundant. If we accept different types of creativity, then all drama, from the informal dramatic play of preschool children to a finely disciplined Shakespearean performance, and including such mundane activities as lighting and scenery construction is, in fact, creative.

In this book, dramatic activities are described as spontaneous. That is intentional, to point out the necessity of an intuitive, flexible adapting, and dramatic experience which is truly spontaneous. A dictionary definition reveals that *natural* is listed as one synonym for spontaneous, and it is a good word to use in describing the experiences we are considering here. Drama leaders are concerned with evoking in children a natural, spontaneous response to the chosen motivation. This is akin to the free, unstructured response of young children's imaginative play, so respected in nursery school and so quickly discouraged in first grade. The teacher-leader does not formulate ahead of time what the children's response to the material ought to be, but rather plans a motivation and builds a dramatic experience as the children's natural responses to that motivation come forth. This use of the term, does not, however, mean that the drama *program* is spontaneous, or unplanned. The spontaneous drama leader realizes children need some sort of stimulus to be creative. Many writers have pointed out that children cannot create in a vacuum, but must be exposed to some sort of stimulus.[6] So the role of the drama leader is one of locating and selecting from among the available motivations the one which he thinks will be most effective. This requires preplanning, but not of the entire lesson.

The foregoing is a general definition of spontaneous dramatics for children. There are, in addition, some quite specific related terms which will help to further clarify the nature of this art form.

Another term widely used throughout this chapter is *leader*. This term is used because for too many people, the role of "teacher" is

---

[6] Maurie Applegate, *When the Teacher Says Write A Poem* and *When the Teacher Says Write a Story* (Scranton, Pennsylvania: Harper and Row, Publishers, 1965). The opinion about the necessity of triggering creativity is widely held; it is as well expressed by Applegate as by anyone. Several of her books are listed in the bibliography for the next chapter and are of interest, though they are not directly related to dramatics activities.

largely a didactic one, mainly occupied with dispensing of information. The too common picture is of the teacher standing in front of a group of children and talking *at* them. This is not a role congruent with the goals of spontaneous drama, and so you, as a teacher interested in becoming adept at leading a group, will want to notice carefully the differences which exist between the two roles. Becoming a spontaneous drama leader requires some different abilities than you customarily use when you are teaching more conventional subject matter. These will be pointed out in following sections.

Interpreting Versus Improvising

To some, the term improvising may seem a cumbersome way to say "act out," and frequently teachers respond to ideas in spontaneous dramatics by saying "But I do that all the time in my reading classes." There is a rather subtle distinction to be made, however, between interpreting a story and improvising one.

It is, of course, true that many elementary teachers encourage literature interpretation in their reading classes. This takes many forms. It may vary from simply assigning certain children to read each of the character parts in the current story to allowing a group excited about their "play" to enact the story, without using the book as a cue card. In these activities a crucial element is successful and accurate interpretation, enactment, or recreation of the author's statement and intent.

In working with "The Fox and the Grapes,"[7] when a teacher talks with children about how they can convey the anger of the thwarted fox, what sounds and bodily movements they can utilize to show this, he is still working with interpreting, not improvising.

When, however, the teacher faces the children, perhaps after simple enactment as described above, with the question: "Can you imagine what might have happened if the grapes *had* fallen into the fox's paws?"—*then* he is moving into the area of creative improvisation. He is asking the children to extend, to extrapolate, to enrich the basic materials with ideas of their own making. This then is the point at which one moves from interpreting to improvising and begins to do

---

[7] The collection of *Aesop's Fables*, selected and adapted by Louis Untermeyer (New York: Golden Press, 1966, p. 23) is particularly useful. The book is large and lavishly illustrated by the Provensens, who have done their usual superb job of capturing the essence of the material and yet providing a unique visual experience.

spontaneous drama with children. Perhaps another example will clarify the distinction. Allowing children to choose parts and read a story interpretively is doubtlessly valuable. In such a story as the *Midas Touch*, children revel in impersonating the greedy king and his pathetic daughter. Some limited attention can be given to voice quality, inflection, and other aspects of oral interpretation. Usually it is the teacher who limits the number and extent of these periods devoted to exploring the dramatic qualities inherent in a story. Since the results of such an experience are less tangible than those obtained when some good solid skill teaching takes place, the typical teacher, even though he may sense that the children are learning from the experience, moves ahead to more practical considerations. Consequently those children who might have been anxious to "get inside" the skin of the avaricious king and explore greed and its consequences are left behind.

Spontaneous *improvisation* is the major emphasis in dramatics. It is entirely different from interpretation as it involves going beyond the basic material. Taking the theme of the *Midas Touch* story, there are a variety of possible questions. Children could easily respond to such questions as:

1. Why do you imagine the king was so greedy? What might have made him this way?
2. How did the king react to other people? (You will recall that in the story we do not see him interacting with other people.) What was he like to his servants, the townspeople?
3. In what other ways could he have solved his problem?

Children would enjoy improvising these ideas. The teacher might use some of these questions to stimulate discussion, others to encourage children to "act out" their responses and to create *other* episodes which could occur before, during, and after the basic story.

No matter what specific questions the teacher used to begin a session, he could move from interpretation to improvisation and provide an experience in dramatics for his children. In essence he is asking them to extrapolate, to extend or expand, to take some basic material and go beyond it. The teacher asks children to draw from within themselves ideas, thoughts, feelings, and conclusions based on, but not found in, the basic material.

One aspect of improvisational drama must be emphasized at this point. That is, though dramatics *may* lead into creative theater, it is a completely separate entity. There should be no intent, for example, that simple improvisation on a new ending for a favorite fairy tale will lead into a fully costumed and lighted adaptation of a scripted play for parents. Children may eventually mature from simple spontaneous creation of a new character in the story "Stone Soup"[8] to authorship of a new version of "Little Red Riding Hood," presented to the rest of the school, but if such does occur, it must happen because of the children's desire to do so.

The teacher-leader, in fact, must be constantly wary that he succumbs neither to his own need nor those of the principal or PTA president to mount a production for an audience.

In a pioneer film done by Rita Crist, the group does evolve a semi-finished play based on the poem introduced by the leader.[9] When this happens naturally, as an expression of interest by the children, there is little harm in allowing the sessions to progress in this direction. It is, however, imperative that the leader continually examine his motives to make sure that it is the children, who are making a more formal "play" seem important.

Throughout this chapter spontaneous drama *sessions* will be mentioned, another purposeful change in terminology. This term is used to avoid calling them lessons, for far too many people bring negative connotations to the word "lesson." Instead, drama sessions are referred to for two reasons:

1. There is not a specific "chunk" of material which must be covered in a given time span, whether that span be a single session, a month's experience, or a year's work. The teacher does have a plan, but, as will be pointed out later, this must remain flexible so that adjustments can be made as the session progresses. This is in contrast to academic lessons, the learning dimensions of which are all too frequently established by curriculum planners, subject-matter experts, textbook writers, and the teacher in the grade higher than the one you teach.

2. The mental "set" of both teacher-leader and students is different than that in a conventional academic lesson. In such a les-

---

[8] Marcia Brown's illustrations of this old tale (New York: Charles Scribner's Sons, 1947) lend a clearly defined aura of the "strange country" in which the story is set.

[9] "Creative Drama—The First Steps," 29 minutes, sound and color film by Northwestern University Films. Representative episodes selected from an entire sequence of drama sessions show in condensed form the procedures for providing children with a variety of drama experiences leading to a rather formal playing of a poem.

son children too frequently "take-in" whatever is presented, even if it is learned as the result of an *inquiry-oriented* process. In a drama session the leader is presenting something, but only for the purpose of motivating children. There is no intent that they should remember content details in the material. Confronted with a visual image, an aural message, or a tactile sensation, children engage in a process of drawing from within themselves responses and reactions, selecting the most appropriate of these and playing them out while interacting with other children. If, after using the material in a session, children do remember details of names, occurrences and sequences, this is a dividend but is not a purpose of the sessions.

The Inclusive Quality of Spontaneous Dramatics

In addition to unique terminology, there are several qualities of spontaneous drama which are unusual enough to require some description.

Perhaps one of the most distinguishing qualities of spontaneous dramatics, setting it apart from other theater activities, is its inclusiveness. Opportunity is provided for all children to participate, and the premium is not on the potential actor but rather on the ability to take an idea and react sponstaneously to it. This latter ability is one which most, if not all, children can develop.

The leader is cautioned that the key word in the preceeding paragraph is opportunity, for it is crucial that, even with very young children, it be an opportunity, and not a requirement. The leader first makes a genuine attempt to involve all children in his group. This includes allowing those timid or as yet unresponsive children to play inanimate objects, if this gives them security.

The leader works diligently to involve all children; sometimes he does not succeed in this. Since we are attempting to release children's creative potential, and *not* simply add another compulsory subject to the curriculum, it is perfectly acceptable if a child wants to retire to a corner with a book, rather than participate. Usually the eavesdropping begins quickly enough, and seeing what fun others are having, the child chooses to rejoin the group.

The goal is to engage all children in this activity. Sometimes the leader bides his time and waits, but he keeps trying to involve all children, since all children can both contribute to the activity and learn from it.

The On-Going Quality of Spontaneous Drama

The dramatics leader has a plan for his session. Among less-experienced leaders this may be rather carefully written out, to detail stimulus, motivation, procedures, and evaluation techniques. With more experienced leaders, this plan may be more simply an idea of the direction in which he is going. In both cases, however, the leader remembers there is another session coming later.

This means that, though the session is by no means devoid of purpose, it is also by no means considered a failure if that exact purpose is not reached in *that particular session*. There will be other sessions and providing something of benefit occurred, the leader can be content and work with his original idea again later. Perhaps an example will clarify this characteristic.

Suppose a leader is working with the idea of mood, using the story of "Little Red Riding Hood."[10] His main purpose might be to help children sense the mystery of the forest and how the trees, growing closely together, allow only dim filtered light to sift through to the narrow and rocky path beneath. Suppose also, however, that in attempting to play this idea with children, they become fascinated with the idea of characterization and considering what Little Red Riding Hood in the story was really like. One group this writer worked with became concerned with how Little Red Riding Hood could be so gullible, so oblivious to obvious danger signals, and so the group decided to work up a characterization of a slightly more alert Little Red Riding Hood. The devious wolf had a much more difficult job in our version when Little Red Riding Hood took on some of the sophistication natural to the children who were improvising. The leader should not be dismayed when changes like this occur. It is true that he intended to work on mood, but it is also true that because there is no specified content to be "covered," the leader can have another session on mood later.[11]

The teacher can, next session perhaps, choose another story. For example, he could use "The Three Bears."[12] Also set in a forest, this

---

[10] The reader might be interested in using the version included in Miriam Blanton Huber's *Story and Verse for Children* (New York: The Macmillan Company, 1967, p. 256). This is another large anthology of children's literature which any teacher in the elementary school would find indispensible.

[11] Perhaps for variety a second session could be based on Nonny Hogrogian's version in which both granny and the ingenuous Red come to a mournful end. See *The Renowned History of Little Red Riding Hood* (New York: Thomas Y. Crowell Co., 1967).

[12] Some leaders have found *The Story of the Three Bears* (London: Frederick Warne and Co., n.d., with drawings by L. Leslie Brooke) to be useful in drama

story is good for work on mood. Because he tailors the spontaneous drama program as he goes, the leader is not bound by considerations of "finishing" something by a given time. And he does not rush on to something else, fearing what the teacher next year will expect the children to have learned.

The Recurring Quality of Spontaneous Dramatics

There are certain basic recurring ideas, strands, or organizing elements which pervade dramatics programs at any level. These are mood, plot, characterization, rhythm, and unity. Because they recur, a kindergarten child as well as juniors in college are concerned with these elements. Once while working with a group of kindergarten children, I used Grace Hallock's poem about snakes.[13]

SNAKES AND SNAILS

by Grace Taber Hallock

Through the grasses tall and slim
All about the water's rim,
Lie the slimy secret trails
Of the water-snakes and snails.

We delighted in moving through the mind-created swamp grasses as threatening snakes. However, this particular group of kindergarten children was ready for more. So we talked about snakes. Some of the questions we considered were:

1. Are all snakes alike?

2. If not, how are they different?

3. How would a heavy, fat old father rattler, soaked in the sun, move?

4. How would this be different from a lithe young grass snake?

---

sessions. The drawings are unique and using them with children is a helpful experience in aesthetics, in addition to drama.

[13] From the book *Bird in the Bush* by Grace Taber Hallock. Copyright 1930 by E. P. Dutton & Co., Inc., Renewal © 1958 by Grace Taber Hallock. Published by E. P. Dutton & Co., and used with their permission.

Also in *The Reading of Poetry*, ed. William D. Sheldon et al. (Boston: Allyn and Bacon, 1966), p. 331. This fine selection of poetry, with whimsical drawings by Don Madden, is prefaced by a brief but helpful section on how to approach poetry, times for using it, how to choose poems, and how they lead to self-expression.

5. Would you move differently if you were hungry, than if you were full of a foolish mouse dinner?

These and other questions stimulated the children to think of differences, and we were on our way to a simple understanding of characterization. Similarly, though they had worked on characterization previously, a sixth-grade class especially enjoyed further chances to develop skills of characterization. This time we used the nonsense rhyme about the old lady so silly she swallowed a whole menagerie.[14]

POOR OLD LADY

Unknown

Poor old lady, she swallowed a fly.
I don't know why she swallowed a fly.
Poor old lady, I think she'll die.

Poor old lady, she swallowed a spider.
It squirmed and wriggled and turned inside her.
She swallowed the spider to catch the fly.
I don't know why she swallowed a fly.
Poor old lady, I think she'll die.

Poor old lady, she swallowed a bird.
How absurd! She swallowed a bird.
She swallowed the bird to catch the spider,
She swallowed the spider to catch the fly,
I don't know why she swallowed a fly.
Poor old lady, I think she'll die.

Poor old lady, she swallowed a cat.
Think of that! She swallowed a cat.
She swallowed the cat to catch the bird.
She swallowed the bird to catch the spider,
She swallowed the spider to catch the fly,
I don't know why she swallowed a fly.
Poor old lady, I think she'll die.

Ordinarily we would consider sixth graders too sophisticated for such a poem, but in this case it proved a good vehicle for character extension. As I read the poem we laughed over it, and then we sang an impromptu version of it children had learned in music class. Then we explored some questions:

---

[14] "Poor Old Lady" (author unknown) in *The Sound of Poetry*, eds. Mary C. Austin and Queenie B. Mills (Boston: Allyn and Bacon, 1967), p. 251.

1. What is the old lady really like?
2. Was she always as silly as she is now?
3. If not, what made her the way she is?
4. What problems has she? How does she react to these problems?

After a spirited discussion of the old lady's foibles, we divided up into small groups. One of the groups was to invent a problem for the hungry old lady, and the other group was to create her response to the problem, thereby establishing their conception of her character. This drama session also provided many opportunities for creating other characters in some way involved with the old lady.

The Process Quality of Spontaneous Drama

In spite of the danger of unnecessarily raising the dichotomy of process versus content, it seems important to point out that spontaneous drama is a process for elementary school children rather than a content area with specific grade or level expectations.

While for college students and teachers there is content *about* drama to be learned, the same is not true in the case of drama used with elementary school children. Drama is primarily a process, used with *many* contents, to attain expressions of artistic merit from children.

Children do learn about such things as characterization, mood, plot, conflict and rhythm. They learn things about these drama techniques, however, using any content. For example, it does not matter whether the leader uses *Snow White* or *King Midas* to develop ideas about characterization. The leader may use *Sleeping Beauty*, or *Pandora's Box* to give children insights about mood; or, if neither of these interests the leader and the group, he may choose an entirely different story, perhaps one seldom or never before used by a drama leader in developing ideas of mood.

Values of Dramatics

Many writers have described effectively and at some length the social and emotional values which accrue when children participate in drama on a regular basis.[15] Almost any of the books mentioned in this

---

[15] A particularly helpful list of references is included in James Hoetker's *Dramatics and the Teaching of Literature* (Champaign: National Council of Teachers of English, 1969), pp. 17–44. The book also includes a capsule history of the creative drama movement in the United States.

chapter include a rationale for establishing dramatics as part of a child's education. An early, and pace-setting book contains a convincing statement of the values of experiences with drama. Though it is old, undoubtedly Geraldine Siks' book remains a basic statement which should be read.[16]

The Siks' book is one of several introductory books dealing with drama in general. Because these statements of the values of drama are widely available and because the emphasis in this chapter is on drama as a language art, only brief mention of the other reasons will be included here. Certainly for a comprehensive view of dramatics, the reader should do some background reading in the other recommended books.

The child's *creativity* can be developed by exposure to drama as was explained earlier in the section dealing with the reason for calling this spontaneous drama. Several people have pointed out the need for encouraging creativity,[17] have discussed the means of doing so,[18] and have identified conditions for encouraging creativity;[19] the reader is referred to these statements.

Another social value developed by dramatics is *teamwork*, the very heart of drama. As he works with other children, the child learns to modify his ideas, plans, and thoughts as he is exposed to the ideas, plans, and thoughts of others. This needs little encouragement by the teacher, as the child soon discovers that the group with candor and impartiality exerts the discipline necessary for effective playing.

Another value often identified is that drama provides children with healthy channels for the *expression of emotions*. When working *on* ideas in drama, the child can also work *out* frustrations, fears, and inhibitions which ordinarily must be kept in during more conventional school classes. Seeing that characters in motivational materials share some of his common problems can be encouraging to a child.

---

[16] Geraldine Brain Siks, *Creative Dramatics: An Art for Children* (New York: Harper and Row, 1958).

[17] Ryland W. Crary, *Humanizing the School: Curriculum, Development and Theory* (New York: Alfred A. Knopf, 1969), pp. 285–312. In a book refreshingly unlike other curriculum books, Crary, instead of focusing on content which is currently taught, examines instead methodological foundations and procedural bases for curriculum improvement. The chapter on the creative-aesthetic dimension of curriculum is challenging.

[18] George R. Kneller, *The Art and Science of Creativity* (New York: Holt, Rinehart and Winston, Inc., 1965). In a brief, readable book, Kneller has examined several theories of creativity, the nature of the creative person and the creative process, and the implications of what is known for the educative process.

[19] Ruth G. Strickland, *Language Arts in the Elementary School* (Lexington, Mass.: D. C. Heath & Co., 1969), pp. 314–16.

Drama also provides for the development of *reasoning powers* for as the child analyzes the appropriateness of what has been done in the session, he begins to evaluate, to formulate alternatives, and to develop the ability to choose the most appropriate of the alternatives.

All these abilities are crucial, but because they have been so well explicated elsewhere, they will not be developed more fully here.

Instead, we turn now to the *language learning* which this art form can foster.

Drama and Language Growth

An experimental study done by William E. Blank points out clearly some of these learnings.[20] Blank studied three aspects of children's development: voice qualities, personality factors, and vocabulary. Under voice qualities he included articulation and flexibility of tone. Using two groups of school children, one which met weekly during the school year for drama (the experimental group) while the other did not (the control group), Blank administered pre- and posttests in the three areas of concern. The findings indicated that in vocabulary and the voice qualities which he measured, Blank found the experimental group showed a mean improvement over the control group with critical ratios significant at the .01 level. Dramatics had been effective in stimulating growth in voice quality, personality factors, and size of vocabulary. The two language factors are of most interest to us, and will be discussed further.

It seems, then, that one approach to justifying dramatics as an integral, rather than a peripheral part of an elementary language-arts program is the possibility it offers for growth in knowledge about language. What particular aspects of language growth does drama encourage?

I. Vocabulary Growth

Blank found that one aspect of language growth drama encourages is that of vocabulary development. Certainly teachers must be concerned with this because of the crucial relationship between vocabulary development and success in school. By vocabulary development we do not mean, however, learning specific lists of words. We have ample

---

[20] William Earl Blank, "The Effectiveness of Creative Dramatics in Developing Voice, Vocabulary and Personality," *Speech Monographs* 11 (August 1954): 190.

evidence this is not effective.[21] What we need, instead, is that passionate involvement with words and the wonder at what they can do which makes coming across an unknown word a challenge rather than a bore.

What is your curiosity quotient about words? Take these as examples.

> Have you ever noticed someone's *obliquity?*
> Have you ever wanted to be a *mugwump?*
> Have you ever *excoriated* anything?

How many of them do you know? Do they intrigue you so that you would like to know more about them?

How are we to get this involvement with words, so that we develop adults whose curiosity is piqued by unfamiliar ones? Certainly not, as mentioned earlier, by drilling children on lists. Spontaneous dramatics can provide one way. Much of the literature used as stimulus for drama will result in an exposure to new and unfamiliar words. Ward says that in using literature to stimulate dramatics, "the children will take hold of as much of the original language as they are able for the sound of it is fascinating to them."[22]

In using drama to further vocabulary growth, the leader is not after specific words to be memorized but a captivating exposure which sensitizes children to the "lure and lore" of words.

Several excellent examples are contained in the book entitled *Push Back the Desks*. In the first of these examples, the author describes how he worked with a group of kindergarten children. Cullum writes as follows:

> From my meagre linen closet I sacrificed a good white sheet to make a dramatic entrance into the kindergarten. . . . As a roaming language-arts teacher I was able to indulge in such activity. . . . There I was in the middle of the kindergarten covered with my last good sheet, in which two holes had been cut out for my eyes. I saw twenty-two pairs of eyes looking at me. "I am a friendly apparition," I slowly stated. "What's that?" asked five-year-old

---

21 Walter T. Petty et al., *The State of Knowledge about the Teaching of Vocabulary* (Champaign: National Council of Teachers of English, 1968). The book examines current procedures for teaching vocabulary and presents and analyzes eleven recent studies. The summary and recommendations are of concern to a teacher interested in improving his techniques in this area.

22 Winifred Ward, *Playmaking with Children* (New York: Appleton-Century-Crofts, 1957), p. 187.

Tony. They all started to talk at once, of course, so I asked them to sit in a circle, and I sat in the center. I proceeded to whirl about in a flashing dervish manner and explained to them that for Halloween I was going to be a very friendly apparition. "What do I look like?" Finally Annette guessed that I was dressed as a ghost. They then took turns wearing the large sheet and . . . flew through the kindergarten air as friendly apparitions. It was simple for them to accept apparition as a good kindergarten word.

Certainly this is simple dramatization—the very beginning steps, but even at this stage the children take delight in responding to words.

It is one thing to let children respond with fervor to words, and it does build a sensitivity to them, but do these words remain with a child? Cullum feels they do and describes the results he achieved with his group of kindergarten children:

> It was exciting to see them go home during the school year as twenty-two eerie apparitions . . . well-trained pachyderms . . . (or) proud, snorting stallions . . . they carried their big words home to astounded parents, grandparents, and older brothers and sisters. They were proud of their new words. Together we had added sixty new words to their speaking vocabulary. At the end of the year I devised a test to see how well they had retained their big words. Without any review, over ninety percent of the class scored one hundred. The words were still alive.[23]

In summary, what the drama leader accomplishes, then, is to share words with children, and as Lewis says so well "the pupils are off their guard . . . and it is then that something is not learned, but absorbed through the intuitive channel."[24]

II. Paralanguage

Another area of children's growth in language through dramatics is that of paralanguage—pitch, stress, and juncture. Leaders work to help children understand *pitch*, the high or low sound; *stress*, the accent

---

[23] Reprinted by permission from *Push Back the Desks* by Albert Cullum, © 1967 by Scholastic Magazines, Inc. In this account of his work with children, Cullum tells how he fostered creativity by using his own creative ability in many subject areas. The book is easy to read and highly recommended for the myriad of ideas it presents.

[24] C. Day Lewis, "The Poem and the Lesson," *English Journal* (March 1968): 321–27.

in a word; and *juncture*, the stops or pauses between words. Children grow to a conscious knowledge of how they can use this expressive overlay on language. Probably all children, except those with severe emotional and/or learning problems, unconsciously assimilate the basic features of paralanguage along with other early language learning. Most children come to school as fully in control of paralanguage as they are in the more basic verbal symbols of language. Beyond this basic mastery, however, the school provides children with scant opportunity for conscious study in manipulating these three elements to convey ideas more expressively.

Why should children learn something of these features of our language? Linguists and other language students agree they are critical factors in communication. For instance, psychologist Albert Mehabian estimated that of the total impact of the message, 7 percent is accomplished by basic verbal symbols, while 38 percent is conveyed by vocal overlays of pitch, stress and juncture—that is, paralanguage. In addition, he estimates that 55 percent of the message is determined by the accompanying facial expressions called *kinesics*, which we will consider later. Apparently only a small portion of the message is transmitted by the basic verbal symbols.

If these extra-verbal factors are crucial in communication, then it is apparent children should learn about them, so that they can grow to be more effective in using their language.

Examination of basic language textbooks reveals that little is done to make children aware of how they can achieve desired effects of manipulating pitch, stress, and juncture. Much work is included in these books about correct usage, but little is done with helping children experiment with these three elements of paralanguage to become more effective speakers of English. There are, happily, a few interesting exceptions among more recent texts.[25]

Children do know about these factors subconsciously, but we are concerned here with their *conscious control* in order to create desired effects. By stimulating children to improvise dialogue for a variety of people, spontaneous dramatics helps raise to conscious level the idea of the diversity of people's language.

Sometimes these learnings come up incidentally as in sessions experimenting with voices necessary to a particular story. In using the

---

[25] See for example: Muriel Crosby, *The World of Language* (Chicago: Follett Educational Corporation, 1970), (Book 6, pp. 152–56, 187–89, and Book 5, pp. 22–31), or Harry W. Sartain et al., *English Is Our Language* (Boston: D. C. Heath and Co., 1968), (Book 6, pp. 48–49 and Book 5, pp. 50–52 and pp. 104 and 105).

Three Billy Goats Gruff with young children, for example, such questions as the following can be explored:

1. What does a troll sound like?
2. Do all trolls sound the same? Does a river troll (as the one in the story is described) sound the same as a forest troll? Would a cave troll sound different?
3. How does a father troll sound when he is content after a filling dinner of succulent goat?
4. How does a mother troll sound when she is nagging her lethargic husband to get a tender goat for dinner?

Children find such questions as these delightful. They provide opportunities to create story line spontaneously, but more importantly, such questions allow children to explore paralanguage, to play with and speculate upon speech of this created troll family and to see how imaginative they can be in creating the trolls with their voices.

Sometimes these learnings can be stimulated purposely, as when we confront children with pictures of people, and ask them to create voices and manipulate pitch, stress, and juncture to make the character live. Confronted with a picture and having only visual clues, the child is challenged to create a person, using the three elements of paralanguage to augment the basic verbal symbols.

In these examples we have seen how children can learn consciously some ideas about paralanguage which were previously known, but at an unconscious level. These are ideas of which far too many adults remain unconscious. We use paralanguage as adults each day and if we can teach children how to manipulate the three elements consciously, we shall be teaching them how to use one of the most expressive devices of a marvelously flexible language.

III. Kinesics

Another aspect of language about which children can learn in spontaneous dramatics is kinesics. Lefevre defines the term to include:

> all bodily gestures, nudges, nods, finger, hand and arm signals, shrugs, and facial gestures such as winks, smiles, sneers and leers —the whole gamut of expressive actions, so important in . . . interpretation and in the small events of daily life.[26]

---

[26] Carl A. Lefevre, *Linguistics, English and the Language Arts* (Boston: Allyn and Bacon, Inc., 1970), pp. 174–75.

You will remember that Mahrabian, mentioned earlier, estimates this aspect of language may account for up to 55 percent of the meaning of the message. Despite this, and the universal use we make of this aspect of language, an examination of elementary language materials reveals that, like paralanguage, kinesics is seldom a matter of much concern to the authors of language series. Using dramatics can make up for this lack, as children examine characters in depth and work to convey their understandings through the use of extralinguistic features.

A group of fourth- and fifth-grade children recently worked with the old folktale entitled "The Stone in the Road" and concentrated especially on the reaction of the villagers to finding the stone in the otherwise meticulously maintained kingdom. Their leader talked with them about nonverbal means they could use to develop characterizations of the villagers as, in this session, each child chose to be one of the villagers. The differences in the shrugs, hand and arm movements, frowns and gestures, and other kinesics used made obvious to an observer the character of the soldier, scholar, carpenter, and other inhabitants. In the evaluation session following the improvisation, the children learned much from comparing the way one child's characterization differed from that of another child's.

IV. Spontaneous Oral Composition

A more encompasing goal than the specific ones mentioned earlier is that of encouraging growth in the child's ability in spontaneous oral composition, that is, impromptu or extemporaneous invention. We work for this goal when we work with plot development. Ward says that giving children experiences in thinking on their feet and expressing ideas fearlessly is an important concern of spontaneous dramatics. She further notes:

> when older children are asked what . . . [drama] is worth to them besides being so enjoyable, they often think first of this objective because they feel so strongly the need both for the poise which comes from being articulate and the power it gives them among their fellows.[27]

One of the ways Ward suggests developing this ability is to allow a child to give a lead sentence, for example: "The boy was uncertain about what to do now." Without allowing the child who contributed

---

[27] See Ward, p. 8.

the sentence to explain it, the leader selects volunteers who want to build an impromptu scene around the lead sentence.

Another successful way to develop this ability to compose orally is to take a standard piece of literature and present an additional problem related to it. For example:

1. What would have happened if the goat couldn't get across the bridge?
2. How else could Midas have solved his problem?
3. What would have happened if the slipper had fit Cinderella's sister?
4. Who could have come to the aid of the gingerbread boy as he rode across the river on the fox's back?
5. Who else besides the knave might have stolen the Queen's tarts—and why?

Children respond easily to this type of problem and, in the process, develop an oral proficiency.

Recently, I used this approach with a group of third-grade children. The motivation was the old Mother Hubbard rhyme. The rhyme, as you remember, reads:

> Old Mother Hubbard went to her cupboard,
> to get her poor dog a bone.
> When she got there, the cupboard was bare,
> and so the poor dog had none.

The question posed to the children was: Instead of simply letting the poor dog go hungry, what *else* might Old Mother Hubbard have done? Among the more inventive responses suggested, which lent themselves to playing in spontaneous dramatics were these:

1. She went to the butcher and asked for a job. He was in need of help, and so he hired her to cut meat from the bones. At the end of the day she got to keep the bones.
2. She planted a garden in which she grew many vegetables. The extra ones she sold at a stand and used the money to buy bones for her dog.
3. She went out begging from door to door, asking for a penny at each house. The townpeople were embarrassed to give her just

a penny, so they gave more, and when she was done collecting she had so much money she built a mansion and bought bones.

4. Since she didn't have bones she made up some porridge, and it was so good, the dog ate that instead.

Sometimes instead of a problem simply describe two people in a situation and let children create story line and dialogue. The results are not always predictable. Children learn through their improvisation, but the improvisations may be more revealing than pleasant. For example, listen to two third graders improvising, one as a mother or father, the other as a child. In a suburban third grade with which I recently worked, all of the improvisations were frighteningly accurate, as these children used words, paralanguage, kinesics and movement to create a story line about adults and children. Despite the fact that the stimulus had been neutral, all of the adults were cast in repressive, controlling roles!

Children can learn to become proficient in spontaneous oral composition, though certainly this is a skill which is slow to develop and difficult to measure. Perhaps the few ideas discussed here will stimulate you to even more creative approaches to stimulating spontaneous oral composition.

Some Other Uses for Dramatics

Now that we have considered at some length the specific language uses of spontaneous drama, we will refer briefly to other uses of drama in the curriculum because dramatics is not limited to the language program.[28] The perceptive teacher is able to see many subject areas in which to use dramatics. One inventive leader interested in social studies helped intermediate children to a better understanding of themselves when they worked with the idea of fear, in interpreting the explorer's feelings as he set foot on the white-grained edge of an unfamiliar continent. Another helped children evolve some sensitive rhythmic patterns based on the concept of number bases in mathematics. His group, divided into different bases, interwove, moved, split, and regrouped and enjoyed working with the concept on paper after they had interpreted it rhythmically.

Still a third leader helped kindergarten children in a simple fashion respond to the ebullience of a Sousa march and later led sixth graders

---

[28] See Hoetker, pp. 31–32.

in a sensitive response to the brooding and evocative counter rhythm in Ravel's *Bolero*.

In science, another leader helped second-grade children explore the possibilities of dramatic improvisation using the life cycle of flowering plants and enriched the topic considerably by helping children understand the rather subtle differences between larkspur and hollyhock, fuchsia and dandelion, and how to interpret what their responses might be to outside influences. The hollyhock and the larkspur responded to the effect of the wind, for example. The children understood and played the differing effects of the sun on the shade-loving fuchsia and the sun-loving dandelion.

Other drama leaders have found opportunities to incorporate drama into the school program in other areas. While there are many applications of this art in the curriculum, the ones of most concern here are those integral to the language-arts program. Readers interested in other uses for dramatics will find the articles written on them of help in explaining the wide scope of drama in the elementary school.

Summary

In this chapter two things have been attempted:

1 To provide a brief description of spontaneous drama, that is, a detailing of the diverse activities included under the general title, so that you may have a clearer idea of the nature of the activities this chapter is encouraging you to engage in.
2 To identify the many types of language growth which may take place as a result of your using drama as an aspect of your language-arts program.

There is no limit to the amount of language growth possible through spontaneous drama—if the leader is willing to undertake such an adventure with the same willingness as his children will.

Suggestions for Further Exploration

1. The definition of drama given in this chapter is informal and process oriented. Assume that you are a teacher interested in spontaneous drama and are asked to explain it at a parent-teacher meeting. Evolve your own definition of spontaneous drama which will be more specific than the one given in this chapter.

2. The chapter makes the point that in longer prose selections, the leader's job is always to condense and tighten the action and plot, to reduce it in length to a manageable size for playing. Choose a folk- or fairy tale and attempt to do this while retaining all the essential action and characters.

3. Where else, besides in the context of drama have you heard the word *creative* used? With a few other people in class, try to establish a denotative meaning for the word, noting what your agreements and disagreements are. Can you agree on a connotative meaning? Reading Paul Torrance's *Guiding Creative Talent* (Prentice-Hall, 1962) might help clarify your ideas.

4. Earlier in the chapter the word mugwump was introduced just to pique your curiosity about an interesting word. Since by now you know what it means, try planning a drama session around the imaginary adventures of a mugwump. How would you introduce the idea to the children? What questions could you ask to motivate them?

5. One of the most successful ways to get children to think about paralanguage is to present them with pictures of distinctive-looking people and let them create voices for the unknown person. Look through magazines to find several of these pictures which you think would stimulate children to create voices and experiment with paralanguage.

6. The Old Mother Hubbard rhyme used in the chapter was chosen because its plot led up to a crisis point at which children could engage in problem solving. Try to locate several other stories which could be used in the same way. Locate the crisis point in each and create some motivating questions to encourage children to solve the problem.

7. In discussing the story of Little Red Riding Hood, reference was made to *mood* as a dramatic element. Choose six other stories you feel would help children understand the concept of mood and create motivation questions related to each, which would help children understand what mood is and different ways in which moods can be evoked.

Bibliography

Allen, Joan Gore. "Creative Dramatics and Language Arts Skills." *Elementary English* 46 (April 1969): 436–37.

The writer reports on her work with a fourth-grade class which wrote a play from a story, of the learnings generated in this activity, and of her belief that teachers do not need to lay down formal rules for this procedure. She feels students, when involved, do not realize the amount of work they are doing as part of the enjoyable activities.

Barlin, Anne and Paul. *The Art of Learning Through Movement.* Los Angeles: The Ward Ritchie Press, 1971.

Written by two dancers with extensive backgrounds in drama, this book offers a wealth of specific suggestions to the teacher interested in movement. Each activity is described clearly, and careful attention is given to preparation, explanation of the movement, further development and musical accompaniment. This last is provided, for many of the activities, on two records which come with the book. A bright, encouraging book, distinguished by clear and open format, designed to help teachers succeed in an area too few try.

Brady, Bee. "The Play's Not the Thing." *Grade Teacher* 85 (March 1968): 82–83.

Brady begins her article by identifying several purposes for creative drama. She advocates using stories to motivate because of her feeling that pictures are too static. Her recommendations for how to choose a story are valuable. Kipling and Stevenson stories are recommended.

Byers, Ruth. *Creating Theater.* San Antonio: Trinity University Press, 1968.

Ms. Byers states at the beginning of the book that her major interest is in experiences which "lead to play creation, writing, and production." As such, the book is an extension of, rather than central to, spontaneous dramatics. Her book is worthwhile reading, however, as a joyful description of the author's thirteen years of experience in motivating children between the ages of eight and thirteen in drama activities.

Chambers, Dewey W. "Storytelling and Creative Drama. "In *Literature for Children,* edited by Pose Lamb. Dubuque: William C. Brown, 1970.

Chambers' book deals very satisfactorily with both arts included in the title and is, hence, of interest to an elementary school teacher. In the section devoted specifically to drama the author identifies readiness activities leading into drama, describes procedures in planning the crucial first session, and relates at length the description of an actual fourth-grade work with an old folktale. The drama leader will find both the section on classroom climate and on the steps involved in creative drama to be of help.

Daniels, Stephen. *How 2 Geribils, 20 Goldfish, 200 Games, 2000 Books and I Taught Them How to Read.* Philadelphia: The Westminster Press, 1971.

A fascinating and first-hand account by a teacher of black ghetto children, which should be of interest to anyone who wants to teach culturally different children. Though the major focus is on reading, the section on role-playing or psychodrama (pp. 74–78) will be of interest to the drama teacher. Daniels' use of this technique to free children to express themselves is truly impressive.

Davis, Sandra S. "Pied Piper Way to Reading." *High Points* (Winter 1968): 8–10.

Working with comparable groups of intermediate grade children, this teacher provided drama and music activities leading to reading for one group; the other group experienced a highly motivating program which did *not* include drama. Scores on a standardized reading test, administered at the close of a four-month treatment period, indicated that the group whose reading activities grew out of drama and music experiences scored higher than did the control group. The author achieved a statistically significant improvement in reading scores.

Dixon, John. "Creative Expression in Great Britain." *English Journal* 57 (September 1968): 795–802.

Dixon discusses both creative writing, and improvisation. He feels that the writing should use feelings as well as thoughts which arise from personal experiences. Improvisation helps students penetrate roles and, therefore, offers the possibility of changing their attitudes about subjects.

Fariday, M. J. "Creative Dramatics: An Exciting Newcomer in the Elementary Curriculum." *Minnesota Journal of Education* 48 (January 1968): 20–21.

Ms. Fariday reports the results of her work, primarily based on literature as a motivation. Her comments on evaluation after the session are helpful. She did an informal test of listening skills which revealed that listening improved after creative drama sessions, and that the greatest amount of improvement occurred among academically slow children.

Harris, Peter, ed. "Drama in Education." *English in Education* 1, no. 3 (Autumn 1967).

A valuable article on drama in primary schools opens this comprehensive yet small publication which gives American readers an insight into the drama program in Great Britain. Teachers would find one article, "Sit Down, Sidney," to be particularly helpful as it deals with children doing seated pantomimes—one solution to the problem of inadequate space. The article "Improvisation" by Dorothy Heathcote, a noted leader in the drama movement, is also of much interest. The magazine is published by the National Association for the Teaching of English, which is the British equivalent of our National Council of Teachers of English.

Hunt, Douglas and Kari. *Pantomime.* New York: Atheneum, 1964.

In simple, nontechnical writing, which holds the interest of one unfamiliar with mime, the authors explore the art from its earliest beginnings among prehistoric cave dwellers to its most recent manifestations on television. Though the chapters are brief (5–7 pages), and specific sources are not footnoted, each of the distinctive forms is treated in a believable and interesting way.

McCaslin, Nellie. *Creative Dramatics in the Classroom.* New York: David McKay Co., 1968.

This small paperback should be of much value to a classroom teacher because of its practical approach to drama. McCaslin speaks of the improvement of speech through drama and how drama encourages vocabulary development. She devotes a section to problems the leader may encounter, and one to pantomime, which is also helpful. The book includes a myriad of specific exercises to do with children.

Side, Ronald. "Creative Drama." *Elementary English* 46 (April 1969): 431–35.

Side views drama as an important phase of oral expression and as a good method for encouraging creativity. He stresses the importance of concentration, imagination, use of the senses, voice, and the emotions.

Tiedt, Iris M., and Sidney W. *Readings on Contemporary English in the Elementary School.* Englewood Cliffs: Prentice-Hall, 1967.

The reader is referred especially to "Learning Through Creative Dramatics" (pp. 36–44) by Margaret S. Woods. This is a good introductory article to those unfamiliar with the major ideas of dramatics and with the leaders in the area. Woods writes convincingly, especially of the conditions necessary to create a climate for the art.

Weisheit, Marilyn. "Knowing Is Experiencing." *Childhood Education* 44 (April 1969): 489–500.

Weisheit relates the experience of a kindergarten teacher using egg-hatching as motivation for a creative dramatics experience. Children pantomimed and developed a story on the basis of their observations.

Author's Comment

Often student teachers are hesitant to try doing drama with children because it seems to an observer to be disorganized and chaotic. Good drama experiences are not so, as the previous chapter pointed out. Nevertheless, the seeming confusion which occurs when children are involved in drama sometimes discourages the inexperienced student teacher from planning drama experiences, In addition, few cooperating teachers do drama, so the student teacher often does not have a model to emulate.

In the following section, written when Mr. Merkel was a junior involved in student teaching, the author reports his experiences in a classroom doing drama with children. He received little encouragement from his cooperating teacher but nonetheless, was able to lead the children in a successful sequence of drama experiences. Perhaps his enthusiasm for drama will encourage you to try planning some experiences for your children.

Chapter Supplement

An Experience with Drama

by Darrell Merkel
Mayflower Mill Elementary School

Children are potentially creative. They have sensitivity, imagination and a desire to express their feeling and responses openly and imaginatively. Too often this creative urge is stifled by the teacher, the school or some other environmental influence; consequently children don't develop their creative abilities. The job of the teacher, therefore, is to develop, not inhibit, the child's creativity, sensibility and imagination. Children need to express themselves creatively. One way they can do this is to experiment with their bodies and voices. A natural outlet for this experimentation is creative dramatics. Through creative dramatics, a child can improve social attitudes and relationships, gain greater self-confidence and emotional stability, improve his vocal and bodily expression and develop independent thinking and personal creativity.

Creative drama is an area of the school curriculum for which a potential teacher or inservice teacher does not need extensive training and background. My interest in dramatics began as a result of my participation in high school formal play productions where I gained an understanding of the underlying elements in drama. I received experience in characterization and learned set construction techniques, costuming and make-up. It was in my second year of college that I was introduced to creative dramatics as a part of the elementary school curriculum. This was in a course I was taking to learn methods and materials for teaching all areas of language arts. I studied the topic of creative drama and found writers described it as a very interesting and valuable part of the language-arts program. It was also in this class that I was a participant in some informal creative drama sessions. My interest was enhanced as a result of this involvement. Because of this, I structured a semester project around this subject. The project involved research, organization of lesson plans for the primary grades and testing them with students in a classroom situation. The lessons were utilized in three traditional classrooms in an average middle-class situation. The positive results obtained encouraged me to take a more active interest in creative drama.

During an eight-week student teaching assignment, I attempted to actually integrate creative drama into a language-arts curriculum. The school was an open-concept building in a rural community utilizing team teaching in grades kindergarten through third. Grades four, five and six combined to form one team with differentiated staffing. In addition, the help of interns, student teachers, teacher aides and paraprofessionals was integrated throughout all seven grade levels. I was assigned to grade four and instructed to teach in all areas of the curriculum excluding art and music. All fourth graders had language-arts instruction for five thirty-minute periods per week, Monday and Friday periods being devoted solely to spelling. The other three days were generally used for grammar. Creative drama had never been introduced in any form and many of the teachers were not aware of its existence as part of the curriculum.

Fourteen children were selected from the fourth grade sections by the two certified language-arts teachers. Chosen randomly from different ability groupings, many of the children had been only exposed to drama through such formal productions as Christmas plays. I began finalizing my plans so I could present a completed outline of my project to the administration of the school for their approval and consent to proceed. The school requested this evidence, being somewhat skeptical as to the values of such a program and of the physical requirements placed on rescheduling room assignments.

I set up a series of eight lessons that could involve the children in sixteen, thirty-minute sessions. For each I organized *group goals*, that is, what a session was to help children learn to do. I also had specific *drama goals* establishing the dramatic abilities each session was designed to encourage. I then selected materials needed to fulfill my objectives including: audio-visual machinery, sources of literary material, pictures, books and props that might be utilized. I then prepared a brief description of the method that might be used. I use the word "might" since these were not rigid guidelines but suggested sequences, including questions and comments for each lesson. Through student reaction, the sessions could proceed in many different directions.

These introductory lessons in creative dramatics ranged from relatively simple activities to more complex dramatizations. They, however, were flexible enough so that they could have been included at any convenient time as an adjunct to the language-arts curriculum, responding to the interests and demands of the children.

The following is a representation of the outline submitted to the administration for approval. It lists session numbers, the main emphasis of that session, and the stimulation or motivational device that was to be used in the presentation.

Session Number	Main Emphasis	Stimulation
1–2	Introduction to creative drama, learning to use the body to do interpretive movement.	present words that describe animal movement. Children become animals indicative of these words. (e.g., slump, slither, glide)
3–4	To increase abilities in interpretive movement, introduction to the idea of mood.	play a tape recording containing many different types of music. Ask the children to assume the mood of each recording through facial expression and bodily movement. (e.g., classical could be light and happy whereas blues is sad.)
5–6	To increase abilities in interpretive movement, further development of mood.	discussion of the poem "The Sandhill Crane,"[1] after which the children will dramatize the animal movements in the poem as it is read.

[1] Mary Austin, "The Sandhill Crane," in *The Arbuthnot Anthology*, ed. May Hill Arbuthnot (Chicago: Scott, Foresman, 1961), p. 53.

Session Number	Main Emphasis	Stimulation
7–8	Major emphasis on mood.	pictures presented that suggest some unspecified danger dealing with the lives of people. Children's discussion of pictures provide basis for dramatic interpretation.
9–10	Characterization is the main emphasis. Plot in-introduced.	children will be presented many different types of hats, some indicative of a specific occupation or role (e.g., cowboy). Others, not indicative, can be whatever the child makes them. Children portraying different roles interact to create a story line.
11–12	Characterization, plot, incidental dialogue.	slides of different kinds of people from which the children will speculate about that person's character. The discussion provides the groundwork on which a later improvisation about this person's life will occur.
13–14	Combining characterization, plot, dialogue and mood.	presentation of mask pictures which, after discussion, will stimulate children to dramatize life in the unnamed culture of which these masks are a part.
15–16	Combining characterization, plot, dialogue and mood.	story line created in response to a picture. Children are in total control of the manipulation of characterization, plot, dialogue and mood. They must create their own material.

Because of omitted and shortened class periods, this project occurring during the Thanksgiving and Christmas seasons, I did not complete the outlined program. Many of my sessions were shortened because of practice for the Christmas play. Others were omitted completely with no available time for "make-up" sessions. As a result, sessions thirteen and fourteen were combined into one session which became the culminating lesson. What follows is a representation of the lesson plan for that session in greater detail.

A. *Group Goals*
1. To correlate creative dramatics with other areas of the curriculum—particularly language arts and social studies.
2. To increase skills of intragroup cooperation necessary for group improvisation.

B. *Drama Goals*
1. To present to children pictures which will stimulate them to create a dramatization of life in this unnamed culture.
2. To continue developing in children increasing competency to use the dramatic elements to create and play a story of their own devising.

C. *Materials*
Slides taken from pictures in:
Hunt, Kari, and Carlson, Bernice. *Masks and Mask Makers.* Abingdon Press, 1961.
Background information from:
Baranski, Matthew. *Mask Making.* Worcester: Davis Press, 1962.

D. *Method*
Begin with a discussion of the artifacts and the lives of their creators to stimulate ideas that will later lead to playing of some aspect of these lives.

Questions and comments for prompting thought:

"By looking at the masks on the screen, can you tell me anything about the people who made them?"

"What are the masks made of? How are they painted? For what purposes could they be used?"

"Although we don't know much about these people, can you imagine: Where they might live? How? Do they live in family units like ours? Are there many children in the family?"

"What could their homes be like? What are they made of? How are they built?"

"What kind of food might they eat? How is this food prepared? How do these people get their food?"

"How could the people travel? Are there roads? How do they get from village to village?"

"What do the people look like? How do they dress? Why? What are their clothes made of? How do they wear their hair? Can we tell their occupation or duty in their community by what they are wearing?"

At any point in the discussion, the children should be free to dramatize their answers. Gradually string these ideas together until the children have created an improvisation about the life, or some aspect of the life, of these unidentified people. The materials, although from actual Indian cultures, need not be identified for the children during the session so as not to stifle creative thought. At another time the correct information may be supplied. I found this most important because the children were able to let their imaginations work and to create their own culture when supplied only with three slides and several flat pictures of masks. I supplied the actual information about the people who were associated with the masks in a social-studies class which followed the creative dramatics sessions. The children were very surprised how near their interpretations were to the real information. A unit on American Indians and in particular, Indians in Indiana, followed in social studies. Dramatics were then utilized in that class to personalize the information they were gaining. In language-arts class we followed up with lessons about Indiana in creative writing sessions and developed spelling lists using words frequently encountered when studying Indiana. In reading classes, the children did independent reading in fictional Indian material, and then reported to the class the subject and possibly the story line of the book through dramatics.

I found the response to my program to be tremendously positive. All of the children involved showed excitement, enthusiasm, and interest and demonstrated a willingness to participate and cooperate. Even those who were more shy began to develop an eagerness to dramatize their ideas and express themselves verbally by the end of my short program. They were beginning to work well as a group and their attitudes toward each other began to improve. Since there were only fourteen children in my creative dramatics program, the other children did not receive this kind of instruction. They, however, talked to my group and voiced to me their willingness to do something with dramatics. This is why I followed my creative dramatic sessions with some related dramatic activities in the classroom so that all of the children could become involved.

The teachers' reactions, disappointingly, were not quite as enthusiastic and encouraging. Throughout my student teaching at the school, despite my invitations, my sessions were never observed by the teachers I was working with. I was rarely questioned as to the purpose or procedures involved in the project, although some did voice their opinion that the program sounded "interesting," but insinuated in other discussions its lack of practicality in their programs.

I, however, found the experience to be very successful and worthwhile. It helped me gain a better understanding of the advantages and limitations of creative dramatics and of the potentiality children have for creative expression. I understand this ability in many of the children as a result of having worked with them in other, more structured subject areas, in which they displayed less creativity. I was pleased, however, to see the reasoning abilities each displayed. Their ideas often times were very sophisticated which prompted my alertness and total involvement throughout each activity. I feel that I could never have gained the depth of insight into creative dramatics I now have if I had only read about it and not become involved. One's ideas grow when watching and listening to children as they work.

The following are suggestions I would make to anyone beginning a program of creative dramatics.

1. Every person has the ability to be creative if he is not afraid to let it show. There can be no right or wrong way in being creative. Therefore, don't fear teaching creative drama. A sincere effort will have successful results.

2. Express to the children that sincerity is the key to their performance. It is hard to judge sincerity so, if in doubt, don't assume the action was insincere.

3. Remember to evaluate an action and not the child. Nothing stifles creative thought, I've found, more than to criticize the child himself. If you feel the action was not good, ask questions that would elicit creative responses that would correct or improve the action.

4. When starting a program, I found it easier to begin with animate objects, since the children are naturally full of motion.

5. Don't expect too much of the children on your first try. Often what looks feasible on paper won't work with a particular group. You need to be willing to adjust to the capabilities of your group.

6. Don't talk about doing it, get involved!

CHAPTER SEVEN

Writing with Children

The writing children do can be divided into two types for purposes of clarification and consideration. Whether these types are labeled creative and practical, imaginative and utilitarian, or innovative and functional is not important; in any case, the writer is simply trying to establish a dichotomy in the reader's mind.[1] In one type the child's power to invent or fashion something new, different, unique or unusual is most important. In the other type, because of a different intended purpose, mechanics and form must be proportionately more important. Each of these types of writing demands slightly different behavior from the teacher. In order to adequately consider each type and point out how you can encourage children to write better, the division will be maintained in this chapter.

What Is Creative Writing?

The question may seem superfluous, and yet to give some attention to a definition seems to be a wise idea. In creative writing, children are asked to make up, invent, devise, originate, or in some other way

---

[1] Although this dichotomy is an artificial one, as Ferris reminds us, it is a useful one. The chapter by Ferris, "Teaching Children to Write," in *Guiding Children's Language Learning*, ed. Pose Lamb (Dubuque: William C. Brown, 1971), pp. 171–208, contains a particularly helpful section on means of motivating children to write creatively.

respond to a stimulus. The response may be a poem, a short story, a descriptive paragraph, or a play. The important element is that the child encounters the motivation and using his own ideas, builds upon it.

Since this is the case, we need to identify more particularly some possible stimuli, or means of motivation. As in other areas of the language arts, if we think of the five senses, we have a point of departure.

1. The sense of *sight*. Teachers frequently use pictures or other visual stimuli to evoke creative writing. Many magazines have pictures which could be used, and a concerned teacher has a picture file to which he can go (or to which children may go) in search of a picture which will evoke creative writing. As a general rule, pictures in which something happens, has happened, or is about to happen, are more effective than simply "beautiful" views or landscapes. These offer little in the way of potential plot development.

2. The sense of *hearing*. Records can be used to stimulate the flow of thought which may lead to creative writing. Sometimes you may want to try using just sounds and then talk with children about such questions as: In what places might we hear such a sound? What kinds of people could be in such a location? For what purposes? What kinds of things might they be doing there? Why? With whom?[2]

At other times, you might use a storytelling record and stop it before the conclusion in order to let children write their own.[3] Even very young children can do well in finishing a story with their own creative ending; this is a technique widely recommended.

A fifth-grade group, working with an unfinished story included in their language-arts textbook, recently wrote the following endings.[4]

Whodinky

I will tell you what it is. First of all, he is green and has two legs and one arm. He has feet three feet long. He has antennas that

---

[2] You might find any of these helpful: *Sounds of Animals* (Folkway Records FX6124), *Sound Patterns* (Folkway FX6130), and *Voices of the Satellites!* (Folkway FX6200).

[3] There are untold numbers of such records available. Three I have found to be special favorites of children are: *Joy to the World* (Christmas Legends) told by Ruth Sawyer (Weston Woods #707), *Best Loved Fairy Tales*, by Charles Perrault (Spoken Arts #847), and *Ruth Sawyer, Storyteller* (Weston Woods, #701–702).

[4] Schiller et al., *Language and How to Use It* (New York: Scott Foresman, 1969), Book 5. This includes several stories to finish, including the one entitled "The Whodinky" (p. 118) which features King Rom, Brian the leprechaun, and a mysterious Whodinky.

tell him where he is going. Now you know what a Whodinky is. I'll give you one more chance to find one, but only five pots of gold is my reward.

So they sat up and still thinking they could find one. In sixteen days they all gathered in the throne room. Bryon danced once again among the men and he said "Did you catch me a Whodinky?" He said "No, because you don't know how to catch a Whodinky." "Well I'll tell you. You get a mirror and you reflect it on the sun and then that night on the moon, and the next morning you will have a Whodinky if you do it right. I will give you one more chance but this time I offer four pots of gold."

In sixteen days they all gathered in the throne room, and again Bryon danced among the men. He said, "Well, did you get me a Whodinky?" The men all replied, "Yes." Bryon said, "Where?" and asked one man, "How many did you catch?" "One," said the man, and he asked another man, "How many did you get?" "Two," said the man, and he asked another man, "How many did you get?" "Two," said the man. This went on for thirteen men. Then he asked King Rom, "How many did you get?" "Fourteen," said the king. "Oh," said Bryon, "Where are they?" The men said in chorus, "You give us the gold first." "No," said Bryon, "You did not catch any. You are ashamed to admit it, like you were so ashamed to ask what they were and how do you catch one. Ah, ah, ah, there is no such thing as a Whodinky. I just wanted to see how many would lie to get money. You are all foolish, foolish, foolish," he said as he and his four pots of gold disappeared.

What Is a Whodinky?

A Whodinky is a foot high and weighs 10 pounds. It has a cow's head, a pig's tail, a dog's feet, and the rest of his body is shaped like a horse. It has four legs. The front ones are longer than the back ones. Its color is pink and purple polka dots.

He can walk, he can run, he can skip, and when he wants to go across the ocean or a river, he flies. He just pulls out his handy wings and hooks them on to himself and starts flying.

He can't really talk but he grunts, squeaks, whistles and makes weird noises with his mouth. When he grunts and he is mad he makes a real low grunt. When he grunts and he feels good he makes a high grunt. He only squeals when he is frightened. He whistles when he's happy. He makes weird noises with his mouth when he's troubled. He turns invisible when he's in trouble.

To catch a Whodinky, you make a sign and spell Whodinky backwards like this: Yknidohw. A Whodinky will come and read the sign, or try to read it. While he reads it, you slip a rope over his head. After you have done that, that's all you have to do because he is very gentle.

3. The sense of *touch*. In developing descriptive skills, it is often wise to give children the challenge of describing the feel of something. In order to isolate the sense of touch, some teachers use blindfolds, so children focus only on whatever information their hands give them. The exercise works with individuals or groups. If working in groups, the children can compose a description and read it for the rest of the children in order to see if they can guess the material being described.

This is an easy exercise to do with children because they delight in bringing items to school to put in the "feel" box. If you keep a box accessible where they can contribute items whenever they see something of interest, you will always have a supply from which to draw.

4. The sense of *taste*. It is a profitable experiment in creative writing to allow children to describe tastes, with the purpose of encouraging them to observe carefully and then develop a telling description. Samples of herbs, spices, vinegar and other substances can be handed out in small paper cups. After children have developed the ability to describe what they have tasted, they can be encouraged to weave this into a story. They can be asked such questions as:

Who could be tasting this? Why?
What brought the person to taste this?
What could happen as a result?
Where might this be happening?

5. The sense of *smell*. Children can be asked to observe carefully the smells at several locations: you might begin having them observe at home, in the school, or outdoors. One teacher led her children blindfolded around the school, to see if they could determine where they were by the smells in different locations. They discussed the places they had been, the smells they couldn't recognize, and later wrote a group description of the smells of the school.

6. *Combination* of the senses. Teachers often find that using more than one sense results in increased ideas for writing. They have used such films as "Rainshower,"[5] "The Hunter and the Forest"[6] and "Let's Write a Story"[7] to good advantage in motivating writing. The charming "Alexander and the Car with the Missing Headlight"[8] which fea-

---

[5] Dimension Films, 15 minutes, color, sound.
[6] Aktiebvlaget Svensk Film, 8 minutes, black and white, sound.
[7] Churchill Films, 11 minutes, color, sound.
[8] Weston Woods film, 14 minutes, color, sound.

tures strikingly original art work by children, can be used effectively to motivate other adventures for Alexander. "The Loon's Necklace"[9] is especially good when working with older children in having them write their own folktales.

These are simply some possible motivations to encourage children to write creatively. No one author can give you all the ideas you will need for creative writing. There are several other sources included in the chapter bibliography which will help as you start children on the journey toward becoming effective creative writers.

The Necessity for Wide Reading

The process of creative writing can be thought of as a two-part process, a *taking-in* part, and a *giving-out* part. The teacher is active in stimulating the second, or *giving-out* part, as the previous section pointed out. There is a more far-reaching and less-direct way in which he is influential in the *taking-in* part, however. It is this part of the program which entails reading to the class on a regular basis.

It is crucial that the teacher read to his group: every day is really minimal. *What* he reads is not nearly so crucial as the fact that he does read poetry, fiction, biography, newspaper articles, perhaps a diary excerpt or even something interesting from an encyclopedia—anything and everything. He does this because some of this reading will touch a child in a way that more direct motivation closely linked to the actual process of creative writing may not touch him.

The rationale for this reading, plus some comments about reasons teachers don't read to children are put forth in delightful if slightly acerbic fashion by Root.[10] As he so aptly describes it, there are at least three reasons why reading is crucial.

1. There are many types of writing which must be heard in order for their full beauty to be accessible; poetry and plays fall into this category. Without such reading aloud of these and other forms, children may never be exposed to the particular delights available in these forms.

2. Many books are appropriate from the point of view of content before the reader is able to cope with the complexities of the

---

[9] Crawley Films, Ltd., 11 minutes, color, sound.

[10] Sheldon Root, "What's Wrong With Reading Aloud?" *Elementary English* (December 1967): 929–32.

printed page which they offer. Root mentions White's *Charlotte's Web,* and to this should be added the delightful works of Milne, and *The Wind in the Willows.* Share these with your children, or, by the time they become competent enough to cope with the print, they may be put off by the topic. No one should have to wait until they're adult to discover these joys!

3. There are exciting bits of literature too far from the beaten track for most children to discover them alone. If you doubt this, look back over the list of Newbery and Caldecott winners, for a start. How many of these have your children exclaimed over? Each of them has something unique to offer—perhaps you can widen your children's exposure by reading to them. In addition to these, make sure your children encounter *The American Institute of Graphics Arts Awards* books, and the *New York Times Book List.* The *Lewis Carroll Shelf Awards* list provides the names of some other excellent books children may not have explored.[11]

Probably the most difficult thing for the teacher to do is to have the restraint to keep quiet after he has shared something with his group. The natural tendency is to talk about the work, to point out the imagery, the figurative language, and to belabor all those "interesting" vocabulary words. To do so often destroys the magic of the moment and turns the reading time into yet another teaching time.

The relationship between what you've read and creative writing will be, for the child, tangential if not nonexistent on a conscious level. That's fine—leave it that way. The purpose here is not to provide conscious patterns for children to emulate, or direct instruction in forms, but rather to provide an enriching experience which may affect some children. The key word is "may," for we have no real way of knowing what effect all this reading has on individual children. And this is the way our work frequently is when we are concerned with learning in the affective realm. We are not concerned here with things easily measured, with missing addends to be found or with elusive pitches to be matched, but rather with enlarging a child's consciousness by exposing him to experiences he might not otherwise encounter. In this, as in much of our teaching, we are offering a child a chance to grow beyond what he was when he came to us, and, in the final analysis, the decision

---

[11] Dewey W. Chambers, *Children's Literature in the Curriculum* (Chicago: Rand McNally, 1971). Another comprehensive list of award-winning books is included in this volume. Chambers describes pertinent details about thirty-two awards, knowledge of which would help a teacher in book selection.

to accept or reject must be his. What we do know is that, as teachers of creative writing, we are sure that an enlarged and expanded self may lead to writing which is more creative, and that is our goal.

Since we have been considering creative writing at some length, it is important to be aware of some problems in this area.

Changes in Creative Writing

The relative importance of creative writing in the schools today can legitimately be questioned. While much has been written about it, even a cursory look at most elementary language-arts programs reveals that creative writing has yet to carve out for itself more than an un-directed position in the elementary curriculum. Why is this the case?

A look at the history of creative writing suggests some answers to this question. Early in the 1920s, many writers began to emphasize the need to add writing experiences of a creative nature to the elementary curriculum. One of the first people pointing out this need was Hughes Mearns, in a book which still makes fascinating reading.[12] Mearns' book was the beginning of a whole series of encouraging books put out by gifted teachers, blessed with insight into the conditions necessary for encouraging children to create and skilled in drawing from children writing of rare insight and beauty.

Generally these early books shared three concerns. They all gave some attention to the *conditions* necessary for encouraging creativity. They addressed themselves to the role of the teacher, the means he could use to stimulate writing and what he should avoid doing.

Second, these books all emphasized the necessity of *accepting* all efforts and encouraging the children. Burrows in a quotation fairly typical of this group of writers said:

> it follows that because we permit each child to say what he wants to say in his own way, we, for our part, must accept graciously whatever he writes . . . an eager acceptance of their stories . . . we accept them as we would any other gift—with warm appreciation. Criticism is as inappropriate in this situation as it would be at Christmas time.[13]

Third, these writers all agreed on the minimal importance of *mechanics*. The idea was suggested that work on the skills, punctuation,

---

[12] Hughes Mearns, *Creative Power: The Education of Youth in the Creative Arts* (New York: Dover Publications, Inc., 1958), 2nd edition.

[13] Alvina Treut Burrows et al., *They All Want to Write* (New York: Holt, Rinehart and Winston, 1964), p. 88.

spelling, or grammatical considerations, must take place in periods separate from creative writing. The feeling is that marking papers for these points will surely destroy any impetus a child has to create.

Sharing these three common concerns, the books also shared a common shortcoming—they did not generally provide for any kind of a *sequential development* in children's writing. The teacher was left with interesting ideas, which when put into use often did result in evoking creative expression. Basically there was one element missing— a progression or sequence of development. That is, though a child's writing may have improved in some ways, perhaps due to maturity, there was little or no discernible improvement because of the program through which he progressed. As a result, the teacher garnered occasional pieces of genuine beauty but could see no observable growth towards writing power.

This may be one reason why creative writing has remained a stepchild in the curriculum: a pleasant endeavor of interest to both the teacher and child, but not a central concern.

A Newer Approach

Within the last few years we find creative writing taking a new direction. There are three instances which can be cited as evidence of this new direction in writing. These three, and others which could be located, spring directly from the uncomfortable awareness of many adults that, although many children have had some experience with creative writing as part of the language-arts curriculum, all too few write well as a result. Indeed, as Hochstetler says so emphatically, far too many children:

> reach sixth-grade level without being able to construct good clear sentences either orally or in writing. What is probably more detrimental to the . . . expression is his inability to examine and edit his sentences critically.[14]

Robert Evans' article is a succinct and forceful statement of the need for a planned program to develop writing skills.[15] When talking

---

[14] Ruth Hochstetler, "Facets of Language—Grammar and Usage," in *Guiding Children's Language Learning*, ed. Pose Lamb (Dubuque, Iowa: Wm. C. Brown, 1971), pp. 283–323.

[15] Robert Evans, "A Glove Thrown Down," *Elementary English* (May 1967): 523–27. The author points out the fallacy of assuming that children can write significant prose without direct instruction and makes a convincing argument for structuring beginning writing experiences around careful observation of objects.

201

about skills he is not concerned primarily with the basic mechanics of punctuation, grammar, and syntax, but rather with developing in children the ability to write tellingly about what they have observed carefully. While he does not in the confines of his short article describe the exact nature of the organized writing program he advocates, his plea for consciously teaching children how to observe, write, and rewrite is a compelling one.

Two other authors have expanded their ideas into a sequential program. James Moffett, in an excitingly different book, has challenged his readers to rebuild the language-arts curriculum around writing.[16] He shares with Evans a desire to have children observe keenly, describe analytically, and revise critically. In addition, he writes convincingly of children's ability to work in small groups as they help each other edit, to a more extensive degree than is usually the case. He makes a clear distinction between editing and correcting, which is helpful to teachers trying to experiment with his ideas.

Finally, the Fournier series puts into sequential workbook format the ideas of this new approach to creative writing.[17]

The basic problem involved is that so far no sequence of writing skills to be mastered at the elementary level has been identified and agreed upon. People in mathematics and music education, for example, have identified quite definitively the specific skills and their order of acquisition. In language arts, skills in spelling and handwriting have also been ordered sequentially. No such ordering exists for creative writing, though the three writings mentioned here begin such a task.

Actually, the foregoing dichotomy between free and more structured approaches to creative writing is an artificial one, set up primarily to throw into relief the distinguishing characteristics of each point of view. It is possible to take the best of each approach and weld them into a richer experience than either would provide alone. It seems apparent that neither provides a completely satisfactory approach, but together they provide a means of improving the creative-writing program.

---

[16] James Moffett, *A Student-Centered Language Arts Curriculum* (Boston: Houghton Mifflin Co., 1968).

[17] Raymond Fournier, *Thinking and Writing: An Inductive Program in Composition* (New York: Prentice-Hall, Inc., 1969). The series attempts to develop in children the skill of selecting, organizing, and presenting information. It leads a child through five different levels of increasingly complex problems designed to develop this skill. While no claim can be made that these are unique skills, apparently this is the first time they have been organized in sequential fashion.

Editing and Correcting

In order to understand this new approach to writing, the teacher must understand a fundamental but often overlooked distinction between two terms: *editing* and *correcting*.

It is undoubtedly safe to say that most of what happens to writing after the first draft falls into the category of correcting. For far too many children, writing is a two-step process—creating or setting the ideas down and correcting or repairing the way these ideas look on paper. Thoughtful teachers have long been aware that such attention to the mechanics of proper punctuation, spelling and even more sophisticated matters as phrase relationships, seems to have one effect— that of discouraging pupils from wanting to write more. In fact, Trauger reports the results of an interesting study which substantiates empirically what some teachers have known intuitively for years: the more emphasis placed on mechanics or correcting, to use our term, the less writing may ensue.[18] This places the teacher in a dilemma: How to encourage writing which abounds in creative and vigorous ideas, and yet which presents these ideas in a form which communicates well?

The skillful teacher knows that giving back papers to be corrected should occur as an option for those children who receive satisfaction from seeing papers displayed in the room or around the school. Naturally if they wish such pleasure—and children can understand this— then they must do their potential reader the favor of putting the writing into standard English, or risk remaining unread.

The skilled teacher also knows, however, that there are myriad ways writing can legitimately be improved, through improving or clarifying the thought expressed. We shall call this process *editing*. Undoubtedly the most complete and definite statement about editing has been given by Moffett, who places creative writing at the very core of the language-arts program.[19] While such emphasis on writing is interesting, such a curriculum in language arts may not be possible for most teachers. In Moffett's book, creative writing *is* the language program, to oversimplify a bit. If as a teacher, you are not comfortable with such a single-minded position, perhaps the materials in this chapter will

---

[18] Wilmer K. Trauger, *Language Arts in Elementary Schools* (New York: McGraw-Hill Book Company, 1963). In this very useful book, which deserves to be better known, Trauger deals most helpfully with characteristics of the language which children can learn. The section on playing or experimenting with ideas in writing is one of the best sections.

[19] Moffett, *A Student-Centered Language Arts Curriculum*.

serve to give you some ideas about how writing can be a more vital part of the language-arts program. Considerable time will be spent on editing because of its importance in the creative-writing process.

Whenever a child has written something, it can probably stand some editing. Note please that the previous sentence does not read "should be edited." There is a vast difference between pieces which *can* be edited (all writing, at all times) and those pieces which *should* be edited (some writing, sometimes). It is the fine discernment in telling when and how which cannot be legislated.

What do we mean by editing? Very precisely, we mean changing, altering, adapting, adding to, or taking away from what was originally there. We mean revising, reshaping, relocating, and redoing in order to say more exactly what we wanted to say originally.

In the relatively relaxed time after the first creative inspiration and haste to write their thoughts, children can be led to ask themselves some questions:

1. Which of my sentences say what I want to say the "best" way they can? Are there some which don't really say anything at all? Are there places where I've expected a reader to jump wider gaps in action than anyone can safely jump? Is there a way I can rearrange my sentence to make it more interesting (funny, engaging, descriptive, unexpected, shorter, longer, tantalizing)?[20]

2. Are there words in my story which need to be made stronger? For example, *nice*, that pale modern-day ancestor of the vigorous Middle English adjective meaning wanton, is now so anemic it can seldom hold its own in a sentence. Children can be helped to see that many words need to be weeded out of their writing vocabulary because they are today too feeble to be effective.

3. Is there anything in my story as a whole which: a) needs to be somewhere else or b) doesn't need to be in the story at all? In this, of course, one is trying to get children to do basic plot revision, to think about what happened to whom, when, and why.

---

[20] The materials included in *Language Explorations for the Elementary Grades* (A Curriculum for English) (Lincoln: The University of Nebraska Press, 1966), are particularly helpful in developing this sense of how sentences can be edited.

All of this is so different from the usual, rather picky insistence on mechanics, on harping about, for instance, agreement of verb tense with subject (which incidentally is more profitably approached from the point of view of the thoughts expressed than from the side of "correctness" or rules). It is also so different from asking children to follow through such uninspired activities in a language-arts book as asking them to pick out the "best" topic sentence, an uncertain task at best.

What we are asking children to do is to step back from their work, to take a hard look at it, and then to impartially make some value judgments about the quality of that work. This is, as anyone who has ever attempted it knows, an exceedingly difficult task. It is, however, one which in the long run proves to be worth the time expended on it. The teacher should realize that this ability develops slowly over a long period of time. If he wants to develop the ability in a group which has never worked this way before, he may well spend an entire year bringing children to the point of achieving the objectivity necessary for successful editing.

The teacher, thus, is aware of his goal—stimulating children to write more—and he feels that it is only by writing and then editing that children learn how to write better.

This editing procedure which is more important than mechanical correctness in creative writing, profits from the teaching of specific mechanical skills, which is done when children are engaged in practical writing. That is, having received specific, organized, and sequential exposure to the mechanical skills in the other segment of their writing program, the children are able to use these skills as they do their creative writing. Techniques for teaching such skills will be discussed later.

Evaluating Creative Writing

There are three types of evaluation which need to be considered. These include: 1) the children evaluating their work, 2) the teacher evaluating children's work, and 3) the teacher evaluating his work. Whether the teacher prefers having children work at editing alone or in groups, this procedure leads naturally into evaluation. Children evaluating their own work is listed first because it is the most important type of evaluation. This type is closest to the way adult writers work. That is, writers seldom rely mainly on extrinsic evaluation but, as is the case with other creative people, rely primarily on their own intrinsic evaluation of their work. This is not to deny the importance of such people as editors in helping writers examine their work, but simply to say that the major evaluative effort rests with the creator.

Our job then is to help children learn how to evaluate their own work. Basically, of course, that is what the following series of questions is designed to do: help children evaluate an individual piece of work.

The term *evaluation* suggests an extensive procedure taking place over a period of time. This is facilitated by having children keep a folder of their work so they can evaluate at intervals the progress they have made. If the teacher encourages children to keep samples of writing, he can have individual conferences with children in which they evaluate their writing.

In reviewing the creative writing a child has done, the teacher can help him think about some of the following questions.

Questions related to the plot

1. Are the ideas in my stories becoming more interesting? Am I learning to make things happen sequentially so the reader can follow easily?

2. Am I learning how to make plots go in more than one direction? Can I sometimes start at the end of my story and work backwards, or in the middle and go in both directions, instead of always having to start at the beginning and work toward the end?

3. Am I learning how to write different kinds of plots including both realistic and fantasy ones? Am I learning how to write plots which both boys and girls find interesting?

Questions related to characterization

1. Do my stories show I am learning how to write about a variety of people?

2. Are my people becoming more believable? Do they do and say things which *might* happen within the confines of my story as I've written it?

3. Am I improving in my ability to make people more real? Do the details I include seem to make the people alive, rather than flat like silhouettes?

4. Do I ever try to personify something? Can I convincingly make something inanimate come to life?

Questions related to setting

1. Am I improving in my ability to look at some object and write a clear, concise description of it which will share my impressions with a reader?

2. Am I becoming able to combine descriptions of several objects into a unified paragraph which helps my story?

3. If I write made-up descriptions, are they getting better at making a reader "see" the objects or situation I am describing?

4. Am I developing the ability to reread what I have written and to eliminate detail which I may like but which doesn't help my story?

The teacher makes use of some of the above questions as he has conferences with his children. He may not necessarily use all of these, or use them in the order presented. In addition, further questions need to be written for:

mood in the story,
climax and conclusion in the story, and
conversation in the story.

As the teacher helps children evaluate their own work, he is also evaluating so he can decide which children need further work in specific writing skills. These conferences are used by the teacher to determine which children need to be grouped for more experiences, perhaps in a group working on description, for instance. In a review of a child's work he may decide that the child doesn't need further work on description but does need further work on plot or dialogue. Thus the teacher, in addition to using the conferences as a time to help children evaluate their own work, also uses them as a time to determine what the child needs to do next.

The teacher also uses the conferences as a way of evaluating his own work, to assess strengths and weaknesses of the creative-writing program as a whole. If he discovers that few, if any, children can write convincing dialogue, he knows his planning of the program must have been weak in that area. If he discovers that many children are able to write convincing climaxes and conclusions, he knows he can shift focus to emphasize some other aspect of writing. Thus while his major purpose in the conferences is to help children develop the power to analyze their own work, he also uses conferences as a technique for evaluating *his* own work.

Children and Literary Forms

Related to the idea of a structured and sequential program is the thought that children can and should be taught to write specific literary forms.

One of the most accessible of these is the *simile*, because making comparisons using the terms *like* or *as* is relatively simple. Many language-arts books teach this form to children.[21]

One easy way to teach this idea is by using an audio-visual approach. We have had singular success by using the text, *A Picture Has a Special Look*.[22] Though originally intended to sensitize children to a variety of art media and their distinctive characterteristics, this text is written using many similes. The available film-strip is used as motivation, followed by a discussion of the author's similes. To follow up, a record about similes is used.[23] Some third-grade children recently created the following similes after this introductory motivation:

1. as simple as   writing *a*
                            an egg
                            pulling grass

2. as tight as: a belt that is too small for you
                        shrunk pants

3. as thin as: the letter *i*
                        a stamp

4. as mean as: a horse that kicks

5. as small as: plankton

6. as tall as: a giraffe on stilts

7. as stupid as: a potato

8. as lovable as: my relatives

---

[21] See, for example, *The World of Language* (Chicago: Follett Education Corporation, 1970), Book 3, p. 100, and Book 5, p. 345.

[22] Helen Borten, *A Picture Has a Special Look* (New York: Abelard-Schuman, 1961). This is also available as a filmstrip-record combination (LTR-054) from Weston Woods Studios.

[23] "Similes" from *Developing Language Arts Skills*, available from The Society for Visual Education, Chicago, Illinois. Also of use is #9, "Metaphors and Similes —Imagery!" from the record and filmstrip set, *What Is Poetry*, CFS-501, available from Caedmon Records.

This motivation seems effective at all levels. Recently some college juniors in a language-arts methods class, trying the motivation themselves before using it with children, wrote the following similes:

As misunderstood as a cat in a fishbowl.
As cozy as a kangaroo's pouch.
As disappointing as an empty mailbox.
A character as fake as a frozen TV dinner.
As monotonous as a piece of ruled paper.
As definite as a little boy with his first tricycle.
As creative as a burned-out lightbulb.
As simple as a bald head.
As soft as the drop of an eyelash upon your cheek.
As promising as a bag of jelly beans.
Silent as butter melting on a steaming ear of corn.
As mean as a father early Sunday morning.
As busy as an electric typewriter.

Another form children can be taught to write is the *metaphor,* although this is a bit more difficult because the comparison is not directly stated.[24] An examination of any good poetry anthology will result in many samples to use with children. You might want to begin with the charming poem entitled "Metaphor"[25] or with some of the poems by children included in Nancy Larrick's book.[26] These works demonstrate effectively to children that they can become adept metaphor writers. An article by this author may offer some suggestions of help when you attempt to motivate children to write metaphors.[27]

In addition to literary forms, there are many specific poetic forms children can enjoy writing. There have been many periodical articles describing approaches to writing haiku, sigo, cinquain, and diamante.

---

[24] Some series do attempt to help children with this idea. See, for example, *Language and How to Use It* (Glenview, Ill.: Scott, Foresman & Co., 1969), Book 6, pp. 156–58.

[25] Eve Merriam, *It Doesn't Always Have to Rhyme* (New York: Atheneum, 1965), p. 27.

[26] Nancy Larrick, selector, *Green is Like a Meadow of Grass* (Champaign: Garrard Publishing Co., 1968).

[27] John Warren Stewig, "Metaphor and Children's Writing," *Elementary English* (February 1966): 121–23.

These articles are often written by classroom teachers reporting on successes they have had, and so they generally are very helpful and need no further word of explanation here.[28]

Practical Writing

In this second half of the chapter we are concerned with the other type of writing children do. Though it is called practical, it is important to remember there should always be creative elements in any writing a child does. Even in something as prosaic as writing an invitation, children can be creative if the teacher allows for some flexibility.

A pervading concern in this section is teaching children specific skills of use in writing. This section will begin with some ideas about skill groups and mechanics and then consider specific forms children may need to know to write.

Skill Groups and the Mechanics of Writing

We need to make a distinction here between the way children usually learn skills and the method this chapter advocates. Unfortunately, the too-common approach is to have children progress page by page through the language-arts textbook. This is most frequently done because of the mistaken belief that such an approach to mechanics will be effective. Such procedures persist despite the fact that thoughtful writers have pointed out for a long time their questionable merit.[29]

The most helpful approach to mechanics is one which can be called *diagnostic*. That is, the teacher watches his children's written work, notices which problems recur, keeps a record of the frequency of these errors, and finally prescribes a remedy. In the last stage of this procedure, he puts children in small groups to do intensive work on the specific problem they share. The characteristic of these groups is their ephemeral nature; children work together only as long as necessary to master the needed skill.

---

[28] Several of these are included in the chapter bibliography.

[29] Miriam E. Wilt, "Organizing for Language Learning," *The National Elementary Principal* (November 1965): 6–12. Wilt describes clearly the need for such a "diagnostic" approach to skills as described here.

Time Problem

The most frequent cavil against individualizing any instructional program is lack of time. This is indeed a problem if one sees the textbook as equivalent to the instructional program. Indeed, this is perhaps one reason so little individualization is done in elementary schools.[30]

If however, the teacher can bring himself to see the textbook as a reference aid, a source of ideas and exercises for children to do, time will be no problem. This is because all those large blocks of time currently spent leading children page by page through the text will now be free time for work on individual problems.

An example may serve to illustrate this point. While observing a student teacher recently, I saw her give a unit test concerned with contractions, and especially with the use of *it's* as a contraction for *it is*. As anyone who has observed signs, billboards, and adult writing of all kinds can attest, this is one of the things which schools are apparently least adept at teaching—yet it is a simple phenomenon which is easily taught. One child, a fifth grader, failed the test, but the next day the student teacher was scheduled to move on to another topic. When I asked her what would happen to the child who got so few right she said: "Oh, it doesn't matter, they'll get contractions again next year." And so they will—and the next year and on ad infinitum, because of the abuse of the spiral idea so widely espoused in elementary language-arts texts. And the child will probably graduate from high school without knowing how to use contractions because no one is sufficiently interested to break this cycle of indifference, stopping to help him learn this simple skill. The student teacher had dutifully "covered" the pages prescribed in her series at her grade level, so she was content to let the next teacher worry about this problem. Instead of determining which small group of children needed help on this specific skill, she held the whole class together, boring some and not reaching others, until the five pages were covered. Then, inexorably, she moved on.

An unsatisfactory approach? Yes, but because she felt the entire group had to use the whole book, she thought this approach appeared to be logical. Had she tried the skill-group approach described above, she might have been more successful in meeting children's needs.

---

[30] A recent survey indicated that in 81.5 percent of the classrooms responding, the textbook *was* the language-arts curriculum. Such a lack of individualization of the program unfortunately results in a poorer program than is desired. See *The Status of Language Arts* (Dansville, N.Y.: F. A. Owen Publishing Co., 1965).

Sources of Errors

It was mentioned earlier that children's writing indicates areas needing individualized work. This work on mechanics always takes place in a period separate from creative writing time, however, and while examples drawn from children's writing may be used, these are never identified by author.

The teacher may well want to use some sentences or paragraphs taken from the writing turned in to him because this lends an air of reality to the skill practice. The teacher does this anonymously to protect the child who wrote the example from ridicule. He may copy the material on a ditto master, write it on a transparency to use in an overhead projector, or use the paper itself (with the name masked out) in an opaque projector. Using such real examples has the advantage of being more interesting to children than using examples given in a text or made up by the teacher.

Yet another way to accomplish this purpose, if you are concerned that children will discover who wrote the example being used, is to work with another teacher on this project. If you notice some of your children having trouble with subject and verb agreement, for example, you can borrow some samples another teacher has gathered. If some of his children are having trouble with misplaced modifiers, he can borrow from you. Usually there will be enough overlap of problems in children of any grade level, so that it will not be a problem to obtain samples in this way.

Duration of Groups

There is no stigma attached to being put into a skill group if two conditions are met:

1. Each person is working in a skill group of some kind. It is a rare classroom which has many children without some kind of problem. If you do have some children whose written work needs no help, they may need skill group work in other subject matter.

2. The groups have to be viewed as *temporary*, not permanent. The teacher groups children to learn a skill; when they have learned that skill the group disbands and children regroup to learn a different one. Unfortunately, it may seem some children are always in a skill group. This will be a problem, unless you have been able to meet condition one, above. If you have

not been able to, and some children feel self-conscious about this, perhaps you need to re-examine your priorities and see which of the skills you are expecting these children to learn are most crucial.

Letter Writing

Though letter writing has been included in the part of the chapter dealing with practical writing, in essence it belongs as logically with creative writing because the best letters are indeed creative.[31]

Teachers need to be aware that one reason why teaching anything beyond some basic structural considerations related to letter writing is difficult is that ours is not, and has not been for some time, a nation of letter writers. Few children have a model to emulate in this skill. It is a rare person, indeed, who has the leisure, or perhaps more accurately decides to use his leisure, in creating compelling communication in written form. In fact, though many elementary texts still deal at length with teaching children to write invitations and thank you notes, such forms of communication are becoming increasingly more rare in today's society. Consider when you as an adult last received a written invitation of the type still too frequently included in language-arts textbooks. Perhaps such consideration might change your mind about the need to teach such forms to children.

Though there is no particular justification for attributing this decline in letter writing to the manner in which the skill has been taught in schools, such is at least a reasonable assumption. It is true that there are certain basic forms which need to be used when doing business letters. These forms can usually be learned at the time children have need of them. In informal letters however, the emphasis on content which will capture a reader's attention far too infrequently takes priority over a punctilious attention to mechanical details. Children can be helped to an understanding that a letter can be as exciting to read as a story.

One way of stimulating children to edit their own personal letters is to have them write a letter, to a real person, and then let them work on the letter with a classmate. With their partner, they can edit

---

[31] Alvina Burrows makes this point, and offers several suggestions about encouraging children's writing in "Involving the Child in the Language Arts," Album 3 from *Listener Inservice Cassette Library*, available from Listener Corporation, Hollywood, Calif. The album of cassettes also offers help in oral language development.

the letters by using some of the questions proposed on pages 204 and 206–7, in order to increase the effectiveness of their writing. After such editing has been accomplished, and the letter recopied, it must be mailed to give the child a feeling that this is a worthwhile task.

Report Writing

Report writing is frequently a problem for teachers, and most reports written by children are badly done because techniques of report writing are frequently taught too hurriedly and too late. It is difficult for many children to understand that writing a report is not equated with copying from an encyclopedia.

A brief anecdote will illustrate the problem. While supervising a student teacher recently, I listened to some reports of the usual kind—painful readings of long transcripts from encyclopedias, much of which was unintelligible to both the reporter and the victims. As one particularly inept fourth-grade reader struggled with his list of principal products, faltering over: "The principal products are coffee, tea, and . . . and . . . and . . . ," he was unable to read the long word he had copied verbatim but uncomprehendingly from the encyclopedia. Into the painful silence came a very up-to-date future stewardess who obligingly supplied: "and milk?"

One reason children often fail to learn to write good reports is that far too few understand how helpful outlining can be. Outlining is basically a simple skill and can be taught in first grade if approached correctly. There are two easy ways to do this. First, when a teacher works with the idea of sequence in doing an experience chart with children, he is providing a useful introduction to outlining. Outlining is, after all, nothing more than setting information down in logical order. After a trip, perhaps to a bakery, the teacher helps children write down in order some ideas they want to include in their experience story; this is beginning outlining. Second, it is helpful as an introductory technique to have children rewrite in their own words a story which has been read to them. Any simple story will do. As the teacher helps them make an orderly list of the characters to be included, he is providing a painless introduction to a skill which, if well learned, will prove eminently useful to children.

Multiple Sources

The teacher lays the groundwork for intelligent report writing in sixth grade, when, in kindergarten, he uses several versions of a favorite story.[32] When he reads a variety of settings of "The Three Billy Goats Gruff" for example, and discusses with the children which they enjoyed most, he is helping them see, even if indirectly, that one source is not a final authority. The teacher continues going to more than one source, talking about likenesses and differences between them in order to inculcate the idea that multiple sources add richness to our thinking and experiences.

Children later use their practical writing skills when they send letters to newspapers around the country, ordering single copies of a variety of papers in order to see how differently the same events are reported in different parts of the country.[33] Imagine the shades of opinion represented in newspapers, for example, the day the Supreme Court action on segregation was taken! Though such a project as this is more closely related to social studies, it does entail language-arts skills. Whether in using actual materials to gather data or in using reference books, children can begin to sense the need for more than one source, if the teacher sees this as important.

Questioning

One of the most helpful habits a teacher can instill in students is that of making a list of questions to be answered before starting to do a report. Instead of simply allowing children to sign up for a topic, the teacher helps children frame a series of questions which should be answered in the report. In doing such a report, children too frequently tend to simply copy the section in the encyclopedia about this topic. There are however, a whole variety of more particular or specialized questions to which children might want answers, if they were encouraged to speculate about the general topic. For example, in considering a report on the products of Italy, children might explore such questions as:

Are there other products, not of major importance economically, but which are important for other reasons, perhaps aesthetically?

---

[32] Any card catalogue should reveal multiple versions of a single story. The major purpose of using several versions is the enrichment of the literature program which results. A collateral benefit is establishing in children's minds the value of using more than one source.

[33] The teacher can consult Robert U. Brown, ed., *The Editor and Publisher International Yearbook* (New York: The Editor and Publisher Company). It lists all newspapers published in English throughout the world and gives the necessary ordering information.

Are there some which can be produced only in certain places because of geographical features?

Are there some which are becoming less important? If so, for what reasons?

When children go out to find answers to questions *they* have asked, the tendency to copy from an encyclopedia is less, no matter what the topic.

The only problem with this approach is that the teacher must avoid "implanting" his questions in children's minds. He too, should be able to suggest some questions, as an ex-officio member of each planning committee, but the process must not turn into a thinly disguised guessing game designed to place his questions at the head of the list. If he can help his children with these three ideas: note-taking, outlining and the use of multiple sources, the teacher is likely to be successful in stimulating children to do reports with interesting content and ones which are respectable as examples of the child's ability in language arts as well.

Summary

This section has dealt rather briefly with some problems involved in helping children become more adept at practical writing. It has been concerned with some larger issues, rather than focusing on specific skills which should be taught. This is because, in actuality, it is impossible to specify in a meaningful way the exact skills your children ought to learn. Certainly in a very real sense the practical writing skills necessary for a group of lower-class children living in a city area are very different from those needed by advantaged middle-class children living in an upwardly mobile suburb. In addition, the time of acquisition will be different for those skills which the two groups do share. This is the reason for the emphasis at the beginning of the section on skill groups. What may be the focus of a skill group in one situation may be a truly irrelevant skill for another group of children. Thus, it is up to you as the teacher to analyze your children within the context of the community, the school, and the parents; determine what practical writing skills you think your children may need; and proceed from there. Of course, it is impossible in one of the most fluid societies the world has ever known to predict what writing skills your children will need as adults. But this procedure of analysis and skill-group treatment makes more sense than to assume, a priori, that any set of skills can be established as necessary for all children.

Finally, this chapter must be seen simply as an introductory statement of a few possibilities in this facet of the language arts. Writing, unlike some of the more easily definable and teachable skills of language, is both more elusive and finally more rewarding for teacher and child. Because of its complexity, the writing process is more difficult to write about, to read about, and to encourage than the more routine aspects of a total language program. For you, as a future teacher of writing, all this chapter can do is to identify some possibilities, raise some questions, and refer you to some other sources which will do the same. Hopefully the chapter will have met this objective and launched you on the frustrating but rewarding task of becoming an effective teacher of writing.

Suggestions for Further Exploration

1. Obtain some samples of children's stories. In each case, try to determine which aspects of the story need the kind of editing described in this chapter. Remember that it is crucial to pick the elements *most* in need of attention: belaboring the details in one piece of writing too extensively can cause children to lose interest.

2. Select a motivation of your own in one of the five sense categories mentioned in the chapter. Plan carefully the questions you will ask to encourage children to think about the motivation. Make sure that the majority of the questions are open-ended ones which will allow for a wide variety of responses. If possible, use the motivation with a group of children to determine the effectiveness of your questions.

3. A good way to understand the difficulties inherent in any art form is to try doing it yourself. Study the materials available about some of the structured poetry forms, and then try to write some poems yourself. After you have done this, analyze the difficulties you encountered. Does being aware of your own difficulties change how you would approach these forms with children?

4. Gather a collection of unrhymed poetry to use with children. Try to find poems of this type at different levels of complexity, appropriate for use at different ages. This is important according to Walter (see book bibliography) because children too frequently feel that to be poetry, writing must rhyme. Most poetry writing is bad because of this idea.

5. Select some common object you are used to seeing frequently. Examine it as if it were the first time you were seeing it. Write a description of it including any observations you make with your senses. Visual descriptors will probably occur to you first: the surface texture, the contours of the object, its dimensions. Do not neglect the other senses: can you describe how it feels, how it tastes, what noises it can make? Don't neglect the off-beat or unusual: the taste of a light bulb, the sound of a leaf (as you rub your hand against it), the smell of a toothbrush, or the feel of uncooked macaroni.

6. To develop the ability to write convincing details and description (created as opposed to observed, as in question six) take a myth you find interesting and develop it into a fully detailed story. Expand the setting, plot, and characters, trying to retain the essence of the original.

7. Find several versions of the same folktale. Share these with children, and then have them choose which one they like best and analyze in writing what they liked about their choice. You might try several versions of "Rumplestiltskin" (including the charming new version of it by Evaline Ness, "Tom Tit Tot," New York: Charles Scribner's, Sons, 1965). Another good one is "Cinderella," and be sure to share with your children the unique version by Beni Montressor (New York: Alfred A. Knopf, 1965). His version, with the more complete descriptions of the Baron of Montefiascone, his daughters Tisbe and Clarinda, and poor Angelina (renamed Cinderella) make fascinating reading.

8. Take any story which includes several characters. Mary Norton's "The Magic-Bed-Knob" (New York: Hyperion Press, 1943) is a good example. If you have access to a group of children, share the story with them, and then let them choose which character they would like to be. Let them rewrite an episode in the story from that character's point of view.

Bibliography

Inexpensive Paperbacks
about Children's Writing

Many people have written on children's writing. The following list of paperback books—all inexpensive, full of ideas, and easily accessible—is recommended in the hope that you will read further.

Applegate, Maurie. *When the Teacher Says Write a Poem.* Scranton, Pennsylvania: Harper and Row, Publishers, 1965.

The potential audience for this book is junior high school students, and Applegate's argument is that "poetry is for you." The sections on rhythm, and the pictorial nature of poetry are especially good. Though designed for an older age group, the book has many ideas of interest to elementary teachers.

———. *When the Teacher Says Write a Story.* Scranton, Pennsylvania: Harper and Row, Publishers, 1965.

The book, written in Applegate's usual evocative style, includes both adult and children's writing in copious amounts. The chapter on character development and the section on checking writing before considering it finished, contain many useful ideas.

Arnstein, Flora J. *Children Write Poetry: A Creative Approach.* Dover, N.Y.: Dover Publications, 1967.

The author reports on many years of experience in sharing poetry and helping children to write it. She deals deftly with the problem of the ideas children develop about themselves which interfere with creative expression. A good section is included on helping children evaluate their own standards, both for their writing and for adult poetry.

———. *Poetry in the Elementary Classroom.* New York: Appleton-Century-Crofts, 1962.

The author's suggestions about how to interest children in poetry, how to encourage poetry writing, and how to compensate for inadequate backgrounds in poetry are designed to bolster teachers' confidence in their ability to handle this topic. It includes many examples of poems written by children.

Brandt, Sue R. *How to Write a Report.* New York: Franklin Watts, 1968.

It is difficult to determine which is crisper: the author's style or the illustrator's drawings, but there is no doubt that both contribute to making this an extremely valuable tool in teaching what is too often a dull subject. The author's approach is straightforward and the material is well organized, while the humorous illustrations help to hold wandering attention. If any book could interest children in the topic, this one should.

Burrows, A. T. et al. *They All Want to Write: Written English in the Elementary Classroom.* New York: Holt, Rinehart and Winston, 1965.

This older book, frequently updated because its message is so basic and so fresh, reports the work of four teachers who concerned themselves with writing before it became generally accepted in the elementary curriculum. A concern for the mental health of children and the release which creative writing can be permeates the book though practical writing is not neglected.

Carlson, Ruth K. *Sparkling Words,* 1965. 1718 LeRoy Avenue, Berkeley, California. (Also available from National Council of Teachers of English.)

The author deals with fostering divergent-thinking creative approaches to poetry writing. Most of the approaches recommended have grown out of classroom teachers' experimentations.

———. *Writing Aids through the Grades.* New York: Teacher's College Press, 1970.

The author provides teachers with valuable help in getting and keeping the flow of expression going through motivations keyed to the children's own personal experiences and with suggestions for overcoming the difficulties of grammar, structure, and spelling without stopping the creative flow. She recognizes the importance of relating the child's other creative impulses to his writing, and emphasizes the value of group experience, both in developing projects and in discussing each other's work.

Corbin, Richard. *The Teaching of Writing in Our Schools.* New York: The Macmillan Co., 1966.

One in a series planned to answer questions parents ask, this book gives a teacher insights into particular aspects of the creative-writing program which may need explaining to parents. The chapter on reasons for a creative-writing program could be used to good advantage, as could the many suggestions in the chapter on evaluation.

Dawson, Mildred, and Choate, Mary Alberta. *How to Help Children Appreciate Poetry.* Palo Alto, Calif.: Fearon Press, 1960.

The book includes 100 poems for interpretation through choral reading, finger plays, painting and drawing, writing, acting and dancing. Selections are included from Rosetti, Dickenson, Kipling, Whitman, and others. The book offers seasonal and holiday poems, thoughtful, tranquil, nonsense, and humorous poems.

Foster, Joanna. *Pages, Pictures and Print: A Book in the Making.* New York: Harcourt Brace Jovanovich, 1958.

Though not technically a paperback, this small book details in interesting fashion the process from idea to printed page. The author deals easily with the complexities of blanket cylinders, Quoin keys and

Smyth sewing, all the while retaining the reader's interest by her deft style and eye for descriptive detail.

Glaus, Marlene. *From Thoughts to Words*. Champaign, Ill.: National Council of Teachers of English, 1965.

Another book of ideas compiled by a classroom teacher as enrichment activities to stimulate an interest in language. The first section encourages observation in a variety of situations, the second concentrates on word activities and the third presents ways of introducing children to authors.

Henderson, Harold G. *Haiku in English*. Champaign, Ill.: National Council of Teachers of English, 1967.

The author's modestly sized volume is illustrated throughout with tasteful black and white drawings. Henderson begins with a lucid explanation of Japanese Haiku, and another chapter on English Haiku presents a clear contrast with the first. Teachers will find the chapter on how to teach haiku particularly helpful, as much because of the sample poems which are included as for the instructions which are clear and easy to follow.

Jacobs, Gabriel. *When Children Think*. New York: Teachers College Press, 1970.

The author describes his experiences in eliciting creative thinking from nine-twelve year olds through having them keep journals of their ideas. Selections from the children's journals show the range of their thoughts, the honesty of their views of themselves and their world, and the excitement of recognizing and developing an idea that is new to them. A description of the techniques the author and his colleagues have developed is included.

Leavitt, Hart Day, and Sohn, D. *Stop, Look and Write*. New York: Pathfinder-Bantam, 1964.

The book of black and white photographs is divided into twenty sections, each of them prefaced by some comments directed to the high school students for whom it was originally intended. Described by the authors as a "beginner's course in how to see," the book provides a wealth of photographs of use to the elementary teacher, who will find the comments of interest.

Mearns, Hughes. *Creative Power: The Education of Youth in the Creative Arts*. Dover, N.Y.: Dover Publications, 1958.

The book, a reprint of the original edition, detailing the author's innovative work many years ago at Columbia University, is an amazingly fresh treatment of writing, poetry, plays, and other creative expression. Mearns brings a truly gifted insight into the potential of children to create, and his book is inspiring encouragement to all who want to go and do likewise.

Petty, Walter T. *Slithery Snakes and Other Aids to Children's Writing.* New York: Appleton-Century-Crofts, 1970.

> The contents are as useful as the title is catchy. The chapters on building blocks and on tools of the trade are full of useful ideas. The authors deal with transforming and combining at the sentence level, and with larger forms, including poetry. A section on helping children out of a writing slump should be useful as will be the concluding chapter of evaluation.

Smith, James A. *Creative Teaching of the Language Arts in the Elementary School.* Boston: Allyn and Bacon, 1967.

> Smith's book (from a series of seven devoted to all curricular areas) is primarily a handbook of techniques, which includes many examples written by students. His list of ways to motivate children, the section on judging quality in writing, and the material about using questions are particularly helpful.

Stegall, Carrie. *The Adventures of Brown Sugar: Adventures in Creative Writing.* Champaign: National Council of Teachers of English, 1967.

> This is Mrs. Stegall's spritely account of her pupils' encounter with creative writing on an extended basis—from the moment the idea of their book was conceived, through the many sessions of learning skills, to the final culmination in their own book. A delightfully encouraging account of how an insightful teacher can make language arts come alive.

Studacher, Carol. *Creative Writing in the Classroom.* Palo Alto, Calif.: Fearon Publishers.

> The book includes practical suggestions and procedures for enriching the creative climate of the classroom. There are chapters on description, writing stories and poetry, creative-writing projects, and setting and maintaining the creative climate. Methods applicable to students at all levels of achievement in the elementary grades are included, as well as many examples of student writing.

Walter, Nina W. *Let Them Write Poetry.* New York: Holt, Rinehart, and Winston, 1962.

> The author, who believes the surest way to develop appreciation of poetry is through experiences in that art, reports of her efforts in teaching children. She begins by explaining how to establish a creative environment and concludes with a section on evaluating poetry.

Wolsch, Robert A. *Poetic Composition in the Elementary School: A Language Sensitivity Program for Teachers.* New York: Teachers College Press, 1970.

> The author, a language-arts consultant, encourages the teaching of poetic composition as a means of developing the whole child because he believes that poetic composition heightens children's awareness of themselves, their surroundings, and their language. This book reports

his experiences with children and provides a much needed guide for elementary school teachers.

Yates, Elizabeth. *Someday You'll Write.* New York: E. P. Dutton and Company, 1969.

This charming small book, directed especially to the elementary child, gives us an introduction to the author as well as to the art of writing. She stresses the importance of reading as preparation and the need to establish clearly a time reference when beginning a story. The section on style is particularly helpful as is the one on selecting the right word for the right spot.

Periodical Bibliography

Ackerlund, Sylvia. "Poetry in the Elementary School." *Elementary English* 47, no. 5 (May 1969): 583–87.

The author stresses the necessity of including poetry in the language-arts program and the misuse of poetry at the present time. She offers suggestions on how to teach poetry more effectively. Included are such ideas as: relate poetry to classroom situations, use poems for pantomime and dramatization, and encourage children to write their own poems. She also discusses how the teacher can better prepare himself for teaching poetry.

Allen, R. Van. "Let Not Young Souls Be Smothered Out. . . ." *Childhood Education* 44 (February 1969): 354–57.

Creative-writing experiences can help the child realize no one else can really say anything for him. Each child should be allowed to develop a style of expression all his own. Creative writing can develop imagination, build self-confidence, provide for emotional expression, develop the aesthetic sense, deepen appreciation of other people, and bring balance to educational activities.

Dearmin, Jennie T. "Teaching Your Children to Paint Pictures with Words." *Grade Teacher.* (March 1965): 26–27.

The article relates the experiences a classroom teacher had in using the cinquain form with her fourth- and sixth-grade children. This brief report, dealing with what the author calls a "dwarf poetry" form, is nonetheless sufficient to whet the appetite of a teacher interested in motivating his children to write this type of poetry.

DeVries, Ted D. "Writing Writing and Talking Writing." *Elementary English* (December 1970): 1067–71.

This article recounts an experience using tape recorders to help children move through three states: saying something, hearing it back, and seeing it in writing. Essentially this reports a variation on the language-experience approach used for writing purposes instead of reading. The article offers suggestions about how to increase students' desires to write, including the novel suggestion that teachers write for and with their students.

Glickman, Janet. "A First Grade Hiaku Project." *Elementary English* 47 (February 1970): 265–66.

Haiku, an old Japanese poetry form, is made of seventeen syllables consisting of three lines of five syllables, seven syllables, and five syllables, respectively. Simple in form and direct in thought, it requires that children be very exact in what they are saying. This article relates a beginning attempt which integrated art and oral language using this form in the first grade.

Hopkins, Lee Bennett. "Two Creative Verse Forms." *Instructor* 78 (March 1969): 76–77.

The *Sijo* poetic form was produced by the Yi Dynasty of Korea in the fourteenth century. In English translation it is written in six short lines, each line containing seven to eight syllables, for a total of forty-eight syllables.

The first part of the word *cinquain* means the number five in French and Spanish. This refers to its five lines, each of which has a specific number of syllables and a specific purpose. The author offers suggestions for how to teach these forms to children.

Olson, Helen F. "Using Reading to Teach Creative Writing." *Education Today*. Elementary Literature Bulletin #25, Columbus: Charles E. Merrill Publishing Company.

The article deals with examples chosen from children's literature which can be used to motivate various types of writing. The author sees value in the standards of excellence which these examples set for children. She outlines procedures for teaching paragraph writing and myth writing by using literature and makes a clear and valuable distinction between emulation and imitation.

Shapiro, Phyllis P. "The Language of Poetry." *Elementary School Journal* 70, no. 3 (December 1969): 130–33.

The author speaks of poetry as an experience and suggests ways the reader may gain the most from experiences with poetry. She also stresses the important use of sound and meter in poems as compared to their use in normal language communication.

Sharples, Derek. "The Content of Creative Writing." *Elementary School Journal* 68, no. 8 (May 1968): 419–26.

The article deals with the question of how creative writing should be judged. Sharples states that since judgment must stem from individual development, the degree of progress made in creative writing must be based on the child's previous performance. He also suggests that the teacher must present the stimuli to encourage the child to make this progress.

Smith, Lewis, and Willardson, Marilyn. "Communication Skills through Authorship." *Elementary English* 2 (February 1971): 190–93.

The authors recognize that a young child has always had to be dependent on adults to record his thoughts. The article presents one solution to this problem, using portable cassette recorders. Separate units were set up in one corner of the classroom, and children were encouraged to dictate any time they wished. Teachers or teacher aides typed up the recordings. These typed materials later became the source of reading activities.

Tiedt, Iris M. "A New Poetry Form: The Diamante." *Elementary English* 46, no. 5 (May 1969): 588–89.

The author introduces a new form of poetry writing—the diamante—which is produced in a diamond shape consisting of seven lines, the result of using a formula whose elements are nouns, adjectives, and participles. The general idea is to start with a subject noun as the top point of the diamond, e.g., country, describe it with adjectives and participles and then as the diamond tapers down to the bottom point, e.g., city, use participles and then adjectives to describe the city. The middle line consists of nouns that relate to the top subject noun.

True, Sally R. "Sijo." *Elementary English* 42, no. 3 (March 1966): 245–46.

This article introduces the Korean poem form, the Sijo. In English translation it is a six-line, nonrhyming poem dealing with deep thought and revealing emotions. This is done mainly by using such contrasts as sun to rain, mountains to water, or earth to sky. The teacher who introduces Sijo to his students will not only be sharing with the students the beauty of nonrhyming poems, but also encouraging the child in using symbolism from nature.

An Integrated Language-Arts Unit

by Carolyn Holland,
Klondike Elementary School

It was with a great deal of enthusiasm for audio-visual techniques that I plunged wholeheartedly into a project which proved to be a wonderful learning experience for all of us who were involved in it.

My student teaching was in a departmentalized situation in which my cooperating teacher and I taught reading and language arts to three classes of fifth graders. Each group spent half the period reading and working in an individualized reading program. The other half of the period was devoted to language arts, and this was the area of my focus.

My supervising teacher gave me a book, *The Lion, the Witch, and the Wardrobe* by C. S. Lewis with the comment that I was to use this book as the core of my language-arts instruction for the next eight weeks.[1] I was free to design the unit in any way I felt would facilitate the teaching of it.

After reading the book, I decided that the story would lend itself well to condensation, and that the children could probably take the main idea from each chapter and make a poem of it, carrying the

---

[1] C. S. Lewis, *The Lion, the Witch, and the Wardrobe* (New York: The Macmillan Co., 1950).

thread of action from stanza to stanza. Each class would compose its own, and the resulting narrative poem would then furnish us with a script. This would be taped by the children and illustrated with a slide set.

Since there were three different groups of children involved, I decided to use three different mediums for the pictures so that I could have the varied experience, and so that there would be a basis for comparison of the techniques. One group posed in living pictures for their slides; another made paper bag puppets; the third group used magazine pictures and original art to illustrate their poem.

It was an ambitious project, and somewhat experimental, so I allowed my plan to be flexible enough to change and grow with classroom developments.

Building Interest in Poetry

Since I had selected poetry as the device to use in the project, my first step was to try to stimulate interest in poetry—in reading it, writing it, listening to it. I put up a brightly colored bulletin board using poetry books from the library. These were carefully chosen for their splashy pictures, shortness of verse, and clarity of thought. The books were opened out flat and secured to the bulletin board in random fashion. The object of this was to get the children to stop and look at the illustrations and see that much indeed, can be said in just one line. The board was entitled, "What is a poem . . . ?"

To supplement this, other interest centers were set up. On the window sill we had a collection of poetry books, started with volumes from the library. Before long, the children were bringing their own favorite poetry books to share with classmates, and our window library became quite representative of all types of poetry.

On a worktable we set up a listening post. This is a box that is wired for sound to which several sets of earphones are connected. This box allows more than one child to listen at once. Eight children could listen at one time to poetry records from the library. For some of these records, there were accompanying books. Poetry tapes were also available from our school library. The children signed up to listen, and each child had the opportunity to listen to each record or tape before a change was made.

Out of these exposures to poetry grew the desire for expression. The children began to hand in unsolicited original poetry. We felt this needed recognition, so we invited all classes to participate in making an original poetry book. The children were to write the poems. This was completely voluntary and absolutely no pressure was brought to bear. The poems were not altered or changed by the teachers, nor did we question their motive, style, or content. The poems were free form, and most of our corrections and suggestions were punctuation. Our purpose was to motivate. The response was amazing. Three poems from among the many written are included here.

The Wind

Have you ever felt the wind?
It can be as soft as a kitten's purr.
At times I don't even know it's there.
But when a trickle of wind goes up my spine,
    I know it's there, somewhere.

Have you ever felt the wind?
It can be as fierce as a lion's roar.
I always know it's there.
The wind practically blows me when I try to talk,
Have you ever felt the wind?

Barbara

Rain

Rain!
It is very beautiful.
Rain!
It tingles your nose.
Rain!
It clatters on the roof.
Rain!
Children go splash! splash!
Rain!
When it rains, mothers worry
That you'll catch cold.
Would you catch cold from rain,
No!

Tina

The Rolling Clouds

The rolling clouds I see above my head,
As they float over the mountains and
    through the valleys,
Make me wish that I were one of them,

So I could float and see the roaring
    streams and lakes below.

The rippling streams and lakes I see below,
As they wind and wiggle through the
    mountains and vales,
Make me wish that I were one of them,

So I could watch the trees color their
    leaves.

The painted trees I see that drink the
    water from every stream,
As I go winding by.
Make me wish that I were one of them,

So I could stand so straight and tall,
    and watch the birds fly by.

Jim

We had the poems typed, each on an individual sheet, and each child had the privilege of illustrating his own, if he chose to do so. A ditto was made so there could be a copy of the book for each child. The best cover for the book was selected from among many submitted, and the activity culminated with a beehive of activity in assembling the book.

Starting to Work

With this introduction, it was time to begin our main project. I introduced *The Lion, the Witch, and the Wardrobe* by telling some interesting facts about the author and his other works. Then I explained to the children briefly, in outline form, the successive steps we would take in making a slide set.

Again, we started by putting up a large bulletin board depicting the main characters, which aroused much interest and speculation about the story. One of our most stringent requirements for reading aloud to the children was that they give their undivided attention, so desks were cleared, and we began to read the first exciting chapter of our book, discussing a few points as we proceeded.

Immediately then, working on the chalk board, I asked the children to help list the main ideas in the first chapter so that we could use them as a starting point for our poem. This done, we began to try to make rhymes or couplets out of the ideas. For example, the story begins by telling about four children who were sent away from

London to the countryside during World War II so they would be safe from the Blitz. We turned this into:

> Once four children were sent to stay
> At a house in the country not far away.

This was a good start. The next part told about the house they went to, the old professor they stayed with, and their feelings about being there, and this description evolved:

> It was big and spooky with rooms galore,
> All of it was theirs to explore—
> Boy! This is better than any old war!

They began to get the feeling. Right away the children could see the possibilities, and we raced ahead, completing the poem for that day. I was pleased. So were the children. Enthusiasm was high.

Each day thereafter, we read one or two chapters, always drawing out the main ideas to form a framework for our poetry. To write a poem every day was a demanding assignment for middle graders, so we used various methods to give variation. Some days, the children were allowed to work in small groups of three or four to make a poem at school; sometimes they did it as homework. Frequently, we combined parts of the work from various groups or individuals; sometimes the class was divided and half would work on today's poem, half on tomorrow's. Always there was the privilege of individual work for the more talented.

Also, there was the need to assemble this work daily and make the decision about the final form. We needed today's poem to add to the previous day's poem, which was mounted on a bulletin board so the children could read and reread it and make suggestions for change. An editing committee of volunteers was formed for this work, and it was surprising how adept they became at sorting and assimilating the material.

By the time we finished the book, we had the narrative poem also and were ready to turn our attention to making the slide sets. We gave a ditto copy of the completed poem to each child at this point and explained that the poem now had to be divided into scenes so that a picture could be obtained to represent each segment of the action. They did not find it hard at all to decide upon the scenes and this was accomplished rather quickly. In one group, it happened that there were five pages of poetry and five rows of students, so one page was assigned to each row as their responsibility. This insured uniform participation. Each page included at least five scenes. From this point, each of the three classes was involved in different kinds of things that would contribute to their own particular project. I will treat each separately now to better describe the steps taken.

Three Groups at Work

The *Living pictures group* was now ready to make their background scenery. Our room had several large four-by-four-foot bulletin boards, so we decided to draw the backgrounds, paint them and mount them on the bulletin boards, and to create whatever props were needed from things at hand or from home. Each row was responsible for creating the scenes on its page of poetry. We found that some of the scenery was useable throughout the story, and as it turned out, each row created one scene. This allowed more focus for the children, and the backgrounds they created were most imaginative.

A list of all the characters was written on the board and the children drew lots for the parts. All the children were free to draw for any part until he got one. The list was extended to include things like trees, flowers, and animals; this gave everyone a responsibility, a costume to make, and a picture to be in. Drawing lots seemed to work better for us and get more different students involved, even the less capable, than tryouts and popular selection. Each one felt he had an equal chance.

The children made their own costumes from things at hand. If anyone needed an item he didn't have at home, we asked the class, and it was amazing how all our needs were met—and with such imagination and ingenuity.

Now, we were ready to take the pictures. Each row posed the characters into the pictures they thought would best represent the scenes in their part. Remember, each row worked on only one page. By using the row system, which included only five or six students at any one time, we could keep commotion at a minimum.

We used a Kodak Instamatic camera, completely automatic, two reflector lights, and colorchrome slides, all furnished by the school. The teacher took the pictures, as we felt that it was important to protect the quality of the pictures. Each group was allowed thirty slides.

Some of the students who seemed more adept or interested evolved as helpers of various sorts, assistant directors, prop people, costume or make-up helpers. This afforded a wonderful opportunity for us to delegate responsibility and really involve everyone.

While all this was going on, the students who had speaking parts were practicing individually and together, using a tape recorder to check their progress. A tape recorder is indispensible in doing this because a student is most sensitive to his own recorded voice and performance, faults and all. The recorder was available to the students individually and as a group, and it didn't take long for them to become quite critical and begin to "iron out" their difficulties.

As the practice for recording went on, we asked for volunteers from each of the three classes to make one musical background, which would be used by all three groups, under the direction of the music teacher. We obtained a chorus from the combined classes, and they selected background music from among songs they knew, practiced and recorded it in a humming, drumming style. This was dubbed in as background music for the narrative poems.

I might add here that the mechanics of running the recorder, dubbing the music and sound effects were done by the students themselves. The crew practiced right along with the students who were reading the parts, and by the time the final recording was done, they had all practiced enough together to perform like clockwork. They arranged their desks in a close circle so they could spread out their scripts to eliminate paper noises. The microphone was set up in the middle of the group for uniform recording. This, of course, was under the constant supervision and guidance of the teacher. It required self-discipline and cooperation, but they felt like movie stars and directors, and they loved it!

The *puppet group* made their characters out of lunch bags. We used the small sacks to get uniform puppet size. The trick to making these puppets is to fix a large head about five or six inches in diameter to the bottom of the sack. The legs, body or costume can be made quite small to fit onto the side of the sack. It seems that this proportion makes the most effective puppet.

We provided the children with plenty of sacks, colored paper, scissors, and paste and told them to make whatever character they wanted to. I made several samples, showing the children how to curl strips of paper to use for hair, how to make animal whiskers, to fringe the paper and use scraps and buttons for trim.

Finally, the class selected from among all those made which ones should be used to represent each character. This class used the basic scenery the other class had made but made changes in it to suit their script and their puppet size.

We again used the row system whereby each row directed one page of script, and again it worked out fine. We did find out that while one row was working, the others should be occupied reading or with some assignment. At this point, much of the work has been done, and if they are not working on something specific, they sometimes bother the ones who are.

My original intent was for the *third group* to illustrate their poem with magazine pictures, collages, and original drawings. We found out fairly early that this story did not lend itself to magazine pictures, and decided that original art would be better. Each day, after we read the chapter from the book and outlined the main ideas on the board, the children would select something from that chapter that they wanted to draw a picture of. Sometimes the entire class would have the assignment. Often, half the class would do the pictures one day, the other half the next day. In this way, we had some pictures for every chapter to choose from, plus the magazine pictures they brought in. We kept a good supply of eight-by-eight-inch paper available for these pictures so they would be of a fairly uniform size.

We used a Kodak Visualmaker for the filming. This is a special outfit which includes a camera and a metal stand. The camera, which attaches to the metal stand, has a special lens which enables it to make perfectly focused slides of any picture which is centered under the stand. The picture must be no larger than eight-by-eight inches, however. This equipment is specialized, but it is easy to use, and many schools have it in their media centers. A Visualmaker camera is virtually foolproof and each child was allowed to photograph the drawings he had contributed.

By the time this group finished the book and their story poem, they also had most of their pictures done. It is a good idea to have each child write a title for his picture on the back of it, and the chapter number for proper identification. After a while, there are enough pictures that this becomes necessary.

We then selected a picture committee whose job it was to select the most representative picture to illustrate a chapter. When these were selected, the class helped with final selections and culling.

We used a slide sorter for all groups to arrange the pictures in order according to the script. Then we played the recorded poem, showing the slides at the same time, making any necessary changes and marking on the script the exact time to flick to the next scene.

Sharing the Results

The results were impressive. Now, we had three original narrative poems, each illustrated in a different medium. The children were delighted with results, but they wanted to see each other's work. They also wanted their parents to see the show, so we decided to have a premiere showing. The project had been fun to do, and the party we had was a fitting climax. The children baked dozens of cookies, made gallons of Kool Aid, cleaned and decorated the room, moved and arranged the furniture, set up equipment, and served happily on any committee.

Their enthusiasm was reflected on the day of the party in the presence of an appreciative overflow crowd. I am sure that none of these children will ever forget their involvement in this project, no matter how small the role they played. It was a real learning experience for all of us.

CHAPTER EIGHT

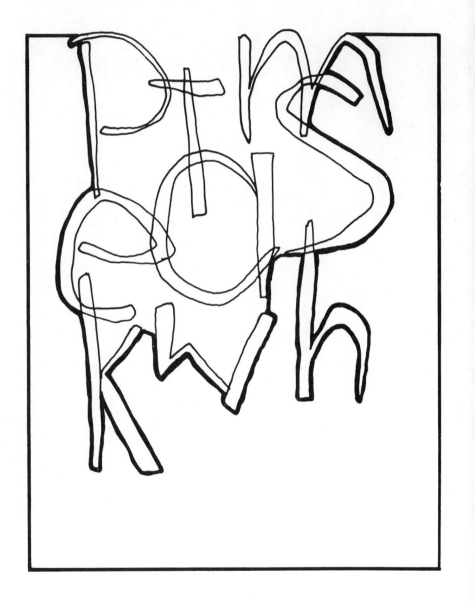

Handwriting

Handwriting is an art open to any amateur for the delight he gets from it himself, and for the further pleasure he gives to others.[1]

The above quote by Lewis Mumford—that delightfully wry commentator on the American way of life—seems strangely out of date now, though it was written less than fifty years ago. It's a rare individual who has the leisure today to savor the art of the proper shaping of letters. If we do notice good penmanship as we read, we may unconsciously be grateful for it, but seldom do we pause to reflect upon the skill of the writer. Even less often do we think consciously about out own writing.

Yet, though our world is unlike Mumford's, and delight in an attractive page is minimal, some valid reasons remain for being concerned with handwriting and how to teach it to children.

Practical Reasons

Is the street address 732 Vineland Place, or 132 Vineland Place? Is the client on whom you are to call Mr. Tomaus or Mr. Tomans? Is

---

[1] Lewis Mumford as quoted in Robert O'Brien, "The Moving Finger Writes —But Who Can Read It," *Saturday Review* (July 18, 1959): 8.

the cough medicine for which you're searching called Myoncl or Myond? In such situations and countless others, we find ourselves each year staring in bewilderment at the scribbles on the paper in our hand, unable to decipher the marks. Hours, time, and money are lost as we make the effort to interpret our own scrawls or those of others. Postal clerks, pharmacists, plant managers and secretaries all share the same frustration in dealing with the products of a society which sees no intrinsic value in handwriting, yet pays the penalty for illegibility. The problem of unreadable writing is nationwide and apparently not getting any better.[2]

Adult handwriting may range from such clear and legible samples as Figure 5 to the completely illegible scratches of Figure 6, taken

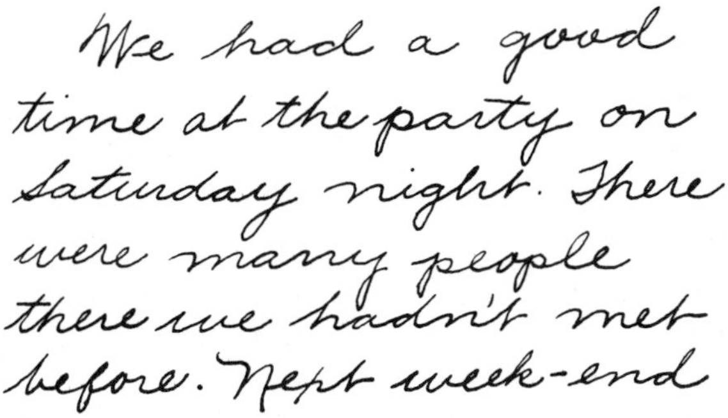

We had a good
time at the party on
Saturday night. There
were many people
there we hadn't met
before. Next week-end

Figure 5

unfortunately from the writing of a professor who communicates daily in writing with many colleagues and students.

The teacher in the elementary school is similarly faced with a wide range of handwriting competency, as demonstrated by the samples included in Figure 7, all taken from one class of fifth-grade children.

Given the reality that widely differing competencies exist among young children's handwriting and apparently continue to exist among adults, the need for some sort of handwriting instruction is evident. To whom should it be given and for how long? These among others are the questions with which this chapter will be concerned.

---

[2] O'Brien, *Saturday Review*, July 18, 1959. As far back as 1959 the estimate made was that U.S. businesses lose about $1,000,000 *per week* because of scrambled orders, lost time, missent deliveries, and clerical mistakes which are the result of poor handwriting. It is safe to say the problem is of even greater magnitude now.

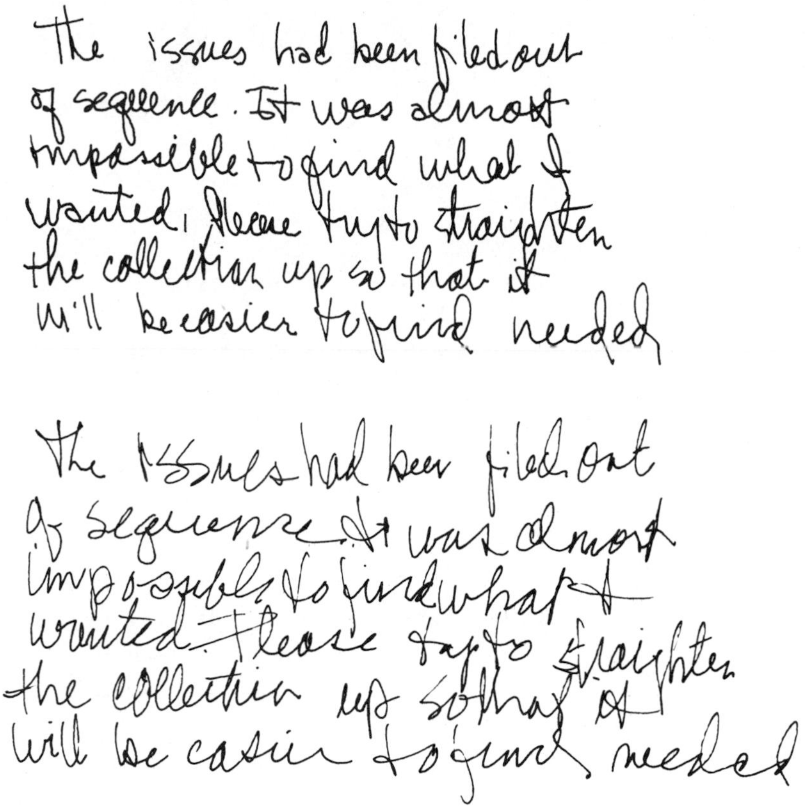

The issues had been filed out
of sequence. It was almost
impossible to find what I
wanted. Please try to straighten
the collection up so that it
will be easier to find needed

The issues had been filed out
of sequence. It was almost
impossible to find what I
wanted. Please try to straighten
the collection up so that it
will be easier to find, needed

Figure 6

How is Handwriting Taught?

Since much of what goes on in schools is evolutionary from ideas and practices of earlier times rather than implementation of new ideas,[3] some investigation of the history of handwriting instruction may help the future teacher understand current programs.

For many years, children in this country learned only *cursive* writing (Figure 8). This is the connected form of writing we most commonly call "writing." Though young children learned to read from

---

[3] An articulate statement of this contention is included in Margaret Ammons, "Communication: A Curriculum Focus," in *A Curriculum for Children*, ed. Alexander Frazer (Washington: Association for Supervision and Curriculum Development, 1969), pp. 105–22.

Florida did not always belong to our country. In Chapter 2 you learned how Ponce de Leon discovered and claimed Florida for Spain. About forty years before English settlers built Jamestown in Virginia the Spaniards started a settlement in Florida. They called it St. Augustine. It was the first permanent settlement in our country. Find it on your map on page 205.

Florida did not always belong to our country. In Chapter 2 you learned how ponce de Leon discovered and claimed Florida for spain. About forty years before english settlers built Jamestown in Virginia the spaniards started a settlement in florida. They called it St. Augustine. It was the first permanent settlement in our country. find it on your map on page 205.

Since the climate of Florida was unually warm the family could use their patio all the year round, here they planted lovely flowering fruit trees which they had brought to the new world from Spain, among these trees were figs, lemons, limes, and oranges

Figure 7

242

materials which were set in printer's type, quite unlike the script they wrote, no attempt was made to begin writing instruction with a form similar to type.[4]

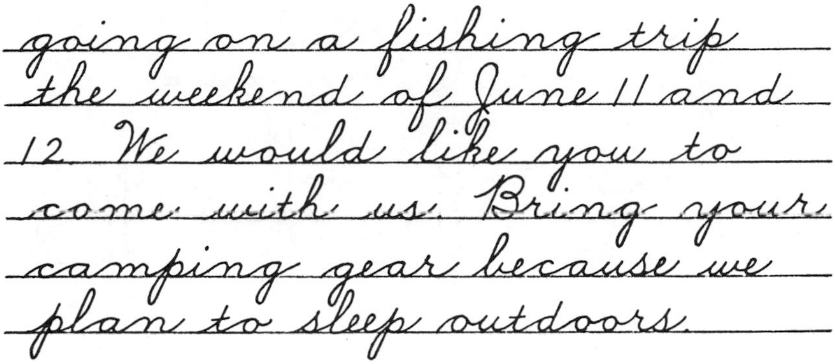

going on a fishing trip the weekend of June 11 and 12 We would like you to come with us. Bring your camping gear because we plan to sleep outdoors.

Figure 8

From *You Can Write*, Book 6, by Aubrey Haan and Bernadine C. Wierson. © Copyright 1966 by Allyn and Bacon, Inc. Reprinted by permission of Allyn and Bacon, Inc.

It was not until early in this century that children began to be instructed first in one kind of writing (close to print type, Figure 9) and then were required to learn another form (the form widely accepted among adults).[5]

The acceptance of *manuscript* writing, the unconnected form made essentially of straight lines and circles, is remarkable for two reasons:

1. We can pinpoint with accuracy both the date and the person responsible for introducing the idea. One cannot help but marvel at the pervading influence of a dynamic lady from England, Miss Marjorie Wise, who first taught a course in this new method at Teachers College (Columbia University) in New York in 1922. From this beginning manuscript has spread until its use is almost universal.

---

[4] An interesting exception to this is the series of books about Babar, the elephant, which are not set in manuscript-like type, but rather are printed using cursive writing. See for example, *The Story of Babar* (London: Methuen and Co., Ltd., 1955).

[5] It is interesting to note that though almost all American children learn both styles, in a number of European countries children learn only one form, cursive.

Figure 9

From *You Can Write*, Book 2, by Aubrey E. Haan and Bernadine C. Wierson. © Copyright 1965 by Allyn and Bacon, Inc. Reprinted by permission of Allyn and Bacon, Inc.

2. The degree of acceptance of this two-form approach to teaching handwriting is almost complete. It is a rare idea or innovation in education that receives almost universal acceptance in schools. A study done some time ago indicates that at that time, almost all children learned both forms of writing.[6] While the study is admittedly an older one, there has been no replication of it. Informal observation does not suggest that the situation has changed much.

Thus we see that handwriting instruction is fairly well codified into one approach: that of using an introductory mode (manuscript) and a permanent mode (cursive).

Time Allotments

While there is no general agreement about the amount of time which should be spent on handwriting instruction, it is probably not too unfair to characterize it as minimal. Though school schedules and

[6] Virgil Herrick, *New Horizons for Research in Handwriting*, (Madison, Wisconsin: The University of Wisconsin Press, 1963), pp. 19–20. The study revealed that 79 percent of all children learned both forms, with 14 percent learning cursive only and a miniscule 7 percent learning only manuscript.

time durations vary widely, one element which pervades many class-rooms is the need to teach many language arts in a limited amount of time. The teacher must provide experiences in reading, creative writing, creative drama, usage exercises, oral language work, listening instruction, practice and drill on mechanics, *and* handwriting. Certainly it is easy to see why the teacher, innundated with so many things to do in so short a time, turns to the sequentially organized handwriting series. Pressed for time and faced with the need to teach the skill effectively, he seeks a set of materials which will do this easily and quickly. It seems fair to generalize about handwriting instruction as being fairly well codified in approach and taught in minimal amounts of time. What are the reasons for this?

Probably one reason for the state of handwriting instruction today is that neither teachers nor students find it a very rewarding subject. One author has identified the reason for teachers' attitudes toward the subject:

> Handwriting is an unpopular subject with teachers, probably because adult handwriting tends to be inferior to that of students. . . .[7]

In addition to the problem of teacher attitude, a recent study indicated that children find very little of interest in handwriting study. Inskeep and Rowland questioned 550 children in grades four through six and discovered that handwriting was next to the bottom in a list of preferred school subjects.[8]

Commercial Materials

It is important to be aware of the commerical series available for handwriting instruction since the teacher typically chooses one to use, rather than fashioning his own program. Indeed, some authorities have

---

[7] Kendrick B. J. Noble, "Handwriting Programs in Today's Schools," *Elementary English* 40 (May 1963): 511.

[8] James Inskeep and Monroe Rowland, "An Analysis of School Subject Preference of Elementary School Children of the Middle Grades," *Journal of Educational Research* 58 (January 1965): 225–28. An interesting aspect of this study is that through an examination of correlations between I.Q. and preferences, the authors discovered that this dislike for handwriting pervaded all intelligence levels.

taken the position that the most crucial determinant of the nature of the handwriting program is the commercial series which is used.[9]

When the teacher, perhaps while serving as a member of a textbook adoption committee, examines these materials, he is struck immediately by the quantity which are available. There are in excess of sixteen companies manufacturing handwriting materials, and among this array it should be possible for every committee to find something to their liking.

Typically these commercial materials differ in three respects.

1. They differ in the individual letter *forms* which are presented as the model to be followed.[10] For instance, we find that both capital and lowercase letters are made differently depending on the series. The letter *B* may, for example, be made in any of the ways illustrated in Figure 10.

Figure 10

The letters *P*, *W*, *X*, and *R* are others which vary from one series to another.

2. They differ in the *sequence* in which individual letters are presented. Some series introduce all the lowercase letters first,[11] others introduce a mixture of lowercase and capitals,[12] and still others introduce all the capital letters first.[13] In each case, the rationale for the mode of presentation is "difficulty," though exactly how this is determined is not always clearly explained.

---

[9] Herrick, *New Horizons for Research in Handwriting*, p. 27.

[10] One of the factors to keep in mind in selecting a series to use is *simplicity* of form. There is good evidence that most adults tend to modify the style they learned in school in the direction of more simple forms. See Eunice Askov's "A Decade of Research in Handwriting: Progress and Prospect," *Journal of Educational Research* 64 (November 1970): 99–111.

[11] Mary Elizabeth Bell et al., *I Learn to Write* (Indianapolis: Bobbs-Merrill Company, 1968).

[12] *Peterson Handwriting* (Greensburg, Pennsylvania, 1968).

[13] B. F. Skinner, *Handwriting with Write & See* (Chicago: Lyons and Carnahan, 1968).

3. They differ in the recommended *method* for making the letter. For example, a child learning to make a manuscript *W*, may learn one of the three ways illustrated in Figure 11.[14]

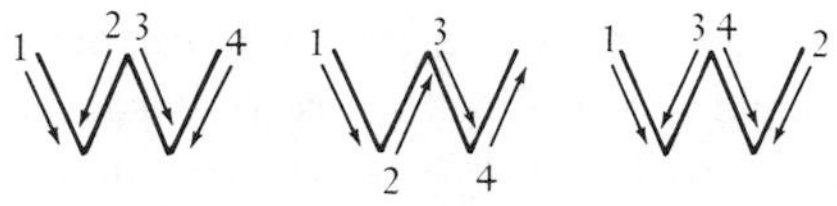

Figure 11

Choosing a Series

Making a decision about which series to use is indeed difficult, because, despite several small differences in the three points mentioned above, the materials are characterized more by their similarities than their differences. In fact, one author maintains that because of this: "a teacher using one series rather than another might be somewhat hard-put to identify specific advantages of the adopted series. . . ."[15]

The decision-making process is further complicated by the fact that research in the area is limited. We do have some indication of which letters are most difficult, and this information can be used in assessing the materials. The Lewises did a study in which they determined the difficulty of *manuscript* letters and discovered that *q, g, p, y,* and *j* are the most difficult, while *H, O, L, o,* and *l* are the least difficult.[16] Burns examined the difficulty of cursive letters, and as a result of his study determined that *a, e, r, t, v, n, o,* and *s* are the most difficult.[17] These studies provide a teacher with some data to use in selecting a

---

[14] The three methods respectively from left to right may be found in: Marion Monroe, *Writing Our Language* (Chicago: Scott, Foresman, 1969); Morton Botel et al., *Spelling and Writing Patterns* (Chicago: Follett Educational Corporation, 1971); Aubrey Haan and Bernadine C. Wierson, *You Can Write* (Boston: Allyn and Bacon, 1965).

[15] Pose M. Lamb, "Handwriting in Elementary Schools," in *Guiding Children's Language Learning* (Dubuque: William C. Brown, 1971), p. 225.

[16] Edward R. Lewis, and Hilda P. Lewis, "Which Manuscript Letters Are Hard for First Graders?" *Elementary English* 41 (December 1964): 855–58. Difficulty was determined by the number of times a letter form was written incorrectly.

[17] Paul C. Burns, *Improving Handwriting Instruction in Elementary Schools* (Minneapolis: Burgess Publishing Company, 1962), p. 24.

series, as he will check to see if these difficult letters are among those taught first or whether they are delayed until later in the sequence when a child has more confidence in his skill.

Beyond these studies, there is little controlled, empirical research to justify materials and methods in handwriting. There is a great quantity of nomothetic writing by experts, but unfortunately little of this is backed up by "hard" data. Until more research is available, decisions about what materials to use and how to use them will probably continue to be made on intuitive bases.

There are two series unusual enough to deserve mention. The first of these is *Writing Our Language* by Marion Monroe,[18] unusual because of its use of actual student handwriting samples. The remainder of the available handwriting materials present a model of unblemished perfection, which at times looks as though it might have been created by a machine. The question should be raised about the effect such unrelenting perfection has upon children, and especially upon boys, for whom such perfection is not easily acquired and by whom it is seldom desired.

The second series, based on theories of programmed instruction and utilizing the technique of immediate reinforcement, is *Handwriting with Write and See* by B. F. Skinner (Chicago: Lyons and Carnahan, 1968). By use of a special pen which causes a chemical reaction on treated paper, the child gets immediate positive response in the form of a *grey* line as he makes the properly formed letter. If he makes the form incorrectly, a *yellow* line appears. The advantage of this approach is that the student does not wait until the teacher can check his writing but can tell as soon as the letter is finished if it is made correctly. This feature helps eliminate the child's making the incorrect form over and over again until the teacher can get around to each child.

Individualizing the Handwriting Program

Typically handwriting instruction has been given in total-class situations. The teacher most frequently presents the new letter or combination form using the handwriting series as guide, and all the children work on the same letter at the same time.

---

[18] Marion Monroe, *Writing Our Language* (Chicago: Scott, Foresman & Co., 1969). The series makes use of student writing in its evaluation sections, and also of handwriting by famous adults. This technique lends considerable reality to the materials.

Given what we know about the range of individual differences likely to be present in any elementary classroom, such a procedure cannot be of maximum effectiveness. What are the alternatives? Some scheme of individualized instruction seems to be desirable.

When considering the problem of individualization, one must be aware that there are basically two types which are involved. The first of these is *rate* individualization, the easier to accomplish. Especially with such new materials now available as the Skinner "programmed" writing series, it is very possible for children to move through a specified content at their own speed.

The more difficult type to implement is *content* individualization, probably due to the difficulty with which we as adults relinquish ideas of certain contents being necessary for everyone. It is probably a fair generalization that most individualized learning programs in effect today are ones of rate, not content.

Askov is firm in pointing out that there are definite advantages gained when individual instruction in handwriting is provided.[19] Her review of research revealed that, especially for older children, more gains are made when children's individual problems are diagnosed and specific study strategies are created than when everyone progresses through the same program in the same way.

The Open Concept and Individualization

The idea of open-concept, or multi-age grouping, arousing such interest among educators now because of the positive and pervading influence of the British Infant Schools,[20] can lead to individualization of handwriting. One interesting aspect of this new approach is that it puts into practice ideas suggested some time ago by forward-looking educators.[21]

---

[19] Eunice Askov et al., "A Decade of Research in Handwriting: Progress and Prospect," *Journal of Educational Research* 64 (November 1970) 99–111.

[20] For a description of how such a grouping facilitates language learning, and especially how one child with more mature skills helps one with less mature skills, see Ann Cook and Herbert Mack, "The British Primary School, *Educational Leadership* 27 (November 1969): 140–43.

[21] Miriam Wilt, "Organizing for Language Learning," in *Issues & Problems in the Elementary Language Arts*, ed. Petty (Boston: Allyn & Bacon, 1968), pp. 39–46. The most striking fact about Wilt's article is that it discusses ideas only now becoming accepted. Her suggestions for multi-age grouping with younger children learning from older children in a very free environment were made some time ago, though they are only now being implemented on a wide scale.

Such organizational arrangements capitalize on the help older children, whose skills are firmly established, can be to younger children who may still be learning basic skills. It should certainly be possible for the teacher in such situations to guide the older and more capable students in helping the younger ones to move at their own rate in acquiring the skills of handwriting. The teacher may need to present initial lessons in the mechanics of making a particular form, but follow-up practice can be done alone.

One program needs special attention here because it provides not only individualization of rate, but also of content (manuscript symbols, cursive symbols, or typewritten symbols).

An Experimental Program

One of the most noteworthy programs in handwriting, the Hawaii program, was begun a few years ago. It is experimental and of interest for two reasons.

The first of these reasons is that, after they have progressed through a series of group readiness activities, children entering the handwriting program are allowed to chose in which mode they will learn: manuscript writing, cursive writing, or typewriting. Recent correspondence with a member of the Hawaii English Project casts doubt on the strongly held belief on the part of handwriting experts and classroom teachers that children need to learn manuscript writing and then switch to cursive. Data collected over a five-year period indicates that over 90 percent of the kindergarten children in this state are able to go directly to the cursive script.[22] Follow-up studies on the children who attempt cursive and do not succeed indicates they also have trouble with the manuscript form, suggesting a need for further readiness activities.

A second feature which distinguishes the program is that it is highly individualized and auto-instructional. Although handwriting experts have for years pointed out the importance of individualization, in actuality one finds that group instruction, as mentioned earlier, is the more usual method employed.

---

[22] Information in this section adapted from mimeographed reports and correspondence from Mr. Donald Y. Enoki, Curriculum Planner, Hawaii English Project, Summer 1971.

In the Hawaii program, after children have chosen the mode (manuscript, cursive, or typewriting) in which they will learn, they make a further choice. They elect to learn using *Flock Cards, Writing Books,* or *Film Loops.* All the materials have been prepared or especially adapted for this program. The learner uses his Flock cards, which include specific directions for making each letter enhanced by the kinesthetic or tactile element; the Writing Books, which are similar to conventional handwriting materials; or the Film Loops, each of which presents a single letter in an easily used format which the child may view as frequently as he likes. Children work individually and progress at their own rate. The teacher in the classroom does no group instruction. Instead, he uses the amount of time set aside daily for handwriting practice to assist individual children. After practicing until he feels he has mastered the particular letter or combination of letters on which he is working, the child can go to a checker who examines the material.[23] The checker either recommends that the learner go on to another letter, or that he practice further. The steps in this program are diagrammed in Figure 12.

Paraprofessional Help in Individualization

Few teachers work in programs as experimental as the one described above. Yet, even in a more conventional program, with some planning and recruiting among parents, more individualization can be effected than if the teacher tries to do the entire program himself. A brief review of school admission forms will reveal which mothers have proficient enough handwriting to serve as assistants in the program. These women can be contacted about helping with the handwriting program. The teacher can spend a few hours on initial instruction with this group of mother-volunteers, who can come into the classroom on a regularly assigned basis. The teacher will undoubtedly do the initial presentation on the letter forms. After this is done, these mothers who have been instructed in how to supervise practice can help individuals work at whatever forms they need to practice.

---

[23] Note: These are salaried staff members who also perform other paraprofessional tasks. The teacher helps with checking but is not alone responsible for all the children.

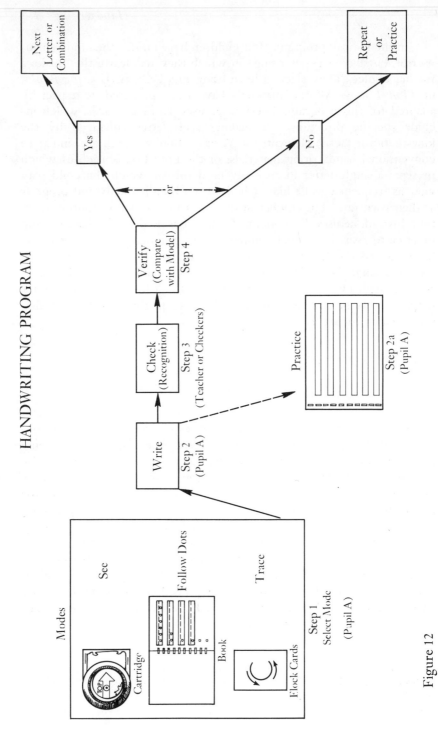

HANDWRITING PROGRAM

Figure 12

252

The Issue of Transition

Much of the foregoing, concerned with how handwriting is taught and the materials necessary to accomplish this, is based on a tacit assumption: the use of two forms. It is important to question this practice, despite the evidence cited earlier that the use of two forms is almost universal and despite the fact that few commercial series even admit that perhaps some children should be allowed to learn only one form.[24]

The reasons given for teaching manuscript are logical, to be sure. These include:

1. There are only two basic shapes to be mastered, the circle and the straight line.
2. There is time for the child to rest between letters, since each letter is disconnected from the others.
3. There is much similarity between this style of writing and the print children read.

Considering the inherent logic of these reasons, we must ask if the advantages gained by learning cursive writing are strong enough to warrant burdening children with learning two systems.

We have empirical evidence that manuscript writing is superior to cursive in some ways. It is more legible than cursive writing, it can be written as fast as cursive, and it can be learned more easily.[25]

In addition, it is difficult to read the research of Templin without wondering about the wisdom of requiring children to learn both manuscript and cursive writing. Templin examined the handwriting of 378 adults and concluded that:

> the transition from the manuscript to the cursive style of handwriting at any age or at any grade level tends to result in less legible adult handwriting.[26]

---

[24] One pair of authors does conceed that "Some children never wish to change. This may be especially true of the slow child and the artistically talented child." See Aubrey Haan and Bernadine C. Wierson, *You Can Write* (Boston: Allyn & Bacon, 1965), p. T–6.

[25] See Don W. Anderson, "Handwriting Research: Style and Practice," in *Research on Handwriting and Spelling*, ed. Thomas A. Horn (Champaign: National Council of Teachers of English, 1966), pp. 18–28.

[26] Elaine Templin, "The Legibility of Adult Manuscript, Cursive, or Manuscript-Cursive Styles," in *New Horizons for Research in Handwriting*, ed. Virgil Herrick (Madison, Wisconsin: The University of Wisconsin Press, 1963), pp. 185–206.

The main, and indeed only, reason which justifies this duo-system of instruction is the societal pressure brought to bear on those who use manuscript once they are adults. There are all sorts of reasons given for making a transition, e.g., cursive is faster, it is more individualistic, it is a legal requirement on documents. None of these reasons can be defended by empirical data. We are thus confronted with the fact that we ask children to learn two systems simply because many in our society look upon cursive writing as more "adult" than manuscript. The question to be considered by teachers is: How long must we use a cumbersome two-style approach which results in reduced legibility, in order to satisfy an illogical societal demand? The amount of time wasted when one well-developed skill is discarded and another must be learned has to be weighed against the value of this time being spent in more profitable pursuits.

Changing the Status-Quo

Naturally the change from using a two-style system of instruction to teaching a single form or to allowing children to choose which form they will learn needs to be made at a school-district level. No teacher can effect such a change himself. All the teachers and administrators must agree on the wisdom of having children learn one, not two styles. Once such a decision is made, specific plans must be developed for explaining to parents the rationale for the decision and for enlisting their aid in making the program a success.[27]

It seems to be an especially appropriate time now to consider this problem in view of the interest in accountability which seems so common.[28] Parent groups throughout the country are requesting and receiving specific statements of what schools are attempting to do and reports about the effectiveness of these attempts. Along with demands

---

[27] This will not be easy. Patrick Groff ["Preference for Handwriting Style by Big Business," *Elementary English* 41 (December 1964): 863–64] reports that though business executives expressed a preference for manuscript, parents felt two systems were necessary ["Parents' Opinions about Handwriting Styles," *Elementary English* 43 (December 1966): 873–76].

[28] Accountability, the idea that schools must assume responsibility for the results of their work, is widely treated in the professional literature. See for example: R. E. Burgett, "Accountability: Just the Teacher?" *School and Community* 58 (December 1971): 30–31, or R. J. Nash, "Accountability: Next Deadly Nostrum in Education?" *School and Society* 99 (December 1971): 501–4. Either provides a good introduction to the problem which needs careful consideration by teachers.

that schools increase their effectiveness, should go some reconsideration of this issue in handwriting.

Accepting the Status Quo

Realistically, it is probable that teachers and principals may be unwilling to effect the change to a single style of handwriting, or to allow children a choice of modes as is done in the innovative Hawaiian program. If this is the case, the school staff needs to consider *when* the change from manuscript to cursive is to be made.

Educators need to be aware of research which demonstrates quite conclusively that the *later* the transition is made, the better off the child is. Wilson speaks for those who believe this in stating that "The delay of the cursive writing skill increases the mastery of written language each half year it is delayed."[29] Her research indicated that children in her study ($N = 147$) wrote more words the later they made the transition. She discovered that children who changed as second graders wrote on the average of 2623 words; those who did not change until the end of third grade wrote on the average of 7681 words. Clearly, then, the later the transition, the better for the child.

The teacher will want to be aware that several of these series do suggest optional times of transition in the program, and some decision about which of these to adopt will need to be made. In addition, all series give very specific suggestions which the teacher will find helpful for how to make the transition.

Developing Legibility

When working with older children who have learned cursive writing, the teacher will find that two approaches to practice are possible. He may decide to use the handwriting series essentially as it is, or he may decide to work on legibility by concentrating on the problems his children have, which is a diagnostic approach.

Research on handwriting has demonstrated that there are some letters which are quite apt to give children problems. The teacher may want to analyze the children's writing to determine which of his children have such problems. He can then put the children into skill-

---

[29] Louise Ada Wilson, *The Journal of Exceptional Education* 31, no. 4 (Summer 1963): 371–80.

development groups to work on their specific problems. Children can work with their small skill group until they have mastered the particular troublesome form and then move to another group. When all the children have mastered the form, the group is disbanded.

Horton made a study of difficulties in cursive writing among 1000 sixth-grade children.[30] As a result of the study it is possible to predict that the following letters will probably be of some difficulty to your children:

letter

r—This is the most difficult and accounted for 12 percent of all illegibilities.

These letters accounted for 30 percent of all illegibilities.

h
l
k
p
z

Given such a large percentage of difficulties caused by a small number of letters, Horton concluded that "concentrated effort on a few troublesome letters would produce greater legibility in cursive [writing]. . . ."[31]

Beyond working on specified form problems, however, the teacher is always concerned with a larger problem, that of helping children *regularize* their handwriting. Legibility is to a large degree dependent upon this regularization or the predictability the reader can expect while reading a particular sample.

There are basically four aspects of handwriting which need to be regularized. These are 1) slant, 2) size, 3) form, 4) spacing.

The question of amount of *slant* forward or backward is not as important as the question of the regularity of the slant. Though some authors are adamant in recommending elimination of a backhand slant, it is difficult to see the justification for this position, provided the backhand slant is regular, i.e., consistent.

While there is no doubt that excessively small or excessively large handwriting may present problems of legibility, again the question of regularity of *size* is more important.

---

[30] Lowell W. Horton, "Illegibilities in the Cursive Handwriting of Sixth Graders," *Elementary School Journal* 70 (May 1970): 446–50.

[31] Horton, *Elementary School Journal* 70:449.

Similarly, while there may be certain *form* irregularities or peculiarities so unusual that the teacher may feel it necessary to help a child eliminate them, it is more crucial that a child be consistent in the form that he uses. That is, if the reader can begin to anticipate that the form of a particular letter will always be made the same way, he can minimize the problem of reading the writing. If, for example, in a single sample the letter *a* is made three different ways and at random, the problem of legibility is greater.

Finally, helping children work on regularity of *spacing* is essential. Again it matters less whether the spacing is very compact and tight or if it is very loose and relaxed, providing it is regular. It is when one encounters irregularity of spacing that legibility diminishes.

Children can check the regularity of their own slant, simply by drawing lines through the spines of the letters; these lines should be parallel. Figure 13 indicates a desired regularity of slant.

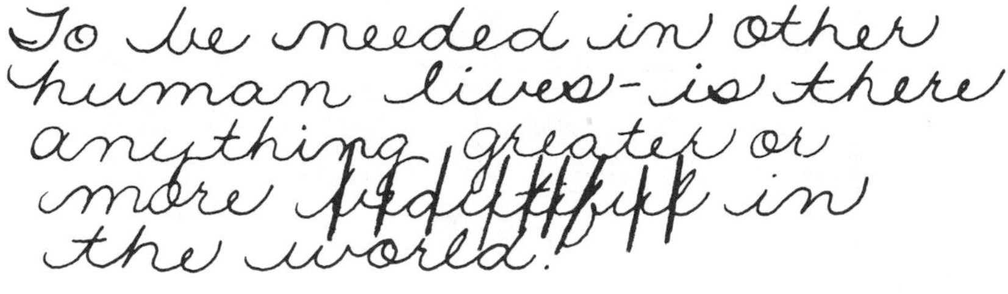

Figure 13

What one wants to help children overcome is the sort of irregularity in Figure 14.

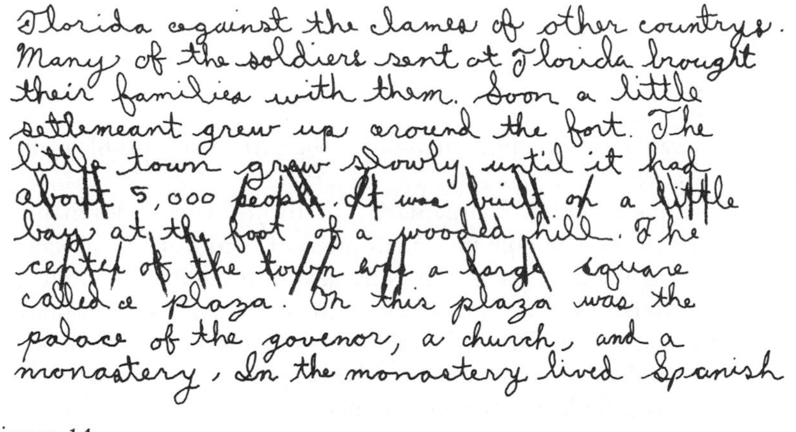

Figure 14

Whether one has large handwriting or small is less crucial than that the size is regular. Drawing guide lines (Figure 15) can help children check on the regularity of size in their writing.

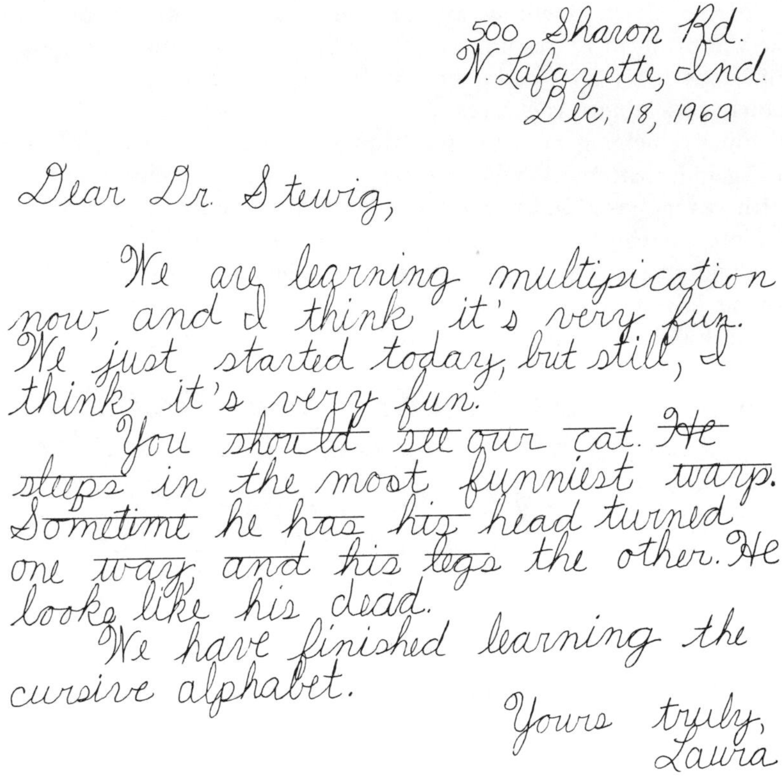

> 500 Sharon Rd.
> N. Lafayette, Ind.
> Dec, 18, 1969
>
> Dear Dr. Stewig,
>
> We are learning multipication now, and I think it's very fun. We just started today, but still, I think it's very fun.
> You should see our cat. He steps in the most funniest ways. Sometime he has his head turned one way and his legs the other. He looks like his dead.
> We have finished learning the cursive alphabet.
>
> Yours truly,
> Laura

Figure 15

What one wants to help children avoid is the sort of size problem illustrated in Figure 16.

It is simple to check on regularity of form—have children use a paper punch to put one hole in a small piece of cardboard. This can be moved along a line of writing as it is used to check on the legibility of individual letters. The cardboard serves to block out the surrounding letters. While it is true that within the context of a word we can often make out an individual letter, the goal is complete legibility apart from context. To accomplish this children need to work on regularity of form.

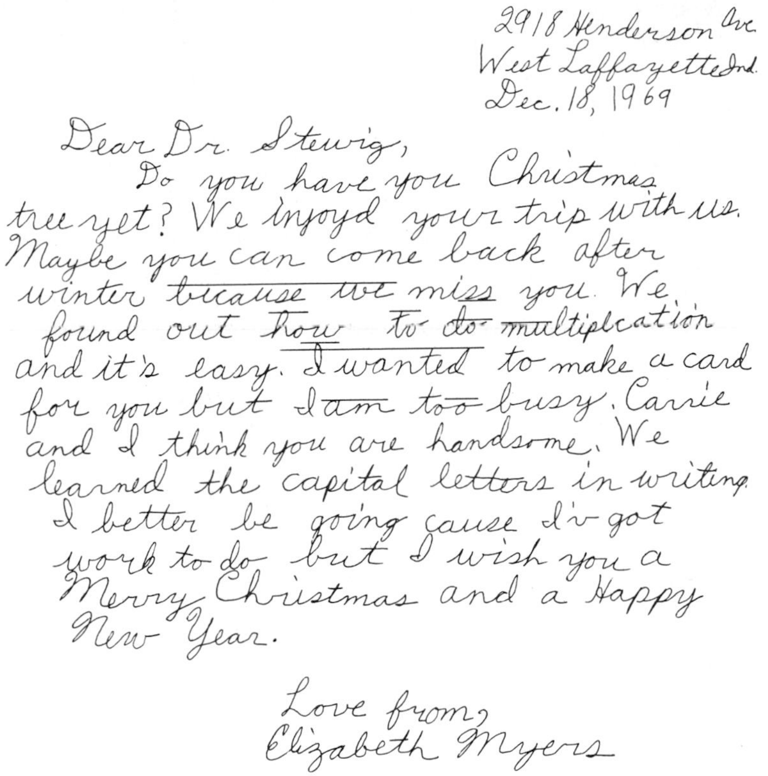

2918 Henderson Ave.
West Laffayette Ind.
Dec. 18, 1969

Dear Dr. Stewig,
Do you have your Christmas
tree yet? We injoyd your trip with us.
Maybe you can come back after
winter ~~because we~~ miss you. We
found out ~~how~~ ~~to do~~ multiplication
and it's easy. ~~I wanted~~ to make a card
for you but ~~I am~~ too busy. Carrie
and I think you are handsome. We
learned the capital letters in writing.
I better be going cause I'v got
work to do but I wish you a
Merry Christmas and a Happy
New Year.

Love from,
Elizabeth Myers

Figure 16

Regularity of *spacing* is harder to evaluate, because it has to be done visually. The child needs to look not only at single words, but also at lines of writing, to determine if the spacing is regular.

Variability of Standard

In all this emphasis on legibility, it is important to remember one qualification, which is the intended audience for the writing. In this practice work and indeed in most of what he writes in school, the child is writing for someone other than himself and thus must write legibly. This is simple courtesy for the reader.

Children need to have understanding teachers, however, who recognize that as adults we all write differently in different situations. When we write a letter to a friend our handwriting is of better quality than when we scribble a grocery list. So, too, as children take notes for a report or do a first draft of a story, they need to be allowed to scratch out their ideas as quickly as they want, without being concerned about the quality of their handwriting. Obviously if one's goal is a free and untrammeled expression in creative writing, any attention to legibility of copy needs to wait until *after* the ideas are safely out on paper.

Related to the idea of variability of form is variation in speed of writing. Girls apparently gain a speed advantage early in their school careers and maintain this advantage when they are adults. Groff studied over 3000 subjects in grades four through eight and discovered that girls consistently wrote faster than did boys.[32] Another study examined writing speed of college freshmen; girls consistently wrote faster than boys.[33] This fact has apparent implication for the elementary teacher when writing tasks are required of both sexes. Provision will need to be made for extra time for boys, who are apt to take longer to accomplish an identical writing task.

Finally, the moderation advocated by Smith et al. is good counsel for the teacher and will serve to summarize this section.

> It is vital that the teacher keep in mind the great variability among learners and keep ends and means in proper perspective. Children vary greatly in coordination, and their handwriting will reflect these differences. The teacher, in working toward the goal of legibility, must be satisfied with progress and not demand perfection.[34]

Typing in the Elementary School

One can view the question of typing by elementary children either as a very natural phenomenon in our electronic age or as an impractical idea. No matter which position one holds, there are questions to be raised before an intelligent decision can be made on what choice of action should be followed. In this section, several of these questions will be raised.

Interest in this question is not new, though the amount of research is limited.[35] The major question to be answered is: Can children be

---

[32] Patrick J. Groff, "Who Writes Faster?" *Education* 83 (February 1963): 367–69.

[33] Tim Gust and Deborah Schumacher, "Handwriting Speed of College Students," *Journal of Educational Research* 62 (January 1969): 198–200.

[34] E. Brooks Smith et al., *Language and Thinking in the Elementary School* (New York: Holt, Rinehart and Winston, 1970), pp. 237–39.

[35] Ben D. Wood and Frank N. Freeman, *An Experimental Study of the Educational Influences of the Typewriter in the Elementary School Classroom* (New York: The Macmillan Co., 1932).

successfully taught how to type? Wood and Freeman's study gave an affirmative answer to the question, and almost thirty years later another study by Tootle gave the same answer.[36]

What happens to children who are taught to type in the elementary grades? Tootle found they gained in spelling ability and creative writing ability. He further found, and Donoghue also reports,[37] that the *amount* of writing increases. Tootle was reporting on the amount of creative writing, while Donoghue was reporting on the amount of report writing. Donoghue concluded that the reports written by children who type average 3.3 times longer than similar reports written in longhand by nontypists. A further argument in favor of typing is that children can learn to type "at rates which exceed their handwriting rates by as much as two or three times. . . ."[38]

Since it has been established that children can be taught to type at the elementary school level, some methodological questions can be considered:[39]

1) *By whom* should typing be taught? Is this a skill one can expect a classroom teacher to teach? Or is it more logical to expect that teachers with special training of some kind would be needed? Or could such teaching be done by tapes, records, or other audio-visual materials?[40]

2) *When* should it be taught? Is this something else to be included in the school day, or should it be offered outside regular school hours? At what grade level should it be taught? Freeman recommended beginning in first grade, as did another author.[41] Is this in fact the optimum age for beginning such instruction?

3) *To whom* should it be taught? Is this something all children should learn, or should it be offered on an elective basis?

---

[36] John C. Tootle, "Typewriting in the Written Communication Activities of the Fifth Grade" (Ph.D. Dissertation, The Ohio State University, 1971).

[37] Mildred R. Donoghue, *The Child and the English Language Arts* (Dubuque: William C. Brown Co., 1971).

[38] Donoghue, *The Child and The English Language Arts*, p. 269.

[39] For some recommendations by a classroom teacher, see Margaret McCall, "It Worked for Me," *Grade Teacher* 86 (October 1968): 35.

[40] Interest in new means of teaching typing is evident. One publisher recently brought out a series devoted to typing instruction, see *Typing Our Language*, for middle- and upper-grade children, published by Scott, Foresman Publishers.

[41] Ralph Haefner, *The Typewriter in the Primary and Intermediate Grades* (New York: The Macmillan Co., 1932).

4) How are physical considerations to be arranged? The question of financing and where to locate machines are problems which need to be solved.

This section has purposely raised more questions than it has answered. Proponents of typing in the elementary school make convincing arguments for their case.[42] Despite such arguments, the number of children who learn to type in the elementary school remains small. Is typing instruction at the elementary level an educational idea ahead of its time? Or is it a needless frill suggested by the mechanically inclined? Typing may be either, or something else entirely. Could you develop a rationale for typing instruction that might convince a principal or a group of parents of the need to include it in the elementary curriculum?

Studying Writing Systems

Maintaining children's interest in handwriting, even if the teacher's enthusiasm is high, is sometimes difficult. The teacher may find it helpful to develop a unit on other systems of writing to revive flagging interest. Children at any grade level can study such a unit, with some adjustments made for difficulty level. This section will be concerned with some ideas for such a unit. These must be viewed as suggestions, provided simply to start you thinking. As you work with children other ideas will occur to you.

It is logical to begin such a unit with a study of other writing systems currently in use. Children can examine samples of other alphabetic systems.[43] They will find it interesting to compare similarities and differences among such alphabets as the Cyrillic, Korean, or Arabic. They can make charts illustrating these and practice making some of the more unusual ones, including trying to write words or sentences in one of the alphabets.

While doing this children can study the different pronunciation marks which are used in other languages, including the tilde /ñ/, the macron /ō/, the breve /ŏ/, the diaeresis /öö/, and the cedilla /ç/. Such

---

[42] You might like to read: Thelma Martin, "Have You Considered Typing," *The Instructor* 78 (May 1969): 20. Or see Joan Klyhn, "Tiny Typists," *Times Educational Supplement* 2785 (October 1968): 607.

[43] There is a plethora of such materials available. Some of the trade books on the topic are included in the bibliography.

typographic symbols as the ellipsis /. . ./, the dagger /†/, and the section mark /§/, can be noted. For older children a study of editing marks can be included.[44] Also, they can read about such *ideographic* systems still in use as Chinese and Japanese. Children find it intriguing to learn to make their name, or to make symbols for some common words, in one of these communication systems (Figure 17).

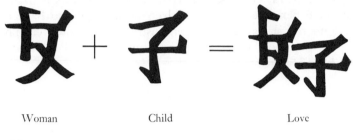

| Woman | Child | Love |

Figure 17

In such a unit, classroom visitors can augment research in books. For example, within your community there will surely be someone who could demonstrate how to write Hebrew (Figure 18). If you live

שְׁמַע יִשְׂרָאֵל

יְיָ אֱלֹהֵינוּ

יְיָ אֶחָד.

Figure 18

[44] See: Joanna Foster, *Pages, Pictures and Print* (New York: Harcourt Brace Jovanovich, 1958). The entire book, devoted to the processes involved between manuscript and published work, is of interest to children. The chart of proofreaders' marks on page 33 is particularly useful for this unit.

in a large enough community, perhaps there will be writers of other languages. A foreign student from a university or perhaps the grandparent of one of your children will know how to write another language.

Children are interested in learning how people who are blind write. It is often possible to borrow a braille typewriter from the local association for the blind. One kindergarten teacher provides a particularly meaningful experience for her children in arranging to have a blind person come to her classroom to demonstrate the typewriter. Then the children in her room usually continue to correspond the rest of the year with their visitor.

BRAILLE ALPHABET

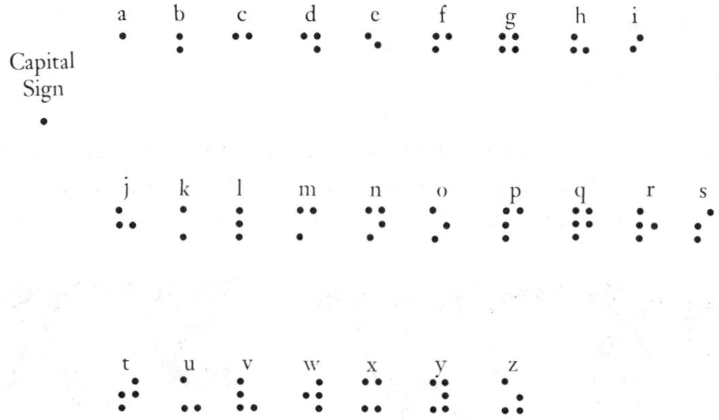

Figure 19

In addition to these writing systems, children also can learn much about *notation systems,* or ways people communicate ideas using written symbols which are nonalphabetic.

It is useful to expose children to some of the following:

1. a secretary, who can illustrate how to take shorthand. Children are always fascinated to see how their name looks when written in shorthand. They delight in writing their name this way and older children like to try writing entire words (Figure 20).

2. a dancer, who can illustrate how to write *Labanotation,* the system for recording choreographic ideas. Perhaps the dancer could write out a few steps and then show how a dancer translates this into movement (Figure 21).

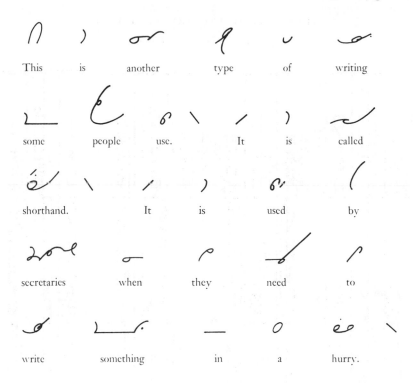

Figure 20—*Shorthand*

3. a court reporter, who can illustrate how to use a stenotype machine. This ingenious device, which allows him to record as fast as a witness can speak, always amazes children (Figure 22). Older children can be allowed to use the machine after they have been instructed in correct procedures.

4. a composer (or perhaps a music teacher or professor) who can show children how this symbol system can record intricate ideas.

5. an architect, who can show children how he indicates with written symbols many details of importance to both builder and client. With fifth- and sixth-grade children, such study could lead to a coordinated unit directed by the art teacher on house planning, so the symbols can be used.

After studying current writing systems, the teacher may want to involve children in studying ancient writing systems. There are many of these which interest children.

STUDY IN BODY AND ARM MOVEMENTS

Suggested music: Brahms' "Lullaby."

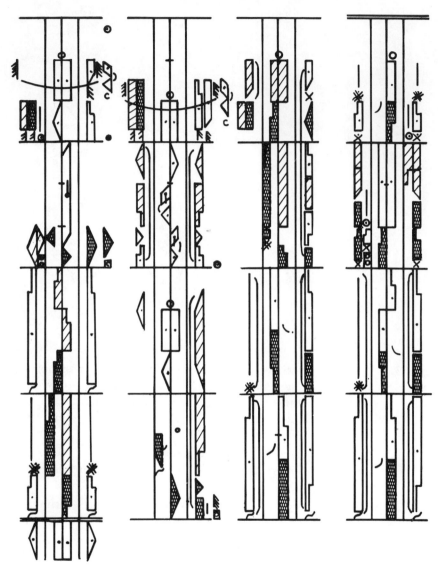

Figure 21—*Labanotation*

266

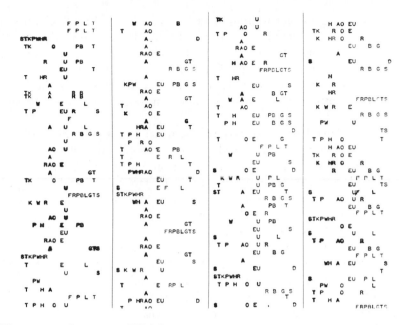

Figure 22—*Stenotype Writing*

An immediate attention-getter is the boustrophedon arrangement of the ancient Greeks,[45] which involved writing alternate lines backwards (Figure 23). The challenge writing in this fashion provides will intrigue children.

Come over to my house

a gnivig m'I esuaceb

party tomorrow.

Figure 23

---

[45] A particularly delightful explanation of this is included in *Look and Learn*, the 1966 Childcraft Annual (Chicago: Field Enterprises), pp. 64–65. One of the freshest approaches available to a wide spectrum of language ideas, this bright, colorful, innovative and imaginative volume belongs on every teacher's desk.

In studying ancient writing systems chronologically, one can begin with the caves of Altamira in Spain and Font-de-Gaume in France, to which language historians trace man's first attempts to "write" his ideas. The boldly executed paintings, flung from one end of the mammoth caverns to another, represent attempts to record exploits of the hunt. These early attempts are acknowledged in both trade books[46] and series books.[47]

Several correlations are possible between language study and the art program, though the art teacher may not look upon these as "art" per se. After reading about the clay tablets on which the Mesopotamians wrote, children may fashion replicas of the tablets and the V-shaped gouges with which they wrote.[48] Interest is high as children try their hand at communicating in this unusual, albeit cumbersome, fashion. Vegetables can be cut into a variety of letter forms and printed as two-dimensional visual compositions.[49] Any firm vegetable, such as potatoes, carrots, parsnips, etc., can be used. Even first-grade children, who can safely use blunt knives for this purpose, may take part in a project of this type. The printing process may use just letters or may incorporate children's drawings and paintings for more visual interest.

Children can search for typeface samples from magazines, which illustrate visually the quality of words. For instance, they might find examples of lettering which is:

tense	open
elegant	crowded
relaxed	thick
tall	squashed
complex	simple
curving	spiky

To begin, you may suggest certain qualities like those above. Later, children suggest qualities and find examples. In addition to stimulating an interest in writing, this activity also can build visual sophistication.

---

[46] Frances Rogers, *Painted Rock to Printed Page* (Philadelphia: J. B. Lippincott, 1960).

[47] See for example the treatments in *The World of Language*, ed., Muriel Crosby (Chicago: Follett Education Corp., 1970), Book 6, pp. 10 and 11, or Andrew Schiller et al., *Language and How to Use It* (Chicago: Scott, Foresman & Co., 1969), Book 5, pp. 10–13.

[48] Any type of clay (including plasticene) works and tongue depressors make good gouges.

[49] Harvey Weiss, *Paper, Ink & Roller* (New York: Young Scott Books, 1958) is of help in this area. A pleasant visual layout and clear instructions distinguish this eminently practical book which should encourage even the most timid of teachers to adventure into printing experiences of all kinds.

Several other ideas of this nature have been suggested by John Holt, who addresses himself to the question of building and maintaining interest in writing.[50] In the engagingly written section devoted to handwriting, Holt puts much premium on exploration. The question he asks is one we could ask ourselves more often: "How many different ways can you think of to do it?" He suggests we can take a single letter and vary it in three aspects: proportion, slant and weight (thickness). Some ways an *A* could be varied are included in Figure 24.

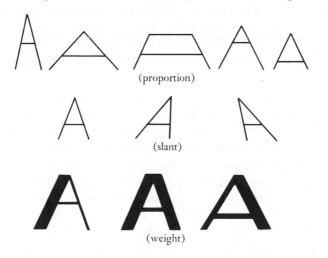

Figure 24

His ideas about making letters out of a variety of materials are also exciting to read and should result in unusual and stimulating experiences for children.

To conclude this section on developing a unit of study of different types of writing, we could profit by keeping in mind a comment Holt makes:

> nothing, not even a task as seemingly cut-and-dried as making letters, needs to be monotonous, frightening, dull, cut off from the rest of learning, and of life, or from the possibility of imagination, experiment, invention, play.[51]

---

[50] John Holt, *What Do I Do Monday?* (New York: E. P. Dutton & Co., 1970). The author, who has worked with students from elementary through graduate school, offers a unique way of looking at his topic. The chapters related to the development of self are particularly thought-provoking as are his comments on basing creative writing on oral language.

[51] Holt, *What Do I Do Monday?*, p. 200.

Suggestions for Further Exploration

1. Try an experiment with some materials easily at hand. For the next two weeks, keep all the handwritten envelopes which come to you through the mail. At the end of that time take these (and one *you* have addressed) and arrange them from most to least legible. After doing this, try to identify the factors you see as most crucial in legibility.

2. Using a copy of the guidelines provided in Burns et al. (pp. 364–66), analyze two of the handwriting series available to you. Which of them ranks highest, according to their guidelines? After reviewing the series, decide if there are any important factors which are not included.

3. You might be interested in reading something about *graphology*, the study of handwriting for the purpose of character analysis. Be sure to read several sources. Are there areas of both agreement and disagreement among those who write about this topic?

4. Innovative suggestions concerning handwriting are few. One worth examining is that made by Frank N. Freeman ("On Italic Handwriting," *Elementary School Journal* (February 1960): 258–64). Read his article and try to identify both the strong and weak points in his argument which favors adoption of this different system.

5. A piece of research referred to in the chapter reported that handwriting was among the most disliked of school subjects. Try to interview three or four children in each of several different classrooms. Find out what their attitudes are about handwriting and the reasons for these attitudes.

6. Using magazines as suggested on page 268, find examples which illustrate to your satisfaction the list of adjectives and make these up into a poster or chart you can use with children. Could another list of *verbs* be made up and illustrated in the same way?

7. Find a copy of *Words and Calligraphy for Children* by John Cataldo (Reinhold Book Corporation, 1969). This is an excellent source of motivating activities related to words and writing. Try his idea of using the letters in the word to depict the animal visually. If possible, try the project with a class or a small group of children, to get their reactions to the idea.

Bibliography

The Art of Writing. Paris: UNESCO, 1965.

An elegantly designed catalogue for a traveling exhibition, this publication surveys the whole history of written communication. Though the illustrations are only black and white, the paperback book is exciting to look at; the commentary is brief and within the reading level of most intermediate grade children. The book is an invaluable source of illustrations.

Cataldo, John W. *Words & Calligraphy for Children*. New York: Reinhold Book Corporation, 1969.

This is a lavishly illustrated record of the ways in which words and art materials can be unified into finished visual expressions. Examples of art work by children from ages six to seventeen demonstrate how words and letters can become integral parts of paintings, drawings, and other art forms. While some of the techniques, like batik, are not explained in sufficient detail, most of the projects are well within the range of a classroom teacher.

Chappell, Warren. *A Short History of the Printed Word*. New York: Alfred A. Knopf, 1970.

Primarily of value as a resource book for the teacher, this extensive and scholarly book will be of interest to intellectually mature intermediate grade children. Illustrated profusely with diagrams, drawings, samples of typefaces and scripts, and with photographs, the book is a rich source of examples in planning a unit on writing. Of particular interest is the quite complete section on printing: machines, processes, tools and reproduction techniques are described and illustrated.

Fairbank, Alfred. *The Story of Handwriting*. New York: Watson-Guptil Publications, 1970.

This small, but lucidly written and profusely illustrated book begins with an account of Sumerian writing from 3100 B.C. From that point, the book deals concisely (from two to five pages) with all the major writing forms. The writing presupposes no background on the part of readers but details with interest and with few oversimplifications the development of writing.

Fraenkel, Gerd. *Writing Systems*. Boston: Ginn & Company, 1965.

In brief compass, the author explores the history of writing from earliest times, concluding with a treatment of the need for spelling reform in our current alphabetic system. Scattered throughout the book are line drawings, diagrams of ancient syllabaries, and photographs of remnants of writing from several civilizations. The accompanying teacher's handbook includes a bibliography.

Gourdie, Tom. *The Puffin Book of Lettering*. Baltimore, Maryland: Penguin Books, 1961.

This delightful little paperback should prove of much interest in motivating intermediate grade children. It deals with pen, brush, and simple carved letters, and explores a variety of forms. The child with determination should enjoy the lettering skill this book encourages.

Mellor, Ann. *Children's Printing*. Newton, Mass.: Educational Development Center, 1969.

Part of the Elementary Science Study project, this slim paperback describes in convincing fashion the encouragement which experiences with the printing process offer to the creative writing of children. Procedures for moveable type and silkscreen printing are clearly explained and illustrated with samples by children. Such use of a press is highly motivating to children learning manuscript who need extra practice in recognizing forms.

Montessori, Maria. *Dr. Montessori's Own Handbook*. New York: Shocken Books, 1965, pp. 51–52, 134–58.

An educational pioneer whose ideas still have much to say to the classroom teacher, Montessori's presentation of her theory of handwriting instruction is unique and challenges traditional approaches. The section with much emphasis on kinesthetic methods is of interest as is one devoted to the acquisition of vocabulary.

Mother Tongue Series. "Problems and Remedies." Segment # 4, Time-Life Films, New York City.

This series, produced for BBC-TV, examines all facets of the newly popular British Infant School movement. The first ten minutes of this segment are devoted to the type of integrated handwriting program using italic writing common in these schools. Because both the approach and the materials are so different from what is used in American schools, the film is particularly informative.

Ogg, Oscar. *The 26 Letters*. New York: Thomas W. Crowell Company, 1971.

The author begins with a recounting of the discoveries of the treasures in the caves of Spain and France, wall and roof paintings which are man's earliest attempts at written communication. Between that chapter, and the last on printing and typefaces, is a fascinating account of man's struggle to record his thoughts in written words. Ogg's style is casual but informative; the abundance of two-color illustrations enhance the topics.

Scott, Louise Binder. *Developing Communication Skills*. St. Louis: Webster Division, McGraw-Hill Book Co., 1971.

Teachers will find the book, long on practical suggestions and short on theory, to be of immediate usefulness in the classroom. The sections on readiness activities for, and kinesthetic teaching of, handwriting are helpful.

Thomson, George L. *Better Handwriting.* Middlesex, England: Penguin Books, Ltd., 1967.

A brief but intriguing explanation of italic handwriting, explained in terms simple enough for older intermediate children. The directions and illustrations are clear and easy to follow. Samples written in this hand by both adults and children serve as encouragement for those trying to master the skill. The paperback format is inexpensive, and this, plus some simple pens could launch interested children on a challenging undertaking.

Periodical Bibliography

Bell, Mary Elizabeth. "Manuscript Writing after the Primary Grades." *Education* 89 (September 1968): 81–83.

This article gives a brief account of how manuscript writing began and advocates the use of manuscript and cursive writing by children throughout the school year. The author feels that manuscript writing should not be pushed to one side after learning cursive, but should be used in daily lessons. The author noted that immature children are not capable of doing cursive, so they should be allowed to use manuscript.

Enstrom, E. A. "Instructional Goals for Handwriting." *Elementary English* 85 (January 1969): 84–85.

This article discusses guidelines for designing a worthwhile handwriting program. Legibility, speed, and efficiency in performance are three subgoals, according to the author. In teaching motor skills one must: (1) *teach* the skill, (2) *teach the use of the skill,* and (3) motivate the importance of *using* the skill. Also he stresses the importance of "overlearning" the skills, in practice sessions. According to Enstrom, the teacher's skill is the first essential in the teaching of handwriting. This author has written extensively about handwriting. Check out the author entry in *Education Index* for the rest of his work.

Enstrom, E. A., and Enstrom, Doris. "Signs of Readiness." *Elementary English* 48 (February 1971): 215–20.

It is not uncommon to find a child entering kindergarten who has already had some exposure to handwriting. The kindergarten teacher must make sure that any previously learned incorrect ways these children have are corrected. He should not force the children to write but should satisfy the needs of those who desire it.

Furner, Beatrice A. "Recommended Instructional Procedures in a Method Emphasizing the Perceptual-Motor Nature of Learning in Handwriting." *Elementary English* 46 (December 1969): 1020–30.

According to Furner, the method of instruction utilized in handwriting must stress perceptual development. The students should observe the teacher's movements in making the letter. This instruction involves the use of a problem-solving approach. The visual sensation is reinforced by a verbalization of the process involved in forming a letter. According to the author, in learning any handwriting procedure visual, auditory, and kinesthetic stimulation should be employed. Letters having common formational characteristics are introduced in groups. The sequence of instruction for grades 1–3 was summarized.

Gaforth, Francis, and Hunnicutt, C. W. "A New Slant on the Second R." *Today's Education* 59 (February 1970): 45–46.

The authors contend that good handwriting is dependent on muscle training to only a limited degree and that handwriting seems to be primarily a mental process or an internalization of legible external models.

Learning handwriting in the beginning is more like drawing and the larger the drawing the easier it is to form internal images, so use of the blackboard is good. Individual work is best after an initial group presentation. Work on the most obvious and easily corrected errors should be done first so the child can achieve success. When legibility is satisfactory, the child can be excused from handwriting instruction.

Krzesni, Joseph S. "Effect of Different Writing Tools and Paper on Performance of the Third Grader." *Elementary English* 48 (November 1971): 821–24.

This study attempted to determine if primary students performed better with a felt pen, a ballpoint pen, or pencil, and to see if there was a difference in performance between students using lined paper and those using unlined paper. The sample consisted of 120 third-grade pupils. The children wrote a short story about a camera and were given a spelling quiz. There was no significant difference when lined paper instead of unlined paper was used. The performance was better with ballpoint pens and felt pens, than with pencils, and felt pens were superior to ballpoint pens.

Otto, Wayne. "Effect of Time of Transition from Manuscript to Cursive Writing upon Subsequent Performance in Handwriting, Spelling, and Reading." *The Journal of Educational Research* 62 (January 1969): 211–16.

The purpose of the research was to determine the best time for the transition from manuscript to cursive writing. The researchers selected children who fell within one of the four common transition periods: first half of the second grade, second half of the second grade, first half of the third grade, and second half of the third grade. The results indicated that late transition was connected with rapid handwriting and early transition with legible writing.

Smith, Martha. "Project that Writing Lesson." *Texas Outlook* 53 (April 1969): 24–25.

The author experimented with an overhead projector in first-grade writing classes in an attempt to increase student interest. She found children grasped the writing technique easier with the use of the overhead projector. It helped greatly to have the kinesthetic practice of writing in the air while she demonstrated the proper forms on the projector. With this approach she also felt she could give more individual help.

Strahan, Mary Anne. "Film Loops to Teach Handwriting." *Instructor* 80 (May 1971): 70–71.

The author reports favorably on the use of film loops which students can work with by themselves, and which teach specific techniques like holding a pen or pencil correctly and the proper formation of letters and words.

The advantage of this approach is that teacher supervision is not needed as the student keeps track of his own performance, finds his weaknesses, and then works on a program that will give the needed help.

Umbach, Walter O. "Teaching Penmanship." *School and Community* 56 (November 1969): 48–49.

The author feels the main problem with penmanship instruction today is the poor handwriting of the teachers; teachers aren't being proper models.

The theories and the materials used for handwriting are good, the subject matter is relatively easy, therefore the fault must lie with the teacher. Students whose teachers write well have the advantage, because many students learn to write by copying their teacher. Teachers who scribble tend to produce students who scribble.

Wilson, Louise Ada. "Helping Children with Manuscript Writing." *Peabody Journal of Education* 47 (September 1969): 72–76.

This article looks at both types of handwriting from the kinesthetic point of view. The problem of transition from manuscript to cursive is noted, and a suggestion of how the transition can be made easier for the child is given. An explanation of how the two writings are comparable should help the child. Research results are given to back up the suggestions. The article also includes suggestions on how to help the child develop proper motor skills and how to evaluate one's writing through descriptive expressions.

Appendix 1

What Help for the Sinistral Writer?

The problem of the left-handed child is a recurring one, primarily because of the instructional questions raised when the right-handed teacher must attempt to teach the left-handed child. This problem occurs frequently. Though estimates vary according to sources checked, it seems likely that the teacher is more apt to encounter more left-handed children today than ever before.[1]

Teachers often wonder about how to determine handedness, about the wisdom of attempting to change handedness, and about appropriate instructional techniques. Though there is some research which indicates that the final *product* of the left-handed child may be equal to that of the right-handed child,[2] the problem of how to help the left-handed child remains.

In order to help the teacher with this problem, the following bibliography is presented. Space limitations prevent comprehensive summarization of the ideas included, but the interested teacher will want to read further in this crucial area.

Anderson, Verna D. et al. *Readings in the Language Arts.* New York: The Macmillan Co., 1968, pp. 172–74.

Burns, Paul C. "Language Arts Research that Should Make a Difference." *Elementary English* 41 (March 1964): 279.

Burns, Paul C. et al. *The Language Arts in Childhood Education.* Chicago: Rand McNally and Co., 1971, pp. 351–53.

Dallman, Martha. *Teaching the Language Arts in the Elementary School.* Dubuque, Iowa: William C. Brown Co., 1966, pp. 143–45.

Dawson, Mildred. *Guiding Language Learning.* New York: Harcourt Brace Jovanovich, 1963, p. 330.

Donoghue, Mildred R. *The Child and the English Language Arts.* Dubuque: William C. Brown, 1971, pp. 276–79.

---

[1] Estimates range from a low of 2 percent, to a high of 11 percent, given by Gertrude A. Boyd, *Teaching Communication Skills in the Elementary School* (New York: Van Nostrand Reinhold Co., 1970).

[2] Patrick J. Groff, "Who Are the Better Writers—The Left-Handed or the Right-Handed?" *Elementary School Journal* 65 (November 1964): 92–96. The author compared writing samples from children in fourth through sixth grade and concluded that the right-handed children did *not* write better than the left-handed ones.

Drummon, Harold D. "Suggestions for the 'Lefties.'" *Elementary School Principal* 24 (February 1959): 15.

Enstrom, E. A. "The Extent of the Use of the Left Hand in Handwriting." *Journal of Educational Research* 55 (February 1962): 234–35.

————. "In Left-Handed Handwriting: The Little Turn that Makes the Big Difference." *Elementary English* 43 (December 1966): 865–68.

————. "Misconceptions Regarding Teaching the Left-Handed." *The Catholic Educator* 35 (February 1966): 46–48.

————. "Research in Teaching the Left-Handed." *The Instructor* 73 (October 1964): 44–46.

Gardner, Warren H. *Left-Handed Writing*. Danville: The Interstate Publishing Company, 1958.

Green, Harry A., and Petty, Walter T. *Developing Language Skills in the Elementary School*. Boston: Allyn & Bacon, Inc., 1971, pp. 447–49.

Groff, Patrick. "Spelling and Language Achievement of Left-Handed Children." *Elementary English* 39 (May 1962): 446–69.

Trauger, Wilmer. *Language Arts in Elementary Schools*. New York: McGraw-Hill Company, 1963, pp. 90–91.

Williams, Neil W. "What Do You Know about Lefties?" *Grade Teacher* 81 (June 1964): 44–45.

Wills, Betty. "Handedness." *Encyclopedia of Educational Research*. New York: The Macmillan Co., 1960, pp. 613–15. See also the section on this topic in the 4th edition (1969) by Otto and Anderson, p. 573.

CHAPTER NINE

Spelling

A criticism with which we are all familiar . . . is that our schools fail to make good spellers. It is undeniably true that there is a great deal of bad spelling in our schools . . . results lead one to doubt seriously the efficiency of the methods of teaching spelling. . . .[1]

Such a condemnation of the school's apparent inability to teach children to spell is not unique. Criticism of poor spelling is commonplace among parents, the general public, and those responsible for hiring secretarial and other office help. Yet, it's ironic that the complaint was voiced well over thirty years ago! Concern over spelling continues, as does the search for the most efficient methods of helping children master this language skill. Definitive answers needed by the teacher are not yet available, but some tentative indications of helpful techniques can be considered. This chapter will examine the nature of the spelling problem and suggest some ways of helping children acquire the skill of accurate spelling.

---

[1] Ethel Mabie Falk, "Interpretation of the Language Arts Program to the Parents and Community," *Teaching Language in the Elementary School*, Forty-third Yearbook, Part II (Chicago: National Society for the Study of Education, 1944), pp. 241–51.

The Situation Today

Are children today poorer spellers than those who studied in the one-room school of yesteryear? Sherwin analyzed nine studies which attempted to answer the question: How effective is spelling instruction today? The studies were published between 1926 and 1951 and dealt with different school populations in a variety of ways. Unfortunately, the general conclusion Sherwin reached was that the researchers shared a common conclusion—"the results are beneath what they regard as their legitimate expectations."[2]

Why should we be concerned with inaccurate spelling? The contention was made in the oral language chapter that oral language is the

"They ought to do something about the quality of education some kids are getting these days!"

Reprinted by permission of Newspaper Enterprise Association

---

[2] J. Stephen Sherwin, *Four Problems in Teaching English: A Critique of Research* (Scranton: International Textbook Company, 1969), p. 37. A complete annotation of this essential book is included in the bibliography.

most common, the most essential form for the child to master. If this is so, why is spelling important at all?

The spoken word, quickly uttered and more quickly lost, has an impermanance which allows for more deviation from a set standard than is possible in writing. Mispronunciations and usage errors are in many situations overlooked, or noticed but tolerated.

The same is not true for the written word. The simple procedure of encoding one's thoughts gives a permanance and thus a specious authority to writing. Errors last longer and because of this are more roundly condemned. People tend to look down upon those who cannot spell accurately. Because of this, and despite the fact we know spelling is a skill not necessarily related to general intelligence and ability, we must help children learn to spell.

Some children have little trouble with spelling; others find it a mystifying task and mortifying trial. There are a variety of reasons why this is so.

Some Causes

Often spelling difficulty may not be caused by a single reason; several factors may account for continued problems. The teacher will try to determine the causes for spelling problems. Once this is accomplished, he can attack the problem from more than one direction.

Many children spell poorly because they *listen inaccurately*. In social situations and in weekly spelling lessons, these children listen inattentively. Thus they do not hear correctly and when confronted with a word in a spelling list, may spell it as they have heard it. For example, if a child listens inattentively, he may spell *probly* instead of probably.

Similarly, the child who writes *reconize* may *not* be hearing the /g/ sound in the middle of the word. Spelling problems caused by poor listening habits show up when children omit syllables, drop endings, and reverse syllables or letter order. For such children, increased practice in listening may well result in improvement in spelling.

A child who listens poorly to others may also listen poorly to his own speech. Thus, others may be saying *umbrella*, but the child, in hearing the word inaccurately may also not hear himself add a syllable as he says *umberella*. This also leads to spelling problems. Sessions designed to improve listening habits may need to be accompanied by increased attention to the accuracy of a child's oral pronunciation.

Children with *poor reading ability* are apt to be poor spellers. Though the exact nature of this interrelationship has yet to be defined, it has been documented that children with reading problems are seldom good spellers.[3] Apparently through wide reading which results in seeing words over and over again in context, good readers unconsciously assimilate the spelling of more words than do children who read less widely. For children with reading problems, increased in-class practice or perhaps referral to a reading specialist may result in reading *and* spelling improvement.

As to the *type* of reading instruction which results in the most impressive gains in spelling, one carefully controlled research study indicates that children who learn to read using the language-experience approach to reading become significantly better spellers than do pupils who use basal readers. This superiority is evident in both spelling done in written compositions and in spelling lessons.[4]

The child with *poor handwriting* is also apt to have spelling problems. As he practices writing words during spelling classes, such a child encounters difficulties because words can easily be miswritten. This is not because of any cognitive problems of misunderstanding the spelling but because of the purely mechanical problems involved in putting words on paper. For such a child, an increased amount of time devoted to handwriting practice may also result in increased spelling proficiency. Another way to help children with motor skill problems is to allow them to use manuscript writing during spelling tests, which makes the spelling procedure easier. Even with intermediate grade children who have made the switch to cursive writing, allowing the use of manuscript on spelling tests frequently minimizes some of the problems of handwriting which complicate the spelling task.

The teacher should be aware that in this, as in other areas of learning, *sex differences* will be apparent. As with handwriting, so it is with spelling: boys regularly do less well than do girls. This was first noted in 1897 by a researcher named J. M. Rice; it is also commented upon by writers of our own day.[5] Though it is probably not necessary to institute sex-segregated spelling classes to compensate for this difficulty, the

---

[3] The converse of this is apparent in reports that children's spelling and reading scores have been correlated as high as .63, indicating that those who read well are often superior spellers. Thomas D. Horn, "Spelling" in *Encyclopedia of Educational Research*, Fourth Edition, ed. Robert L. Ebel (New York: The Macmillan Co., 1969), p. 1289.

[4] Ronald L. Cramer, "An Investigation of First-Grade Spelling Achievement," *Elementary English* 47 (February 1970): 230–37. See bibliography for a complete annotation of the article.

[5] Carl Personke and Albert H. Yee, *Comprehensive Spelling Instruction* (Scranton: Intext Educational Publishers, 1971), p. 67.

individualized spelling techniques described later in this chapter will help boys achieve more than will more traditional methods.

In these examples we have been concerned with problems individual children might have. There is a larger and more universal problem related to spelling English which affects all children.

The Problem of "Fit"

All of spelling can be summarized as a problem of fit, between the sounds we make as speakers of the language and the symbols we use to write down what we have said. The discrepancy between sounds (phonemes) and symbols (graphemes) is the crucial determinant of how easy or difficult it is to spell a language. Stageberg defined phoneme:

> The phoneme is easily understood; it is a speech sound that signals a difference in meaning. Consider, for example, the words *dime* and *dine*. They sound exactly alike except for the /m/ and the /n/, yet their meanings are different. Therefore, . . . the /m/ and /n/ . . . are thereby established as English Phonemes.[6]

The words *can* and *cap* are two other examples.

In contrast, the term *grapheme* is used to describe the letters used to write down the sounds we make. While the sound in two words may be the same, the way in which it is written may be quite different.

Every language has these two elements, though the similarity of fit between the elements varies in different languages. In some languages, all or almost all of the sounds are recorded in one unvarying way. For example, in such languages as Hawaiian, Turkish, Spanish and Finnish, there is close correspondence between sounds and letters. Finnish children have minimal trouble spelling because for nineteen phonemes, they have twenty graphemes. Thus the correspondence between sound and written symbol is almost 1:1.

The Problem in English

It becomes apparent that English children will have more trouble writing their native language than will Finnish children when we con-

---

[6] Norman C. Stageberg, *An Introductory English Grammar* (New York: Holt, Rinehart & Winston, 1965), p. 10.

sider that though English has 41–45 phonemes,[7] we have only 26 symbols (the alphabet letters) to record what we have said.[8] What causes these sound-symbol irregularities? There are basically three reasons for this phenomenon.

First, because English is an eclectic language, we have borrowed many words from different *countries*. Because the sources are different, the letters for representing the sounds are different. Borrowings in English account for up to 40 percent of the total stock of vocabulary words. This may seem large, until we consider that other languages borrow even a larger percentage of their words. Albanian, for instance, contains only 8 percent native Albanian words; the remaining 92 percent are borrowed.

Words have entered our language at *different times*, and this has also resulted in different spellings for similar or identical sounds. One elementary series helps children understand the reason why one group of words, which ends in the same sound, is spelled with two different written endings, -ent and -ant.[9] The reason is because these words entered our language at different times.

Third, spellings and pronunciations for words have *changed* since they were first introduced. The words *know* and *knight*, for example, were first pronounced with /k/ sounds at the beginning of the words. What was once an essential phoneme has, over the years, become a troublesome silent letter.

This problem has been of concern for some time, both to the casual observer and the serious scholar. The following poem illustrates the problem well.

Our Queer Language

When the English tongue we speak
　　Why is not break rhymed with freak?
Will you tell me why it's true
　　We say sew but likewise few;

---

[7] There is some difference of opinion about the number of phonemes in English. Estimates vary from 37 (Norman Stageberg) to 45 (Paul Roberts). The exact number is not so important as the fact that even with the lower estimate, much discrepancy exists in number between phonemes and graphemes.

[8] It has been noted that American-English spelling consists of 41 sounds represented by 26 symbols. Yet over 500 different spellings of these 41 sounds exist. For more detailed description of this, see: "Phonemic Notations and the Roman Alphabet," by Godfrey Dewey in *Education* 88 (4) (April 1968): 296–99.

[9] This point and the preceding one are dealt with in the sections on etymology by Paul Roberts, *The Roberts English Series* (New York: Harcourt Brace Jovanovich, 1970). See particularly Book 6, pp. 182–83 and 192–93.

And the maker of a verse
Cannot cap his horse with worse?
Beard sounds not the same as heard;
Cord is different from word.
Cow is cow but low is low,
Shoe is never rhymed with foe;
Think of comb and tomb and bomb;
And think of goose and not of choose;
And since pay is rhymed with say,
Why not paid with said, I pray?
We have blood and food and good;
Mould is not pronounced like could,
Wherefore done but gone and lone?
Is there any reason known?
And in short it seems to me
Sounds and letters disagree.[10]

Lord Cromer

It has been assumed for a long time that such discrepancies as these resulted in English being essentially irregular. We are apt to notice these words (of low regularity) because they occur so frequently.[11] What we are apt to ignore, as casual observers of the language, is the large body of words which are highly regular and occur frequently. Because they are less distinctive, they are less noticeable.

As a result of the assumed irregularity in spelling, materials and emphases in spelling programs formerly made children learn spelling word by word—indeed a formidable task! Little emphasis was placed on learning the predictable patterns which exist in English. As a result, children, especially those with little intuitive grasp of how our language patterns, were overwhelmed by the spelling task and often gave up. It has been estimated that when this practice was common and a child was handed a list containing fifteen words, each of which had to be learned separately, a spelling program from grades two through eight could include an overwhelming total of more than 3000 such separate acts of memorization.[12]

---

[10] From Martin Henry, *Letters and Sounds* (London: Oxford University Press, 1942).

[11] Teachers are aware of them, because they cause endless problems for children. Anyone who has attempted to teach children how to spell *one, acre, iron, myth,* or *laugh* can attest to the difficulties caused by irregular spellings.

[12] Wilbur S. Ames, "A Comparison of Spelling Textbooks," *Elementary English* 42 (February 1965): 146–50.

Other Complications

As if the pervasive problem of discrepancy between sound and symbol were not enough, there are other problems a child faces in learning to spell.

One of these is that we sometimes say words in one way, but write them in other ways. An example of this—independent of dialect which will be discussed later—is the word *February*. In America it is almost universal in informal speech to omit the first /r/, while the spelling has remained as if the /r/ were said. We most often say the word: /feb' $\overline{yoo}$ er' $\bar{e}$/, while it is still written as if it were said: /feb' $\overline{roo}$ er' $\bar{e}$/. Such eliminations of sounds are a problem for some children.

A child's *dialect* must be considered because it may make learning to spell more difficult.[13] Several examples may serve to clarify this point. In north central Indiana, many speakers make no difference in the medial sound of two words: /pin/ and /pen/. Since the child *says* only one sound, he will have to learn consciously that this sound is *written* two different ways if he wishes to communicate. In eastern New England the words /tot/ and /taught/ are often homophones. In parts of the eastern United States, the terminal /r/ is often completely lost, though of course it must still be represented in writing. The child may well say /ka/ but he will be expected to write car. The reverse problem, that of an inserted /r/ must be dealt with when children realize that it may be acceptable to say /idear/, but the word must be written *idea*. In parts of the South, the word which is written *tune* is pronounced /ty$\overline{oo}$n/ with only minimal similarity between sound and spelling. In some parts of the north central area of our country, *horse* and *hoarse* are pronounced as homophones, which complicates spelling for children of that region.

A further problem for all children is that of the "schwa" sound.[14] Four examples are given below. In each case the sound is the same, but the mode of representing it in graphemes is different.

The word:

/but ' ən/   where ə is written as o, button
/vur' jə nəl/   where ə is written as a, virginal

---

[13] Of course his own dialect, particularly as the teacher dictates words during a spelling test, may also complicate the spelling problem. Recently, while working with a group of teachers in Florida, I heard /repoat/ for report, /libry/ for library, and /mere/ for mirror. This was in informal conversations but it does raise the question of how these teachers pronounce such words on the spelling test.

[14] The indeterminate vowel sound or sounds of most unstressed syllables of English, however represented; a neutral vowel written in a variety of ways.

/wor′ dən/   where ə is written as e, warden
/foun′ tən/   where ə is written as ai, fountain

Influence of Linguists

Recently, linguists of many sorts have become interested in the problem of the relationship between the symbols and sounds in our language.[15] One study, notable for the extensive treatment it gives the problem, is sure to have much influence on spelling materials and methods.

Paul Hanna and his associates have done a study made possible through the use of computers, which indicates that in fact a large percentage of the words we use are regular. The researchers analyzed over 17,000 common American-English words and as a result concluded that vowel and consonant sounds and their symbols have regular spellings approximately 80 percent of the time.[16] Such elements as position within a word lower the percentage, however. Only about 49 percent of the words were spelled correctly using the rules. Hanna and his coworkers have created a spelling series[17] and written a professional book[18] making practical application of the ideas developed in the study. Because of the recency of the work, follow-up research studies which indicate the effectiveness of this approach have yet to be done.

Spelling Generalizations?

Is it helpful to teach children phonetic generalizations? As pointed out earlier, the act of learning each new word as a separate task is such a formidable one that it may overwhelm some children. Yet, the question is: Does it do any good to teach children sound-symbol generalizations? The research evidence regarding this, summarized in Personke and Yee's recent book, is equivocal. After examining many research

---

[15] The term linguist is an "umbrella" word, a general term including many separate entities categorized together for convenience. There are structural, transformational, comparative, historical, and descriptive linguists, among others.

[16] Paul R. Hanna et al., *Phoneme-Grapheme Correspondence as Cues to Spelling Improvement*, U.S.O.E. Cooperative Research Project, #1991 (Washington, D.C., Superintendent of Documents, U.S. Government Printing Office, 1966), 1716 pp.

[17] Paul R. Hanna et al., *Power to Spell* (Boston: Houghton-Mifflin Co., 1967).

[18] Paul R. Hanna et al., *Spelling: Structure and Strategies* (Boston: Houghton-Mifflin Co., 1971). See bibliography for a complete annotation.

studies, the authors could not find undisputed evidence that time spent in teaching and learning spelling generalizations resulted in superior performance. In reporting one of their own studies, the authors summarized: "The hypothesis that phonetic instruction provides a positive difference in spelling achievement was *not* confirmed in this study."[19]

Despite lack of evidence which points to the efficacy of teaching spelling generalizations, teachers have for some time taught children generalizations about the relationships between sounds and letters. Such attempts have been concentrated in instruction during reading classes, with the idea that understanding such generalizations would help children read better. Certainly there is substantial difference between the decoding process in reading, and the encoding procedure in spelling. Nontheless, it is interesting to consider the validity of the sound-symbol generalizations children have been learning.

Clymer studied basal reading series and located 121 different sound-symbol generalizations which were taught.[20] Of these, he selected 45 for further study. These were analyzed to determine the percent of utility or the frequency with which the generalization did indeed apply. This was done by comparing the number of times they did apply with the number of exceptions which existed. As a result, Clymer concluded that only 18 of the generalizations had a 75 percent utility and were thus worthy of being taught.

While Clymer is himself prudent in cautioning that his research cannot be viewed as completely conclusive, it does raise interesting questions about how many and which kinds of sound-symbol generalizations children should learn. We need, apparently, to re-examine some of our cherished old shibboleths. Generations of children learned the old saw: "When two vowels go walking, the first one does the talking." This seems hardly worth teaching when we consider that it has only 45 percent utility. Apparently, we must be careful in selecting generalizations to teach. One must always balance the time taken up in teaching and learning these generalizations against the other uses to which such time could be put.[21]

A related, but slightly different approach, is that of teaching spelling *patterns* to children. Several authorities maintain that this ap-

---

[19] Personke and Yee, *Comprehensive Spelling Instruction*, p. 66.

[20] Theodore Clymer, "The Utility of Phonic Generalizations in the Primary Grades," *The Reading Teacher* (January 1963): 252–58.

[21] Many other studies dealing with this problem have been done. Among the most recent is Lillie Smith Davis, "The Applicability of Phonic Generalizations to Selected Spelling Programs, *Elementary English* 49, no. 5 (May 1972): 706–13.

proach results in increased spelling competencies. It has been contended that there are basically four patterns of enough utility to be worth a child's time.

Pattern One: CVC

Examples of this pattern are the words *cat* and *sad*. This is the most common spelling pattern, a short vowel preceded and followed by a consonant. Once children have played with this pattern, creating many words from the basic pattern, they can experiment with the variations: substitute consonant blends for the initial consonant (such words as *clan*) or for the final consonant (such words as *hand*).

Pattern Two: CVCe

Examples are the words *save* and *plane*. In this common pattern the long vowel sound, surrounded by two consonants, makes a word in which the final e is silent.

Pattern Three: CVVC

Examples are the words *pain and leaf*. In this pattern the two medial vowels produce a dipthong or a long vowel sound between the initial and final consonants. Children can substitute consonant blends for the initial consonant (such words as *brain*) and substitute consonant blends for the final consonants (such words as *beast*).

Pattern Four: CV and CVV

Examples are such words as *be* and *go* (CV) and *may* and *see* (CVV). In the second of the patterns children may substitute consonant blends for the initial consonant (in such words as *flee*).

Once children have explored these four patterns, there are innumerable others which they may explore, depending on the amount of time available and the inclination of the teacher.

Exceptions to the Pattern

Having children experience patterns in spelling is not the complete task, however. As they progresss through the spelling program, children must be exposed to the idea that in addition to patterns, there are exceptions. The danger in any generalization is that the pattern may be overextended or applied to words for which it is inappropriate. Much inaccurate spelling results from overzealous application of generalizations. The child who spells *bizzy* (for busy), *honer* (for honor), and *ankshus* (for anxious) is only trying to apply what he has learned.

Trying to explain the logic behind some of these exceptions is largely futile; many exceptions must simply be learned on a rote basis. For example, children are often taught the pattern: When words begin with an initial /k/ sound, they are spelled with the letter *k* when the letters *i* or *e* follow, and are spelled with the letter *c* in all other cases. The alert child will soon notice, however, that there are exceptions. In such words as *chaos, character,* and *chorus,* the initial ch spelling is necessary to represent the initial /k/ sound. This is because such words are borrowings from the original Greek spelling, with the ch retained, instead of modified to fit the more general English system.[22] Does this make sense? Of course not, if one is searching for logic in a system which developed in piecemeal fashion. The child simply has to learn that there are exceptions to the system. While it would be more convenient for everyone concerned if some of these obscure borrowings were changed in written form to conform to the system, this is unlikely. Therefore, the onus of learning not only the system but also the exceptions falls on the child. An unfair requirement? Probably, but one which is unlikely to be changed! The teacher's job is, therefore, to make the learning of the system as palatable as possible.

Developing Word Families

The position taken later in this chapter is that individualization is the key to a successful spelling program. Such a position does not negate, however, the value of some group experiences designed to help children learn about the basic spelling patterns of high frequency.

For instance, developing the concept of word families with children is a good idea, both for the help it brings in understanding underlying spelling patterns, and also for the self-confidence it can foster. The idea is that given a basic pattern, the child is automatically able to spell many other words. He may be unaware of this family feature of English, and it should be called to his attention, in informal group situations. For example, the teacher may take Pattern One: CVC as

---

[22] This and other material related to the complexities of the spelling system are clearly and concisely presented in Gertrude B. Corcoran, *Language Arts in the Elementary School* (New York: The Ronald Press Company, 1970), p. 120.

an example. Given the fact that the child can spell *cat*, he can discover that he can also spell: *fat, gat,*[23] *hat, mat, pat, rat, sat, tat,* and *vat,* or a total of ten words, rather than one. Children should be able to come up with nine other words in the family for the word *save* (Pattern Two), six other words in the family for the word *pain* (Pattern Three) and ten other words in the family for the word *may* (Pattern Four). The challenge of finding new words intrigues children, and the resulting contests to see who can come up with the longest list of family words helps children internalize the idea of patterns in spelling and also acts as a helpful motivating device.

All of the foregoing assumes that English spelling is quite rigid and as a generalization this is true. Spelling is undoubtedly one of the least creative aspects of language. Yet, there is some evidence of more flexibility in spelling than is commonly acknowledged.

The Need for Flexibility

At one time, English spelling was more flexible than it is now. Written records from the sixteenth century reveal that the word we can only spell *guest* today was then spelled in a variety of ways: gest, geste, gueste, ghest, or gheste.[24] Such individuality of approach is not condoned in our era.[25]

Today, it is certainly true that there is a body of basic words with invariant spellings which all who wish to be considered educated must learn to spell the "right" way. Spelling is, however, by no means as invariant as most spelling series and too many teachers have led children to believe. The frequency with which people refer to a dictionary as the ultimate authority in determining the "proper," and only way to spell a word is unwarranted spelling dogmatism.

---

[23] In developing word families with children, they will frequently suggest words the meaning of which is unfamiliar to them. Since it makes no sense to isolate spelling from other language arts, the teacher uses such occasions to do some informal vocabulary teaching. He widens the experience of children with words, though no attempt is made to fix these in a child's use vocabulary. Rather, talking about what a gat is and who uses the term, is simply a way of expanding the child's world.

[24] Pei, Mario. *All About Language* (Philadelphia: J. B. Lippincott, 1954), p. 115.

[25] Some language series attempt to help children gain historical perspective about language. Early variability in spelling is explained in *New Directions in English* by Anderson et al. (New York: Harper and Row, Publishers, 1969) Book 5, p. 138.

Some time ago one researcher compared the variety of spellings listed in several different dictionaries. As a result Emery concluded that there are many fairly common words which may be spelled in more than one way, and even the dictionaries do not agree on the number and spelling of acceptable variant forms.[26] He reported that in many cases it was not possible to determine which was considered the common spelling and which the variant.

More recently, this writer examined a currently available dictionary, in an attempt to identify what types of options exist for the speller.[27] One dictionary was used; several would undoubtedly reveal many more options in the spelling of our language.

Spellers have options at all three positions in words; initial, medial, and final. In the *initial* position, we find impale or empale is used. In *medial* positions we find the following possibilities: pygmy or pigmy; brier or briar; extrovert or extravert; and knowledgeable or knowledgable. In the *final* position we find theatre or theater; debonair and debonaire; and plow or plough. We find further that as spellers of English we have other opitions. When we *pluralize*, we may use either colloquiums, or colloquia. When we *change tense* from present to past we may use focused or focussed. There are innumerable examples such as these in our language.

As teachers, we must be flexible enough to accept such differences for the richness they add to English, and not ignore them because they represent a spelling with which we are unfamiliar. As Sherwin has said, "it is difficult enough to teach spelling without dissipating one's efforts in correcting supposed errors which are merely alternate forms. The spelling lesson is not an occasion for indulging one's linguistic prejudices."[28]

The Changing Role of Dictionaries

Despite the reverent attitudes of Scrabble and crossword buffs, manifest changes in ideas about dictionaries are taking place now.

For hundreds of years, dictionaries were looked upon by those who made them (lexicographers) and those who used them as *prescrip-*

[26] Donald W. Emery, *Variant Spellings in Modern American Dictionaries* (Champaign: National Council of Teachers of English, 1958), pp. 14–15.

[27] Jess Stein, ed., *The Random House Dictionary of the English Language* (New York: Random House, 1967).

[28] Sherwin, *Four Problems in Teaching English* . . ., p. 104.

tive tools, that is, as the ultimate authority in prescribing how words should be spelled, pronounced, and what they should mean. This attitude about the function of dictionaries is summarized by Noah Webster who wrote in the preface of his dictionary:

> It has been my aim in this work . . . to ascertain the true principles of the language . . . to purify it from some palpable errors, and reduce the number of its anomalies, thus giving it more regularity and consistency in its forms . . . to furnish a standard of [language] . . . redeemed from corruptions . . . and degradations. . . .[29]

In contrast, current dictionary makers view their function differently, that of *describing* what people actually do with the language, rather than attempting to tell users what they *ought* to do. This newer approach is summarized by the editor of the edition of *Webster's Dictionary* which stimulated such controversy when it was published.[30] In emphasizing the *recording*, rather than the *prescribing* aspects of the new dictionary, the editor comments: "It does not attempt to dictate what usage should be . . . [it is] the record of this language as it is spoken and written."

In addition, he points out that "a definition, to be adequate, must be written only after an analysis of usage. . . ." Finally, in commenting on the elimination of the descriptive labels identifying level of usage[31] the editor points out that "it is impossible to know whether a word out of context is colloquial or not. . . ."[32]

The whole issue of the purpose of a dictionary is dealt with in a book of use to teachers.[33] You may want to read this to expand your understanding of dictionaries. The authors describe in admirably objective fashion the point of view of the lexicographers, and also

---

[29] *An American Dictionary of the English Language* (New York: S. Converse, 1828).

[30] Phillip B. Gove, editor-in-chief, *Webster's Third New International Dictionary* (Springfield, Massachusetts: G and C. Merriam Co., 1961).

[31] This issue was one of the most heated when the dictionary was first published. Previous dictionaries labeled words as colloquial, slang, nonstandard, idiomatic, etc. *Webster's Third* was the first major dictionary to eliminate many of these labels, feeling that such evaluation was not part of its major task, which was seen as reporting.

[32] See pp. 6a–7a of the preface.

[33] Richard R. Lodwig and Eugene F. Barrett, *The Dictionary and the Language* (New York: Hayden Book Co., 1967), pp. 48–65. This interestingly written book provides a pleasant introduction to the wealth of variety available in dictionaries.

of their opponents, who contend that in refusing to prescribe usage the dictionary makers are abrogating their rightful authority.

The idea that a dictionary should be looked upon as a recording device, not a law-giving one, is certainly a concept teachers will want to share with their children when doing a unit on dictionaries.[34] With older children such a unit must include several different dictionaries, so children can become aware that whether it is pronunciation, syllabication, meaning, or etymology, there are differences depending upon which dictionary we use.

Approaches to Teaching Spelling

Several questions must be considered when planning how to teach spelling. The first is: How much *time* can be optimally devoted to the skill?

There seems to be agreement, the result of various research efforts, that a maximum of seventy-five minutes per week can be most effective in teaching spelling.[35] While this generalization is subject to the same dangers as any educational generalization, it seems that for most average groups more time than this results in a sharp falling off of learning. The diminishing returns in terms of test scores do not seem worth the additional time and effort involved.

Another question to be considered is: *Which words* should be taught? The most common instructional procedure is for the teacher to use one of the commercially produced spelling series. How do such series arrive at which words to include?

Interest in which words children should learn is not new. It has been well established by several researchers that a small core of words accounts for a large percentage of those we need to know as adults.[36] Horn speaks of the necessity of children learning what he calls the "security segment," which "may be provided by 3000-4000 highest-

---

[34] The teacher will enjoy reading about the controversy aroused when the editors of *Webster's Third New International Dictionary* stated strongly their position about being reporters rather than arbiters of correctness. See James Sledd and Wilma R. Ebbitt, *Dictionaries and That Dictionary* (Chicago: Scott, Foresman and Company, 1962).

[35] This and many other ideas of interest to the teacher are included in Ernest Horn's *Teaching Spelling* (*What Research Says to the Teacher* series #3) (Washington, D.C.: Department of Classroom Teachers, N.E.A., 1967), 35 pp.

[36] See Thomas D. Horn, "Spelling," in *Encyclopedia of Educational Research*, ed. Robert L. Ebel (New York: The Macmillan Co., 1969), pp. 1282-99.

frequency words which are needed in and out of school by children and adults."

What words are included in this fundamental core which all children will find of such utility when they are adults? Many researchers have concerned themselves with this problem, and a chart summarizing this research is included below.

WORD LIST STUDIES

Researcher	Year	Number of Words	Basis for Inclusion
L. P. Ayres	1915	1,000	words used in literary writings and adult correspondence.
E. L. Thorndike	1920	10,000	most commonly used words in samples of textbooks, literary and other published materials.
E. Horn	1926	10,000	adult writing needs, surveyed letters, minutes of meetings, newspaper and magazine communications.
E. L. Thorndike and I. Lorge	1944	30,000	samples were drawn from magazines, the 1920 list by Thorndike, a group of 120 juvenile books, and miscellaneous adult and children's writing.
H. D. Rinsland	1945	14,571	children's writing, both informal letters and assigned theme writing, from grades one through eight.
J. A. Fitzgerald	1951	2,650	compiled from a number of both children's and adults' lists, these words and their repetitions comprise 93 percent of the Rinsland list.
P. Hanna et al.	1966	17,000	incorporated the Thorndike list of 1,920 plus other, less common words.

Teaching the Basic List

Most spelling series use one or more of the above lists as a source of words. Since this is so, it would seem a simple enough task to administer a spelling program. All the teacher need do is to use the commercial speller which provides the basic words children need to know. The problem is that such a circumscribed program, though unfortunately too common, meets the needs of very few children.

Capable teachers frequently make some adaptation of the basic program presented in commercial spellers because they observe on an informal basis what has also been established through research, that often using only these lists is a waste of time. Frequently, many children already know part or most of the words on the list.[37]

For this reason, teachers interested in meeting individual needs experiment with plans, using a basic list as a departure point and providing opportunities for children to learn other words of interest to them. Three such plans will be described; each is different but each provides a needed grounding in the "security segment," or basic word list, which Horn has reminded us is so crucial.

Changing the Pattern

In each of the following plans for spelling programs, details and general procedures are drawn from actual classroom situations in which experienced teachers, unsatisfied with conventional approaches, evolved new methods of spelling instruction.[38] There is no intent to provide a recipe for you to follow verbatim. Rather these descriptions are included to demonstrate that given one teacher, thirty children and a self-contained classroom, it *is* possible to provide for differing abilities.

An Approach to Grouping

If the teacher does not feel that a totally individualized spelling approach is possible, grouping may help to meet the varying spelling abilities which exist in any classroom. The following account is illustrative of what can be accomplished.

---

[37] This problem is explained by James W. Hughes, "The Myth of the Spelling List," *National Elementary Principal* 46, no. 1 (September 1966): 53–54.

[38] As a contrast, see the account included at the end of this chapter, written by a student teacher who began an individualized program.

The teacher, who had been working for about eight years in an upper-middle-class university community, wanted to challenge his children. To do this, he set up a two-group program, in which children qualified to enter the "special" group.

Each week all children took the pretest in the spelling series from the unit for that week. If they met the criteria the children could elect to enter the special group.[39] Even if he qualified, the child did not have to enter the special spelling group. The teacher felt the child should be free to choose which group he would be in, depending on what he had to do that week. If the child was engrossed in an independent science project, or in making a construction for social studies, or in reading a particularly compelling book, the teacher wanted him to be free to devote major attention to that.

During spelling lessons on Tuesday through Thursday (of the same duration as in ordinary programs), the teacher devoted all his time to helping individuals. Children were encouraged to work together, though this happened spontaneously, rather than being planned. Children in the regular group did the exercises in the spelling book. Children in the special group studied the words they had missed on Monday, in addition to working on the words in the special spelling list.

Where did the special group words come from? They were contributed by children, who delighted in finding difficult words to put on the list. Words were drawn from conversations, television programs and commercials, billboards, books children were reading, subjects being studied, hobbies, and any other sources to which children wanted to turn. The teacher contributed no words to this list.

The only day this spelling approach took more time than usual was on Fridays when the final tests were administered. The teacher began by reading the basic list. Children in the regular group wrote all the words. Children in the special group wrote only those they had missed on Monday. When this list was finished the children in the regular group went on to other work they needed to do, while the teacher administered the special group word list. After the tests were administered, each child checked his own, in order to receive the valuable feedback which results.

---

[39] The criteria differed, depending on the difficulty of the spelling list. If it was an especially difficult list, children who had five wrong could still qualify for special spelling. On weeks when the basic list was easy, however, perhaps only one could be missed in order for a child to qualify. The criteria could change each week. It was set by the teacher and all the children knew what it was.

Though only two groups were involved in this plan, it does represent one way of meeting individual needs more adequately than having all children work on the basic list. The next program provides for even more individualization.

The Multi-Level Approach

The following recounts how one fifth-grade teacher in a self-contained classroom set up such a system in his room.[40] The teacher, who had taught for three years, was working with a heterogeneous group of urban children encompassing a wide range of intelligence and ability levels.

After feeling for some time that a conventional spelling approach was not really challenging able children, though it was frustrating slow children, the teacher decided to establish a spelling level for each child and let the child work at that level until he could move to another level. The procedure was a simple one.

Children were first tested, using the unit tests from the commercial spelling series available in the school. The testing began with the third-grade book, the first available in that series. A few of these tests were given each day at the beginning of the school year. It was arbitrarily decided that when a child missed more than half of the words, he should stop at that level. Testing went on, using more advanced books, until a spelling level was established for each child. Though these were fifth-grade children, several of them were spelling at levels far beyond this, while several could not cope with the fifth-grade spelling words.

When this initial placement was accomplished, each child received a copy of the book at his level.[41] Children worked at their own level, though if two children happened to be at the same level, working together was not discouraged. The same amount of time was devoted to spelling each day as in the conventional approach used in other classrooms. The teacher presented no group lessons, but was available throughout the entire spelling period to give individual help.

---

[40] There are research reports describing the details of this approach which attest to its success, though the method has not attained wide popularity. As long ago as 1923, a principal reported the success he had with this method, see Ben J. Rohan, "An Experiment in Spelling," *Journal of Educational Method* 2 (June 1923): 414.

[41] This was facilitated by the fact that the school used the soft-bound consumable type of workbook. No attempt was made to conceal from the children the level at which they were working.

The testing procedure was designed to be as simple as possible. The teacher gave the test to those children working at the highest level. They in turn gave the test to those at the next level, and so the testing proceeded. After each child was given his test, he corrected it himself to determine what his errors were.

Another feature distinguishing this program was durational flexibility. Children worked the same amount of time each day, but if they could do two lessons in one day, it was possible to finish a unit in less time than is ordinarily the case. As soon as children mastered one unit in the book they moved on to the next.

Probably the most positive advantage of a program of this nature is the realistic challenge it provides to the participants. For the child who finds spelling easy, more difficult words (and thus more interesting ones) lie ahead. For the child who finds spelling difficult, the realistic challenge of words at a level he can master provides a sense of accomplishment. It is true that such a child is working below "grade level," but only until he can work himself up to grade level. Since no one has to stay at a particular level for a specified amount of time, there is a continual challenge the individual sets for himself to work his way to the next level.[42]

There are, to be sure, some disadvantages to such a program. One of the most formidable is the problem of convincing the principal, parents, and other teachers of the worth of the approach. The principal's support is necessary in order to sell the plan to parents, who will resist the idea of their child working below grade level. The justification for such a program can be made on the basis of amount of improvement.

In the particular instance described here, all children in the room made a year's improvement, though in some cases the child was still below grade level.[43] The problem of convincing other teachers, not involved in the plan, remains a major one, especially if they have rather firmly established grade-level expectations.

If a teacher is successful in eliciting the cooperation of his principal and coworkers and the parents, he can set up this program, responsive to individual needs, by using conventional materials.

---

[42] The whole question of the "level" of spelling words is an artificial one, as is pointed out clearly in a methods book of much usefulness to teachers. See Ruth G. Strickland, *The Language Arts in the Elementary School* (Lexington, Massachusetts: D. C. Heath and Co., 1969), pp. 401–3. Little or no agreement exists among publishers of spelling materials about how to determine word difficulty.

[43] That is, they managed to master the content of at least thirty-six lessons, the number prescribed for one academic year. The question of what constitutes a "year's improvement" in spelling is, of course, a rather artificial question.

The Spelling "Buddies" Approach

One third-grade teacher adopted an approach capitalizing on children's interest both in working with a buddy and in learning words of special interest to them. All children were given a partner with whom they worked during spelling periods.

On Mondays, all children took the basic test from the commercial series being used. The words missed on this pretest constituted a beginning list for each child.

To this list, the child added words from his word box (a three-by-five metal recipe box kept in his desk). The child put any word in the box he liked; choice of words from the box for any particular week was also up to the child.

On Tuesday through Thursday the children worked with their buddy, dividing words into syllables, writing the words in sentences, analyzing words to see if they followed the patterns of words already learned, and other related activities.

On Friday, each child gave his partner the test and then the process was reversed. The teacher employed self-checking for the additional learning it encourages, though each week she did spot-check several tests to make sure accuracy of correction was being maintained.

Two advantages resulted from this approach. *First*, motivation was exceedingly high. Children enjoyed working with their buddy and for the most part work proceeded in a business-like fashion. The teacher did reserve the right to change partners in the few instances where disagreements arose.

Second, many children incidentally learned the words their partners were learning. Each child was responsible only for the words on his own list. In actuality, the teacher found that working together with his buddy for three days often resulted in a child's unconsciously assimilating some of his friend's words. Though no effort was made to provide for this or to measure frequency of occurrence, it happened often enough for the teacher to remark on it to the other teachers.

Spelling and Attitudes

Can the teacher interested in improving his spelling program be sure more children will learn more words in the same amount of time as do children in a conventional program? To give a very candid answer: No. All of the programs tried here were evolved by classroom teachers simply because they were bored with more conventional programs. None was set up in a scientific manner to assess in sophisticated fashion the amount of learning which occurred.

Then why bother? Again, the answer is a simple one: attitude. In all three cases, and in that of the student teacher who wrote this chapter's supplement, improvement in children's attitude toward spelling was noted. Those children who were gifted in spelling less often slid listlessly through the list with no challenge. Those who were slow in spelling less often feared the spelling period as a time to be embarrassed by their inadequacies. Though each plan was different, each did accomplish what ought to be a major purpose of any spelling program—nurturing positive attitudes toward spelling.

An additional fact to be noted relates to word difficulty. When children set their own challenges, word lists tend to become more difficult. We find with individualized approaches that children often choose more difficult words than are included on commercial word lists. A group of third-grade children quite "average" in terms of I.Q. and background, voluntarily included these words on their individual lists.

chariot	distinguish
celebration	delicious
inseparable	hasten
keenness	unquestionably
accordingly	antelope

Is it wise to advocate the use of a method which has not been scientifically researched? Specifically, is it wise to try a program the major advantage of which seems to be something as tenuous as "attitude"?

The best response to such a question comes from some authors who examined the most significant studies related to the question of method and concluded: "Evidently one still must 'make his choice and place his bets' as to what spelling strategies work best!"[44]

Package Programs

The teacher can find available commercial programs designed to individualize the program.[45] A teacher of spelling may not feel he

---

[44] Harold G. Shane et al., *Interpreting Language Arts Research for the Teacher* (Washington, D.C.: Association for Supervision and Curriculum Development, 1971), p. 72.

[45] Typical of such programs is the *Spelling Progress Laboratory*, available from Educational Progress Corporation, Tulsa, Oklahoma.

knows how to individualize his program, or he may wish to concentrate his efforts in a different academic area. If such is the case, he can easily find several commercial packages or kits, which will in organized fashion provide an individualized spelling program.

Whether or not this is the approach a teacher *ought* to use is something the individual teacher will have to decide. The approach to curriculum planning outlined by Professor Huenecke in Chapter Two, which puts a premium on the teacher knowing the individual child well enough to plan objectives for him, questions an approach of this nature. The basic if unstated underlying assumption of this book is that the teacher chooses from an array of possibilities those more appropriate to his children. Nevertheless, it is important that the teacher be aware such prepackaged materials are available, should he choose to use them.

Spelling Games

Because teacher and child alike too frequently fail to find spelling challenging, teachers often resort to spelling games to make the program more interesting.[46] The basic motivation is laudable, but unfortunately these games need to be selected with much care; too many are simply not worth the child's time.[47]

Many teachers have grown up with the "spelling bee," or "spelldown," which regardless of the title applied to it must be regarded as a waste of children's time. Thousands of children have wasted untold amounts of valuable time in this occupation as they grew up, simply because the teachers who used it as motivation ignored two important requirements of any valid spelling game.

Requirement One

The game must require the child to respond in a way which approximates normal, adult spelling procedures. It is seldom as adults that we spell standing up in a line, with a coterie of peers to cheer us and an opposing team to jeer us. We seldom must spell a word correctly in a limited amount of time with this attendant confusion around us.

---

[46] Sherwin, *Four Problems in Teaching English* . . ., p. 101 summarizes this point in reviewing research studies of children's and teacher's preferences for school subjects. He concludes that teachers rank spelling lower in their list of preferences than do children.

[47] For a helpful section describing several worthwhile spelling games, see the section in Mildred R. Donoghue, *The Child and the English Language Arts* (Dubuque: William C. Brown Company Publishers, 1971), pp. 342–45.

Requirement Two

A valid game must engage the child in spelling, not in waiting. In a spelling bee, as in too many other "games," the child spends the majority of his time waiting. If you doubt this, compute the amount of time the child actually concentrates on spelling, as compared to the amount of time he spends in line, jiggling on one foot, waving his arms, whispering to his friends or laughing at someone on the other team.

These two basic requirements for all valid spelling games have been explained with the context of a bad game, the spelling bee. Many of these so-called games actually do little to improve spelling ability and even less to further the self-concept of the poor speller.[48] Keeping these two important qualifications in mind, however, the perceptive teacher will be able to examine those games he encounters to determine if they will accomplish the desired purposes.

A plethora of such games is described in periodical literature,[49] though if the criteria suggested above are applied, many such games will be found wanting. There are, in addition, commercially produced games which are characterized generally by their careful planning, sequential structuring, and variety.[50]

Suggestions for Further Exploration

1. Do some research on alternative forms to T.O. (traditional orthography). Several systems exist, including i/t/a/ and Unifon. A helpful introduction to this idea is included in *Reading in the Elementary School*, by George D. and Evelyn B. Spache (Boston: Allyn and Bacon, 1969, pp. 490–97). What advantages do these systems offer as alternatives to T.O.?

---

[48] Another author has described this problem and has dealt incisively with "Spelling Baseball." See Jules Henry, *Culture Against Man* (New York: Random House, 1963), pp. 297–302. This commentary on American society in general makes stimulating reading. The section entitled "Golden Rule Days: American Schoolrooms" (pp. 283–322) raises important questions about conventionalized school behavior.

[49] See, for example, F. J. Savage, "Play Ball with Spelling," *Instructor* 79 (April 1970): 135–36 or M. J. Flasch, "Spelling Games," *The Grade Teacher* 88 (October 1970): 83–85.

[50] Typical of such materials is the *Spelling Learning Games Kits* put out by Lyons and Carnahan, Chicago, 1969. Provision is made for the slow and fast learner, and for a high level of involvement of all children playing. A scope and development chart allows teachers to prescribe particular games to help children with individual problems.

2. Locate a copy of George Bernard Shaw's *Androcles and the Lion* (Harmondsworth, Middlesex: Penguin, 1962). This edition includes a version of the text printed in an alphabet designed by Shaw as another alternative to T.O. Do you see it as more or less possible than some of the systems described in Spache? Does it offer some advantages none of the other systems do?

3. The discrepancy between sounds and written symbols was discussed in this chapter. Examine several spelling series to determine how and at what levels this idea is explained to children. Which materials explain this phenomenon in a way which seems easiest to understand?

4. Design a worksheet or a series of exercises which would acquaint children with the idea that many English words are borrowed from other languages. Could you explain to a group of interested parents why such an idea is important to children?

5. Make up a list of words containing silent letters. Look these up in James A. H. Murray, ed., *A New English Dictionary on Historical Principles* (Oxford: The Clarendon Press, 1933). This monumental ten-volume dictionary, a standard reference tool available in libraries, offers extensive etymological information about words. What can you learn about when the letters ceased being pronounced in the words included on your list?

6. Helping children understand the idea of homonyms (both homophones and homographs) is a difficult task which recurs throughout the spelling program. Create a homonym dictionary for children, using pictures cut from magazines. Or, if you have contact with a group of children, have them make up their own dictionary.

7. The contention was made that spelling is best taught through an individualized approach. There are, however, articulate writers who feel that such an idea can be overdone. Read Lawrence Deacon's "The Teaching of Spelling Can Become Too Individualized," in *Issues and Problems in the Elementary Language Arts*, ed. Walter T. Petty (Boston: Allyn and Bacon, 1968). Are there advantages or disadvantages which are ignored in the arguments? Which side seems to present the stronger case?

8. Interlingua and Esperanto are two proposed universal languages which use our standard English orthography. Write for information about each one. What factors have accounted for the acceptance or lack of acceptance of these forms? (Interlingua Society, 80 East 11th Street, Room 627, New York, New York. Esperanto Association of North America, 1827 N.E. 49th Avenue, Portland, Oregon.)

Bibliography

Book Bibliography

Avedon, E. M., Sutton-Smith, Brian, et al. *The Study of Games*. New York: John Wiley and Sons, 1971.

This book represents the most comprehensive source of information about games now available. The book offers a complete section on the history of games, drawing on information from anthropology and folklore. The uses of games in many sectors of life is included: games in business and industry, psychology, the armed services among others. The final very comprehensive section, treats the theory and structure of games.

Boyd, Gertrude A., and Talbert, F. Gene. *Spelling in the Elementary School*. Columbus, Ohio: Charles E. Merrill Publishing Co., 1971.

A succinctly written and noticeably practical paperback which teachers will want to have when planning a spelling program. There is a brief but interesting section on historical approaches to teaching spelling. The chapters on activities and spelling games, and on individualizing the spelling program are particularly helpful.

Cooney, Barbara, illustrator, *The American Speller*. New York: Thomas Y. Crowell Co., 1960.

The artist's charmingly evocative illustrations, done in two colors, bring to life a different world, one shaped by the pervasive influence of Webster's original blue-backed speller, of which this is an adaptation. Of value for intermediate grade children, the book presents information about sounds and letters which most children will already know, but the words and sentences used are sure to stimulate interest in spelling. A brief biographical sketch about Webster is included.

Hanna, Paul R. et al. *Spelling: Structure and Strategies*. Boston: Houghton Mifflin Company, 1971.

This valuable handbook for teachers, written in two parts, should help improve the teaching of spelling. The first part deals with theoretical foundations of spelling and provides much background material which is interestingly written. Topics include spelling as encoding, the alphabetic principle, origins and orthography of English. The history of spelling in American schools is also detailed. The second half of the book outlines an eight-level spelling program, sequenced to expose children to all of those spelling generalizations which the earlier Hanna research has revealed to be useful to children.

Kohn, Bernice. *Secret Codes and Ciphers*. Englewood Cliffs: Prentice-Hall, 1968.

Though not related to conventional spelling, this book serves well in motivating interest in writing. Middle grade children will be fascinated by this examination of the types of ciphers and will be challenged to learn and use these intriguing ways of disguising written communication. Though many of these codes are old, the author concludes the book with a chapter on codes of our century.

Sherwin, J. Stephen. *Four Problems in Teaching English: A Critique of Research.* Scranton: International Textbook Company, 1969.

The author has identified four areas of concern: Latin and its relation to English, spelling, grammar, and diagraming. In each of these areas he has searched out the well-known and the obscure research reports, and analyzed them meticulously. His thoughtful reporting of his conclusions, written in a delightfully readable style, results in an invaluable sourcebook for the future teacher.

Steig, William. *C D B!* New York: Simon and Schuster, 1968.

A wonderfully whimsical creation, this small book with ideas and illustrations by Steig is certain to capture the imagination of young children. Working with the idea that only letters, not entire words, can communicate ideas, Steig evolves many cryptic communications which will challenge children to make up more of their own. By pronouncing the letters which are printed, the message becomes apparent. N–Q = Thank you. D N S 5 X = The hen has five eggs. Can you make up another?

Taylor, Margaret C. *Wht's Yr Nm?* New York: Harcourt Brace Jovanovich, 1970.

Prolifically illustrated with black and white line drawings, this book for middle grade children presents a capsule history of the evolution of writing. Ancient alphabets are examined and of particular interest to children will be the section on how to write their names using these alphabets.

Periodical Bibliography

Ammon, Richard I., Jr. "A Practical Way to Teach Spelling." *Elementary English* 46 (December 1969): 1033–35.

The author believes no child needs to learn to spell every word on a predetermined class list. Words a child should learn to spell should be drawn from the words he misspells in his writings.

Ammon suggests that as the teacher finds misspellings he should write both the error and the correction on a separate slip of paper (e.g., egzakly/exactly), which prevents the child's paper from being marked up. In the beginning of the year each child is given a pack of index cards and a recipe box in which he is to make a personalized dictionary. After the child collects from twenty to forty words he submits a list for study. After having the list approved and studying the words, the child is ready for a quiz which is dictated and corrected by a partner.

Blake, Howard E. "Some Spelling Facts." *Elementary English* 47 (February 1970): 271–79.

Children use many approaches when learning to spell: by reading, by studying meanings of words, by writing words in and out of context, by oral spelling, by using phonic and linguistic aids, and by using a combination of some or all of these.

Teachers of spelling *should* know thoroughly the intricacies of each approach and the terminology of each. Blake believes that only when teachers have acquired this knowledge as well as an understanding of the potential contribution of the various approaches are they adequately qualified to teach spelling.

Bronstad, Travis, and Earp, N. Wesley. "Break Rules." *The Texas Outlook* 52 (May 1968): 32–33.

These authors deal with ways to vary spelling to meet individual capacities, interests, and needs. They point out that the conventional spelling program bores the good spellers and defeats the poor spellers.

The authors discuss five different suggestions for providing for these individual differences. The requirements for each child should be adjusted to his potential. For instance, perhaps the slower student need only spell five out of twenty words correctly in order to be successful. Another necessity is that teachers help students transfer spelling skills from drills to their writing. The authors suggest that in evaluating children's spelling progress, the teacher should consider his initiative in proofreading and correcting spelling in his own writing.

Brothers, Aileen, and Hosclaw, Cora. "Fusing Behaviors Into Spelling." *Elementary English* 46 (January 1969): 25–28.

The authors list five spelling behaviors to be incorporated into written work: copying a printed model, proofreading, rewriting to correct the errors found in proofreading, writing a word from memory, and spelling automatically without thinking. A spelling program should provide practice in all of these areas. However, the traditional method of teaching spelling does not adequately satisfy these behaviors. The authors identify many weaknesses of such traditional programs.

Cramer, Ronald. "An Investigation of First-Grade Spelling Achievement." *Elementary English* 47 (March 1970): 230–37.

This study tested the facility with which two groups of first-grade children spelled phonologically regular and irregular words and the possible influence of reading instruction on spelling achievement. Spelling achievement was examined on lists of regular and irregular words and in written composition. The reading methods used were the Language-Experience Approach and the Basal Approach. The sample consisted of twenty-one first-grade classrooms.

The Language-Experience Approach results showed that these students were better spellers, had less difficulty with the irregular orthography of standard American English, and their written compositions contained less spelling errors. The Basal Reader Approach students had more difficulty with irregular orthography of standard American English and achieved lower scores on lists of regular and irregular spelling words.

Groff, Patrick. "Research on Spelling and Phonetics." *Education* 89 (November 1968): 132–35.

The investigator attempted to test the validity of research which demonstrated that auditory discrimination plays a causal part in spelling disability and that phonetic knowledge and skill play an important part in spelling ability. Several studies have shown that children given unusual amounts of phonetic training did significantly better in spelling achievement than groups who haven't had this training.

Groff's research attempted to determine if phonetics instruction for one semester would bring greater than ordinary results. His study replaced an ordinary Wednesday spelling test usually given in the textbook program. No other change from textbook procedures was used. The findings indicated that the middle-grade pupils in this experimental program made somewhat greater spelling gains than did matched groups in the customary program.

Laurita, Raymond E. "The Road to Better Spelling." *New York State Education* 58 (February 1971): 23–24.

The author feels that poor spelling ability is due in part to the learner's failure to develop a consistent method in developing an organized spelling vocabulary.

The key to spelling success is viewed to be early mastery of a spelling process which facilitates the development of spelling categories during the early period of exposure to language. Once an organized method has been established, the child can begin the lifelong task of adding words to already formed categories.

Lightbody, Patricia, and Day, Katherine. "Order Out of Spelling Chaos." *Instructor* 79 (April 1970): 60.

The author's propose a logical and sequential approach for teaching spelling and relate several practices and characteristics of a linguistic program they have used.

This program focuses on three classes of spelling words: "Predictable" words, "unpredictable but frequent" words, and "unpredictable but rare" words. Since the program is designed to stress the regular or predictable rather than the exceptions, the authors contend that this approach teaches the child to rely heavily on the "sound-to-spelling relationship."

These authors contend that "order" in spelling is achieved by means of a sequential linguistic approach. By guiding children to discover the regularities in our sound-symbol relationship, teachers can instill more confidence in young writers.

Sharknas, Jenevie. "I Individualized Spelling," *Instructor* 79 (March 1970): 64.

The author found that even though her class did well on tests, their compositions, letters, and other written work were full of errors.

Details of each day's spelling activities are included. Results of the program were positive. The author reports a great improvement in word awareness—of pronunciation and meaning as well as spelling. There was a definite carry-over to other written work and sentence structure greatly improved, as did the appearance of the papers.

Smith, R. J. "Spelling in the Elementary School." *National Elementary Principal* 50 (September 1970): 44–51.

English contains both irregularities and regularities for which the spelling program must provide. Spelling introduction should teach the basic structural properties that underlie the spelling of many words. This can be done by incorporating spelling into many language-arts activities. The teacher should find methods of motivation and reward that stimulate children to learn to spell correctly. Several such methods are described.

Unbach, Walter O. "Get Your Spelling Program Out of Its Rut." *School and Community* 57 (December 1970): 18–19.

The author views our present spelling programs as routinized but he does not blame the authors of spelling texts as they have given teachers what they want—security in a stock program.

Many materials can be used to teach spelling, but the important point is not the materials, but how teachers adapt these materials to their students.

The author gives many suggestions about ways to vary the spelling program. For more honesty regarding the report card grade, Unbach suggests that it should be based on the professional teacher's evaluation of the student's ability to spell in real, meaningful *writing* situations.

Appendix 1

Analyzing a Spelling Series

This appendix is included with the idea that, even if you do individualize your spelling program, you will probably use a commercial series as the basis for the program. If this is so, choosing the best text for your purposes may become a crucial issue. This form is one way of evaluating spelling series. As you work with these series you may think of other points which need to be considered in arriving at a final decision.

	SERIES A					SERIES B				
	Poor	Fair	Good	V Good	Excellent	Poor	Fair	Good	V Good	Excellent

I. *EXERCISES*
1. Quality, including interest level and variety.
2. Involves activities other than just spelling—dictionary work, handwriting, etc.
3. Drill: amount, type and interest level.
4. Reviews—frequency and quality.
5. Unit tests.
6. Provision for individualization.

II. *TEACHER'S MATERIALS*
1. Quality of suggestions.
2. Quantity of suggestions.
3. Accessibility.

III. *PHYSICAL FEATURES*
1. Size and variety of type, contrast with paper for visibility, ease of use over a continued period of time.
2. Page layout—interesting and eyecatching, but not cluttered.
3. Illustrations—quantity and quality, amount and distribution of color.
4. Indexing—of topics, reviews, adequacy of table of contents. Can you find things in it easily?

Some Other Points to Consider

You will also want to notice the following points. While the series cannot necessarily be ranked on a continuum, concerning these points, in the same way you ranked them in the first three sections, you will be able to jot some notes about these points to help you see what differences exist.

Orientation

Is the series linguistic? How effective is it in making apparent sound and symbol relationships and divergent forms?

Or does it use a story or thematic approach—with less emphasis on patterns?

Rationale

Does the series include any information about:

a. How the words were chosen? What source did the authors use to determine which words to include?[1]
b. How the authors decided on the difficulty levels of words?[2] How did they decide what grade level was right for a particular word?

---

[1] Several researchers have investigated the problem of which words a child "ought" to know. This has been done by investigating the words children use, the words adults use in writing, words most common in printed materials, and composite lists. Probably a composite list is the most sensible approach, since there is overlap between the other lists.

[2] There is not a great deal of consistency in the grade level placement of words. Studies by Betts, Wise, Spache, and Greene have concluded in the same general way: it is difficult if not impossible to determine with any accuracy the "grade level" of a particular word.

Appendix 2

Alphabet Books

One of the most successful ways of interesting young children in spelling is to share with them some of the many available alphabet books. Several can be looked at and compared; discussions can ensue about which ones children liked best, and why. In addition to stimulating oral language, such an experience generates interest in learning how to make the letters.

A second use to which such books can be put is encouraging children to think about the diversity of form possible within one letter. An A, for example, can be made in many different ways. Within the basic form there are many variations possible, by changing the size, shape, proportion and weight of the parts of the letter. You can use alphabet books with older children to show the different ways artists made the letters. After you have examined with children the variety which is possible, the group can be encouraged to experiment with making their own letters.

Another use to which these books can be put with older children is as a stimulus to create their own alphabet books, which can be shared with younger children in the school. A variety of art media can be used; crayons, paint, cut paper, stencil prints, and mixed media all work well in making such books. After the books are made, their creators enjoy the experience of seeing younger children use the books with delight.

Following is an annotated list of alphabet books. By checking with more than one library you should be able to find several of these, or others, to use in the ways suggested above.

Barry, Katharina. *A is for Anything*. New York: Harcourt Brace Jovanovich 1961.

> The whimsical little children populating this small book encounter a variety of unusual people, including an enigmatic Indian, a jester, and rotund king. Black ink line combines effectively with large blocks of color used by the artist, to create illustrations easily as effective as the rhymes accompanying each letter.

Burningham, John. *ABC*. Indianapolis: The Bobbs-Merrill Co., 1964.

> In a bright book, the illustrations for which are reminiscent of Wildsmith's, this artist takes the reader to Africa, where sultans ride elephants; to sea, where yacht sails bloom in the sun; to the top of an erupting volcano; and to an audience with a dyspeptic queen.

Chwast, Seymour, and Moskof, Martin. *Still Another Alphabet Book*. New York: McGraw-Hill, 1969.

Designed to be a puzzle and game in addition to an alphabet book, this bold, vibrant effort catches and holds one's attention, as an attempt is made to solve the puzzle running across the bottom of all pages. Children spend hours with the captivating pictures as they learn to play the game.

Cranstoun, Margaret A. *Let's Look at the Letters*. New York: Holt, Rinehart and Winston, 1967.

The eye-catching illustrations in full color will capture children's attention, as will the open format of this unusually attractive book. The rhymes, some from Mother Goose, and others created by the illustrator, will keep children's interest.

Duvoisin, Roger Antoine. *A for Ark*. New York: Lothrop, Lee and Shepard, 1952.

A simple but expressive retelling of the Noah story, this full color book exposes children to some unusual animals: vipers, nuthatchs, ocelots, and jararacas. The illustrations, rhythmic with a minimum of detail, recreate the adventure with élan.

Falls, C. B. *ABC Book*. Garden City: Doubleday and Co., 1923.[1]

The strength of these woodcuts with their bold, blocky forms, heightened by a vigorous use of color, makes this a powerful statement. Letters and words march determinedly across the bottom of the page, while above the reader meets unusual animals: xiphius, yak, and unicorn, among others.

Gag, Wanda. *A B C Bunny*. New York: Coward-McCann, 1933.

Done in the artist's well-known style, this charming pastoral adventure takes the bunny through several different places, until he finally returns safely home. It is done in black and white, but the bright red letters will catch children's eyes. A song about the rabbit, created by the artist, is included.

Gordon, Isabel. *The ABC Hunt*. New York: Viking Press, 1961.

Two children, whose adventures began with a bowl of alphabet soup, find themselves in a variety of places looking for letters. The black and white photographs are very clear; the book is for the literally minded child.

Greenaway, Kate. *A Apple Pie*. London: Frederick Warne and Co., Ltd., n.d.

Another book with one theme running through from beginning to end, this may need some brief introduction to explain the illustrations.

---

[1] Despite its date, this book is still in print, as is the Gag book.

The wide-eyed children, comely in their formal clothing, are often set against a strangely empty background, adding to the air of unreality.

Kuskin, Karla. *ABCDEFGHIJKLMNOPQRSTUVWXYZ*. New York: Harper and Row, Publishers, 1963.

This diminutive book is a visual winner. Delicate black ink line adds detail to a bold use of color. The hand-drawn letters are of interest for the variety they introduce.

Lear, Edward. *A B C*. New York: McGraw-Hill, 1965.

An exact reproduction of Lear's original manuscript, these black ink drawings and verses written in script make a book very unlike any other alphabet book available. The illustrations, of another era, depict kerosene lamps, ices to eat, conical beehives, and tops. The letters in color are large and clearly made. There is typeset copy at the end of the book in case Lear's cursive writing proves difficult to read.

Matthiesen, Thomas. *A B C*. New York: Platt and Munk, 1966.

One of the few picture books done with photographs, this is a calm and ordered look at the world in which children live. The photographs are clear, in full color and unfortunately lacking the kind of excitement generated by artist's conceptions. It is undoubtedly for the pragmatic child. A matter-of-fact text accompanies each illustration.

Miles, Miska. *Apricot A B C*. Boston: Little, Brown, 1969.

The story about the life of an apricot seed, through maturity and back to the seed again, is tenderly depicted in soft colors. The story is an interesting one.

Moore, Margaret and John, *Certainly, Carrie, Cut the Cake*. Indianapolis: The Bobbs-Merrill Co., 1971.

Another of those strange amalgams of children's format but adult sophistication, this unusual little book features cleverly contrived poems for each letter. The drawings are populated with intriguing and bizarre people from some indeterminable time and place.

Montresor, Beni. *A for Angel*. New York: Alfred A. Knopf, 1969.

Despite the angel in the title, there is nothing saccharine in this unworldly collection of the unexpected and the unusual. The artist's drawings, employing a limited palette, liberally laced with black, evoke a strange land where grandma plays a green guitar while a giraffe gulps grapes.

Munari, Bruno. *A B C*. Cleveland: World Publishing Co., 1960.

Munari's color, splashed boldly across the pages, illustrates simply but with verve, several objects beginning with each letter. Some of the alliteration is as ear-catching as the illustrations are eye-catching.

Newberry, Clare Turlay. *The Kittens' A B C*. New York: Harper and Row, Publishers, 1965.

With a limited palette but using a very facile wet and dry brush water color technique, the artist has created a kindle of kittens sure to delight. From alley cats to Siamese, this group is entrancing, though some of the rhymes are strained.

Rees, Ennis. *The Little Greek Alphabet Book*. Englewood Cliffs: Prentice-Hall, 1968.

A quatrain introduces each of the letters and provides some description of the visual material. Unfortunately some of the quatrains are simply bad poetry, but the book is a good addition to a unit on the alphabet.

Russell, Solveig Paulson. *A is for Apple and Why*. New York: Abingdon Press, 1959.

Not an alphabet book per se, but rather a simplified retelling of the evolution of the alphabet, the book covers several centuries in forty-eight pages. Such an attempt necessitates omissions and generalizations, but despite these the book is a valuable introduction to a topic children can explore in more depth later.

Schmiderer, Dorothey. *The Alphabeast Book*. New York: Holt, Rinehart and Winston, 1971.

The dynamic graphics in this book done in bold silhouette may not appeal to everyone but are certain to leave an indelible image in the child's mind. In a series of ingenuous steps like the panels in a cartoon, each letter is transformed into an amorphous animal painted in an assertive red and blue.

Tudor, Tasha. *A is for Annabelle*. New York: Oxford University Press, 1954.

One thread, the adventures of the doll for whom the book is named, runs through this charming pastel look at an uncomplicated world. Probably of interest only to little girls, who will be enchanted.

Wildsmith, Brian. *A B C*. New York: Franklin Watts, 1962.

The artist's usual carefree splashes, abandoned strokes of color, and infinitely subtle gradations are here turned to an enchanting picture book sure to capture children's interest from apple to zebra. Some of the animals are less well-known: iguana, yak and jaguar; all will delight the reader by their freshness.

Author's Comment

Often both student teachers and classroom teachers feel that mechanics, spelling and handwriting, are dull and uncreative. Nevertheless, these are subjects children are often drilled on with regularity. Perhaps this is one reason so few children really enjoy expressing themselves in writing. The author's feeling that the act of writing is more important than the skill areas is reflected in the placement of the three previous chapters. The chapter on writing precedes (being more important) the two skill chapters. It is hoped that motivating children to write and developing an interest in writing, will precede and remain more important than mechanical considerations when you begin to teach.

Still, skills must be taught. A creative and energetic student teacher, dauntless in most things, was concerned over her responsibility to teach spelling. This was a subject she disliked, as did her children. In the next section, Mrs. Simsohn relates how she made spelling an exciting challenge for children. She launched this ambitious program at the end of her first week of student teaching. Could you plan a challenging approach to teaching one of the skill areas?

Chapter Supplement

Individualized Spelling—
It Can Be Done

by Ellen Simsohn,
Hebrew Academy of Tidewater

Think of this: a class of third graders learning to spell words like lieutenant, schizophrenia, ballerina and rhinoceros; every student's mind working to its capacity in spelling; twenty-eight children having twenty-eight different spelling lists each week. Impossible? Idealistic? Idealistic—yes. Impossible—NO! Such results as imagined above are possible through the use of an individualized spelling program. And such a program is practical, for I instituted and successfully ran an individualized spelling program during my eight weeks of student teaching.

This was not done with a small, extraordinary group of third graders at an experimental school. The school was in a rural area. The class was made up of fourteen boys and fourteen girls, whose talents and home environments were varied. This was not a unique class by any means.

I was gradually eased into my student teaching. The first week was spent in observation. The second week, I was given the responsibility of teaching one subject, the third week I was given two subjects, and so on, until I was teaching all day. My first assignment was teaching spelling—probably chosen because it seemed to be the most straight-forward teaching task.

I decided that initially I would teach spelling in the manner I saw it being taught during my week of observation. The students used a workbook called *Spell Correctly*, published by Silver Burdette (1968). They all took a spelling pretest on Monday, followed by assignments in the book on Tuesday and Wednesday, a practice test on Thursday and the final test on Friday. It took less than a week for me to see that the spelling program was not all that it could be.

It was Monday's pretest that really got me thinking. The pretest was a folly, as it served no useful purpose. For although it indicated which spelling words the students already knew, they *all* did the same work during the week and they *all* took the same test on Friday. So what was the point of taking the pretest? The pretest, however, made me aware of the basic inefficiency of this way of teaching spelling. Because some of the children already knew many of the words, they were not all learning the same number of new words each week. Some students were learning only eight or six or possibly even three new words for Friday's final test, while others had to master eleven or twelve new words. Because of this inequity, you could always predict, with a reasonable degree of accuracy, who would be getting the highest grades on those tests. This just was not fair. But even more important, this inequity in learning tasks seemed to violate much that I had learned in college. I had learned that we, as teachers, should always help each student learn the most he can. Supposedly, he would grow the most when we gave him material slightly above his level, so that he would have to "reach" a little. Yet in this classroom, the brighter students were not learning as much as they could. They were not stretching their minds at all! In a very real sense, the spelling program being used allowed a gross injustice to be done to these children. So these observations—the pointlessness of the pretest, the inequity in the learning tasks, and the failure to "stretch" the minds of all the students—made it clear to me that a change was needed. But to what would I change?

It was lucky for me that the previous year I had done a research project on "The Teaching of Spelling" for my language-arts methods course. I had combed the literature for different methods of teaching spelling, and this was a useful resource for me in developing a new approach to spelling. There were many different creative spelling programs from which to choose, and I found that almost all of them were a form of individualized spelling. An individualized program seemed to be the right thing to try, for it would ameliorate the shortcomings of the spelling program previously being used. Individualization could equalize the number of new words learned and could give each student the opportunity to stretch his mind to its limit. How to go from the concept of individualization to a workable individualized program was another problem! To solve it, I again referred to my research project. I gleaned the best (or most workable) ideas from all the articles on individualized spelling, and the resulting synthesis was my very own individualized spelling program.

My program was basically quite simple. Each Monday, each student would compile his own twelve-word spelling list for that week. His list would be composed of words missed on the given pretest plus some words of his choice. During the week, the student would do work to assure his understanding of the meaning and spelling of these words. And on Friday, each child would be tested on his list of words.

With the mechanics of my program well thought out, I went to my cooperating teacher for advice and approval. She was not quite as thrilled as I was with my plan and was somewhat hesitant about its success. But she wanted me to try it. So after some minor revisions regarding the testing procedure, she sent me out into the classroom to try my new way of teaching spelling.

Preparing the students for a major change in the spelling routine was my first job. I explained the new program to them, saying that from now on they would not all be learning the same words. I told them that some of their spelling words would be words that *they* wanted to learn. We discussed the question of where to find interesting words for spelling. Possible places were books, television, and conversations. The students needed a place to compile these interesting words they found. So they each made a Spelling Wordbook from construction paper and notebook paper. Fearing that these wordbooks would not be in school when they were needed, or that they would get lost, I made the rule that Spelling Wordbooks were to stay in school. Interesting words found at home were to be jotted down on paper and transferred to the wordbook on the following day. It was suggested to me by another teacher that I prepare supplementary word lists, since the children might have difficulty finding words for their wordbooks at first. Using various spelling texts, I compiled lists of third-grade words, fourth-grade words, and spelling demons, which I could later give to the children if need be. Supplementary word lists also contained words from current math, science, and social studies units. The final preparation was the creation of a Word Tree, affixed to a prominent bulletin board. The Word Tree started out as a huge, leafless tree. But it would end up full of leaves, each leaf emblazoned with a spelling word that the owner was proud of having mastered.

The students were now ready to begin. On Monday, a pretest, on one of the spelling lists from *Spell Correctly*, was given. The class graded the tests together. Each student then made his own list for the week, on a new sheet of paper which was numbered from one to twelve. He first wrote down all the words which he had missed on the pretest and then added words from his wordbook and my posted word lists, so that his total number of spelling words was twelve. A second copy of the list was also made, to be retained by me. This second copy was a necessity. I needed it for preparing the final tests as well as for those times when students lost their own copies.

Tuesday and Wednesday were devoted to activities which would enhance the students' understanding of the meaning and spelling of their words. As a group, we worked through the exercises in the spelling book, since these exercises often emphasized phoneme-grapheme relationships, inflected forms of words, and homonyms, synonyms, and antonyms. Each student wrote sentences using his spelling words. This proved to be doubly beneficial, as spelling practice for the students and as an indication to me of their understanding of their spelling words. Mastering the spelling words was done at home during the week.

Practice spelling tests were given on Thursday. Each child was given a "spelling buddy," whose reading level was about the same as his. The buddies gave each other the spelling tests. I corrected these tests, although it was apparent the students had not fully realized that these lists which they had compiled on Monday were their actual spelling lists, to be learned by Friday! The remaining part of spelling time on Thursday was devoted to preparing the class for Friday's final tests. This was most crucial, for the tests were to be given in a completely new way!

In order to give twenty-eight separate tests, I utilized two portable tape recorders with earphones. Each recorder had fourteen tests on it. On the tape, I greeted each child, then gave the test as I normally would, leaving enough time for the child to write each word. The word was said three times, so that no replaying was necessary. At the end of the test, I told each child to turn off the tape recorder, hand in the test, and get the next person to be tested.

This testing procedure had to run exactly on schedule, since we had a fixed amount of time in which to do the testing. It also had to proceed without me, as I would be teaching reading groups while the testing was taking place. Therefore, the class had to be thoroughly prepared for the testing experience.

So, on Thursday, the students were given a complete run down on what to expect the next day. They were shown the testing area and told who would use which tape recorder (the tape recorders being labeled Tape Recorder #1 and Tape Recorder #2). A time schedule for the use of each tape recorder was posted. The children heard a tape of a spelling test just like the one they would hear the next day. Three rules which I instituted were discussed and their importance was stressed. Rule Number One was that no one except the two children being tested was allowed in the testing area. Rule Number Two was that there was to be *no* touching of any buttons on the tape recorder except the Play and Stop buttons. This was imperative if the testing was to go smoothly without my help. The students were told that disobeying this rule would be punishable by throwing away the test of any offender. Rule Number Three was that the completed tests were to be immediately deposited on my desk. To wind up this preparation session, all questions from students regarding the testing procedure were answered. With all this done, we were ready for Friday—final test day.

Frankly speaking, I was afraid that the first testing session would be a disaster. I was quite doubtful that my grand scheme would work as planned. But I had to go on with it. Before the actual testing started, all the children prepared their papers, noting at the top the time of their test and which tape recorder they were to use. And then we began. Seventy-five minutes later, I was ecstatic. It had worked without a hitch. I practically flew through the halls of the school to share my good news with my fellow student teachers.

In the weeks to follow, we followed the same Monday through Friday schedule, with some minor changes. Each Monday, the previous week's tests were returned, along with big, green, construction paper leaves. On the leaf, the child was to write one word from the test which he was proud of having mastered. The diversity in words was fantastic —ballerina (from a little girl who had just started taking ballet lessons), lieutenant (which took at least three weeks to master!), Viet Nam (from a boy whose father was stationed there), to name a few. These word-leaves were, of course, pinned to the Word Tree, which was bare at first but which "grew" more leaves week by week. Since Thursday was no longer needed for explaining the testing procedure, we used part of Thursday's spelling time for some good-natured competition in spelling games. Finally, every few weeks we gathered around the Word Tree to share words. This was one of the most enjoyable activities we had. We shared words with each other, as well as discussing meanings, related words, etymologies, and unusual spellings. It was quite informal and a lot of fun both for myself and the students.

So, my individualized spelling program worked. There were some problems, however. Some were major; some were minor. Some I solved; some I didn't. One problem was the children's choice of words. Surprisingly, they did not choose words that were too easy. Rather, at first they picked ones that were too hard. After the first few weeks, however, most of the children were able to pick words that were within their capabilities. I would never discourage a child from trying an overly hard word. Instead, I would let him try it for a week or two, and if his attempts proved unsuccessful, I would then suggest he drop the word. Usually the students would be more than willing to do this. There was another big problem involved with the children's choice of words. This was making sure that they understood the meanings of their words. I had the students write sentences using their spelling words in order to evaluate the degree of understanding of each word. Then I worked with those students who needed help. I found that students who drew upon their own interests and experiences in choosing spelling words did not need this sort of help as much as those who went to the dictionary looking for "hard" spelling words.

I had a problem finding activities which would promote the learning of the spelling words. Although the students were to work on their spelling words at home every night, there was also some time during the school day for spelling work. What kind of individual work would best help them learn those words? I tried sentence writing, story writing, sheer drill-type practice, and exercises in which the students noted the number of syllables, long and short vowels, and silent letters in each spelling word. None of these activities seemed to be very helpful.

In many spelling texts, such as *Spell Correctly*, spelling words are grouped according to some spelling pattern, e.g., words having the long /a/ sound, or words having the suffix -ly. If one used only the text, it would be easy to teach spelling generalizations, since everyone would be learning words exemplifying a particular generalization. With my spelling program, there was a problem. Since everyone was learning different words, I thought that group work on spelling generalizations would be impossible. And so, for eight weeks, we did no work of this kind. This was a terrible mistake; for if our goal is independence in spelling, it must be based on a thorough grasp of the spelling generalizations. I know of two ways to remedy this situation. The first is to somewhat circumscribe the children's choice of words, instructing them to choose words with a particular vowel sound or a particular suffix, or whatever. Everyone would then have spelling words that had something in common, and group teaching of spelling generalizations would be relatively easy. Another possibility is to let the children be completely responsible for learning their weekly spelling words at home, and then spend class time to work on this other aspect of spelling—learning generalizations. This second choice, however, does not directly tie the learning of generalizations to the weekly spelling words. Instead, it is hoped that the generalizations would carry over to the learning of those spelling words.

I found that my spelling program was not related to the other language arts. Students continually handed in stories containing misspelled words. This problem was easy to remedy, although it took some time. I kept a notebook and jotted down each child's misspelled words as I graded papers. These words could then be used in making up part of his weekly twelve-word list.

My cooperating teacher saw a problem in grading. Would we give letter grades, as always? The children were learning, or trying to learn, much harder words than usual. Would it be fair to give a child in my program a B, when he could receive an A in a traditional program? This was a hard problem to resolve. The cooperating teacher felt that we ought to stretch our grading scales to take into account the additional difficulty of the words. I felt, however, that you grade a child on how he does *relative* to his ability. Thus, the child who already knows the third-grade words, should not get an A for doing what is easy work for him. He should only get an A when he excels at a learning task which is challenging for him. You will have to decide this question for yourself.

There were also a few procedural problems in my spelling program. When the practice tests were given on Thursday, I had to make sure that each child knew how to pronounce his buddy's words correctly. And when I prepared the tape for the final tests, I had to give certain children a longer time to write their words. I felt that it was certainly not fair to penalize a child because he worked somewhat slower than the rest. Our goal is spelling accuracy, not spelling speed.

What were the results of this individualized spelling program? The students learned to spell the "required" third-grade words plus many more advanced ones. Hopefully, the program created an interest in words. Certainly, our discussions at the Word Tree helped promote such an interest. And finally, the program was more fair and more challenging than the previous one. Every child was stretching his mind.

Certainly, this is not *the* best way to teach spelling. I don't know *the* best way. But I do think it is a better way than the usual or traditional way of teaching spelling. Many teachers hesitate to institute an individualized spelling program because it is too much work. Granted, there is more work involved. But the benefits are so great that it is well worth the extra effort. Do try some kind of an individualized spelling program. I am sure that you can create variations on my program, just as I created my program as a variation on the programs of others. But do try individualized spelling—it can be done.

CHAPTER TEN

Learning about Language through Literature

by Harlan S. and Ruth Mork Hansen

The purpose of this chapter is to highlight the literature available to both teachers and students which will aid them in an in-depth study of various aspects of our language.

Children's literature is a study in and of itself. That study is best served by other books which have already examined the various content categories. To be consistent with the purpose of this text—language as an art for effective communication—the discussion here will concentrate on how literature enhances an appreciation and understanding of our language beyond a professional's concern for proper usage.

To accomplish this purpose, the chapter will examine several aspects of literature and language. First, we will examine the functions of children's literature. Second, various aspects of our language will be defined and discussed. And last, a sampling of literature illustrating these aspects of language will be highlighted.

Functions of Literature

Literature in the classroom has three distinct functions: (1) to provide a literary experience, (2) to impart information, and (3) to provide a vehicle for developing language-related skills of memory, sequence, description, expression, comprehension, interpretation, analysis, synthesis, and evaluation. Because of the misunderstanding regarding these three functions, which is common among teachers, it is necessary to describe each function before proceeding to a discussion of presentation and content.

The Literary Experience. The literary experience has as its sole objective the enjoyment of a book. It treats the book as something written from the heart of the author—a combination of words and ideas put together by one who selected what *he* considered the right combination to make the characters come alive and to excite the reader to greater insights about himself and his world; past, present, and future.

The child should be allowed to take from the literary experience no more or no less than he chooses to acquire. And he should be allowed the same reading privileges adults exercise in their recreational reading.

An adult browses and selects a book. After starting the book, the adult might tire of it and put it away for a while, or perhaps forever. Or when reading, an adult may temporarily be led to daydream if the story is reminiscent of some personally related experience, characters, or situation. If some unusually dull sections occur, an adult might skip over those to get on to the more exciting segments. In the end, each adult takes from a book exactly what he chooses to take.

Children must be afforded these same freedoms. The professional who insists that all children look to the front while listening to a story or who treats assigned book reports as guarantees that pupils read more than the dust cover, robs children of a vital experience.

The literary experience is the very heart of literature. It provides what educators and librarians have called "that spark between the reader and the story" which is unique to every individual.

Time should be devoted each day in every classroom to providing literary experiences for children. Literature is the most valuable content material to use in impressing young children with feelings concerning the past, present, and future. This experience nurtures productive minds and builds a desire to see, hear, and understand the ideas of others. Only through a systematic acquaintance with books can a teacher make an effective contribution to children's impressions of literature. Extensive reading is the foundation of the teacher's preparation.

It is obvious why teachers must provide literary experiences for children in initial education programs—children lack the necessary reading skills. Somehow, in too many classroom situations, children's gaining skill in the decoding process parallels a gradual phasing out of the teacher's oral reading. This is most unfortunate. What about children who have not mastered the reading skills? It is equally important for teachers in all grades to provide group literary experiences so that all children have an opportunity to enjoy the vicarious experiences written especially with their age group's interests in mind. Perhaps this listening enjoyment will also serve as a motivation to acquire reading skills once a child sees what literature has in store for him.

Why should this literary experience occur daily? There is ample evidence that children who have been read to regularly since birth exhibit a greater initial interest in books and school and continue to exhibit a positive reading attitude in later years.[1]

The purpose of reading is to effect a positive, lifetime, independent reading behavior, not, as some educators seem to imply, the highest measured achievement of specific reading skills. Therefore, a child must constantly see skills in light of the broader objective. A regular literary experience is the most effective guarantee that this broader objective will be met.

The Information Experience. This classroom function of literature is self-explanatory—to present factual knowledge. Information books differ from trade books because the intent of both the author writing the book and the teacher selecting these books is different than when writing or selecting a book simply for enjoyment. The author's purpose is to give an accurate and meaningful picture of a specific topic, and he limits his thoughts and vocabulary to the subject and audience for which he has chosen to write. The teacher also has a different objective in mind. He may now want to measure in some way the information obtained from the book. While the literary experience is the relationship between a child and a book, the information experience is a relationship between the teacher, the child, and a book. Teachers read or assign these books for specific purposes. Information experiences are needed as often as information has to be transmitted or is sought by individual children.

When the child seeks information for the sheer sake of seeking, the reading experience runs a fine line between being an information or, more probably, a literary experience.

---

[1] Harlan S. Hansen, "The Impact of the Home Literary Environment on Reading Attitude." *Elementary English* XLVI (January 1969): 17–24. This study related parent's early literature behavior—reading to children, encouraging reading, providing materials, and model example—and its effect on fourth-grade reading attitude. The bibliography refers to several other studies.

The Language Experience. The language experience uses literature to aid in developing specific language skills. A teacher might read an accumulative story and then ask the children to recreate the exact sequence. Or he might assess recall and retention by asking children to recall different parts of the story. The story could serve as a basis for extended discussion of children's related personal experiences. Or children might create different story endings. The main function of literature in this experience is to use content merely as a vehicle for the development of language-arts skills.

Where is the confusion? The major problem is that teachers have not seen these functions as three separate and distinct functions of literature and have not understood the purposes of each. A teacher may say he is providing a daily literature experience for children but frequently because of the zeal for "instruction," such an experience becomes an information experience or a language experience. Even worse, the experience sometimes becomes an indigestible mélange of all three.

Perhaps the greatest abuse is to use the literary experience to accomplish one or both of the others. For example, picture the teacher who selects a story and begins, "Once upon a time, there was a baby lion named George." (Teacher, putting book temporarily out of story-reading position: "How many of you have ever seen a baby lion?" Children responding: "I saw one at the zoo." "I saw a rabbit the other day." "We have a new dog," and so on). "George lived in the jungle." (Teacher: "How many of you know what a jungle is?" Children: "I saw an old Tarzan movie." "I played on the jungle gym yesterday." "My mom says our garden looks like a jungle." and so forth). After a half hour of that, who can remember the story? Why should an author spend time putting down his best combination of words and ideas only to have them dissected and distorted in this manner?

Unfortunately, teachers see their role as providing children with an experience in which the gain can be immediately measured.

The *literary experience* is impressional. It is measured years later by assessing the reading attitude and involvement which has resulted from a regular exposure to the best literature available. The *information experience* is foundational, providing information which, when added to other information, builds a firm foundation for further information. And the *language experience* is given skilled treatment so that the skills of listening, expressing, thinking, and sequencing become overlearned and therefore help facilitate the intake and analysis of many communication experiences.

Literature Presentation

Presentation of literature to children needs only a brief mention. When involving children in the three functions, the printed page has unfortunately assumed the highest priority.

Children can benefit from a multi-exposure through varied media. Films, filmstrips, records, tapes, radio, television, and storytelling are available methods. These media forms can extend and enrich the three literature functions in several ways.

First, they provide a common experience for all children regardless of their reading ability. They enable children to visually experience what they may be incapable of reading. This not only makes literature available to all children but builds self-confidence as it allows them a mode of common communication with their peers. An intermediate grade boy who loved the outdoors but who lacked reading skills was able to experience the excitement of Jean George's, *My Side of the Mountain,* through the filmed version.[2]

Second, exposure to literature through various media has stimulated children to go to the original source for more and continued enjoyment. "Book Trails" and "It Happened When" literature programs over the Wisconsin School of the Air state radio network stimulated extended reading experiences of the books used on the programs. In a sixth-grade class, taught by one of the authors of this chapter, the showing of the eleven-minute film, "Story of a Book,"[3] resulted in the book *Pagoo* having continuous circulation for the remainder of the school year.[4]

Third, multi-media approaches provide for discussions of the appropriateness and value of different media. The other chapter author unfolded the same story of Pagoo through film, filmstrips, record, storyreading, and storytelling to a kindergarten class. This laid the foundation for individual judgments of which medium best sparked individual children. It led to the discussion of disadvantages perceived in each method of presentation. The main accomplishment was an extension of literature as a study in itself—in addition to the content as written or presented.

Finally, in this day of changing and advancing technology the use of different media expands the definition of "book" or "literature" be-

---

[2] Jean George, *My Side of the Mountain* (New York: Dutton, 1959).

[3] This film and several others are annotated in the list of films following the chapter.

[4] H. C. Holling, *Pagoo* (New York: Houghton Mifflin, 1957).

yond the mere printed page form. Some children have perceived themselves as failures because they couldn't adequately decode the alphabet system. These children need the positive feeling that they can "read" by decoding alternate systems.

Language and Literature about Language

Language is the process by which human creatures communicate with each other. In the lower animal life forms, communication takes the form of signals which relate to the basic areas of desire, pleasure, pain, and fear. In human life language adds a unique aspect to these other areas—the conveyance of an idea.

Because language is basic to all human relationships it is necessary that man understands his language at a conscious level, as well as merely use it on an intuitive level. The study and understanding of the various aspects of language provide the foundation for better usage and clearer understanding.

A vast amount of literature is available for use in exploring, examining, and understanding our language. The initial involvement with this literature in a classroom study will fall into the *information experience* category. Hopefully, this organized exposure to content about language will spark a host of individual literary experiences as children seek and explore information beyond that which is expected.

When should a study of language be initiated in formal education programs? The preschool and kindergarten level are not too early to provide some impressions about the nature of language and the various code systems. An impressional exposure at this age level not only provides early insights into a lifetime activity but hopefully puts into a broader perspective the decoding skills to come. Literature about language at this stage of study must be presented to children. However, they can be involved in much of the content through appropriate activities.

As children learn to read they can begin more in-depth study of the history and nature of language and can become much more involved in its various facets. Language is similar in characteristic to literature about language. The more often we become involved with it as we reach different ages and stages, the more new insights and adventures are opened to us.

How can children study language, and what literature is available to assist this study? Two suggested methods of study provide children with a look at language on two different inquiry levels. The first is the study of the means of expression or *language forms*. The second is the study of the *nature* of all language forms in our past, present, and future.

Language Forms

Language forms are (1) oral communication, (2) written communication, (3) nonverbal communication, and (4) mechanical communication. A brief discussion of each form of language communication follows.

Oral Language. A focus on the *dialects* and *idiolects* of oral language unfolds related aspects of vocabulary and usage. *Dialect* refers to a regional variety of language distinguished by features of vocabulary, grammar, and pronunciation different from other regional languages and constituting together a single language. *Idiolect* is the language or speech pattern peculiar to each individual.

No man can change the place of his birth or the generation in which he lives. That language which he acquires early will reflect his own personal phonemic style as well as the family or regional language style around him and will provide his basic lifetime speech pattern. The education he receives, the people he associates with, and the language uses he needs to master for particular occupations will enable him to change certain aspects of his personal and cultural speech, yet the opportunities to make drastic changes are not great.

Children exposed to the various regional dialects are provided experiences in understanding and appreciating the roots from which specific dialect characteristics grew as well as the opportunity to become sensitized to the dialect variation they hear in their everyday environment. Literature on records provides excellent possibilities for dialect and idiolect study. Locating one story, perhaps a folktale, narrated by many famous storytellers such as Carl Sandburg, Basil Rathbone, Danny Kaye and Boris Karloff enables children to hear different dialect and idiolect patterns of the same words. Reading the Laura I. Wilder series of books on early pioneer life[5] or *Corrie and the*

---

[5] See for example, Laura I. Wilder, *Long Winter* (New York: Harper and Row, 1971); *Little House in the Big Woods* (New York: Hale, 1932); or *By the Shores of the Silver Lake* (New York: Harper and Row, 1953). Once children discover the delights of the author's writing, they want to read all the books in the series.

Yankees about Civil War days[6] will add another dimension to this study. *Roosevelt Grady, Boss Cat, Lonesome Boy, Uptown,* and *Stevie* provide examples of Negro dialect from the migrant fields to New Orleans to New York. *David He No Fear* and *Every Man Heart Lay Down* are told as heard from African people newly acquainted with English. *A Feast of Light, I am Here Yo Estoy Aqui, The Year of Small Shadow* and *A Little Oven* deal with situations where children from other countries experience the problems of meeting a new culture, country, and a new language. *Always Room for One More* and *The Merry Adventure of Robin Hood* show speech patterns from other countries and from the past. Finally, *The Surprise Party* illustrates that classic example of how a secret changes in meaning as whispered from one animal to another. Idiolect and dialect study will be further enhanced by finding within stories several words which are used to mean the same thing—baby buggy, baby carriage, perambulator, pram, and others. Within regional dialects, social dialects can be frequently detected. These result from wealth, education, travel experiences, and/or the banding together of nationalistic groups.

The study of dialects and idiolects extends the usual skill program of vocabulary, grammar, and pronunciation through an in-depth exposure to its various regional and personal diversity. It also puts the term "correct speech" into proper perspective as acceptance of and tolerance for many speech patterns reinforces each child's unique pattern.

Written Language.   Written language uses an intermediate written symbol in transmitting a thought to someone else. The various aspects of written language include: (1) graphic, (2) idea codes, (3) word-picture codes, (4) the alphabet, and (5) special code systems.

Graphic writing uses pictures as the basis for communication. Cave writing has enabled man to capture much information regarding early man and his life. The writing of the American Indians employed signs and picture clues which provided a meaning. These graphic code systems function to give information as well as to provide aesthetic representation found in expressive art. Obviously, these graphic forms need to be realistic representations if they are to effectively communicate. Herein lies their limitation. While the writer of the graphic form may feel he's communicating specific information, through this form of written language, he is actually providing possibilities for varied inter-

---

[6] This book, and most of those subsequently mentioned, are annotated in the list included at the end of the chapter.

pretation on the part of the "reader." This limitation is an important one for children to examine.

How Medicine Man Cured Paleface Woman and *The Sioux Indian* are representatives of books which portray the graphic form of communication. *Talking without Words* and *God's Man* are examples of children's stories told in picture only.[7]

Idea writing employs symbols which represent an idea. The curve sign on the road tells us not only that a bend is ahead but which direction the road is turning. The symbols in our number system are idea markings which reflect a quantity which has a common meaning. This idea code system is sometimes called "memory aid writing" in that it helps us keep track of items and time with a minimum of symbols. This form of writing condenses the idea into a single symbol for fast and accurate interpretation. Comic books offer possible examples of this form ("light bulb" signifying an idea) as do highway manuals. *Signs and Symbols Around the World* provides a good foundation for both idea writing and word writing.

Word-picture writing involves children in the study of those pictures which represent a specific word. Brand name symbols are examples of this form of writing. Many grocery stores, fast food chains, department stores, and other community businesses have identifying symbols which are interchangeable with their name. Children "read" them daily in advertisements, billboards, or on store signs. This symbol-word name study capitalizes on the children's previous experiences within their environment. Newspapers and magazines provide numerous examples of word-writing.

The study of the *alphabet system* takes children through an understanding of the evolution of letter code systems. An alphabet expresses the single sounds of a language and therefore can encompass many languages in addition to our own.

A Is for Apple and Why, The 26 Letters, What's Behind the Word, The Romance of Writing, and *A Study of Writing* look specifically at the alphabet code while discussing it in light of other language forms. A host of trade alphabet books which feature content and styles ranging from Brian Wildsmith to Marcel Marceau are readily available for children's perusal and enjoyment.[8] Many children's books

---

[7] A pamphlet entitled "Books without Words," which includes an annotated list of two dozen such books, is available from the Minneapolis, Minn. Public Library.

[8] An annotated list of such books is included in Chapter 9 on p. 312.

are now available in foreign languages so children can compare various alphabet symbols.

Special code systems include such forms as shorthand and music. Music books are available in most classrooms. A shorthand book or *Alice in Wonderland* in shorthand, as well as a secretary as a resource person, will highlight the study of this special code system.

Nonverbal Language. Man has developed a system of nonverbal communication which operates parallel to or in place of speaking or writing.[9] These nonverbal means are grouped into three categories: (1) haptics, (2) kinesics, and (3) paralanguage.

Haptics is the study of communication by touching. Embracing, kissing, patting on the head, shaking hands, nudging, and caressing all convey a message. These messages vary from culture to culture and are sometimes of an opposite nature. To pat an American boy on the top of the head is a sign of endearment. However, the top of a Thai's head is where his soul is connected with heaven and a pat there would be a grave offense. Illustrations in books and advertisements which show examples of haptics are good study possibilities. Young children as well as older children can decode and discuss this nonverbal language form.

Kinesics is the study of body posture and movement.[10] All moveable parts of the body are involved and the message communicated may be unintentional or directed by gesture or movement. Nodding the head, winking, raising the finger to the mouth for silence all transmit an idea to the receiver. In addition, a stance might be termed masculine or feminine. It might denote happiness or unhappiness. It could show elation or anger.

Some of these movements are either spontaneous or directed movements which are unique to each individual's expression pattern. However, some body movements are used for directional or interpretive purposes. The policeman, the referee, the music conductor, the deaf person, the hula dancer and the ballet dancer all have special gestures which have a common basis for communication. These are learned rather than acquired and are a part of a child's out of school environ-

---

[9] If you are interested in launching a study of nonverbal communication, this article may help: L. A. Landsman, "Man behind the Mask," *Instructor* 80, No. 79 (February 1971). This interview with the mime Marceau gives valuable insight into the art form.

[10] A valuable book by the best-known expert in this newly developing field is Ray L. Birdwhistell's *Kinesics and Context* (Philadelphia: University of Pennsylvania Press, 1970).

ment. The study of both forms of kinesics—the spontaneous or learned —is vital, as observed body movement is an integral part of every person's language pattern, whether spontaneous or realized.

Talking without Words, Marcel Marceau's ABC, and *Talking Hands* are several of a growing number of books which deal with gestures. Referee's handbooks, music conductor's books, police handbooks, and deaf sign-language books all highlight the many facets of kinesics. The newer encyclopedias also include materials on gestures as communication.

Paralanguage is a signal system produced by the nonarticulated voice track. It is identified not by the oral language utilized but by the intensity, pitch, and tempo employed. Coughing, crying, and giggling are other examples of oral sounds which communicate an idea. Children might look for words in their stories which give clues to the paralanguage used, such as "she hollered" or "they giggled as they talked." The study possibilities of paralanguage are interesting and exciting because of these subtleties, and because many people have not seen them as separate communicators.

Mechanical Writing.   This is one language form which has recently emerged. Films, filmstrips, records, tapes, radio, and videotape all add a new dimension to language in addition to the content presented. Moods, feelings, and extended visual stimulation add new impact to the message. A film grammar is emerging which provides children ways to analyze and interpret the mechanical language form. David C. Davis of the University of Wisconsin School of Education is currently systematizing this film grammar.

The use of puppets, animation, shadow figures, live animals and humans, and the iconograph means of panning the camera over book illustrations affect the film grammar. Students can compare one story in these many forms and arrive at personal value judgments. Typewriters, adding machines, braille writers, and computers are other mechanical means of communicating as well as flashing lights and teletype transmitters.

While the communication of all the above-mentioned mechanical media forms utilize either oral language, written language, or nonverbal language, children can profitably study the advantages and disadvantages of using a mechanical writer as well as the extent to which the message is changed in mechanical transmission.

The four language forms provide an abundance of study possibilities for many ages and many interests as our daily life is filled with examples of each. The study of language creates that necessary one-to-one correspondence between what is going on inside the classroom with what is going on outside of the classroom. This study will not only enable children to appreciate the richness of our language heritage but to better communicate and understand others.

The Nature of Language

The study of language has another aspect—the nature and role of language in past, present, and future. This approach cuts across language forms and sees the variability of language forms within each component.

A study of the nature of language could include the following concepts: (1) history, (2) acquisition, (3) organization, (4) change, (5) roles, (6) norms, (7) acculturation, and (8) relativity. While these concepts overlap with the earlier discussion of language forms, they approach language study from another point of reference. The nature of language will be examined here to provide some ideas on which to build a more in-depth study.

History examines the origin of various language forms. Children can role-play the problems early man faced in his need to communicate with other people. Gestures, grunts, formation of words, and pitch of voice all come into play. The importance of this historical view of language will give children insights into why man needed language, the first forms available to him, and how this basic system showed the need for more sophisticated means of conveying needs, desires, information, feelings, and questions.[11]

Acquisition deals with the manner in which young children acquire language. While many areas of this study are too complex for any but highly trained researchers, some aspects fall within elementary school-age children's understanding. Children with younger brothers and sisters can report on their manner of communication and include information on how this communication was gained. Family speech patterns, how frequently parents talk with their children, if they verbally label household items, how many new words are being learned from television, as well as exposure to brand words in the everyday environment are possible investigation areas. The start of idiolects and how these relate to dialects can be examined. The way children acquire language in other countries or cultures may be of value in this study, especially

---

[11] Another writer who believes this is important has suggested other ideas to try. See G. G. Duffy, "Teaching the History of Our Language," *Instructor* 80 (Nov. 1970): 87–88.

in relationship to the availability and emphasis of public schooling. There are some excellent books available on child growth and development to assist in this study.[12]

Organization stresses the idea that language can be defined using word labels for its various parts. Paragraphs, sentences, phrases, nouns, pronouns, adjectives, and adverbs are some of the labels in use. Studying the advantages and disadvantages of this organization, including social implications, may allow children to see value in this study of organization as contrasted to the usual sentence dissection method. A study of organization may well motivate children to learn the specific labels, while appreciating how these labels fit into a larger conceptual framework.

Change is inherent in language. One generation cannot always see this change taking place, especially through the adolescent phase of life. Yet, children's present language provides an excellent vehicle for contrasting common words children use today with those of the past. The idea that usage is an important agent of change along with man's seemingly natural desire to coin new words will facilitate understanding of this concept. The role government, technology, and the media have played in areas of usage and change is essential to examine. Resource people can greatly add to this study as can literature which utilizes language common to various times in history. Books such as *Words from the Myths, Why You Say It, People Words,* and *Culture, Class, and Language* all show how usage has changed over the years.

The concept of *roles* examines the language that accompanies various roles, whether they be social or occupational. Carpenters, plumbers, policemen, engineers, teachers, athletes, and others all use language appropriate to their occupation. This language then becomes a part of the common language. For example, in a city which has a professional football team, for several months of the year, words and phrases such as "split T," "tight end," "wishbone I," "free safety," and "audibles" become the language of people on the street and in the stands. Children interested in the sport will study the meanings of these words with far greater zeal than they will the word study pages prepared for them in school.

Norms deal with language which has come to be acceptable to groups of people. The child's, teen-ager's, and adult's needs to adapt their

---

[12] Brief treatment of this is included in C. M. Kirkton, "Language Acquisition and Development: Some Implications for the Classroom," *Elementary English* 48 (March 1971): 406–12. Two books offering more complete statements about language acquisition are Andrew Wilkinson, *The Foundations of Language* (London: Oxford University Press, 1971), and James Britton, *Language and Learning* (Coral Gables: University of Miami Press, 1970).

language to the usage pattern of their peer group is one example of developing language norms for specific groups.[13] The positive or negative value placed on speech patterns at different social levels is another. How these normative patterns develop and solidify into language patterns is important for children to examine. If this examination motivates children to develop extended language patterns beyond the confines of what is expected, so much the better. Literature, with its tremendous availability of vocabulary and usage can provide a powerful tool for a child's personal language expansion.

Acculturation focuses on how our language is a part of a larger usage pattern of many people. This study also examines the way language has changed as various cultures have merged or come into proximity with each other. Such change has added new words, new sayings, new acceptance, and new usage. Books dealing with children's experiences in meeting new language situations should be utilized.

Finally, the *relativity* of language demonstrates that language means different things to different people and that the person initiating the communication and the person receiving the communication must have the same thing in mind if the communication is to succeed. This relativity summarizes the aforementioned concepts which constitute the nature of language. Where you were born, how and how early you acquired language, the roles and norms available and expected in certain situations, as well as the regional cultural variations all play a crucial role in a person's language pattern. Language becomes a relative factor when talking with others whose patterns were developed from a different base. If children can appreciate and understand this relativity early, they might attempt to develop their language forms to more accurately communicate what they really mean, while remaining tolerant of those who still are vague in communicating and receiving other's messages.

Indeed, language has many facets. Too often we bypass a study of these facets at the elementary school level in favor of working on decoding, encoding, and language usage skills. Whether you use the *language forms* approach or the *nature of language* approach, each intertwines around and through the other. Since we are involved with language throughout the majority of our lives, an understanding of the nature of our language and the various language forms will hopefully provide children with a broader foundation from which to begin extended individual language development.

---

[13] One writer has reported positive results in having children study slang. See L. D. Kennedy, "Teaching Dictionary Skills in the Upper Grades; Preparing a Dictionary of Slang," *Elementary English* 49 (January 1972): 71–73.

Suggestions for Further Exploration

1. Take a neighborhood walk to look for graphic, idea, and word-picture writing on street signs, store name symbols, numbers, billboards, and other places.

2. Collect pictures of, or write words or phrases in as many different code systems as you can. For example, four, 4, ////, a hand with four fingers exposed; or a picture of a road with a curve, the word curve, road sign with the symbol for a curve.

3. Talk with several senior citizens in the community. Listen for word usage or speech patterns which reflect language of the past, regional dialects, and foreign language accents.

4. Select a folktale which emerged in a similar form in several countries. For example, the Gingerbread Boy is American, the Pancake is the same character in Norway, the Bannock delights children in Scotland, while the Bun is the Russian version of the story. Record on tape the story versions in their native language.

5. Tape record persons with different dialects reading or telling the same story. This provides opportunities for dialect comparison with a common word base.

6. Locate resource people who use gestures (kinesics) in their occupations: referee, music conductor, airline ground crewman, dancer, and others.

7. Begin a picture file of people using haptics and kinesics to use in discussion with children. Newspaper and magazine ads and pictures are good starting sources.

8. Select some common items that are known to have many different words applied to them in everyday usage—baby buggy, car, stream of water, evening meal, swim suit, and others. Show pictures of these items to at least five different people. Record the words used by each person to label the items. Are these mostly dialect or idiolect patterns?

Bibliography

Aiken, Joan. *The Wolves of Willoughby Chase*. New York: Doubleday & Co., 1962.

This suspenseful Victorian melodrama about the misadventures of two young girls in the English countryside brings out the tongue-in-cheek language patterns that are a part of this literature form.

Adolf, Arnold. *MA, DA, LA*. New York: Harper and Row, Publishers, 1971.

The author has composed a song in praise of mankind—the cycle of the family and of life. Resonant soundings form the basic chant which allows readers to add words and soundings of their own.

Amon, Aline. *Talking Hands—Indian Sign Language*. New York: Doubleday & Co., 1968.

This book tells how to speak in authentic Indian sign language. In addition, sample sentences describe the life of a typical plains boy and show how to use signs today.

Asimov, Isaac. *Words from the Myths*. Boston: Houghton Mifflin Co., 1961.

In addition to his book *Words of Science* (Houghton Mifflin 1959), Isaac Asimov in this book explores the Greek myths to discover the roots of hundreds of words which entered into our daily language. Included is an index of many theological terms and of modern words that come from them.

Bleeker, Sonia. *The Sioux Indians*. New York: William Morrow & Co., 1962.

The life of the Indians includes a description of a winter count, a historic record painted on a buffalo robe highlighting a memorable event of each year. The events are equivalent to ideographs and Indians "read" these winter counts.

Blue, Rose. *I Am Here   Yo Estoy Aqui*. New York: Franklin Watts, 1971.

The story of a five-year-old Puerto Rican child whose family moves to America. When she arrives at school for the first time she feels alone and strange because she does not understand the language and the things she sees are unfamiliar.

Bontemps, Arna. *Lonesome Boy*. Boston: Houghton Mifflin Co., 1955.

This is the story of a young black boy who is lonesome without his trumpet and the lesson he learns about lonesomeness. It has some flavor of the New Orleans regional dialect, especially in the speech of the boy's grandfather.

Brasch, R. *How Did It Begin?* New York: David McKay Co., 1965.

This fascinating book explores the customs and superstitions, mores, and habits that influence us today. In so doing it looks at the reason behind many words and sayings.

Brooke, L. Leslie. *Johnny Crow's New Garden.* New York: Frederick Warne, 1964.

All the animals who come to Johnny Crow's new garden are a part of the amusing rhyming words that tell their story.

Brown, Marcia. *Peter Piper's Alphabet.* New York: Charles Scribner's Sons, 1959.

This alphabet book has a tongue twister for each letter. Excellent illustrations by Marcia Brown.

Burnett, Frances Hodgson. *Little Lord Fountleroy.* New York: E. P. Dutton, 1962.

This classic story written in the 1880s utilizes the language appropriate to England and America at that time.

Burnett, Frances Hodgson. *Rachelty-Pachelty House.* New York: Dodd, Mead & Co., 1961.

This short book about dolls and fairy's "real lives" when people turn their backs, uses vocabulary peculiar to a time when language had a more formal flavor and different slang.

Caldecott, R. *R. Caldecott's Picture Book No. 1.* New York: Frederick Warne, 1879–1885.

Spelling unique to old England is sprinkled throughout this well-known storybook.

Carroll, Lewis. *Alice in Wonderland.* New York: Random House, 1969.

This classic story in its many languages and code systems provides unlimited examples of language usage in forms for study.

Canfield, Dorothy. *Understood Betsy.* New York: Holt, Rinehart & Winston, 1916.

This well-loved story deals with Betsy's life on the Putney farm with its use of country slang common to Vermont at the turn of the century.

Charles, Robert H. *A Roundabout Turn.* New York: Frederick Warne & Co., 1930.

This amusing tale of an adventurous toad who wants to see if the world is really round has such words as heather, gorse, braken, and feathery fronds for which children can seek out the meanings.

Cleaver, Vera and Bill. *Ellen Grae.* New York: Lippincott Co., 1967.

A story, both serious and funny, about Ellen's adventure in a Missouri town, is told in dialect.

Coggins, Jack. *Flashes and Flags, The Story of Signaling.* New York: Dodd, Mead and Co., 1963.

This is an account of signals and signaling devices in everyday use—by ships, planes, trains, in sports, traffic and weather warnings—along with a glance at those of by-gone days. Helpful in looking at basic code systems.

Cox, Plamer. *The Brownies: Their Book.* New York: Dover Publishing, 1964. (First published, 1887)

This entire book in verse presents opportunities for studying the use of language in a forced verse situation as well as an opportunity for viewing language representing the late 1800s.

Davis, A. L., ed. *Culture, Class, and Language Variety.* Urbana, Illinois: National Council of Teachers of English, 1972.

This resource book for teachers contains articles written by well-known researchers and educators. The purpose of the book is to help teachers improve their insights and methodologies to deal more effectively with language problems of disadvantaged children. Obviously, the implication for all groups of children is there.

DeAngeli, Marguerite, *Yonie Wondernose.* Garden City, New York: Doubleday & Co., 1944.

A charming, colorful picture book reflecting Amish family traditions and speech patterns.

DeVar, A. *Talking Words.* New York: Bobbs Merrill, 1969.

This book shows how words can be converted into many different code systems; for example, by putting eyes in the two o's in the word look. It can be used at different levels of study with all age groups.

Epstein, Sam and Beryl. *The First Book of Words.* New York: Franklin Watts, 1954.

See annotation in Bibliography, Chapter 11, p. 380.

Estes, Eleanor. *A Little Oven.* New York: Harcourt Brace Jovanovich, 1955.

Helena and Genevieve get a little oven mixed up with a little loving. This story for younger children brings out the misunderstandings in language.

Ets, Maria Hall. *Talking without Words.* New York: Viking Press, 1968.

Demonstrates the use of gesture in everyday life. An excellent book for the study of this too-often ignored aspect of communication.

Garrison, Webb. *Why You Say It.* New York: Abingdon Press, 1955.

See Annotation in Bibliography, Chapter 11, p. 380.

Gelb, I. J. *A Study of Writing.* Chicago: University of Chicago Press, 1952.

The complete story of writing is included in this resource book for teachers. Discussions concentrate on early writing, the evolution of the alphabet system, the relationship of writing to speech, and the future of writing. Well written and illustrated, this will give teachers good background information.

Goodall, J. *The Adventures of Paddy Pork*. New York: Harcourt Brace Jovanovich, 1968.

This humorous story told in pictures only, enables children to "read" this graphic code. Paddy is lost in the woods and nearly becomes dinner for a wolf.

Graham, Lorenz. *David He No Fear*. New York: Thomas Y. Crowell Co., 1946.

The fearless story of David and Goliath is written as the author heard it told in Africa, using the storyteller's language.

————. *Every Man Heart Lay Down*. New York: Thomas Y. Crowell Co., 1946.

This is the story of the birth of Jesus in words and speech patterns of African people newly acquainted with English.

————. *I, Momolu*. New York: Thomas Y. Crowell, Co., 1966.

The story of an African boy's trip with his father from a remote Liberian village to the coast city of Cape Rogers for not only his first look at "civilization" but his first experiences with people who did not speak or understand his language.

Greet, Cabell et al. *In Other Words—A Beginning Thesaurus*. New York: Lothrop, Lee and Shepard, 1969.

This treasury of words is tailored especially for children. Based on the hundred words commonly used by children in elementary school, the book gives more than a thousand others that students might use.

Harris, Joel Chandler. *Uncle Remus*. New York: Schocken Books, 1965.

Humor, fun, wisdom and humanity are combined in these superbly told stories of nineteenth century rural South.

Hautzig, Esther. *In School*. London: The Macmillan Co., 1969.

This offers a lesson in language by introducing familiar words in English, Spanish, French, and Russian in describing a first day in school.

Helfman, Elizabeth. *Signs and Symbols around the World*. New York: Lothrop, Lee, and Shepard Co., 1967.

See annotation in Bibliography, Chapter 11, p. 381.

Hunder, Kristin. *Boss Cat*. New York: Charles Scribner's Sons, 1971.

A new pet cat causes much commotion as it becomes a member of the Tanner family. This book sheds light on the dialect patterns in the characters' language.

Hutchins, Pat. *The Surprise Party*. New York: The Macmillan Co., 1969.

"I'm having a party tomorrow," whispered Rabbit to the Owl. "It's a surprise." By the time the owl passes the message to other animals who in turn pass it to others, the story changes because the message is misunderstood.

Irwin, Keith. *The Romance of Writing*. New York: The Viking Press, 1956.

From Egyptian hieroglyphics to modern letters, numbers, and signs, the book examines every form of writing man has known. From cave writing to the alphabet to numbers to musical notes, this book with over one hundred illustrations presents a deep insight into the topic.

Kerr, Judith. *When Hitler Stole Pink Rabbit*. New York: Coward, McCann & Geoghegan, 1972.

This is the story of a Jewish family separated in Germany during the war and finally reunited in Switzerland. They embark on an adventure that lasts years and takes them to several countries where they learn new languages, see things, and learn how to cope with wild confusions.

Kredenser, Gail. *The ABC's Bumptious Beasts*. New York: Harlin Quest, 1966.

From Aardvark to Egret to Iguana to Quail to Xenopus, this collection of journeyed creatures takes children through the alphabet. Charming illustrations by Stanley Mach.

Laker, Russell. *Anatomy of Lettering*. New York: The Viking Press, 1966.

This lettering manual offers children an opportuniy to see letters in all styles as well as to examine the basic shapes which form the Roman alphabet.

Lampman, Evelyn. *The Years of Small Shadow*. New York: Harcourt Brace Jovanovich, 1971.

This book tells the story of a young Indian boy's stay with a white family and the problems the boy had with the new language and way of life.

Lear, Edward. *ABC*. New York: McGraw-Hill Book Co., 1965.

See Annotation in Appendix Two, Chapter Nine, p. 314.

Lenski, Lois. *Bayou Suzette*. New York: J. B. Lippincott Co., 1943.

A charming story told in dialect about a little French girl who lives on the bayou path in a Louisiana village and an Indian girl whom she befriends and takes to her home to live.

———. *Indian Captive*. New York: J. B. Lippincott Co., 1941.

This story of Mary Jemison, a white girl who lived in Indian captivity for many years, gives a remarkable picture of Seneca Indian life from the inside.

Levy, Mimi. *Corrie and the Yankees*. New York: The Viking Press, 1959.

The language of the South during the Civil War tells this story of Corrie who shelters and aids a wounded Yankee soldier.

Longman, Harold. *Would You Put Your Money in a Sand Bank?* (Fun with Words). New York: Rand McNally & Co., 1968.

The author examines homonyms through riddles, silly questions, nonsense conversation, and other means to involve children in words that sound alike but are spelled differently.

Longman, Harold, *What's behind the Word?* New York: Coward, McCann & Geoghegan, 1968.

This book does much to clear up the mystery of where our words come from. It tells the story of thirty-nine words in a witty and humorous fashion and deals with the manner in which new words replace old ones.

McGraw, Jessie. *How Medicine Man Cured Paleface Woman*. New York: William Scott, Inc., 1956.

This story in Indian pictographs tells how one winter a lost, sick, paleface woman was discovered by Indians, brought to their camp, and cured. This book's unique value is that it is written entirely in real Amerian Indian pictographs—the oldest form of known writing.

McGrath, Thomas. *The Beautiful Things*. New York: Vanguard Press, 1960.

Danny's sister Laura gave him the word "beautiful" for his birthday. To celebrate they went out to see all the things they could find that fit the word.

Mayer, Mercer. *Frog, Where Are You?* New York: Dial Press, 1969.

This delightful story is one of several books, the story of which is told only in pictures. A boy and his dog wake one morning to find their favorite friend is gone.

NicLeodhas, Sorche. *Always Room for One More*. New York: Holt, Rinehart & Winston, 1965.

An hilarious tale of kindness told in a Scot dialect. Lachie MacLahen invites every weary traveler who passes by to be a guest of himself and his family of twelve in their already bulging house.

Norris, Gunilla. *A Feast of Light*. New York: Alfred A. Knopf. 1967.

This story of a nine-year-old girl's arrival in the United States from Sweden has excellent examples of language in transition as she learns the English language.

Nurnberg, Maxwell, *Fun with Words*. New York: Prentice-Hall, 1970; *Wonders in Words*. Prentice-Hall, 1968; *All About Words*. New York: New American Library, 1968.

These three books deal in a lighthearted manner with words, their origin and meaning, and word tricks and games. Covering grammar, spelling, punctuation, and vocabulary, these books are as educational as they are entertaining.

Ogg, Oscar. *The 26 Letters*. New York: Thomas Y. Crowell Co., 1971.

See annotation in Bibliography, Chapter Eight, p. 272.

Poe, Edgar Allan, *The Fall of the House of Usher and Some Other Tales*. New York: Franklin Watts, 1967.

Poe uses highly descriptive language to tell these stories. His lengthy sentences contain many complex word patterns and reflect the more formal language of the time.

Potter, Charles. *Tongue Tanglers. More Tongue Tanglers and a Rigmarole*. New York: World Publishing Co., 1964.

America's foremost authority on tongue tanglers has put together these two collections of this verse form. Included are notes in sources and variants. These tongue tanglers can provide common reference points for dialect and idiolect analysis.

Preston, Edna. *Pop Corn and Ma Goodness*. New York: The Viking Press, 1969.

An alliterative nonsense saga about love and marriage, birth and death, summer and winter and tears and laughter. Told in tongue-tripping words that demand to be read aloud.

Prokofiev, Sergei. *Peter and the Wolf*. New York: Alfred A. Knopf. 1940.

The print used in this children's classic is calligraphy hand lettered by Hollis Holland.

Pyle, Howard. *Book of Pirates*. New York: Harper & Row, Publishers, 1949.

The colorful language of the sea pirate fills this book of fiction, fact, and fancy concerning the buccaneers and marooners of the Spanish main.

————. *The Merry Adventures of Robin Hood*. New York: Golden Press, 1962.

This children's classic is written in the language of the time.

————. *The Story of King Arthur and His Knights*. New York: Charles Scribner's, Sons. 1903.

King Arthur and his Knights use the best of language such as "thou shalt have the boon although my heart much misgiveth me that thou wilt suffer. . . ."

Radlauer, Ruth. *Good Times with Words*. Chicago: Melmont Publishers, 1963.

See annotation in Bibliography, Chapter 11, p. 382.

Rand, Paul and Ann. *Sparkle and Spin*. New York: Harcourt Brace Jovanovich, 1957.

The authors write about words in many ways, stimulating children to generate new discoveries on their own. They deal with the functions of words in everyday language as well as with how words show feelings.

Rawlings, Marjorie. *The Yearling*. New York: Charles Scribner's Sons, 1939.

This well-known story of a life that is far removed from modern patterns of living is heightened by the language of the simple, courageous people and their wild, hard, satisfying life in inland Florida.

Rees, Ennis. *The Little Greek Alphabet Book*. Englewood Cliffs, N.J.: Prentice-Hall, Inc., 1968.

This book examines the Greek alphabet and relates it to our alphabet. The forced rhyme often detracts from the value of the book—yet the book seems to offer a different dimension to alphabet study.

Reid, Alastair. *Ounce, Dice, Trice*. Boston: Little, Brown & Co., 1958.
See annotation in Bibliography, Chapter 11, p. 382.

Rey, H. A. *Curious George Learns the Alphabet*. Boston: Houghton Mifflin, 1963.

Curious George learns the alphabet in a very unusual fashion. A good book for younger children.

Russell, Solveig. *A Is for Apple and Why*. New York: Abingdon Press, 1959.
See Annotation Appendix Two, Chapter Nine, p. 315.

Scott, Joseph and Lenore. *Egyptian Hieroglyphics for Everyone*. New York: Funk and Wagnalls, 1968.

This book introduces the fascinating realm of Egyptian hieroglyphics. It also teaches the reader how to "read" hieroglyphics for use in present-day museums.

Severn, Bill. *People Words*. New York: Ives Washburn, 1966.

Here is a collection of eponyms—the persons from whom a family, race, city, or nation is supposed to have taken its name. Included are such general subjects as food and drink, clothes and fashions, science and inventions, familiar things, relations with others, mind and body.

Shotwell, Louisa. *Roosevelt Grady*. New York: World Publishing Co., 1963.

Roosevelt Grady was the son of migrant workers who traveled with the crop harvest. Excellent dialect as well as a classic story.

Steptoe, John. *Stevie*. New York: Harper and Row, Publishers, 1969.

A story told in black speech patterns about Robert, an only child, who looks with no anticipation at having Stevie, whose parents work, as a weekday boarder in his home.

———. *Train Ride*. New York: Harper and Row, Publishers, 1971.

An exciting story told in black speech patterns about Charles, who takes his friends on a trip to Times Square. They have a difficult time getting back home without train fare.

———. *Uptown*. New York: Harper and Row, Publishers, 1970.

As two Harlem boys walk through Manhattan where they see junkies, cops, karate experts and hippies they wonder what it might be like to be one of these men. Told in black speech patterns.

Tuer, Andrew, ed. *Stories from Old Fashioned Children's Books*. Detroit: Singing Tree Press, 1968. First published, 1899.

This collection of stories contains many examples of various language patterns both in the narration and the dialogue.

Twain, Mark. *Adventure of Huckleberry Finn*. New York: E. P. Dutton & Co., 1962.

In this classic children's story a number of dialects are used: Missouri Negro dialect, backwood Southwestern dialect, and Pike County dialect.

Ungerer, Tomi. *One, Two, Where's My Shoe?* New York: Harper and Row, Publishers, 1964.

Shoes are hidden in the most unlikely places in this book told only in pictures.

VanGelder, Rosalind. *Monkeys Have Tails*. New York: David McKay Co., 1966.

This book of homonyms is different from others in that many of the words both sound alike and are spelled alike. Told in question form with illustrated glossary.

Waller, Leslie. *Our American Language*. New York: Holt, Rinehart & Winston, 1960.

See annotation in Bibliography, Chapter 11.

Ward, Lynd. *God's Man, A Novel in Woodcuts*. Cleveland: World Publishing Co., 1957.

This story of an ageless tragedy in the society of the twenties and thirties is told without words in one-hundred and twenty woodcuts. An outstanding example of picture writing.

West, Fred. *Breaking the Language Barrier*. New York: Coward McCann, Inc., 1961.

This book deals with language—from caveman grunts to electronic translators. The author shows how inability to speak other languages has handicapped the United States in world competition and dramatizes the way in which ability to speak languages shapes history.

Westcott, Al. *Word Bending with Aunt Sarah*. Mankato: Oddo Publishing, 1964.

Aunt Sarah stimulates us to describe all the possible things certain words make us think of. Teachers can continue this "word bending" with children expanding the process.

White, Mary Sue. *Word Twins*. New York: Abingdon Press, 1961. See annotation in Bibliography, Chapter 11, p. 383.

Films

"Alphabet, The." (Series: Language and Linguistics) 28 minutes.

This film analyzes the English writing system and traces the origin, development, and spread of the alphabet, explaining various writing systems including Sanskrit, Chinese, and Arabic. The film discusses the significance of hieroglyphics in the development of written language. Other films in this valuable series include: "Dialects," "History of the English Language," "Language and Linguistics," and "Sounds of Language." (Indiana University)

"English Language—How It Changes" 11 minutes.

This film shows changes in words; changes in spelling; changes in pronunciation and meaning; and changes in rules of grammar which are presented with examples. Recent changes are used to show how change keeps our language alive, flexible, and a useful communication tool. (Coronet)

"English Language: Story of Its Development, The." 11 minutes.

This film is a visual outline history of the English language from its roots in Anglo and Saxon tongues, through its infusion of French and Latin, and its emergence as a printed language, which is still growing and changing. (Coronet)

"History of Writing." 28 minutes.

This film presents a chronological history of writing as a means of communication, shows how writing evolved from pictures and signs, and illustrates that local materials used as writing tools influenced the methods of sign making and writing. The film explains that symbols for objects and ideas became symbols for sounds; depicts and analyzes significant features of early Chinese, Mesopotamian, and Egyptian writings and contributions of Phoenicians, Greeks, and Romans to our present alphabet. (Encyclopedia Britannica)

"Language and Communication." Color. 16 minutes.

The purpose of this film is to give an understanding of our heritage of spoken and written language and the role of this heritage in the communication of ideas, to encourage the student to develop skills in language communication, and to instill in the student a sense of appreciation of the contributions of past generations. The three historical stages of written language—pictographic, demographic, and phonetic —are described. (Moody Institute of Science)

"Language of the Film." (Series: Film Appreciation) Color. 28 minutes.

> We learn the importance of camera tricks and techniques in visually conveying a director's idea to his audience. Some of the tricks discussed are the dissolve, the fade, camera angle, the type of lens, screenshape, and use of line, distance, and lighting. (OFM Productions)

"Nature of Language and How It Is Learned." (Series: Modern Language Association) 30 minutes.

> This film is the first in a series of five. The film explain the nature of language, how it is learned, and establishes the validity of the "oral approach" to teaching. The living language is shown to be speech. Examples of speech are drawn from the base reservoir of languages of the world. These examples reveal how differently languages function in their sound systems, grammatical organizations and lexical developments. Speech is compared with writing.
>
> This series includes films on "Modern Techniques of Language Teaching," The Organization of Language," The Sounds of Language," and "Words and their Meanings." (Teaching Films Custodian, Inc.)

"Story of A Book." Color 11 minutes.

> By opening a doorway on the intriguing behind-the-scenes creation of a book and by showing the enthusiasm of its author, the film helps children to a new enjoyment and appreciation of books. This film re-enacts the story of the writing of a book. It follows a real-life author, H. C. Holling, through the exciting and satisfying process of creating *Pagoo*, the story of a hermit crab. (Churchill Films)

"Story of Communication." 15 minutes.

> This picture deals with the development of a universal and nationwide system of communication available to all citizens, and it provides the flow of information without which a democracy would perish. Traces methods of communication from very early times to the present day. (Instructional Films Inc.)

"Word Building in Our Language." 11 minutes.

> Through interesting examples, graphically illustrated, the film demonstrates how many of our words are built by adding prefixes, suffixes, or both to a root, and by combining words or parts of them. It also points out that many of our words are derived from other languages, frequently Latin, and generally explores the principles of structural growth of words. (Coronet)

"Who Makes Words." 11 minutes.

> In this film a class investigates the source of words and discovers some are "borrowed," some "invented," and still others come about through changes in spelling or meaning. Important means by which our language grows are learned in their search. (Coronet)

CHAPTER ELEVEN

Vocabulary

The little red-headed boy, with the kind of indignation only four year olds can muster, was intently confronting his teacher at the lunch table. "I don't want these peas, they're despicable," he declared vehemently. The nursery school teacher, with apparent amazement, removed the dish of offending peas as she wondered again at the range of children's interest in words.

The anecdote illustrates well what psychologists and students of language have long known: that children's interest in words, and their intrepid approach to using words is indeed enviable.

How the child's interest in words is first stimulated and later encouraged and how a teacher can continue the growth of this interest is the focus of this chapter.

As Words Are Learned

Children early sense the presence of sound stimuli surrounding them, and soon begin the imitative procedures leading to early development of language. Several researchers have studied the language of very young children, and have helped us understand these early efforts children make at emulating sounds.[1]

Most children utter an intelligible word sometime during the second six months of life.[2] While such words may be difficult for other than a doting parent to understand, the beginning has been made; the growth which follows is truly amazing. It has been estimated that from this simple beginning the child progresses to the point where only twenty-four months later he possesses 77 percent of all the sounds in an adult's language. Strickland reports that by the time a child is three years old, he uses 7600 words per day; this increases to 10,500 words by the time he is five.[3]

Language at Six

Much time and effort has been devoted to determining the size of a child's vocabulary by the time he arrives in first grade. Yet, it may be more confusing than illuminating to examine the results of such studies, for it is difficult to determine just what the first-grade teacher may expect. The chart on page 355 summarizes a variety of studies in this area.

It is apparent from the chart that concensus in this, as in many other areas of research, is not possible. It is interesting to speculate about the factors in the research which may have accounted for these differences. (See item #2, in Suggestions for Further Study, p. 377.)

Probably a first-grade teacher can know for sure only two things after examining this data. *First*, it is likely that the size of vocabulary of children entering school is larger today than in previous years. While most children may not know the 26,363 words which Shibles claims they know, it is safe to assume that children today do have a larger vocabulary than when Canton did his study in 1897. Some observations about society would suggest this conclusion. In the world as Canton studied it, neither television nor radio stimulated vocabulary develop-

---

[1] Ruth H. Weir, *Language in the Crib* (London: Mouton & Co., 1962).

[2] This stage in children's language acquisition is summarized in readable fashion in Green and Petty's *Developing Language Skills in the Elementary Schools* (Boston: Allyn and Bacon, 1971), pp. 63–84. This meticulously researched book with many helpful references is particularly strong in the area of sequential development of language skills.

[3] Ruth G. Strickland, *The Language Arts in the Elementary School* (Lexington, Mass.: D. C. Heath and Co., 1969), p. 87. The section on language growth in the preschool years (pp. 71–103) is a particularly strong one. The section on individual differences is unusual in books of this kind and should be of help to a teacher with atypical children in his room.

Research Studies on Size of Children's Vocabularies

Year Done	*Sample*	*# of Words*	*Researcher*
1897	6 year olds	2,000	Canton
1912	6 year olds	2,500	Terman and Childs
1926	6 year olds	2,562	Madorah E. Smith
1936	First-grade children	2,703	F. W. Dolch
1941	First-grade children	24,000	Mary K. Smith
1957	6 year olds	14,500	Templin
1959	First-grade children	26,363	Shibles
1960	Kindergarten children	3,728	Kolson
1964	First-grade children	12,456	Ames

ment.[4] Books were expensive and scarce—it was a rare child who grew up in an environment providing this stimulus. Further, travel was severely limited so exposure to new ideas and people (consequently to new words) was also limited. Certainly it would be difficult not to agree today that a child's perceptual field is considerably more rich than was that of a child of seventy-five years ago.

Second, it is likely that children come to school with a larger part of their vocabulary made up of words acquired *vicariously*—words for ideas, phenomena, and objects they have never experienced directly. For example, by watching television children may have acquired the ability to use such words as *module, translunar*, and *escape velocity*. Whether the children "know" such words or are simply able to repeat them in context in a superficial way is a matter to be determined by each teacher.[5] It is undoubtedly true that the presence of a large store of vicariously acquired words necessitates a different approach to teaching vocabulary than in other times when more of a child's vocabulary was learned through direct experience.

---

[4] Since television has become an integral part of American life, several researchers have explored its effect on learning. George E. Mason, "Children Learn Words from Commercial TV," *Elementary School Journal* 65 (March 1965): 318–20, studied the relationship between TV and vocabulary growth. He concluded that poor readers gained less vocabulary from watching TV than did good readers.

[5] Dale has clearly defined this problem in an article describing procedures for measuring vocabulary size. (See "Vocabulary Measurement," *Elementary English*, December 1965, pp. 895–901.) To be able to define a word is obviously a different type of skill than being able to choose the correct definition from among several.

Types of Vocabulary

The most typical approach to describing a child's stock of words is to discuss four major vocabularies: those of reading, speaking, writing, and listening (or recognition). While such finite categories are useful for discussion purposes, obviously the areas of overlap are many and the distinctions between vocabularies are blurred.

A child's *speaking* vocabulary is of the most utility to the most children so it will be considered first. As mentioned in the chapter on oral language, we communicate most frequently in speech. Because this is so, a prime concern for the teacher should be to develop, extend, or expand the child's speaking vocabulary.

As the young child grows, correction is constant while he is developing a speaking vocabulary. Despite this correction, usually done by parents in incidental and frequently noncensorious ways, many children use oral language with a fluency adults envy. Preschool children experiment with language, fearlessly try new forms, use new words, and in general feel at home with words.[6] A teacher's role in expanding the oral vocabulary is to increase the stock of words a child can use, while maintaining this fluent approach to speaking.

A child's *listening* vocabulary is intimately related to his speaking vocabulary. This vocabulary becomes increasingly more important as the proportion of each day we spend in listening increases. As we gather a larger percentage of information from listening, the skill of determining word meaning from an oral context becomes more crucial. As is apparent, this is a more sophisticated skill than determining word meaning from print, because while listening we have little time and cannot reconsider and reflect upon words as we can in written context.

Once spoken, the ephemeral words are gone and subtle distinctions, especially of mood or feeling, disappear. We can examine the writer's intent and explore his implications in leisure. No such luxury exists with listening, so expanding this vocabulary is crucial.

A child's *reading* vocabulary, of concern to so many people for such a long time, is the one a child will use almost constantly during his school career. Because of this, a teacher's obligation includes expanding the vocabulary a child can cope with in print.

---

[6] James Bostain comments upon this fearless approach to using language in a delightful series of videotapes entitled *English—Fact and Fancy* (available from National Center for School and College Television, Bloomington, Indiana). A psycholinguist, Bostain's pragmatic approach and dry wit enliven this series which provides much information about language and related misconceptions.

The smallest of the vocabularies, the *writing* vocabulary, is probably also of most limited utility to the majority of school students. Though some of us take delight in finding exactly the right word for the right spot to convey the precise shade of meaning we intend, for the majority of school children, writing will seldom be such an endeavor. This is probably appropriate, considering the small percentage of adults in our society whose careers demand an extensive written vocabulary.

The Need for Vocabulary Development

Considering the size of children's vocabularies when they come to school, why is it important that the teacher concern himself with this aspect of a child's language? If vocabulary develops to this extent before school, can't we consider it a relatively unimportant item of consideration for the teacher? For two reasons, the answer to these rhetorical questions must be no.

First, vocabulary correlates most reliably with success in school. It is important to notice that in the previous sentence, the words read "success in school."

It is apparent that success in life may well be predicated on factors unrelated to size of vocabulary. There are many capable adults who function well on the 500 words on the Horn list, plus a small technical vocabulary related to their field.[7] Given our compulsory school attendance laws, however, and this relation between vocabulary and success in school, the teacher's role becomes clear. Children are required to remain in school and the teacher must do everything possible to excite children about and arouse their interest in words, in order to ensure the children's success in school.

Ames has stated:

> Experiments have shown that vocabulary size is probably the best single index for predicting achievement in nearly all the other language skills.[8]

Ames is considering success in other language arts, but beyond this, we also have evidence that vocabulary size is related to success in other academic areas.

---

[7] As a result of his investigations, Ernest Horn determined that the adult who knows these 500 words will know 99 percent of the words he needs to know, on the basis of words used most frequently. See *A Basic Writing Vocabulary* (Iowa City: State University of Iowa, 1926).

[8] Wilbur S. Ames, "The Understanding Vocabulary of First-Grade Pupils," *Elementary English* (January 1964): 64–68.

Petty has stated:

> In the classroom the achieving students possess the most adequate vocabularies. Because of the verbal nature of most classroom activities, knowledge of words and ability to use language are essential to success in these activities.[9]

A *second* reason for concern on the part of teachers is the increasing rate of language change. Linguists have known for some time that a distinctive feature of any living language is change. As it is used, modified, added to, subtracted from, and in other ways altered, the language becomes unintelligible to speakers of a few hundred years earlier.[10]

Though change as an aspect of language has been noticed and commented upon before, it is a student of our culture rather than a linguist who has summed up the startling *increase* in rate of change which now characterizes English. Alvin Toffler has commented that "of the estimated 450,000 'usable' words in the English language today, only perhaps 250,000 would be comprehensible to William Shakespeare." Thus, in an interval of only about 350 years, if he were "suddenly to materialize in London or New York today, he would be able to understand on the average, only five out of every nine words in our vocabulary. The Bard would be a semiliterate."[11]

This rapid rate of change in language can easily lead to a rather particular danger in vocabulary learning, that of incomplete understanding. Graff discovered, for example, that a group of children with which she worked had indeed "learned" some words. That is, they had learned to recognize some word forms when they appeared on a list. Their learning was limited, however, to the word's commercial use. She gave children the following words, from among others:

mars	lark
mound	dove
crest	raid

---

[9] Walter T. Petty et al., *The State of Knowledge about the Teaching of Vocabulary* (Champaign: The National Council of Teachers of English, 1968), p. 7. This report presents an examination of current teaching practices, an analysis of several studies of vocabulary teaching, and recommendations for more effective teaching in the area; it is concise and readable.

[10] A source of material which makes this principle dramatically evident is *Leaflets on Historical Linguistics,* published by N.C.T.E. (1967). Though the text is too advanced to use with children, the illustrations of pages from such authors as Shakespeare and such works as Beowulf can be used with younger children to augment a study of how language changes.

[11] Alvin Toffler, *Future Shock* (New York: Bantam Books, 1970), pp. 169–72. There is only a small section on language in this provocative book, but it makes stimulating reading as a commentary on our society in general.

From children's responses to the test, she discovered that they knew the words as trade names, but were unfamiliar with the common noun aspect of the words.[12]

An alert teacher needs to be aware of such incomplete understanding of the multiple meanings of words, in order to expand a child's sense of words. Some suggestions about this will be made in the next section.

Encouraging Vocabulary Growth

The key to vocabulary growth, as with so many areas in language arts, is the teacher's own interest. If you were reading, what would your reaction be if you saw the following: *olio, shaggymane, demijohn,* or *nevus?* Would they arouse your curiosity so that you'd want to investigate in order to find out what they mean? If so, you'll probably be able to share that curiosity about words with the children you teach.

The teacher whose curiosity about words sends him with frequency to a dictionary to learn a new word, or a new meaning of a familiar word, is one who can set a positive example for his children. The teacher sets this example in several ways.

1. The first way is by using words without curtailing choice because of difficulty. That is, if *apprehensive* comes to mind, use it. Don't substitute *afraid.* If *courageous* comes to your mind, don't substitute *brave.* This approach necessitates defining the word you have used and there are several ways this can be done. You may simply define it, saying for example: "When Dave came home from Crazy Kate's he was very *apprehensive,* or afraid, of what his dad would say."[13] Or you may give an example. You might say, in using *courageous:* "Remember how Swimmy felt when he was leading the rest of the fish in chasing away the Tunas? That's right, he felt very strong and powerful and brave. Another word for that is courageous."[14] These are probably the two simplest ways of defining a word. Another device you can use is modification. For example, "The light blue

---

[12] Virginia A. Graff, "Plenty of Words," *Elementary School Journal* 68 (October 1967): 9–12. A research report indicating quite conclusively that children frequently can respond on a verbal level, but that real understanding of both words and phrases may elude them.

[13] Emily Neville, *It's Like This, Cat* (New York: Scholastic Book Services, 1963).

[14] Leo Lionni, *Swimmy* (New York: Pantheon, 1963).

color, *azure,* is the most interesting one." You can also use restatement. You could say: "The woman was *frenzied.* Her overwrought state of nervous activity was obvious."[15]

2. Another way the teacher develops interest in words is to have a variety of dictionaries available for children to use. This variety should include several different levels and several different types. Certainly the archaic practice of buying thirty copies of one publisher's dictionary does not encourage the kind of curiosity about words which we are trying to develop. Children enjoy comparing what different dictionaries say about a particular word and learn by being exposed to the sometimes subtle differences in etymology, pronunciation, syllabication, and definition which exist. *Etymological* differences are apparent, for instance, in the word *tom-tom.* One dictionary reports it is of barbaric Eastern origin, while another traces it back to Hindi. *Pronunciation* differences are apparent when we compare /nup shal/ with nup shal/, variations of the word *nuptial. Syllabication* differences show up when we check the words. One dictionary, for example, divides *leisure* as lēzh-r, while another divides it lē′shər Similarly, one elementary dictionary divides *fusion* as fū′zhən, while another divides it as fyüzh′n. *Definition* differences are apparent in the following entries for the term *man Friday:* 1. "a male administrative assistant with diverse duties," and 2. "a person wholly subservient to another, a servile follower." In this case, the connotations are completely different, and children's understanding of the term is enriched by exploring such differences. Even the very youngest children can now be encouraged to turn to dictionaries, as several companies have been manufacturing dictionaries with few words and many pictures.[16] Children who have only one type of dictionary to use may miss the richness of meaning accessible to them when several dictionaries are consulted. An informal examination of dic-

---

[15] These and other ways of defining in context to encourage language growth are discussed at length in Lee C. Deighton's *Vocabulary Development in the Classroom* (New York: Teachers College Press, 1959). An extremely helpful book to any teacher who wants to develop vocabulary strength.

[16] See for example W. Cabell Greet et al., *My Pictionary* and *My First Picture Dictionary* (New York: Lothrop, Lee & Shepard, 1970). The first is a vividly illustrated collection of common objects which are clearly labeled. The second deals with 800 words of high utility in a colorful format. Others appropriate for young children include Wendell W. Wright's *The Rainbow Dictionary* (Cleveland: The World Publishing Co., 1959), Aldren A. Watson's *Very First Words for Writing and Spelling* (New York: Holt, Rinehart & Winston, 1966), Dilla Mac-

tionaries now available reveals this problem. If a third-grade teacher were using the primary level of one of the best-selling children's dictionaries, his children would be limited to seven meanings of the word *cool*. By having a few copies of the intermediate level of that dictionary available, his children would encounter five additional meanings. A copy of the junior level of the same dictionary adds an additional meaning. Having copies of a different manufacturer's intermediate dictionary will add two different meanings, while yet a third manufacturer's product adds another meaning. By having three manufacturers dictionaries, at three levels, the teacher is free to examine a total of sixteen different meanings of this word.

3. The teacher uses and encourages children to use other resource books. There are now thesauruses available on children's levels, though teachers of intermediate grades report good response to adult thesauruses.[17] Investing in an inexpensive paperback thesaurus nets valuable returns in increased vocabulary size and more effective creative writing.

4. By minimizing the importance of correct spelling in written work, the teacher encourages children to use words which may already be in their speaking vocabulary but not in their writing vocabulary. Children can experiment more freely in adding words to their oral vocabulary, simply because knowledge of the peculiarities of how a word is spelled is unimportant in speech. This is not, unfortunately, true in writing. Because of this, the teacher stresses from the first written assignment of the year the idea that in the initial stages of composition, children are free to experiment with whatever words they want to use. Attention to correct representation of the sounds in writing can come later—after the child has gained courage by using the word in compositions.

The Reading Way to Vocabulary

Many benefits were claimed in the chapter on creative writing for reading aloud to children, but it is necessary to reintroduce the topic

Bean's *Picture Book Dictionary* (Chicago: Children's Press, 1962), and P. D. Eastman's *The Cat in the Hat Beginner Book Dictionary* (New York: Random House, 1964).

[17] The eye-catching format of W. Cabell Greet et al., *In Other Words* (Chicago: Scott, Foresman & Co., 1968) makes this thesaurus for children a delight to see.

here in order to point out that children's vocabulary increases as they read and are read to by the teacher.

Whitehead states the role of reading in vocabulary development in the following way:

> Teachers who read to boys and girls . . . will, in the process, expose them to the full beauty and flavor of the English language. The teaching need not be overt, for casual references to a particular word or phrase will often do. Indeed, children often recognize immediately a particularly melodious, rhythmic or emotional word or phrase . . . and thousands of . . . such language elements have been memorized instantly by children.[18]

As the teacher shares books with children, he sets the stage for each book and can do some incidental vocabulary teaching. In introducing Homer Price, the characterization of Homer as *perplexed* when he couldn't get the donut machine to shut off will pique the children's interest. After the teacher has read the chapter to children, there will be no problem in their understanding the word *perplexed*.[19]

With a little work by the teacher, the children can understand what *querulous* means after an encounter with Mole in *The Wind in the Willows*,[20] what *imperious* means after meeting Mary Poppins,[21] what *addled* means after hearing about the Peterkins,[22] and what *pugnacious* means after running into Harriet the Spy.[23]

In addition to the use a teacher makes of vocabulary in introducing or discussing a selection with children, the words used in the story itself will broaden children's understanding. McCloskey uses the following words in his story:[24]

---

[18] Robert Whitehead, *Children's Literature: Strategies of Teaching* (Englewood Cliffs: Prentice-Hall, 1968), p. 81. Teachers will find the leisure-time activity poll included in this book of use in assessing children's reading interests. The list of Juvenile Book Clubs (pp. 49–51) is a helpful resource, as is the sample unit which shows how to develop thinking processes through literature.

[19] Robert McCloskey, *Homer Price* (New York: The Viking Press, 1949). A delightfully comic series of misadventures happen to the hero, Homer. A rather bucolic, small-town setting, unfamiliar to many children, but the humor makes it an unforgettable book.

[20] Kenneth Grahame, *The Wind in the Willows* (New York: Charles Scribner's Sons, 1960).

[21] P. L. Travers, *Mary Poppins* (New York: Reynal & Hitchcock, 1934).

[22] Lucretia P. Hale, *The Peterkin Papers* (Ann Arbor: University Microfilms, Inc., 1966).

[23] Louise Fitzhugh, *Harriet The Spy* (New York: Harper & Row, Publishers, 1964).

[24] McCloskey, *Homer Price.*

"Then the sherrif got *riled*."

"That music has *pixied* these children."

"and provide the *diversion* that the trotting races have."

"Neatest trick of *merchandising* I ever seen."

"The after shave lotion with the *invigorating* smell. . . ."

Children's Independent Reading

As children choose books to read independently, the teacher must avoid the temptation to guide children to choose books on the basis of reading level. It is true that some children with reading problems will need help in selection, to avoid undue frustration because of lack of success in reading books they choose themselves.

On the other hand, for the majority of readers, interest is a more crucial determinant of a child's ability to read a particular book. Since the major purpose of independent reading should be to develop interest in, indeed compulsion for, reading, bringing a child together with a book of interest to him is more important than getting a book on the "right" reading level.

Because the child is highly motivated to read the book he has chosen, the new vocabulary in it will not usually present any major problems. In addition, because he is not limited to books on his reading "level," the child is likely to encounter many new and interesting vocabulary words.

Direct Experiences

There are three types of direct experiences the teacher utilizes because he knows that a word experienced is more likely to be retained than one which is simply encountered on paper.

First, the teacher provides direct experiences with *objects*. Children who have enjoyed cutting open and then eating the succulent flesh of a persimmon or marveling over the treasure of seeds in a pomegranate will seldom have difficulty remembering the words. Children who have explored the surface of pique and percale with the tips of their fingers while their eyes are closed will not have trouble remembering which is which. Any child who has tried to describe the difference in smell between petunias and pansies will have little trouble remembering those words.

Second, the teacher provides contacts with *people* in order to enrich vocabulary. A logical way to do this is in conjunction with the

social studies program. Teachers can be imaginative enough to go beyond the usual mundane units which provide contact with the nurse,
the policeman, and the mailman. Children are no longer challenged by
this tired array of "community helpers." They would be excited to
learn about bobbins, boat shuttles, woof and warp from a weaver;
about prophylaxis, amalgam carriers and wiggle-bugs from a dentist;
about perlite, nodal points and friable soil from a gardner. The use of
resource people in a classroom can greatly extend the vocabulary learning of children in a painless way. An additional advantage of contact
with such resource people is the logical need for practical writing, as
the children write letters to ask guests to visit the classroom and write
thank-you letters after the experience.

Third, a teacher uses encounters in *environments* to encourage
vocabulary development. In addition to having resource people come
to the classroom, the teacher frequently takes children to another location, for on-the-spot learning and vocabulary extension.

A third-grade class enjoyed learning about the job of an architect.
As they toured the office, the children encountered the words *elevation,
perspective, facade, flemish bond,* and *travertine* in a way which made
it easy to remember what the words meant.

Another trip, to a large hotel as part of a study of community
economics, provided a contact with processes (sauteeing) and equipment (quartz ovens and buffalo choppers). Children were fascinated to
see how a professional kitchen is operated and this contact further encouraged their interest in words.

It is important to emphasize that all this experience with unusual
words has a specific purpose: to kindle interest in vocabulary. Its purpose is *not* to add, through study and testing, such arcane words to the
child's vocabulary; few would have any use for such words. The value
of such experiences lies in the stimulation they provide to the student.
These unusual words, some mysterious, some "funny" sounding, some
euphonious, will take root in children's imaginations and keep alive an
interest in and fascination with new words.

Studying Word Parts

The previous suggestions have been aimed primarily at developing
a wide-ranging interest in and curiosity about words. There is, in
addition, place in the language-arts program for more structured
approaches to teaching vocabulary.

One good way to help children broaden their vocabulary is to share with them one of the basic building processes of English, the affixes. Affixes are of three types: prefixes, suffixes, and infixes. Understanding how this word-construction technique works will be of much value to students. Most teachers do something about exposing children to this vocabulary-expansion technique. There are, however, some qualifications which need to be made on how this is most effectively done. It is not as simple as telling children that the prefix *de* means "of" or "from."

Deighton treats this subject very completely in his book, and a few key ideas are included here to help a teacher improve his techniques.[25] The problem with this approach is that there are two dangers in applying the technique. The first is that one may be dealing with a word whose affix is absorbed; that is, the affix no longer means what it meant originally. The de- of desolate no longer means what de- usually means today. Similarly, the pre- of precept or premium, no longer mean what pre- usually means today. The child may be misled if he tries to apply the common or usual meaning of the affix to these words, among others. The second problem is that some words may look like they contain an affix, but they actually do not (for example: the de- of decoy).

In either of these cases, the child will be misled if he tries to apply literally the too often very limited information he has about affixes and how they work.

After extended analysis of English vocabulary, Deighton has offered some suggestions about which affixes should be taught, because of their high utility. He suggests teaching the following list because these 26 will unlock meaning in more than 200 current English words.

anthropo-	hydro-	phil- or philo-
auto-	iso-	phono-
biblio-	lith-	photo-
bio-	micro-	pneumo
centro- centri-	mono-	poly
cosmo-	neuro-	proto-
heter- or hetero-	omni-	pseudo-
homo-	pan-	tele-
	penta-	uni-

[25] Reprinted by permission of the publisher from Lee C. Deighton, *Vocabulary Development in the Classroom.* (New York: Teachers College Press, copyright 1959 by Teachers College, Columbia University), pp. 26, 30 and 31.

The following nine prefixes will help unlock the meaning of 650 words.

circum-	mal-
equi-	mis-
extra-	non-
intra-	syn-
intro-	

Noun suffixes, which always indicate an agent either living or non-living, are also of use because of their frequency of occurrence.

-eer

-ess

-grapher

-ier

-ster

-stress

-trix

Finally, Deighton recommends teaching the following adjective forms with specific and invariant values.

-est	-less
-ferous	-able (-ible, -ble)
-fic	-most
-fold	-like
-form	-ous
-genous	-ose
-scopic	-acious
-wards	-ful
-wise	

Having recommended systematic teaching of these forms, Deighton does warn of the danger in succumbing to analysis. We must remember that "The truth is that most words are more than the sum of their parts." While we give children preliminary help in investigating word meaning through study of the affixing process, we must be careful that we develop a fuller understanding of the richness and multiplicity of word meaning which is not always accessible through simple word building.[26]

Connotation and Denotation

One way to help children understand the richness of our language and develop an interest in words is to explore the idea of connotation and denotation with them. This aspect of language is another adults use regularly, and yet all too infrequently learn to manipulate consciously to make communication more effective.

When we speak of *denotative* meaning (the easier of the two to define) we mean the objective reality of a situation, the physical referent without accompanying value judgments related to it, or the simple and uncomplicated tangible aspects of something.

When we speak of *connotative* meaning (the more difficult term to define) we mean that halo of accumulated meaning, elusive because it refers less to the physical reality and more to our attitudes, perceptions, and feelings about something. Connotative meaning frequently is linked to past feelings or impressions which may remain below the level of consciousness but which, nonetheless, affect how we react to things, people, and ideas.

Some elementary series do a good job of introducing this idea to children,[27] but if your series does not, you may want to plan a unit on these two types of meaning. You can help children see that while synonymous terms may seem to be roughly the same, their connotations make them really quite different. It has been pointed out that talkative, articulate, gossipy, garrulous, rambling, fluent, gabby, and mouthy indeed represent all points on the spectrum from favorable to unfavorable.[28]

Many words have connotations we can learn to use in order to improve language skills. We can convey innumerable shades of meaning

---

[26] See Robert J. Munnelly, "Teach That Word Meanings Are Open," *Instructor* 81, No. 7 (March 1972): 57–58.

[27] See, for example: Chapter Four, "Shades of Meaning," in *New Directions in English* (New York: Harper and Row, Publishers, 1969), Book 5, pp. 51–54; or *The World of Language* (Chicago: Follett Educational Corporation, 1970), Book 5, pp. 81–86.

[28] See Richard R. Lodwig and Eugene F. Barrett, *The Dictionary and the Language* (New York: Hayden Book Co., 1967), pp. 140–48. Though designed primarily for high school students, this well-written book contains much useful information for the teacher and can be read independently by able sixth-grade children. Most of the activities suggested can be adopted for use with elementary students.

when we choose among fat, plump, corpulent, portly, pudgy, stout, obese, and chubby. We even find that people of this physiognomy have been called Rubenseque, after the great Flemish painter whose taste ran to women of ample proportions.[29]

It is a simple procedure when children are involved in creative writing to refer them to one of the thesauruses which are available so they can choose the word with precisely the shade of meaning they wish to convey. After he has introduced the thesaurus and explained how it works, the teacher may reasonably expect that, with practice, the children will become adept in using this tool to help them select from among a variety of words the one which exactly conveys the connotation they want.

Etymological Exploration

One effective way to make words come alive for children and incidentally to help them remember words they encounter is to encourage etymological exploration. Whereas the term *etymology* may sound dull, once children discover the fascinating quirks and peculiarities which lie hidden in the background of even common words, they will become intrigued with the study of word origins. Once they discover the strange original meanings of some words, it will be easier to remember what the word currently means, because the contrast is so sharp.

Two well-known examples will serve as a beginning. When a child says something is *nice*, send him to the dictionary to discover that originally this now-pallid word meant foolish or ignorant. Similarly, we discover that *fond* has its origins in the Middle-English word for foolish.

For many common English words, an examination of origins reveals interesting information. It is surprising to discover that *foyer* originally meant a room with a fireplace. It is easy to remember the word if one thinks about the guests in a French chateau coming in from a cold carriage ride and stopping in the first room they entered to warm themselves at the fire in the foyer. Similarly, it is easy to remember what *recalcitrant* means if one can visualize in the mind its original meaning: the ox kicking back in rebellion—an interesting etymology hidden in the passage of years.

---

[29] If you've not seen a painting by Rubens, find one and see which of the words included above describes the women in the painting most accurately.

In talking about creative writing with children, I wanted to get across the idea of being *succinct*, that is, saying clearly and concisely and in a minimum of words what they had to say. The original meaning of the word is tucking something up out of sight where it won't show. When the children visualized tucking up all the extra words and sentences which were unnecessary to their compositions, they could indeed learn to be succinct.

Does all of the foregoing seem a bit farfetched perhaps and straining to make etymology relevant to children? That may be, but such use of etymological information found in dictionaries is another way to breathe life into words.

Alerting children to the etymologies of words and the aid these can be in remembering what a word currently means can be done in informal fashion as a new word occurs, simply by sending children to the several different dictionaries available in the room. Or, one may develop a unit on etymology to use with children. Few language-arts textbooks for children do much with this idea, though one series is a helpful exception to this statement.[30]

In all these examples, the intent is not that children should be called upon to memorize etymologies. Rather, the purpose of this exploration and resulting discussion is simply to pique children's interest, and in some cases to give them a "memory-hook" or means for remembering the current meaning of a word.

Studying Word Geography

An easily accessible area of exploration for children is word geography, more technically called *dialect* study. The teacher plans experiences in word geography because these experiences abet the teacher's as well as the children's desire to expand vocabulary. One can easily examine with children idiolects, local and regional dialects, and the slang of particular groups.

Children enjoy collecting examples of *idiolects*, their own or those of their families. After that, exploration of *local* words can be made. For example, children in Minneapolis wait at a bus *wye*, and, if driven to school, see parents stop at the *semaphore* until the light changes to

---

[30] Undoubtedly the series for children which does the most with etymology is Paul Roberts et al., *The Roberts English Series* (New York: Harcourt Brace Jovanovich, 1970). Each of the books presents several sections dealing with this topic. Even if the books are not used in your school, you can order single copies and extract the etymological sections to use in a unit.

green. Natives of some parts of Indiana go to farmers' markets in the summer to buy *mangos,* not the yellowish-red succulent tropical fruit usually called by that name, but rather the common bell or green pepper.

There are, in addition, regional words which are interesting to study. Marckwardt, for example, points out the regional manifestation of sweet corn as opposed to roasting ear, gutters as opposed to spouting, and sick *to* his stomach as opposed to sick *at* his stomach.[31] These and literally thousands of other choices can be pinpointed with specificity by dialect experts who have devoted much time to defining regional boundaries.

In a day of rapidly increasing population mobility, a teacher may often have children from several different geographic areas in his classroom. Such linguistic checklists of regional expressions as the one included by Shuy can be used to motivate interest in dialect vocabulary.[32]

In addition to words, students of language geography have noted some sentence constructions, or syntactical variations, peculiar to an area. A bemused new resident of Indiana comments on the following usages which she discovered to her surprise were accepted as standard English in this locale.

"That's because they have so many traffic signs anymore."

"Anymore, the girls wear slacks to class."

"I would like for you to do this."

"I'll have him to call you."

As she points out, such constructions exist in colloquial standard usage in some areas, but students need to be aware that they are localized, and may be scrutinized skeptically elsewhere.[33]

The *slang* terminology of particular groups, which is often not shared by a community in general, is also of interest. Students at one university at which I taught go to "call-outs," organizational meetings held at the beginning of a school year. They complain about classes in

---

[31] Albert H. Marckwardt, "Principal and Subsidiary Dialect Areas in the North Central States," in *Readings in Applied English Linguistics,* ed. Harold B. Allen (New York: Appleton-Century-Crofts, 1964), pp. 220–30.

[32] See Roger W. Shuy, *Discovering American Dialects* (Champaign: National Council of Teachers of English, 1967), pp. 17–24. This paperback provides an easily accessible introduction to the topic of dialect differences.

[33] Betty W. Robinett, "Applications of Linguistics to the Teaching of Oral English," in *Readings in the Language Arts,* eds. V. D. and P. S. Anderson (New York: The Macmillan Co., 1968), pp. 32–39.

rooms far across the campus, assigned by "schedule deputies"—using the word deputy in a way other than it is generally used. Some of the girls become "lavaliered," the preliminary stage to becoming engaged, which involves receiving the university seal or the letters of the boy's fraternity to wear on a chain around her neck.

Many groups have developed these specialized slang "languages," or at least certain specific and unusual uses of words. Children will delight in searching for examples of them.[34]

The Magic of Names

Beginning the school year with a study of children's names, which can then lead to some examination of place names, is an easy way to launch children into a study of words. Their own names hold a fascination for children, and both standard "meanings" of names and family reasons for name choices can be researched and discussed.[35]

In addition to personal names, place names can be studied. From one end of the country to the other, residents of unusually (and sometimes bizarrely) named places are fascinated by the names of their towns. Children find place names especially interesting to study. Whether one is teaching in Riddle, Oregon, or Horatio, South Carolina; Sleepy Eye, Minnesota, or Sour Lake, Texas, the lure of place-name study is the same.

Place-name study can be correlated with *social studies* when one explores the various city names in one's own state or the origin of the state name.[36] A study of cities named by Indians, the Spanish, or French explorers can also be rewarding. It can correlate with *history* as, for example, when one studies the spread of classically named cities across our continent. This classical influence spread as far as Athens, Texas; Attica, Ohio; Corinth, Mississippi; Delphi, Indiana; Rome, Illinois; and

---

[34] You might find *Truck Drivers Dictionary and Glossary* (Jean M. Walker, compiler. Available from American Trucking Association, 1616 P Street, N.W., Washington, D.C.) of interest to your children. A three-part paperback devoted to jargon, illustrations, and terminology children seldom encounter.

[35] There are so many books on the origins and meanings of names that the teacher will have no trouble locating these in any library. In addition, see Appendix 1 in Chapter 3, the letter to parents eliciting information about the child's name.

[36] Pauline Arnold and Percival White, *How We Named Our States* (New York: Criterion Books, 1965). One resource with which you might begin is this volume, which moves chronologically from east to west. Given the limited space available for each state, the writing is quite effective in stimulating interest.

Sparta, Wisconsin. The widespread use of classical names occurred at a particular stage in our country's history and the reasons for such naming can be investigated. Or such study may be undertaken simply as a language-arts activity, for instance, when children study city names to find the longest, the shortest, the most or least phonetic, those derived from people's names, or from words for geographical formations.

In studying local or area names, older residents can be interviewed who may have been present when the names were chosen (or changed, as so often happens). This activity, including planning questions before and writing reports after the interview, helps increase children's interviewing skills.

In studying more remote names, two sources exist. Children may write to the Chambers of Commerce requesting information. This helps provide practice in letter-writing skills. In doing this activity for several semesters with a college methods class, we have experienced between 65 percent and 89 percent response to our letters of inquiry.

It is wise to suggest to children that they write to larger cities, avoiding those tiny settlements which may have a very picturesque name, but may not have a Chamber of Commerce. Even when so warned, children frequently insist on writing to villages, and we have been delighted by responses from librarians, postmasters, operators of the only store in town, ministers, and in one case, a train station master.

In addition to such primary sources, children can go to the books which are available about this topic.[37] There are many of these which the teacher may use to augment the primary sources which children will consult.

Developing Precision

After a teacher has built an interest in words and can see children using and learning new words with vigor, he will probably want to turn his attention to developing an understanding of the precise use of words.

This must be explained further to prevent such a statement from conjuring up unfortunately repressive visions of our own former English teachers. Too many of us began our study of English with teachers who demanded one answer, who were anxious to distinguish between

---

[37] Isaac Asimov, *Words on the Map* (Boston: Houghton Mifflin, 1962). This is another one of the intellectually sound and fascinating books so typical of Asimov's writing. It deals with areas (New England) countries (Greece), states (Tennessee) and cities (Louisville) and in short compass (1 page) gives us a well-researched account of how each came to be named.

right and wrong. The issue of precision is quite different and a valuable one for the child to encounter. That is, being able to choose the word which says precisely what the *chooser* wants to say is an enviable language skill. Too frequently, because of our own imprecise use of words, we give children the impression, albeit unintentionally, that many more words are synonyms than really are.

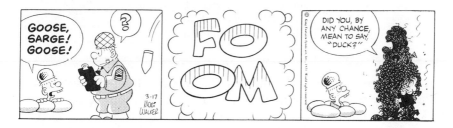

Reprinted by permission of King Features Syndicate Division

Think about your own use of language. Do you use the word *unique*, when unusual is what you really mean? Have you ever used *sad*, when the emotion you were trying to express was a more complex and specific one than that catchall term could express? If so, perhaps your own language precision needs a modicum of attention.

Developing precision in language is not a difficult task, if you can sense opportunities as they arise and work on them. When children use overworked and imprecise terms, it's a simple task to stop, take a few minutes to explore some alternative and more expressive terms, and wonder again at the variety English allows us.

A classroom teacher describes such an activity she initiated with her children when she sensed an overdependence on the word *said*, in her children's writing.[38] After searching for alternatives to the word, alternatives which pinned down more precisely *how* the word was said, the class came up with 104 alternatives, ranging from answered to yelled.

In a similar fashion, the last time I taught sixth graders, we explored the variety of ways one could describe emotion when so many of them were *mad* at one another. We searched for a week, checking with dic-

---

[38] Included in *Guide to Teaching in the Elementary Language Arts* (Charlotte, North Carolina: Charlotte-Mecklenburg Public Schools, 1966), p. 43. Recommended by NCTE as an excellent curriculum guide, this helpful publication, which can be ordered directly from the school district, offers many suggestions about interesting ways to study words.

tionaries, books, families, listening carefully to radio and television, and came up with the following list:

angry	enraged
annoyed	infuriated
perturbed	furious
disgruntled	provoked
"put out"	irritated
frustrated	wrathful
indignant	"ticked-off"
peeved	

At the end of the week when we shared our list, we discussed the rather subtle shades of meaning these terms can convey. We were not looking for right or wrong, and we discovered there were some interesting differences of opinion among students about exact meanings of some of the terms. The exploration proved to be a worthwhile experience which made the multiplicity of language more apparent to this group of children.

Tiedt and Tiedt recommend doing a similar sort of activity using color words, which develops both a color sense and a vocabulary to describe colors.[39] Children, unfortunately, often do not develop the visual sensitivity and the language skill to perceive and describe colors in their environment in ways which would enrich their experience. For children without this ability, such an activity as the Tiedts describe could be very helpful.

The foregoing has assumed, if tacitly, group participation in activities. There are times, however, when a teacher's concern is helping a particular individual improve his mastery of a particular word, by making its meaning more specific.

Pinning Down Meaning

A helpful way of thinking about this problem has been described by Dale, in an article on different ways of "knowing" a word.[40] It is

---

[39] Iris M. Tiedt and Sidney W. Tiedt, *Contemporary English in the Elementary School* (Englewood Cliffs, N.J.: Prentice-Hall, 1967), p. 55. The authors' suggestion for expanding children's color sense and word competency involves looking for words and making up lists of color varieties. Related to red, children might come up with cherry, vermillion, rose, ruby, scarlet, flame, and crimson. A similar approach can be used with all colors.

[40] Edgar Dale, "Vocabulary Measurement: Techniques and Major Findings," *Elementary English* (December 1965): 895–901.

his contention that knowledge of a word can be arranged on a continuum, as described below:

1st stage:	2nd stage:	3rd stage:	4th stage:	5th stage:
"I never saw it before."	"I know there is such a word, but I don't know what it means."	Vague contextual placing, also called the "twilight zone."	The word is pinned down.	Precise refining of differences.

Some examples help illustrate this idea. For most of us, *fundular* belongs in Stage One. To understand it, we would need to look it up in a dictionary.

Stage Two might include such terms as *hugger-mugger* and *laser*. We've heard them at one time or another, but cannot fit them with appropriate referents.

Stage Three could include such terms as *hustings* (it has something to do with elections) and *bask* (it relates to the sun).

Stage Four words are those which we recognize and can both use and define because the meaning is established in our minds.

Stage Five represents further refinement and development of the concept. Some people reach this stage, for example, in their use of *sympathy* and *empathy*, two words separated very subtly by a small but precise shade of difference.

The teacher's job is to help children continue moving words from Stage One to Stage Five. This is done by providing many experiences in which the child can encounter the word in concrete manifestation.

In closing, it is important to reemphasize that the focus of this section is not on a *teacher* deciding right or wrong, but on the *child* selecting more appropriate words to convey precisely the shade of meaning he wishes to express. Such is a sophisticated language skill, but one which can be encouraged by the teacher aware of the rewards of precision.

Vocabulary Games

As with other of the language arts, vocabulary learning can be greatly facilitated through the judicious use of games.[41] The teacher

---

[41] The section on games (pp. 373–76) in Mildred R. Donoghue, *The Child and the English Language Arts* (Dubuque, Iowa: William C. Brown, 1971) will be of interest.

chooses these carefully, in order to make sure they are of educational value, in addition to being fun.

One advantage which many of these offer is that they require little or no material or equipment. A second advantage is that, being of short duration, they can be played in the small bits of time elementary classroom teachers frequently have but seldom utilize.

Many vocabulary games capitalize on children's delight in the ways words and sounds can be manipulated, changed, altered, and experimented with, for the simple joy such experimentation gives. Lefevre points out that interest in words and sounds begins as life begins.

> We all know that infants and children naturally learn language playfully. As they emerge from the cradle, they begin to use among themselves verbal riddles, puns, word plays, rhymes, gags of all sorts as part of their normal play.[42]

This fascination with words continues throughout childhood, a contention documented by the extensive collection of material presented by the Opies in their book.[43] Thus it is easy for the teacher to capitalize on this interest by using vocabulary games with his children. If the teacher knows several of these he can use them in the odd moments of "waiting time," for instance, just before the art teacher arrives, or after the children come back from lunch, the time when a guest speaker is five minutes later, or when part of the group isn't back from the bathroom. Such time is seldom considered or utilized but it can be put to good use by the teacher who knows several vocabulary games.

One author has suggested several games which help develop an interest in vocabulary.[44] Our results are described here, and you may want to try your luck with a group of children.

Lake describes "Hinky-Pinky," in which a definition must be answered by two rhyming words. Examples given include: an obese

---

[42] Carl A. Lefevre, "A Multidisciplinary Approach to Language and Reading: Some Projections," in *The Psycholinguistic Nature of the Reading Process*, ed. Kenneth S. Goodman (Detroit: Wayne State University Press, 1968), pp. 289–312.

[43] Iona and Peter Opie, *The Lore and Language of School Children* (London: Oxford at the Clarendon Press, 1959). The results of an extensive survey of 5000 children in over seventy schools in different parts of Great Britain, this is a compendium of the rhymes, word tricks, riddles, parody, nicknames and epithets, jeers and torments, and secret languages used by children. It may be read for its intrinsic interest, or to notice the universality of children's language: many of the forms used have American English equivalents.

[44] Mary Louise Lake, "First Aid for Vocabularies," *Elementary English* (November 1967): 783–84.

rodent (fat rat); a wet hobo (damp tramp); and profound slumber (deep sleep). Trying this with a college methods class, we elicited the following:

frigid fungus:	cold mold
elevated pig pen:	high sty
squashed chapeaux:	flat hat
rodent abode:	mouse house
thin bird:	narow sparrow

Several students in class wanted to try the idea, and from a group of fifth-grade children, they got the following results:

small evergreen:	wee tree
recorded rock group:	canned band
nodding bird:	bobbin' robin
animal's false hair:	pig wig
pale red soda:	pink drink

In addition to the games mentioned above, there are other, frequently more elaborate, games which are available from commercial manufacturers. The teacher may want to examine those which are available and select some to have for children to use in their free time.

Suggestions for Further Study

1. To become more aware of how adult writers use vocabulary, choose two whose work you enjoy and select a sample of writing from each. Analyze the two samples in any way you like, to determine what differences exist between the two writers. You might examine word length, use of compound words, amount and type of slang or nonstandard terms used, the number of different words used, different levels of speech represented, or inflected words used. After you have done this, select two children's books, and determine how these authors' use of vocabulary differs.

2. The chart on page 355 summarizing the studies of children's vocabulary at age six is incomplete. Draw up a list of the other information you would need to know to determine which of the studies you should believe. What would you need to know about the children, the procedures, the research conditions, and the data gathered, to determine which of the studies is most helpful? Then choose one of

the studies to read and find out how much of the information you need to make a decision about the study is actually included in the report of the research.

3. The Lake article suggests doing the game "Tom Swifties" with children. Methods students have created these: "I'll never be promoted in the Navy," Tom said admirably. "I'll always be a composer," Tom noted. "Which side of the penny did you call?" Tom asked flippantly. "I don't like wringer washers" Tom said crankily. Can you make up some Swifties as original as these?

4. Gather some data which you can analyze on children's vocabularies. You might tape record conversations with children at three different grade levels. Analyses might include incidence of various parts of speech, use of concrete and abstract terms, use of polysyllabic words, or use of compound words.

5. The contention was made in the chapter that the rate of language change is accelerating. A bit of linguistic detective work could reveal this. Talking with friends your own age, make up a list of words which are currently much used by your peers. Interview a group of high school students, to see which words are in wide use among them. Then ask some people your parents' age, and your grandparents' age, to make up a list of words common when they were young. Are there any which are common to all lists?

6. Graff's article (see footnote, page 359) was written in 1967. Read it to learn about her procedures, and then replicate the study with a few children to see if her conclusions also apply to your group.

7. Reference was made in the chapter to thesauruses written for children. Could you make one, using pictures from magazines? Using it with a small group of children would give you feedback about how successful you had been.

8. The material on affixes from Deighton (see page 365) could be of much help in developing vocabulary. Could you make up a game which would be fun for children to play and would, in addition, help them learn one of the lists he suggests teaching?

Bibliography

Belloc, Hilaire. *The Bad Child's Book of Beasts*. New York: Dover Publications, 1961.

Another of Dover's fine reprints, this book contains three of Belloc's small books bound as one. The whimsy of both the verse and the drawings which are reminiscent of Lear appeals to children. Vocabulary learning can be stimulated by the many unusual words the poet uses, and by contact with such unusual animals as the yak, marmozet, viper, and chamois. The last of the books, *A Moral Alphabet*, is for older children and could be used to motivate the creation of another alphabet.

Blumberg, Dorothy Rose. *Whose What?* New York: Holt, Rinehart and Winston, 1969.

Designed primarily for adult readers but accessible to older intermediate-grade children, this delightful accumulation of the odd-bits of naming in our language will capture the imagination. Such terms as Custer's Last Stand, Gresham's Law, Hudson's Bay, Jacob's Ladder, and Mary's Little Lamb are included. An unbelieveably dull format should not deter you.

Bombaugh, C. C. *Oddities and Curiosities of Words and Literature*. New York: Dover Publications, 1961.

Of use primarily as a word game source book for teachers, this reprint of an early work contains such well-known forms as palindromes and such lesser-known forms as lipogrammata. The reading is too difficult for children, but is fascinating for the teacher. The section on emblematic poetry will be of help in motivating creative writing.

Brown, Amy et al. *Dictionary* (Primary Dictionary Series). New York: Pyramid Publications, 1971.

This interesting new series includes four paperback books intended for children from five to twelve years of age. Each successive book contains, defined in greater depth, the words included in the preceding books. The illustrations are only adequate, but the inexpensive format is of much value, since each child could have his own copy.

Charlip, Remy. *Arm in Arm*. New York: Parents Magazine Press, 1969.

A winner of the AIGA Award for distinguished illustration, this unusual book which examines endless tales, reiterations, and other echolalia, is sure to delight children. After enjoying it, children may be challenged to create their own words and pictures.

Dale, Edgar, and O'Rourke, Joseph. *Techniques of Teaching Vocabulary*. Chicago: Field Educational Publications, 1971.

This book contends that systematic study of organized groups of words is needed in instructional programs. The chief contribution of the book is the variety and expressiveness of the word groups put togther for the interested teacher. Teaching suggestions are provided for most of the word groups. Chapters are devoted to suffixes, roots, synonyms and antonyms. Attention is also given to such other aspects of word study as figures of speech, semantic sources of confusion, and word games.

Epstein, Sam, and Epstein, Beryl. *The First Book of Words*. New York: Franklin Watts, 1954.

The book contains historical information, a section on the first writing, the growth of the alphabet, English in the new world and borrowed words. Children will enjoy the sections on "stuck-together" words and tricks with words.

Margaret S. Ernst. *Words*. New York: Alfred A. Knopf, 1957.

Ernst's book makes fascinating reading for a child not bothered by its lack of illustrations. She deals with such topics as roots, accent, slang, and suffixes. Historical information is included in chapters on The Angles, The Norman Conquest and Modern English. The chapters on derivation of words are particularly well done.

Ferguson, Charles W. *The Abecedarian Book*. Boston: Little, Brown and Co., 1964.

Large, elegantly designed full-page letters introduce the esoteric words for which they stand. The drawings, in fine red line, illustrate the unusual words, which range from antediluvian to zoological. A thoroughly delightful book for older children.

Fitzgerald, Cathleen. *Let's Find Out about Words*. New York: Franklin Watts 1971.

Though it covers much the same ground as other beginner's books about words, the writing style and the crisp illustrations in this book recommend it. The origin of words from other countries, the creation of new English words, and a brief examination of how words sound (e.g., "crash is a noisy word") is included.

Funk, Charles Earle. *A Hog on Ice* (1948) and *Heavens to Betsy!* New York: Harper and Row, Publishers, 1955.

Two from among several captivating books written by Funk which detail the peculiarities of English, these are valuable desk references for the teacher to use in explaining the unusual phrases which mean more than the literal meaning. Includes such common (but little understood) phrases as: to bell the cat, a Bronx cheer, a hair of the dog that bit you, and catch as catch can.

Garrison, Webb B. *Why You Say It*. New York: Abingdon Press, 1955.

This invaluable paperback provides the teacher with a wealth of information about unusual words and phrases. The explanations, seldom over half a page long, detail in easily readable fashion the history and derivation of the word. Words and phrases are arranged by categories, but the index helps locate specific words for which one is searching.

George, Mary Yanaga. *Language Art*. Scranton: Chandler Publishing Co., 1970.

The book is a convenient desk-top reference, which will get a lot of use. The chapter entitled "Serendipity" contains a useful collection of alphabet games, both to be played in groups or alone. The chapter on poetry, including student examples, should start ideas flowing.

Helfman, Elizabeth S. *Signs and Symbols Around the World*. New York: Lothrop, Lee and Shepard Co., 1967.

The book begins with the cavemen and concludes with some symbols from the Tokyo Olympic Games. It is profusely illustrated in black and white and to journey through the book is to meet many organized symbol systems not ordinarily encountered. Many of the individual signs are of artistic sensitivity in addition to their use in communication.

Hudson, Peggy, compiler. *Words to the Wise*. New York: Scholastic Book Services, 1967.

A combination information and workbook for intermediate-grade children, this illustrated paperback deals with words from many languages, the Bible, literature, and men's names and place names. The definitions and etymologies are concise and well written.

Lambert, Eloise, and Mario, Pei. *Our Names*. New York: Lothrop, Lee & Shepard Co., 1960.

A handy reference for children to use in looking up what their name means, this interestingly written book can also be read in sequence as a history of naming. The chapters on names of endearment, personal name oddities, and the section on "thing" names contain material not easily available elsewhere.

Lipton, James. *An Exaltation of Larks*. New York: Grossman Publishers, 1968.

An invaluable supplement to the Wildsmith books, this one for adults is illustrated with evocative old black and white drawings. The interesting additional feature is the terms for people, including: a "diligence of messengers," a "sentence of judges," and a "skulk of thieves." The author created a "wince of dentists," and a "shush of librarians" among others. Children would enjoy making up their own.

Matthews, C. M. *English Surnames*. New York: Charles Scribner's Sons, 1967.

Useful primarily as a resource book, this paperback deals exhaustively with the topic. It investigates both chronological development and also such topics as nicknames, occupational and local names; a thorough tracing of each name is given. The teacher may be interested in reading sections of it. For children it will serve as an interest-builder as they check to see what their names mean.

O'Neill, Mary. *Words Words Words*. New York: Doubleday and Co., 1966.

The poet, whose sensitive use of exactly the right word in the right place is enviable, has written a book containing very traditional definitions of parts of speech. Despite the definitions, the charming poems interest children. The feeling-word poems (on such words as mean, precision, forget, hope, and happiness) are the real delight of the book, which should not be missed.

Radlauer, Ruth Shaw. *Good Times with Words*. Chicago: Melmont Press, 1963.

Designed to help a child retain his own original way of saying things, the book emphasizes ways words can add colors, sounds, smells, and feelings to what the child says and writes. The illustrations, in full color, show some of the funny ways words work. The book suggests several activities to involve children with words.

Reid, Alastair. *Ounce Dice Trice*. Boston: Little, Brown & Co., 1958.

From the opening page dealing with sounds of words, to the closing page detailing the uses of firkydoodle fudge, the reader will be delighted with this book. The whole gamut of curious words from *ananals* to *ugwob* is included. The sensitive and sophisticated black and white drawings entrance the eye.

Shanker, Sidney. *Semantics: The Magic of Words*. Boston: Ginn & Company, 1965.

A paperback with accompanying teacher's handbook and key, this brief examination of the topic provides valuable background for a teacher. Designed for the adult reader, the material included should enrich the teacher's understanding.

Spieka, Arnold. *A Rumbudgin of Nonsense*. New York: Charles Scribner's Sons, 1970.

A delightful collection of whimsical verse detailing the exploits of such diverse characters as the zinzerfoo, Milly O'Hooley (whose hair was unruly) and Little Miss Squinch. Children, who love to play with words, will enjoy Spieka's ability to do the same.

Taylor, Elvin. *A New Approach to Language Arts in the Elementary School*. West Nyack, New York: Parker Publishing Co., 1970, pp. 77–108.

A teacher in search of games and activities for vocabulary development will find two chapters in this book of help. In addition, the chapters on creative writing and spelling provide many new ideas to use.

Waller, Leslie. *Our American Language*. New York: Holt, Rinehart and Winston, 1960.

Designed especially for young readers, this book presents a simple history beginning 2000 years ago in England. The contribution of many countries is noted as is the growth of idioms and created words.

Webber, Helen, illustrator. *What Is Sour?* New York: Holt, Rinehart and Winston, 1967.

A book with much visual impact, this deals with opposites and contains no words. It could be used very effectively for language development, especially with young children.

Weekley, Ernest. *The Romance of Words*. New York: Dover Publications, 1961.

Another quality reprint of an early work, this fascinating, if at times eccentric, book is a good reference tool for the teacher. He may use it to look up terms from *abet* to *zwilch*, or to learn about a variety of topics including semantics, word wanderings, homonyms, and metaphors. He may also use it to whet the appetite of good readers in fifth and sixth grade.

White, Mary Sue. *Word Twins*. New York: Abingdon Press, 1961.

Illustrated in a pleasantly slap-dash manner, this four-color book introduces children to homophones—that group of words which sound alike even though their spellings are unlike. It is useful in motivating children to think of other pairs and make up a book of their own.

Wildsmith, Brian. *Birds* (1967) and *Wild Animals* (1967). New York: Franklin Watts.

Two large and lovely collections of the usual lush and sensuous illustrations Wildsmith does so well. Digging through old books, he came up with many unusual terms for groups of animals—unused now but common in other eras. A *sloth* of bears, an *array* of hedgehogs and a *skulk* of foxes inhabit one book; a *rafter* of turkeys, an *unkindness* of ravens and a *congregation* of plovers are among the birds. Either would launch children on a study of words.

CHAPTER TWELVE

Grammar and Usage

Few topics evoke quick responses on both ends of a continuum, ranging from ill-concealed boredom and contemptuous indifference to zealous proselitizing for one's dearly held views. Yet the word *grammar* arouses such responses. Elementary school children respond with groans, a job applicant thinks nervously about it, a mother nags when her child says a sentence incorrectly. Are they all reacting to the same thing? To what does the term grammar refer?

What Is Grammar?

One definition will not serve because the phenomena it describes —language—is so inordinately complex that complete descriptions elude even professional linguists. The term itself is an old one, from the early Greek *gramma*, a word for letter. This ancient word has earlier antecedents, in the word *graphein*, meaning to write or draw. When pluralized, *grammatá*, the word included a range of meanings from letters of the alphabet to the rudiments of writing.[1] Perhaps a

---

[1] For those with historical bent, this and much other information about early grammars is included in Karl Dykema, "Where Our Language Came From," in *Perspectives on Language*, eds. Rycenga & Schwartz (New York: The Ronald Press Co., 1963), pp. 98–111.

collage of definitions will begin establishing the parameters of the term. May defines grammar as:

> a way of signaling; a way of showing relationships within a sentence; a way of organizing meaning. Grammar is also a collection of subconscious rules—rules of word order (syntax) and word form (morphology)—which guide us in the creation of new sentences.[2]

A linguist has defined grammar as:

> the set of formal patterns in which words of a language are arranged in order to convey larger meanings. It is not necessary that we be able to discuss these patterns self-consciously in order to be able to use them. In fact, all speakers of a language above the age of five or six know how to use its complex forms of organization with considerable skill; in this sense of the word, they are thoroughly familiar with its grammar.[3]

Another linguist has said that grammar is:

> a set of statements saying how a language works. It includes, for example, a description of the principles for combining words to form grammatical sentences.[4]

From the above, we can see the necessity of developing a multifaceted definition for a complex phenomena.

The Grammar and A Grammar

If we distinguish between these two terms, a clearer understanding may result. When speaking of *the* grammar, we are referring to the structural system or organization which underlies the totality of the language. This structural system is made up of several components and controls in fairly rigorous ways the utterances possible in a language and those which are not possible (or considered ungrammatical).

---

[2] Frank B. May, *Teaching Language as Communication to Children* (Columbus: Charles E. Merrill, 1967), p. 27.

[3] W. Nelson Francis, "Revolution in Grammar," in *Readings in Applied Linguistics,* ed. Harold Allen (New York: Appleton-Century-Crofts, 1964), p. 69.

[4] Ronald W. Langacker, *Language and Its Structure* (New York: Harcourt Brace Jovanovich, 1968), p. 6.

In contrast, *a* grammar is someone's (or some group's) written description of this language structure. The written description may range from simple to exceedingly complex, though one author has pointed out that even complex descriptions seldom deal completely with the language.[5]

Perhaps the distinction can be clarified through an example. In mathematics there is both *number*, the actual quantity itself, and *numeral*, the written description of, or symbol for, the quantity. The comparison can be made:

> Number is to "the" grammar as
> Numeral is to "a" grammar.

One widely respected linguist describes these two grammars in the following quotation:

> Grammar 1 [*the* grammar] is the system itself. This has everything to do with language performance; without that system the language could not exist. . . . The study of grammar, . . . is the investigation of how the system operates. It is not, and never has intended to be, a miscellany of shibboleths of usage.
>
> Grammar 2 [*a* grammar] is some kind of a description and explanation of that system. This has nothing to do with language performance . . . we are able to use it without being able to explain how the system works.[6]

Components

There are many ways of writing *a* grammar of English; the most influential of these grammars will be described later. No matter what one's persuasion, it is incumbent upon any grammar-maker to describe the three basic components of language: phonology, morphology, and syntax. These are components in any language, though the nature and importance of each varies according to the language being considered.

---

[5] Norman C. Stageberg points out that even the description by Jesperson which runs to seven bound volumes does not deal with all aspects of grammar. See *An Introductory English Grammar* (New York: Holt, Rinehart & Winston, 1965). A college textbook in programmed format, this explains structural and transformational grammars.

[6] Andrew Schiller, "A Few Words about Grammar in General and this Book in Particular," in *Language and How to Use It*, ed., Schiller et al. (Chicago: Scott, Foresman and Co., 1969). (Book 5, Teacher's Edition, p. x.)

Phonology is a first consideration because sound is basic to language. The word *phonology* means the study or science of speech sounds. It comes from the ancient Greek word *phone,* meaning voice. Any grammar will include some description of phonology, the sound system of the language. The basic sound unit is the phoneme, defined as:

> [a class] of sounds that contrast with other classes of sounds, and a single phoneme can be defined as a class of sounds whose phonetic differences are incapable of distinguishing one meaning from another.[7]

Phonemes are the smallest distinctive speech sounds. In the words *dip* and *din,* the /p/ and the /n/ are identified as separate and distinct phonemes.[8]

These small speech sounds, phonemes, are also called *segmentals,* or segments of sound. There is another way we add meaning to this basic set of speech segments, through the use of *suprasegmentals.* This term refers to three ways we vary the basic segments to give more definitive meaning to speech. The three suprasegmentals in English are pitch, stress, and juncture.

Pitch refers to the different levels of sound between the highest and the lowest sounds any given speaker can make. Two speakers will have different vocal ranges, with some overlap. For example, women's voices usually have a higher vocal range than do men's (Figure 25).

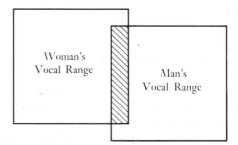

Figure 25

How the speaker changes pitches within his range is an example of pitch variation. In English we most commonly use pitch to distinguish be-

---

[7] Francis P. Dinnen, S.J., *An Introduction to General Linguistics* (New York: Holt, Rinehart & Winston, 1967), p. 35.

[8] It is an agreed-upon linguistic convention that when writing about sounds, / / are put around the letter used to represent the sound. This indicates sounds are being talked about, *not* letters.

tween questions and statements, a falling pitch contour usually signal-
ling a question.

Stress refers to the intensity or loudness with which a word is said.
There are four degrees of stress in English:

1. primary   (╱)
2. secondary (╲)
3. tertiary   (∧)
4. weak   (◡)

Say the following sentences to yourself:

1. The ínvalid was difficult to care for.

2. The ìnválidˇ argument presented by the speaker did not convince
   us.

Did you notice the difference in the way the word was stressed in each
sentence? In addition to stressing speech segments (phonemes) differently, we sometimes stress entire words differently to convey meaning
and indicate parts of speech. Say the following two sentences to yourself:

1. The lóud speàkeˇr was defective and we couldn't hear.

2. He was a lòud spéakeˇr because of an unfortunate hearing loss.

Juncture is the term we use for the suprasegmental which signals a
transition from one phoneme to another, from one syllable to another,
from one word to another, and from one sentence to another. It is the
vocal element which makes it possible to distinguish between the identical segmental sounds in the following pairs of sentences:

1. The *night rate* for sending telegrams is very reasonable.
2. The presence of *nitrate* in the compound was disturbing to the
   scientist.

1. The *ice cream* melted before the diners had finished the main
   course.
2. "*I scream* loudly," Sara said, "but no one ever listens!"

The study of phonology is very complex; indeed, many universi-
ties offer a sequence of courses dealing only with this one aspect of

grammar. While it is impossible to offer anything approximating a complete description in this chapter, additional reading will help further your understanding of this facet of language.

Morphology is another component of the grammar of a language. The term has roots in the early Greek word *morphē*, which means form. English words have a distinctive morphological, or form, system which can be taught to children.

Morphemes, the basic unit in morphology, are the smallest meaning-bearing units of language. In the word goats, there are two morphemes, goat and -s. The example illustrates that there are two types of morphemes:

1. *free,* e.g., the word goat appears independently and carries meaning.
2. *bound,* e.g., the -s does not appear independently, though it does carry meaning: the idea of plural.

Other bound morphemes include the -'s and -s' attached to nouns, the -s, -ed, and -ing attached to verbs, the -est attached to adjectives and the -er attached to adverbs.[9] In each case these bound morphemes signify meaning, though they never appear independently.

You can see that while free morphemes are virtually limitless, bound morphemes are limited in number. Though we can and do make up new words, the number of bound morphemes and their meanings remain relatively constant.

Snytax, the third large component of language, is the word order in sentences. The origin of the word comes through the French *syntaxe* from the Greek word *tassein* which means to arrange or put in order.

English, a word-order or distributive language, offers flexibility of this word order, but not as much flexibility as other languages called inflectional languages. Latin provides a clear contrast. In Latin it makes no difference whether one says:

Puer puellam amat, or
Puellam puer amat.

The meaning is identical, i.e., The boy loves the girl. This is because the endings or inflected forms at the ends of the words tell us who is doing what and to whom. The order, or syntax, is unimportant.

---

9 For an example of how this idea is taught to children, see Andrew Schiller et al., *Language and How to Use It* (Chicago: Scott, Foresman and Co., 1969), Book 5, pp. 197–209.

The same is not true of English. Because English is a positional language, there is a considerable difference between:

The girl ate the hamburger, and
The hamburger ate the girl.[10]

Though all languages are made up of these components, in some, one component is more important than the rest. For example, in Vietnamese (as in other Eastern languages) the direction of the pitch signals meaning. One small two-letter word can mean six different things, depending on how the pitch is manipulated.

| ma (ghost) | má (cheek) | mà (but) |
| ma (tomb | mā (horse) | mā (rice-seedling) |

For English speakers, unused to such subtle meaning-bearing pitch indicators, learning such a language is difficult. We are used to different meaning signals.

Usage

Often people use the term grammar when they are referring to the choices individuals make between two possible alternatives for a particular position in a sentence. We can say either:

1. "I brung the teacher an apple," or
2. "I brought the teacher an apple."

About such choices, one author has said:

The dialect of some groups of people includes "brung" as the past tense of bring. The dialect of other groups includes "brought" as the past tense of bring. Since these two words have equal signaling power, i.e., they both signal the past tense of bring, they are both grammatically "correct." Yet, to most of us only one of them seems proper and elegant.[11]

---

[10] For an example of how the concept of word order is taught to children, see the delightful material in Muriel Crosby et al., *The World of Language* (Chicago: Follett Educational Corporation, 1970). The idea of "scrambled sentences," using a ravenous hamburger, is included in Book 3, pp. 192, 193.

[11] May, *Teaching Language as Communication to Children*, p. 27.

Such a choice is one of usage and does not represent a grammatical error. One may affirm that it is an error; in fact, most standard English speakers would so insist. Nonetheless, it is crucial to remember it is a usage, not a grammatical, issue.

Other usage choices include:

1. "I ain't going," or
2. "I am not going."

1. "May I use the car?" or
2. "Can I use the car?"

The whole issue of usage choices is a very emotional one because people, especially those who have made a conscious effort to improve their language, tend to look down upon those who have not.

Like it or not, language is one way American society makes class distinctions, and less-acceptable usage choices are heavily penalized by those in power. Attitudes about usage are slow to change, though students of language point out that change is occurring.

Perhaps one of the most helpful changes is the increasing use of the term *non*standard English, to substitute for *sub*standard. Though the difference may not be readily apparent, considerable philosophical difference exists between them.

The older term, *substandard*, suggested a hierarchy in which standard English was at the top, and all variants were below, and thus inferior to it.

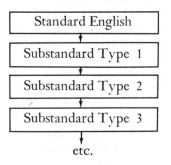

Linguists, and particularly those interested in studying language variations (dialectologists) believe that the term *nonstandard* indicates a different concept of ordering.

Rather than implying or stating the value position that there is one standard to be attained, this position says that several variants of equal worth in different settings are possible.[12]

The question of what schools should do about helping children improve their usage has been debated hotly, and cannot be settled here, though Dr. Huenecke's chapter on language for the culturally divergent (Chapter Thirteen) delineates the problem clearly.

The problem faced by the elementary teacher is: What usage problems are important enough to deserve attention? Within a limited amount of time available, which should be the subject of individual or small-group work?

Any teacher who has tried it will tell you it is difficult to make even minor changes in a child's usage. This is easy to understand if the following are kept in mind:

1. The kindergarten child has spent between four and six years of total immersion in his home culture and language. His language habits are well established and difficult to change.

2. Even the school-age child continues to spend the major portion of his waking hours in the home-language environment. He may spend a maximum of six hours at school, compared to at least ten waking hours at home.

3. Often there are psychological reasons why the child is uninterested in changing his usage patterns. His family and peer groups may exert a tremendous inhibiting force against usage change.

4. Much of the practice he has experienced in school will have been ineffective. Usage drill consists, for the most part, of the written exercises prescribed by language textbooks.

The problem is not simplified by the approach taken in too many elementary language-arts materials. These tend to take a "scattergun" approach and give minimal attention to a wide variety of problems. One thing we know for certain about children's usage problems is that they will not yield to a one-page written drill. Despite this, language-arts books are filled with such drills.

---

[12] One author has stated that while attitudes in this area are changing among language students, little change has occurred among speakers of English, as most still view variants as inferior to standard English. See Phillip S. Dale, *Language Development* (Hinsdale, Illinois: The Dryden Press, 1972), p. 243. This section on sociolinguistics includes much of interest to teachers.

Another reason the teacher must use such materials discriminatively is that even today they frequently prescribe fine points of usage unrelated to the real world of communication.

One elementary book, published in 1968, includes the following:

May and Can
Do You Remember?
   May is used to mean "be permitted to."
   May is also used to mean "have a chance to."
   Can is generally used to mean "to be able to."

While it may be of use for some adults to make this distinction, to recommend that the elementary teacher take up his children's time with such is indeed a mistake.

Another series, published in 1971, recommends some even finer distinctions in its sixth-grade book.

Are you aware of the following *Do's* and *Don'ts?* Careful speakers—

Don't	*Do*
1. Say: What *kind of a* car does he drive?	1. Say: *What kind* of car does he drive?
2. Say: I *sort of* thought you would go.	2. Say: I *rather* thought you would go.
3. Say: I was *kind of* tired.	3. Say: I was *somewhat* tired.

How the authors decided that the usages included in the recommended column are representative of standard English speakers is difficult to determine. Further, suggesting that item 2 or item 3 in the "Do" column are desirable for young children, exposes the authors' lack of contact with the way normal children speak.

A further distinction the book recommends is the following:

this and *these* refer to nearby things.
that and *those* refer to things farther away.

As a result, saying:

"Bill likes *those* kinds of shoes," is incorrect if one is pointing to some on a rack near you.

Is such a distinction any longer a functioning part of English? It is difficult to believe that such is the case.

"Who-o-om, who-o-om?"

D. Hand in the *Christian Science Monitor* © TCSPS

Even methods books for teachers are not immune to such dream-like speculations about the way language ought to be.[13] The following example is taken from a book published in 1972 by a widely known language expert.

Of and *from*

  a. The prepositions *of* and *from* are never used with the adverb *off* such as:

    1. "The men jumped *off* the boat." (correct)
      "The men jumped *off of* the boat." (incorrect)

---

[13] This appellation is applied to much grammar teaching by James C. Bostain, in "The Dream World of English Grammar," *NEA Journal* 55 (September 1966): 20–22. He makes careful distinctions between valid grammatic knowledge and equally useful, but different, social knowledge gained by understanding usage differences.

2. "The men jumped *off* the log." (correct)
"The men jumped *from off* the log." (incorrect)

Such distinctions as these are difficult if not impossible to defend, simply on the basis of common oral usage. The first example is obviously irrelevant in other than literary written English at this time. The form labeled incorrect is, in fact, in widespread use. The second example labeled incorrect could certainly occur in response to a question. For example, "Where did the men jump from?" While the second example may be less acceptable to language purists, it is certainly arbitrary to label it as incorrect. In the final analysis, neither is worth the time of elementary school children.

Realistic Approaches to Usage

Many of the above recommendations, which are found in materials currently widely used, seem unrealistic to the classroom teacher. They attempt to teach children some very fine distinctions of language usage which may be of value to small segments of the adult population but are of questionable usefulness to most children.

Thus, the first thing the teacher must do is to examine critically whatever materials are provided in his school as resources to which he can turn *if* they are appropriate. Once he develops this attitude toward the materials, he can begin at the best place to begin—the children's oral speech.

Diagnosis of children's usage errors is important and must be done in a variety of speech situations. The teacher listens carefully, at first in a general way, to try to pick out the most common usage errors made by the group as a whole. He jots these down, perhaps on a card on his desk. At the end of a week or so of observation, he reviews his list and notes which he thinks are the most serious. Once he has established some priorities, he does more specific diagnosis to determine which children make the usage errors he has elected to focus attention upon. He might again note down these errors on a simple checklist, such as Figure 26, which can be kept on the desk.

The next step is to organize the children into small skill groups, the purpose of which is to provide intensive practice in drill on the particular usage error made by the group. Because problems of this nature are most pronounced in speech, the drill is oral with little or no attention

Usage Error Incidence

Type	Alice	Tim	Margy	Sara	Tom	Roger	Alan	Joyce	Bob
he done									
this here									
she don't									
he was									
brung									
ain't got none									
has took									
they knowed									

Figure 26

given to written practice. The skill group meets together, drilling in a variety of ways, until the teacher feels the children have mastered the particular problem usage. Then the group is disbanded.

Probably many of the children will need work of some nature, and this intensive oral practice in small groups results in more change in usage than does several years of occasional written practice.

Usage is the child's language at work. But what of his *understanding* of his language and how it works? There are wide differences of opinion about how much, if any, understanding a child needs to have about the inner workings and structure of the language he speaks. Eloquent statements have been made by those who claim with accuracy that a child can be enviably fluent with no understanding of how his language works. Equally eloquent statements have been made by those who feel a conscious understanding of the grammar of his language is important for children. In the following section we shall examine three ways to describe *the* grammar, or the structural system of English, and some suggestions about how to teach grammatical ideas to children.

Traditional Grammar[14]

Most of those who read this will have grown up with what is commonly called traditional, or *prescriptive*, grammar, while a few readers will have had the unusual experience of studying one of the other two types described later.

Traditional grammar, with deep roots going back many hundreds of years, is nomothetic. That is, it attempts to tell people, or prescribe, how they should speak. Originally based on Latin models, this type of grammar is concerned with categorizing sentences according to their purposes and words according to their classes, among other more technical considerations. Some of the earlier grammars of English, including those of Jesperson, Curme, Poutsma, and Kruisinga, were lengthy analyses. These were not taught to children, but ideas from them were adapted by textbook writers.

Of course, no school attempted to teach these extensive and highly sophisticated treatments in toto. Instead, a variety of interpreters produced what are called *school grammars*, which diluted and often distorted scholarly efforts. One writer has commented trenchantly:

> Adaptation is really not the right word; bastardization would be fairer, if severer. For the most part they were faulty representations of careful traditional-historical technique . . . presented frequently with gross oversimplifications and . . . the good in them was usually obscured by irrelevant and trivial sections on good manners on the telephone and decorum in the library. . . .[15]

One aspect of traditional grammar, that of diagraming sentences in order to uncover underlying structural/syntactical relationships, has been a part of many children's English experiences in school. This is true, despite the fact that quite conclusive evidence exists that such exercises have no demonstrable relationship to effective speaking or writing.[16]

---

[14] A more complete detailing of the nature of traditional grammar and the problems it presents to the learner is included in John R. Searles, *Structural and Traditional Grammar* (Oshkosh: Wisconsin Council of Teachers of English, 1965), pp. 1–20.

[15] William S. Chisholm, *The New English* (New York: Funk and Wagnals, 1969), p. 52.

[16] This point is discussed fully in J. Stephen Sherwin, *Four Problems in Teaching English* (Scranton: International Textbooks Co., 1969), pp. 169–85. In admirably objective fashion, Sherwin questions the efficacy of newer linguistic diagrams in improving students' language.

Structural Grammar

The year 1933 marked a significant change in direction in grammatical descriptions. That year a leading linguist published a book destined to have profound effects on the work of many scholars for several decades.[17] Bloomfield, and structural linguists who followed him, emphasized the importance of studying spoken language. This is a major difference between structural linguists and traditional linguists who are more concerned with the written language.

A second major difference between the two approaches is that structural linguistics is *descriptive*, rather than prescriptive. Instead of beginning with a written description of how people *should* speak and searching for examples, the structuralists often begin with a corpus of material (recorded speech) and derive from this a description of how people *do* speak. Unlike traditional grammarians, structural linguists are uninterested in making value judgments about how people should speak. Rather, with the dispassionate attitude of a scientist, they study a natural phenomenon so they can record their observations.

Structural linguists have concerned themselves with *sentence patterns*, though there is not universal agreement among them as to the number of patterns which exist.[18] A sample pattern is N V Adj (The tree seems scrawny). The most common sentence patterns include:

Pattern One NV (Noun and verb)
  This is the simplest, most basic pattern in English, e.g., Girls sew. Children are playing. Common variations include: NVA (Noun, verb, adjective), e.g., The door slammed shut; and NVAd (Noun, verb, adverb), e.g., She sang sadly.

Pattern Two NVN (Noun, verb, noun complement)
  This also is a very common pattern, e.g., The girls drank lemonade. Mary eats candy.

Pattern Three NVNN (Noun, verb, noun, noun).
  The girls call the dog Oscar, or Alice gave the chickens corn. A

---

[17] Leonard Bloomfield, *Language* (New York: Henry Holt & Co., 1933). The last chapter of the book is devoted to implications and applications of linguistics to the school curriculum.

[18] For a concise explanation of how this idea can be taught to children, see Verna L. Newsome, *Structural Grammar in the Classroom* (Oshkosh: Wisconsin Council of Teachers of English, 1961), pp. 12–16. Though Newsome's approach is for children in sixth grade and above, her explanation is of help in increasing the teacher's competency in this area.

variation of this pattern is NVNA, e.g., They stained the house brown.

Pattern Four NLvN, NLvA, and NLvAd (Noun, linking verb and noun, adjective, or adverb), e.g., Mary is a singer. The girls are intelligent. Tom is away.

The above patterns have been presented as though they are the only recognized ones. Such is not the case, for in this, as in many aspects of linguistics, there is some difference of opinion. In examining the work of several structuralists, we find the number of sentence patterns given varies from four[19] to ten. [20]

In addition to sentence patterns, structuralists are also interested in word classes, or parts of speech. Rather than relying on traditional means of determining parts of speech, they have evolved an approach using *slot and filler* technique. Sentence, or test frames are created with a word missing. All the words which can fit into the slot, or blank space, belong to that word class, or part of speech.

A noun is a word like *vase* in the sentence: The green *(vase)* is broken.

An adjective is a word like *tall* in the sentence: The *(tall)* tree is blighted.

A verb is a word like *ran* in the sentence: The dog *(ran)*.

An adverb is a word like *sadly* in the sentence: The girl returned home very *(sadly)*.

Structuralists are quick to remind us that this one test is not definitive in determining word class. Some words which do belong in a particular class will not fit in the examples given above. More than one test to determine word class is often necessary.

Nouns as a class are defined quite differently than the conventional definition of "a person, place, or thing." It is readily apparent that this definition is so loose as to be almost useless for teaching purposes, especially for young children. The "or thing" part of the definition contributes to much misunderstanding when children try to work with

---

19 Helen and Carl Lefevre, *Writing by Patterns* (New York: Alfred A. Knopf, 1965).

20 Paul Roberts, *English Sentences* (New York: Harcourt Brace Jovanovich, 1962).

the definition. Structuralists, in contrast, would define a noun in the following ways:[21]

1. it inflects following certain predictable patterns, e.g., nouns are words which accept -s, -'s, and -s'.
2. it is preceded by particular function words, like determiners, e.g., a, an, one.
3. it occupies certain positions in a sentence, e.g., between a determiner and a verb, in the slot and filler construction, a _____ ran.
4. it is formed by the addition of certain derivational suffixes to adjective forms, e.g., add -ness to roots like kind and bold.
5. it sometimes is indicated by a contrast in accent pattern with a similar word in another class, e.g., "I suspéct we will go," as contrasted with "The súspect was in jail."

Transformational Grammar

A more recent development in grammar description was evolved by two linguists, Zellig Harris and Noam Chomsky.[22] Their work has provided the impetus for development of a new direction and has fostered much writing and some research experimentation.

Transformational linguists believe there are two kinds of sentences:

Kernel sentences: which are a relatively small number of basic sentence types which form the core of grammar. These cannot be derived from any other sentences or sentence types underlying them.

Transformed sentences: which are formed, using kernel sentences as a base, by applying a series of transform rules that give direction for changing, adding, deleting, substituting, and combining basic, or kernel sentences.

---

[21] An example of how this idea is taught to children is included in Freeman B. Anderson et al., *New Directions in English* (New York: Harper and Row, Publishers, 1969), Book 3, pp. 24–25.

[22] A statement of the principles of this approach to grammar is Chomsky's *Syntactic Structures* (The Hague, The Netherlands: Mouton, 1957). An admittedly difficult-to-read, technical discussion of the original theory underlying transformational grammar, this book is historically important.

These transform rules, commonly written in a conventionalized notation system, range from very simple, e.g.:[23]

$$S \rightarrow N P + V P,$$

to very complex, e.g.:[24]

$$\text{Aux} \rightarrow \text{tense} + (M) + (\text{have}) + (\text{Part.}) + (\text{be} + \text{ing}).$$

A complete understanding of transformational grammar is beyond the capabilities of young children, but some less-complex aspects of the approach are being taught to children.[25]
The underlying assumptions of the system include:

1. There is a finite number of basic kernel sentence types and transform rules, but an infinite number of variations or actual sentences which can be made, or generated, as a result of using the transform rules.[26]
   For example, if we take the transform rule, which is *finite*,

   $$\text{NP} \rightarrow \text{DAN (determiner, adjective, noun)},$$

   we can generate an *infinite* number of actual sentences from this rule.

2. Everyone possesses an understanding of this process because even young children each day generate many sentences which they have never heard before. They know the rules intuitively and use them in creating new sentences.

---

[23] The notation reads: "Sentence is rewritten as noun phrase plus verb phrase." The arrow is standard linguistic notation for: is made from, consists of, or is rewritten as.

[24] Example is taken from Paul Roberts, *The Roberts English Series* (New York: Harcourt Brace Jovanovich, 1970), Teachers' Edition for the Sixth Book, p. 34, an innovative attempt to introduce linguistic concepts in a systematic fashion to children.

[25] See Ann Kirby's *Elementary School English* (Menlo Park, California: Addison-Wesley Publishing Co., 1967). Children using this series learn such transformational rules as: $\text{VP} \rightarrow \text{tense} + \text{VT} + \text{NP}$.

[26] This use of the term generate, or generation, to make or create using a basic kernel sentence, illustrates why this approach to grammar is sometimes called transformational-generative grammar.

Even Newer Approaches

One aspect of linguistics which makes it exciting to professionals and intimidating to the uninformed is the rate at which new knowledge is being discovered and new ideas generated. Linguists are theorizing, writing, and experimenting constantly. Such new ideas as tagmemics,[27] and stratificational grammar[28] are being developed. Will these new formulations eventually be adapted to the elementary school, as structural and transformational ideas have been? It is too early to tell, but this exciting area of English is apt to continue to be one in which much is happening.

Is Grammar Teaching Useful?

In order to answer this question, another must be considered first: What is the *purpose* of teaching grammar to children? As Professor Huenecke pointed out so clearly in Chapter Two, until one identifies both purposes and underlying assumptions, it is difficult to determine effectiveness of any educational idea. There are two reasons often given for teaching grammar to children.

1. Because grammar exists, it can be and should be studied. Like geography or physics, a body of knowledge exists in linguistics, of intrinsic interest if it is clearly and systematically presented to the learner, at whatever age.

2. Improvement in speaking and writing is, logically enough, often given as a reason for teaching grammar. Conscious knowledge of the structure of language is seen as a means of improving oral and written compositions. Despite the logic, such improvement does not seem to result.[29] Research studies done, beginning with

---

[27] An understandable introduction is included in Carl A. Lefevre, *Linguistics, English and the Language Arts* (Boston: Allyn and Bacon, 1970), pp. 310–13. See entries in the bibliography under Pike, Kenneth for a primary source.

[28] Most grammatical descriptions have to this point been limited to the sentence, or smaller units. A truly adequate description must give attention to units larger than the sentences; stratificational grammar attempts to do this. The description in Lefevre, *Linguistics, English and the Language Arts*, pp. 330–31 is intelligible to the novice.

[29] Though students do get better at grammar exercises, such exercises do not lead to significantly better speaking or writing. A summary of research studies is included in Harry A. Greene and Walter T. Petty, *Developing Language Skills in the Elementary Schools* (Boston: Allyn & Bacon, 1971), pp. 372–74.

one by Hoyt in 1906, suggest that this reason for grammar teaching must be discounted.[30]

The studies mentioned above examine the relationship between knowledge of formal, or traditional, grammar and the expressive arts of writing and speaking. There is certainly the possibility that research examining the relationship between these arts and the newer structural and transformational grammars may well discover some cause and effect relationship. The influence of structural and transformational grammar in schools is as yet too new to have resulted in a significant body of research.[31]

Classroom Applications

Until researchers' findings suggest instructional strategies more clearly for teachers, many will remain uncertain about what to do regarding grammar. While it is difficult to justify a full-scale attempt to teach a grammatical system to children, there are many ideas which can be borrowed from linguists for use in classrooms. These ideas are of interest to children, and exposure to them often results in understandings about language which can be beneficial.

Children can experiment with the *slot and filler technique* borrowed from structural grammar to show the idea of word class.[32] The teacher prepares flash cards with words of different classes on them. Several children take these word cards which can be arranged to make a sentence. The children stand in the front of the room with their cards arranged to make a sentence. After a sentence is made, one child steps out of line. The teacher asks who has a card which will fit into the slot.

---

[30] Franklin S. Hoyt, "Studies in English Grammar," *Teachers College Record* 7 (Nov. 1906):467–500. Hoyt compared the written compositions of two groups of children (one of which had two years drill on formal grammar, the other had none). The groups were equal in compositional ability. Later studies by Rapeer (1913), Boraas (1917), and Asker (1923) have confirmed Hoyt's findings.

[31] This position is well stated in Albert H. Marckwardt, ed., *Language and Language Learning* (Champaign, Illinois: National Council of Teachers of English, 1968), pp. 32 and 33. This paperback is one of a series of six resulting from the Dartmouth Seminar, a two-month project sponsored by several professional associations, which brought together a large number of experts to consider problems in teaching English. The project has had considerable influence on English teaching.

[32] This, and several other ideas are demonstrated with verve and determination by Bernard J. Weiss in a videotape, "Means of Creation: Linguistics Demonstration," in a series, *English for Elementary Teachers*, available from the National Center for School and College Television (Bloomington, Indiana).

This child becomes the filler. Then the teacher sees if anyone else has another word which will fit. This can be repeated several times. The activity can lead into a discussion of what the words which fit into a particular slot have in common.[33]

The idea of *transformation* of basic, or kernel, sentences can be taught to children. Given a kernel sentence, e.g., "The dog chewed on his bone," children can transform it in a variety of ways.

(1) It can be made passive:
   The bone was chewed on by the dog.

(2) It can be made an active question:
   Did the dog chew on his bone?

(3) It can be made a passive question:
   Was the bone chewed on by the dog?

(4) It can be made negative:
   The dog did not chew on his bone.

(5) It can be made a negative question:
   Didn't the dog chew on his bone?

(6) It can be made an emphatic statement:
   The dog did chew on his bone.[34]

Another technique children enjoy and from which they learn is that of *expansion*. Given a kernel sentence, it can be expanded in a variety of ways. One approach to expansion is suggested by Wolfe, who says the technique can either be done orally, or the children may write their responses.[35] He suggests children take a simple (or kernel) sentence and ask themselves several questions, in the following manner:[36]

---

[33] Another approach to this idea is described in Robert Ian Scott, "Teaching Elementary Grammar with Color-Coded Word Blocks," *Elementary English* 45 (November 1968): 972–81. The author reports his experiment with first-grade children who learned word classes by manipulating blocks.

[34] Note that the transforms do not change the tense, but only the form of the sentence. There are other, more complex, transforms which do change tense and other aspects of kernel sentences.

[35] See Don M. Wolfe, *Language Arts and Life Patterns* (New York: Odyssey Press, 1972), Chapter 20, "The Sentence Building Game in Action," pp. 307–20. Though not all writers would agree with Wolfe's assumption that a conscious understanding of grammatical ideas is crucial for children, there is no doubt that his extensive coverage of the topic is effectively designed to capture children's interest.

[36] In this exercise, as in many others, the sentences given are samples and are not the *one* right answer for which a teacher should strive. There are many possible alternatives to most of these processes.

Sentence: I bought something.

1. *When* did you buy it?
   I bought it yesterday.
2. *What* did you buy?
   I bought a pencil yesterday.
3. Can you add a *color* word?
   I bought a yellow pencil yesterday.
4. Can you tell *where?*
   I bought a yellow pencil yesterday at the grocery store.
5. Can you *reverse* the word order?
   Yesterday, at the grocery store, I bought a yellow pencil.

With older children who have had some experience with sentence parts and their functions a slightly different approach can be used:

Sentence: The girl sang a song.

1. Expanding the noun phrase:
   The large girl sang a song.
2. Expanding the verb phrase:
   The girl sang a song very loudly.
3. Expanding both the subject and the predicate:
   The dark haired girl sang a song in a very raspy voice.
4. Expanding through coordinating:
   The girl *and* the boy sang a song and did a dance.
5. Expanding through subordinating:
   Because the girl sang the song, several people left the hall in a hurry.

The purpose of the above techniques is to show children the flexibility and richness of language. It is widely agreed that the major difference between skilled and unskilled communicators is their ability to say what they want to say in more than one way.[37] Rather than being locked into the first way they say something, those children who are fluent speakers and writers seem to be able to recast their thoughts in

---

[37] Walter Loban comments on this flexibility in *The Language of Elementary School Children* (Champaign: National Council of Teachers of English, 1963), p. 88. This report of a study of the language of 338 children, as it developed from kindergarten through grade six, offers many suggestions about the language usage of children and the grammatical capabilities and deficiencies they have.

several ways. Conscious instruction in transformation and expansion should help develop this fluency.

The idea of sentence *moveables,* an aspect of syntax, can be explored with children. It is true, as mentioned earlier, that because English is a word-order language, fewer syntactic arrangements are possible than with other languages. Despite this, many sentences in English can be arranged in more than one way. Adverbs, for example, can frequently be located in several different slots. Such multiple positions allow for stylistic variations.

> Fortunately, the girls were able to maintain happy relations with the villagers.
>
> The girls, fortunately, were able to maintain happy relations with the villagers.
>
> The girls were able to maintain happy relations with the villagers, fortunately.
>
> The girls were able to maintain, fortunately, happy relations with the villagers.
>
> The girls were able, fortunately, to maintain happy relations with the villagers.
>
> The girls were, fortunately, able to maintain happy relations with the villagers.

Each of the above creates a slightly different effect because of the sentence order. This example of an adult sentence has counterparts on a child's level as seen in the Nebraska Curriculum.[38]

Another idea borrowed from linguistics is *sentence combining,* which can be done by grade school children at all levels. It is particularly helpful for children who write short, choppy sentences strung together with "and's." We might take some sentences from the *Story of Ferdinand.*[39]

> His name was Ferdinand.
> He sat down in the bull ring.
> He liked to smell flowers.

---

[38] The Nebraska Curriculum Development Center, *A Curriculum for English* (Lincoln: University of Nebraska Press, 1966). A stimulating attempt to build a curriculum around literature for children, this series of books for teachers includes one entitled "Language Exploration for the Elementary Grades."

[39] Munroe Leaf, *The Story of Ferdinand* (New York: The Viking Press, 1936).

Children can combine these sentences in many ways. Some possibilities include:

1. In the bull ring Ferdinand, who liked to smell flowers, sat down.
2. Ferdinand, who liked to smell flowers, sat down in the bull ring.
3. Ferdinand liked to smell flowers. He sat down in the bull ring.
4. A bull who liked to smell flowers sat down in the bull ring. His name was Ferdinand.
5. His name was Ferdinand and he liked to smell flowers. He sat down in the bull ring.

Summary

Grammatical descriptions of English can be taught and learned by elementary school children. Traditional grammar has been taught, with indifferent results, to decades of children. Now, newer approaches, drawn from the work of structural and transformational grammarians, are being introduced into the elementary curriculum. There is no doubt that children *can* study and learn these new descriptions of language. Should they? This is a larger philosophical question, requiring that groups of teachers think deeply about purposes. Why should children study the nature of their language? Are there better things for them to be doing during the limited amount of time they spend in schools?[40] It would be folly for a writer to prescribe what an individual school system ought to do, without knowing intimately the nature of that system. Perhaps the information presented in this chapter will help you when, as a teacher, you are asked to be on a curriculum committee confronted with such questions.

Suggestions for Further Study

1. The work of the linguist Paul Roberts, who has written an elementary language-arts series, was mentioned in the chapter. Response to

---

[40] Another crucial question is *when* children should study the nature of English grammar. Robert Pooley is among those who feel formal study of grammar should be delayed until junior high school. For an example of the informal study he feels is appropriate for younger children, see "Teaching the English Language in Wisconsin," part of the *Wisconsin English Language Arts Curriculum Project* (Madison: Department of Public Instruction, 1967).

his materials is seldom neutral; people usually respond emphatically. *Elementary English* 47 (April 1970): 493–531 contains several articles about the materials. Read these and review the series to determine if you feel the criticisms are valid ones.

2. Several definitions of the word *grammar*, varying in different respects, were included in the chapter. Examine a number of elementary series for children to see if and how these explain this term to children.

3. Visit a classroom and listen to the children's speech, keeping a tally of the types of usage errors you hear. Tabulate the frequency of these: Which are the most common?

4. Try teaching the idea of expansion or transformation to a group of children. Have another student who can serve as observer work with you. How did the chidren respond to the idea? What, if anything, was difficult about the concept?

5. Find several children's books which can provide sentences to use in the combining process explained in the chapter. Try them out with a group of children to see how many variations can be created using this process.

6. The author of a recent book has identified eight basic sentence patterns. See Catheryn Eisenhardt, *Applying Linguistics in the Teaching of Reading and the Language Arts* (Columbus: Charles E. Merrill, 1972). How do these eight compare or contrast with the patterns described in the chapter?

Bibliography

Clapp, Ouida H. "Why Color It White?" *Instructor* 80 (October 1970): 74–75.

The author comments on the controversy surrounding the question of black children's speech and lists some of the differences between that speech and standard English. She draws attention to the built-in racism underlying bidialectal language programs and makes suggestions for teachers whose black children speak nonstandard English.

Keipe, Ashtoreth, and Wood, Roger. "A Comparative Study of Achievement between a Linguistics Program of Generative Transform Grammar and a Traditional Program of Grammar." *Elementary English* 47 (April 1970): 535–39.

An attempt was made to determine which grammatical description leads to more growth in English and reading achievement. The study was limited by a small sample size (fifty-nine students) and a short (four months) treatment time. There were no significant differences in the gains made by the groups.

Keyser, Samuel J. "The Role of Linguistics in the Elementary School Curriculum." *Elementary English* 47 (January 1970): 39–45.

The author's contention is that grammar study could lead children to make, critically examine, and reformulate hypotheses about language, surely a far cry from typical activity in language classes today. Sample lesson plans are included. The author contends that linguistic information is available to all, thus teachers should be able to plan lessons of this nature despite the absence of commercial materials.

Kreidler, Charles W. "The Influence of Linguistics in School Grammar." *The Linguistic Reporter* (Newsletter of the Center for Applied Linguistics) 8, No 6 (December 1966).

A short article dealing with discrepancies between the Latinate description of our language and newer linguistic approaches. This deals with the work of the NCTE in encouraging language scholarship and the problems of writers in working with publishers. Over twenty new linguistic materials for children are analyzed.

Lamb, Pose M. *Linguistics in Proper Perspective* (Columbus: Charles E. Merrill Publishing Co., 1967).

A conscientious attempt to interpret for classroom teachers linguistic terminology and thought, which is often confusing and forbidding. The book is especially good for the reader with little or no background. The chapters on the relation of linguistics to reading, spelling, and grammar should be of help to many teachers.

Lefevre, Carl A. "A Multidisciplinary Approach to Language and Reading: Some Projections," in *The Psychological Nature of the Reading Process,* ed. Kenneth S. Goodman (Detroit: Wayne State University Press, 1968), pp. 289–312.

> The author has raised the question about whether the newer linguistic diagrams and notation may not simply be a new form of pedantic busy-work. While these may be of interest to scholars, their usefulness for children is questioned. Lefevre considers the question in a dispassionate manner.

Mehta, Ved. "Onward and Upward with the Arts: John Is Easy to Please." *The New Yorker* 47 (May 8, 1971): 44–48.

> A combination of chatty anecdote and scholarly analysis, this presents a many-sided view of the life and thought of Noam Chomsky, a leading transformationalist. Supportive but not adulatory, the article describes in an easily readable fashion the arguments Chomsky's ideas have provoked.

Minnesota Council of Teachers of English. *Linguistic Bibliography for the Teacher of English.* Duluth: The Council, 1968. (Also available from N.C.T.E.)

> A succinctly annotated bibliography dealing with books, periodical articles, videotapes, and other media concerned with linguistics. In addition to specifying target grade levels, the book also indicates difficulty level, a help to novice readers. It provides an invaluable starting point for the teacher interested in expanding his knowledge of linguistics.

Mountain, Lee Harrison. "Telling Parents about Transformational Grammar." *Elementary English* 49 (May 1972): 684–87.

> The author has developed a markedly creative analogy comparing this grammar system with packing clothes in a suitcase. In short compass he explains, in a fashion designed to intrigue middle-grade children and their parents, a rather complex grammatical description.

Pike, Kenneth. "A Linguistic Contribution to Composition: A Hypothesis." *College Composition and Communication* 15 (May 1964): 82–88.

> Another statement appears in Oct. 1964, pp. 129–35. The two articles summarize tagmemic theory with suggestions to teaching composition and literature, including some sample exercises for students to do.

Rycenga, John A. "Understanding Linguistics." *Catholic School Journal* 67 (June 1967): 27–31.

> The writer presents a comprehensible summary of several complex ideas. The ground covered is considerable: from the work of Rask (1818) through the current transformational grammarians. Despite this, the reader is not given a feeling either of being talked down to or of

being rushed. The linguistics reading program appended to the article should be invaluable to teachers.

Shugrue, Michael F. *How the "New English" Will Help Your Child*. New York: Association Press, 1966, 128 pp.

A helpful book to use with groups of parents who may be unclear about why the English their children learn is so unlike what they learned. It describes with clarity and brevity not only several different linguistic descriptions but also usage and the relations between these components.

Sklar, Robert. "Chomsky's Revolution in Linguistics." *The Nation* 207 (September 9, 1968): 213–17.

A very thorough review of Chomsky's ideas and the books in which they are presented. Written in nontechnical language, this thoughtful analysis provides an accessible introduction to the works of a leading linguistic scholar.

Thomas, Owen. *Transformational Grammar and the Teacher of English.* New York: Holt, Rinehart and Winston, 1965.

The author's emphasis is on teaching, rather than theoretical concerns. His purpose is to present those aspects of transformational grammar which have the greatest usefulness to teachers and future teachers. The explanations are clear and numerous illustrations are given.

CHAPTER THIRTEEN

Language and the Disadvantaged

by Dorothy Huenecke

Who are the disadvantaged? What characteristics do they have in common? What makes them unique from the "advantaged?"

To some extent, everyone is disadvantaged, or lacking in advantages. The Army brat who lives in seven states by the age of five lacks the "advantage" of growing up in one neighborhood. The child who does not move until he goes away to college may miss the "advantages" that come with living in a variety of environments. The only child in a family may be deprived of the spirit of cooperation and camaraderie found in large families. These examples illustrate relatively minor disadvantages among people who are not truly disadvantaged in a sociological sense. They serve to point out that disadvantages can be identified for everyone, but this does not qualify a person to thus be labeled "disadvantaged."

Who then are the disadvantaged? Generalizations are hazardous; exceptions abound, but *generally* the disadvantaged can be described as those with low incomes who suffer from economic and social discrimination. In any sense that is meaningful for educators, the disadvantaged are members of minority groups who lack the means to attain many of the privileges of the majority. Because one is a member of a minority group, however, does not necessarily mean he is disadvantaged; the full

415

gamut of "advantaged-ness" can be found in every identifiable sector of American society.[1] However, most of those classified as educationally disadvantaged are members of minority groups including:

1. Blacks
2. Rural and inner-city whites
3. Mexican Americans
4. American Indians
5. Puerto Ricans
6. Migrant workers of all types

In contrast to the relatively minor disadvantages of the middle class, the problems of the truly disadvantaged seem virtually insurmountable. The cumulative effects of social and economic disadvantages permeate every facet of life; defeatism and despair are logical outcomes. In *The Other America*, Harrington depicts the nearly overwhelming difficulties of large segments of the American population.[2] If there is to be a large-scale improvement in the quality of life for these millions of people, education must be integrally and vitally involved.

Problems of the Disadvantaged

Life for the inner-city disadvantaged differs markedly in some respects from that of the small-town or rural disadvantaged; generalizations thus tend to be foolhardy.[3] Several educationally significant problems seem to be common, however:

1. Standard English is frequently not spoken and a nonstandard dialect is used in the home.
2. Experiences upon which school is based are lacking.
3. Community and school conditions are bad and slow to improve.

---

[1] A concurring statement is made in Leonard Kaplan, "Ain't No Such Thing as Culturally Disadvantaged," *Instructor* LXXXI (February 1972): 18–20. The author points out in incisive fashion the importance of the school valuing and building on the experiences the child has had.

[2] Michael Harrington, *The Other America: Poverty in the United States* (Baltimore: Penguin Books, 1962).

[3] Suggestions for teachers of rural disadvantaged are included in R. A. Saudargas et al., "Prescriptive Teaching in Language Arts Remediation for Black Rural Children," *Journal of Learning Disabilities* 3 (July 1970): 364–70.

Language Problems.   Often a child from a disadvantaged home has limited opportunities to hear or speak standard English. Frequently, large families and crowded conditions prevail. Any infant babbles and makes a wide variety of sounds, only some of which will be needed in the language he will speak as an adult. If a child has someone who speaks to him regularly, the appropriate sounds for his dialect are reinforced and random babbling develops into words. The disadvantaged infant seldom has someone who talks to him alone. Thus, for the disadvantaged the process of developing verbal language may be hindered by the lack of reinforcement and inconsistency of models.

A further language problem accrues from the nonstandard dialect spoken in many disadvantaged homes. Loban explains:

> As long as class societies remain stable, the variations in language cause few problems. In fact the language deficiencies support and stabilize class societies. In any kind of society language represents tremendous social power, and the Establishment speaks one kind of dialect, the established standard dialect. . . . Closed societies have always used language and education as one means of maintaining the *status quo* and of perpetuating a large class of peons or peasants. . . . Even in an open society such as ours, however, where individual worth and aspiration are intended to count for more than fortunate or unfortunate birth, language still operates to preserve social class distinctions and remains one of the major barriers to crossing social lines.[4]

Experiential Background.   Consider the following: John and Willie are born on the same day in the same hour. When John leaves the hospital he goes home to an eight-room house where a four-year-old sister eagerly awaits him. His father is an electrical engineer; his mother, a housewife. As John grows up his mother talks to him, reads to him, takes him shopping with her. By the time he enters kindergarten, he will have been to the zoo, the art gallery, symphony concerts, puppet plays, and big-league baseball games. Many times John has ridden in the car with his family to visit his grandmother in another state; several times he has flown there.

Willie leaves the hospital and goes home to five rooms in which his mother and father, grandmother, uncle, five brothers, and four sisters live. Willie's father is a kitchen worker in a large restaurant; shortly after Willie was born a fire destroyed the restaurant and

---

[4] Walter Loban, "Teaching Children Who Speak Social Class Dialects," *Elementary English* XLV (May 1968): 593.

Willie's father was unable to find work for many months. His mother is a domestic worker who cleans houses six days a week. In order to get to the houses which are located in the suburbs, Willie's mother leaves her house at 7:00 A.M.; she rarely returns home before six o'clock P.M. Willie's mother finds great satisfaction in her children but she works such long hours she is able to spend only limited time with them.[5] Willie sleeps in a room with his brothers and uncle, that is stifling hot in the summer and bitter cold in the winter. Although always clean, Willie's clothes are usually worn because he is the fourth or fifth boy in the family to wear them. Willie's family does not own a car and he has never ridden a bus; thus, he has not gone beyond a two-mile radius of his house.

Both children come to school with a background of many experiences. In all probability, only one set of experiences will be built upon by the school. Thus, the disadvantaged do not lack experiences; they do lack the kind of experiences schools typically expect students to have.

Community and School Conditions.   The environment of the disadvantaged is often dismal. Crowded living conditions are the rule rather than the exception. This problem is compounded in the inner city by the density of population in the neighborhood. High noise levels contribute to a state of uproar. Sanitary facilities are often inadequate; visual and olfactory pollution are common.

Schools, which should be of the highest quality to meet the challenge of the disadvantaged, are often of the poorest quality. The following conditions are common, particularly in inner-city schools:

1. There are inadequate facilities for both education and recreation.
2. The buildings are generally older than those in other areas.
3. The schools are less likely to provide remedial facilities and programs than those in higher-income areas.
4. Substitute teachers provide much of the instruction.
5. The high rate of turnover among teachers and the reluctance of experienced teachers to teach the disadvantaged result in a high proportion of inexperienced teachers in these schools.

---

[5] The problem of parent's limited time, especially in relation to influencing school programs is discussed more fully in William R. Harmer, "To What Extent Should Parents be Involved in Language Programs for Linguistically Different Learners," *Elementary English* XLVII (November 1970): 940–43.

6. Teachers spend almost as much time on discipline as they do on instruction.[6]

Another condition in the school occurs because of the double-edged ignorance which exists. Students are ignorant of the system and teachers are ignorant of the cultural mores of the students.

Community and school conditions do not improve rapidly for the disadvantaged. Although there are a number of contributing causes, one stands out above the others: *the disadvantaged have no political leverage.* Sadly, funds allocated to improve conditions have in some cases been misused and abused with few reprisals to the guilty. Feelings of distrust for outsiders, alienation, and helplessness often result.

Positive Education Aspects. Descriptions of the disadvantaged usually revolve around negative aspects of the situation—the word "disadvantaged" itself is a negative word. There are significant positive features, however, which have been identified.

Based on an examination of creativity among the disadvantaged, Torrance found that in many ways:

> the life experiences of disadvantaged children prepare them for creative achievement. Their lack of expensive toys and play materials contributes to their skill in improvising with common materials. The large families and life-styles of disadvantaged families develop skills in group activities and problem-solving. Positive values placed by their families on music, rhythm, dance, body expressiveness, and humor keep alive abilities that tend to perish in more advantaged families.[7]

In elaborating on these ideas, Torrance identifies some "creative positives" he has frequently found among disadvantaged learners:

1. Ability to express feelings and emotions
2. Articulateness in role-playing and storytelling
3. Enjoyment of and ability in creative movement, dramatics, dance, etc.
4. Expressiveness in speech

---

[6] Based on William B. Ragan, John H. Wilson, and Tillman J. Ragan, *Teaching in the New Elementary School* (New York: Holt, Rinehart and Winston, 1972), pp. 210, 211.

[7] E. Paul Torrance, "Are the Torrance Tests of Creative Thinking Biased against or in Favor of 'Disadvantaged' Groups?" *The Gifted Child Quarterly* (Summer 1971): 27.

5. Expressiveness of gestures, "body language," etc.
6. Richness of imagery in informal language, creative writing, etc.[8]

These features suggest exciting possibilities to those who teach disadvantaged youngsters. As specific activities are planned for learners, these data can be considered in establishing an atmosphere which will foster creativity.

Attitude of the Teacher

The attitudes and feelings of people are crucial in situations dependent upon the quality of interaction among people. To focus attention on attitudes, ponder the eight unfinished statements below. How would you complete them? How do you think others might complete them?

1. Most Jews _____.
2. Italians never _____.
3. _____ usually cause trouble.
4. Puerto Ricans are _____.
5. _____ are aggressive, pushy.
6. Mexicans always _____.
7. _____are lazy.

If you were willing and readily able to attribute qualities and characteristics to groups of people in these statements, it *may* indicate an attitude of prejudice. Prejudice is a prejudgment made without adequate basis. If you are prejudiced toward a person, you tend to lump him into a group and attribute characteristics to him without really knowing him. You *assume* certain things to be true about him because you see him as a member of a particular group even though you *know* very little about him as an individual.

The tendency toward overgeneralization leading to prejudice has its origin in the complexities of life. In his classic work, *The Nature of Prejudice*, Allport says:

Overgeneralization is perhaps the commonest trick of the human mind. Given a thimbleful of facts we rush to make a generalization

---

[8] E. Paul Torrance and Pansy Torrance, "Combining Creative Problem-Solving with Creative Expressive Activities in the Education of Disadvantaged Young People," *The Journal of Creative Behavior* VI (First Quarter 1972): 2–3.

as large as a tub. . . . There is a natural basis for this tendency. Life is short, and the demands upon us for practical adjustments so great, that we cannot let our ignorance detain us in our daily transactions. We have to decide whether objects are good or bad by classes. We cannot weigh each object in the world by itself. Rough and ready rubrics, however coarse and broad, have to suffice.[9]

Thus, categorizations and judgments based on scanty evidence abound and feelings of prejudice often result. Allport explains:

man has a propensity to prejudice. This propensity lies in his normal and natural tendency to form generalizations, concepts, categories, whose content represents an oversimplification of his world of experience.[10]

Prejudice is often accompanied by fear. In fact, fear and prejudice often have a reciprocal relationship; one is frequently prejudiced against what he fears and fears what he is prejudiced against. The teacher who plans to work with disadvantaged learners needs to ask himself: Are there factors in this situation that frighten me? If so, what are some of these fears? Are they justified? How can these fears be overcome?

Fear based on ignorance is not uncommon among prospective teachers of the disadvantaged. Very few teachers have experienced a disadvantaged childhood. Most teachers were good students in schools, received the rewards of the system and found satisfaction enough to continue through secondary school and college. It is difficult under such conditions to empathize with students who despise school and teachers alike, and who are unable or unwilling to fulfill the expectations of school.

The discontinuity between the culture of the home and the school makes it difficult to develop in these children the desire for competence in the school environment which is necessary for a continuing positive interaction there. The children have entered school without the skills on which the curriculum is founded, and furthermore, they find it difficult to see the point in making an effort. Thus, for them, the school becomes a place which makes baffling demands, where failure is a rule, and a feeling of competence is rare.[11]

---

[9] Gordon W. Allport, *The Nature of Prejudice* (Garden City, N.Y.: Doubleday and Company, 1954), p. 9.

[10] Allport, *The Nature of Prejudice*, p. 26.

[11] Hilda Taba and Deborah Elkins, *Teaching Strategies for the Culturally Disadvantaged* (Chicago: Rand McNally and Company, 1966), p. 9.

Ignorance of the conditions resulting in such student attitudes can contribute to a subtle fear in teachers of students who hold these attitudes.

If a teacher honestly examines his inner thoughts, he may find feelings of prejudice and fear for the disadvantaged. If he wishes to overcome these feelings, he needs to engage in activities that enable him to remedy his ignorance of the conditions surrounding the disadvantaged. Involvement with the disadvantaged is imperative, so observation and interaction can occur. Tutoring students of disadvantaged groups in their homes offers a unique opportunity to do this. In addition, work in local volunteer groups, perhaps at a community center, or day-care facility, can be most helpful.

Inferences are unfortunately often made about a person's intelligence because of his language. Certain dialects are considered "uneducated" while others are considered to be "educated." If this attitude prevails among teachers, a child may be evaluated as having limited abilities merely because of dialect. According to Russell, although there is a close relationship between language and thinking, they are not identical.[12] Shuy says:

> That people speak different dialects in no way stems from their intelligence or judgment. They speak the dialect which enables them to get along with the other members of their social and geographical group.[13]

It is sad, but true, that teachers too often make such judgments about children's intelligence based upon their language patterns. For upwardly mobile teachers from lower-middle or lower classes, standard English is seen as a means of mobility. Too often such teachers look down upon the nonstandard varieties of English spoken by the disadvantaged children they teach.

As this section has attempted to illustrate, an honest examination of teacher attitudes is essential in dealing with the disadvantaged. One fact stands out above the others: *the attitude of the teacher toward the disadvantaged is the key element in the teaching-learning environment.* The best materials and conditions available cannot overcome the negative attitude of a teacher toward his students. On the other hand, the

---

[12] David H. Russell, *Children's Thinking* (New York: Blaisdell Publishing Company, 1956).

[13] Roger W. Shuy, *Discovering American Dialects* (Champaign, Illinois: National Council of Teachers of English, 1967), p. 5.

lack of facilities will have minimal effect on an educational environment where the attitudes are positive.[14]

Nonstandard Dialects

In examining one's attitude toward the disadvantaged, it is essential to consider honestly one's attitude toward language. The first impression of another person often stems, if unconsciously, to a great extent from his use of language. Based in part on the dialect spoken, a person's language may pique our curiosity and hold our attention or we may conclude that there is little about him to interest us. This impact of language was illustrated delightfully in the musical "My Fair Lady" based on George Bernard Shaw's play, *Pygmalion*. Professor Higgins' modifications of Eliza's dialect could even, with older children, become subject matter for a study of dialect differences.

In all likelihood the most perplexing language-related problem facing the teacher of the disadvantaged revolves around dialects. Typically, disadvantaged students speak a nonstandard dialect which is viewed by many as inferior.[15] Loban says:

> Whereas regional differences in language are usually acceptable and in many respects delightful, social class dialects offer a difficult problem to American schools in which equality of opportunity for all pupils is accepted as an aim. Economic and social lines have always been difficult to cross, and language is one of the strongest barriers to a fluid society . . . all speech communities tend to feel hostility or disdain for those who do not use their language. . . . American teachers acknowledge that most children need to perfect or acquire the prestige dialect — not because standard English is correct or superior in itself but because society exacts severe penalities of those who do not speak it.[16]

---

[14] Other statements of the importance of the teacher's attitude, are included in John Holt, *The Underachieving School* (New York: Dell, 1970); James Herndon, *The Way It Spozed to Be* (New York: Simon and Schuster, 1968); Herbert Kohl, *Thirty-Six Children* (New York: New American Library, 1968); or Esther Rothman, *The Angel Inside Went Sour* (New York: Bantam, 1972).

[15] This is the view held by most teachers of the disadvantaged, according to Doris L. Pertz, "Urban Youth, Nonstandard English and Economic Mobility," *Elementary English* XLVIII (December 1971): 1012–17.

[16] Walter Loban, *Problems in Oral English*. NCTE Research Report No. 5 (Champaign, Illinois: National Council of Teachers of English, 1966), p. 1.

It would appear, then, that a goal of democratic education is that students should be able to use standard English if social and economic mobility are to become realities, ideals espoused in a democratic society. Teachers of nonstandard speakers can best achieve this goal if they apprise themselves of the major ways in which the nonstandard dialects differ from standard English. Figures of school enrollment indicate that speakers of black English are the most prevalent group of disadvantaged students. It is most likely that, if you are teaching or will teach the disadvantaged, the group with which you work will be black. To this end, features of several nonstandard black dialects will be presented.

Not uncommonly, it is assumed that there is a single black dialect. It is equally as absurd to believe there is one black dialect as it is to assume there is one Caucasian dialect. The tendency of some to overgeneralize about dialects in this manner may be symptomatic of prejudice as described earlier in this chapter. This tendency to overgeneralize is illustrated when stereotypes about language are formed; for example, someone using a nonstandard form 20 to 30 percent of the time is often perceived to be using this form 100 percent of the time.[17]

According to Labov, three major phonological variables commonly found in black dialects can be identified:

1. *r-lessness*   When an *r* appears in the medial or final position of a word, it becomes a schwa or it disappears. For example,

   Carol = Cal
   Paris = pass
   guard = God
   terrace = test

2. *l-lessness*   In a manner similar to the loss of the *r* in pronunciation, the final *l* is often not pronounced.

   toll = toe
   rule = rue
   help = hep
   all   = awe

---

[17] William Labov, "Some Sources of Reading Problems for Negro Speakers of Nonstandard English," in *New Directions in Elementary English*, ed. Alexander Frazier (Champaign, Illinois: National Council of Teachers of English, 1967), pp. 143, 148–52, 155–57.

3. *Simplification of consonant clusters at the end of words.* Although many consonant sounds are dropped at the ends of words, those represented by *t* and *d* are very commonly omitted.

past	= pass	mend	= men
hold	= hole	field	= feel
laughed	= laugh	mash	= mass
meant	= men	gasp	= gas

Several major grammatical counterparts of these phonological variations can be identified. For example, l-lessness can result in the absence of the future tense in speech.

you'll	= you
they'll	= they
he'll	= he
she'll	= she

Likewise, the elimination of the final consonant sounds represented by *t* and *d* can result in the absence of the past tense in oral language.

missed	= miss
picked	= pick
raised	= raise

Another systematic examination of a black dialect was conducted by Loban in a longitudinal study. In his conclusions, Loban identifies ten significant variations between the nonstandard black dialect and standard English. The five most prevalent include:

1. Lack of verb agreement, third person singular (excluding *to be*)
   He *say* he's going home.
   They boy *don't* look happy.
   The mother *look* at television a lot.

2. Lack of auxiliary verbs
   He (is) running away.
   How (do) you know he isn't there?
   He (has) been here.

3. Inconsistency in use of tense.
   One time when I was sick my mother *comes* to see me.
   She knew if she *does* something bad he would find out.

4. Nonstandard use of verb forms
   He has *ate*.
   I *seen* him yesterday.
   He *don't* be there much.

5. Lack of agreement using *to be*.
   I *is* going inside.
   There *was* two girls.
   Here *is* two dogs.[18]

Through such thorough analyses of dialects, specific variations from standard English can be identified. Once identified, alternatives can be proposed.

Many teachers of the disadvantaged will not come in contact with the specific deviations from standard English described here. They may teach students with an entirely different set of dialect features. It is highly important that these be identified and described if the problems of nonstandard dialects are to be addressed seriously.[19]

Purposes and Strategies for Language Instruction

The classification of humans into groups labeled "disadvantaged," "advantaged," "genius," or "EMR," stirs the conscience because it is basically *de*humanizing. A number of descriptors can be applied to any one group of people resulting in the multiple classification of individuals. Thus, among other possibilities, a youngster may be classified as male, ten years old, identical twin, average IQ, disadvantaged. The last classification *may* be least relevant. Therefore, to consider teaching strategies for the disadvantaged as though their disadvantagedness was necessarily the most pertinent bit of information about them is unwise.

Disadvantaged students profit from good teaching just as more advantaged students do. This book suggests many good strategies for teaching language to students. All of the suggestions can be incorporated into teaching the disadvantaged because *the basic principles of good teaching are applicable to any level of learning at any socio-economic level.*

---

18 Loban, *Problems in Oral English*, pp. 8, 10, 14, 16, and 20.

19 Such dialect differences are now being described but it will be some time before all major dialects have been analyzed. A description of a different black dialect than the two above is included in Johanna S. DeStefano, "Productive Language Differences in Fifth-Grade Black Students' Syntactic Forms," *Elementary English* XLIX (April 1972): 552–58.

Additional suggestions are presented in this chapter to supplement the others presented in the book. In the sections that follow, a sampling of the many goals for language instruction based on the cognitive, affective, and psychomotor taxonomies is presented.[20] In addition, strategies to attain language goals are described for the skills of listening, speaking, reading, and writing. Most of the strategies are appropriate for individual or small-group instruction as well as large-group instruction.

Listening. Among the important goals for listening are the following:

Cognitive	The student should be able to:
	listen for differences.
	listen for likenesses.
	listen accurately.
	listen critically.
Psychomotor	The student should be able to:
	listen attentively.
	discern relevant sounds (e.g., hear the teacher's voice amid many voices).
Affective	The student should be able to:
	listen appreciatively.

As the suggestions below indicate, students should have an opportunity to hear many sounds, not just the teacher's voice.

The students can talk or read into a tape recorder and listen to their own voices.
The students can listen to musical records and raise their hands every time they hear a specified instrument. (The use of popular records will heighten motivation.)
The students can be given a sheet of paper divided into rows of cells. They can take turns giving such directions as:
1. "Start at the upper left-hand corner. Count 3 squares over, two squares down and draw a cat."
2. "Find the bottom right-hand square. Count four squares up and write your name."
Play "Simon Says."

---

[20] These are the three taxonomies described earlier, on pages 40–46 of Chapter 2. The reader may wish to review the more complete descriptions included there before reading this section.

Stop everything that is going on. Ask students what small sounds they hear (clock-ticking, noises in the hall, etc.) that are usually inaudible.

The teacher can read a list of words all of which begin with the same sound except for one. The students can identify which word begins differently than the others. (This can be done with final sounds, rhyming words, words with a specified number of syllables, etc.)

Play musical records of various moods. Have the students try to express the way the music made them feel, through dancing, creative movement, role-playing, drawing, or painting.

There is a common saying that once you have learned to ride a bicycle you never forget. The same cannot be said for the skill of listening. Once "taught," it does not remain "learned." To acquire good listening skills, activities that explicitly allow for their acquisition are required throughout the school years. Upper-grade teachers cannot logically expect that all necessary instruction in listening will have been accomplished in the primary grades.

Speaking.   Oral language is a major avenue by which man expresses his ideas, feelings, and values. Speaking skills play an important role as man seeks to reach his full potential. The majority of intentional communication is transmitted through speech. One of the major responsibilities of education, then, is the development of students' speaking abilities.

Students need many opportunities to talk in school if they are to develop and refine speaking skills. All adults speak in a variety of "styles," depending upon the situation. We talk differently with husband or wife, with employer, with public official. Disadvantaged students should be able to talk with other students in their classes, with older students, younger students, and people in authority because each situation requires a different speaking style.

The use of nonstandard dialects and the need for standard English to achieve economic and social mobility pose instructional problems for teachers of the disadvantaged. Several questions persist: When should students be taught standard English? How should it be taught?

For early elementary students, the major goal should be free oral expression with little regard to dialects. If there is mutual understanding of what is said among students and between the teacher and students, there is little need to be concerned about dialect. The child should feel comfortable with his dialect and his ability to express himself. As the child advances in school, his ability to express himself in standard English becomes more important. In the later elementary years, in the middle school and secondary school, instruction in standard English is necessary to provide students with an alternative for their dialects.[21]

The concept of alternatives is important. Language and emotions are intertwined. If a person's language is criticized, his inner self may be threatened. The aim of instruction in standard English should not be to *replace* the dialect of the student but to provide an *alternative* dialect if he chooses to use it. Although there may be occasions in the secondary school when standard English is required, the choice is ultimately up to the individual as to whether he will speak standard English. He only has a choice, however, if he knows standard English.

Methods of instruction in standard English vary. The identification of how dialects vary specifically from standard English is prerequisite to thorough instruction. The most common variations can then be altered through drill. Older students can be taught generalizations about language and then can apply them. For example, Loban identified lack of verb agreement, third person singular (excluding *to be*) as a major deviation from the standard English dialect he examined.[22] The standard verb forms for the third person singular can be presented with the students actually memorizing the standard forms. They can then be asked in an analytical approach to substitute the standard forms for nonstandard forms as in the following examples:

She *go* to the store.
He *say* he will be there tomorrow.

Following this, based on synthesis, students can make up their own sentences using the standard form. Clearly, the true indication of students' *willingness* to use standard forms will not likely occur within the classroom, but their *ability* to do so can be ascertained.

Other goals for speaking may include:

Cognitive   The student should:
know a variety of words for expressing his thoughts.
be able to express his thoughts orally.

---

[21] The question of *when* instruction in standard English should be introduced is one of many unresolved questions, discussed by Dorothy S. Strickland, "Black is Beautiful vs. White is Right," *Elementary English* XLIX (February 1972): 220–23.

[22] Loban, *Problems in Oral English*, p. 8.

Psychomotor　The student should be able to:
enunciate clearly.
articulate clearly.
make the sounds of standard English.
speak audibly.

Affective　The student should be:
willing to speak in small and large groups.
willing to speak standard English (at an appropriate age).

The following suggestions may be useful in teaching oral language skills to disadvantaged youngsters:

To provide a set of common experiences to talk about, walks around the school neighborhood and longer field trips can be taken. Films, filmstrips, records, and TV programs can also provide the stimulus for conversation.

The teacher can have the students look at interesting and thought-provoking pictures. The student can make up stories about pictures (individually or in a group) or they can make up questions to ask about the pictures.

A student can be asked to say a word that pops into his head. Another student can repeat this word and say another that has the same beginning sound. This can be repeated until the group has suggested as many possibilities as it can.

The students can sit informally in a circle. One student can start out by saying something similar to the following, "I see a green book. Mary, do you see it?" Mary has to find what the first student saw before she can have a turn.

A student can be blindfolded and asked to describe an object which he can feel.

If students are hesitant to speak before others, they can talk "through" puppets.

The students can be asked to experiment with saying a sentence in many different ways. For example, the sentence "I will be there in five minutes" can be whispered, shouted, stated emphatically, or stammered.

Another way in which the same spoken sentence can have different meanings is through the emphasis put on words. The students can be asked to emphasize different words in a sentence similar to the following: *I* am going home now, *I am* going home now, or I am *going* home now.[23]

Reading. Reading requires breaking the code of a symbol (written word) for something else (object, idea, feeling). Decoding a written word and understanding its intent is a complex process that requires a background of experiences and a knowledge of words.

Many disadvantaged youngsters come from homes where there are no books. They may rarely see a person reading. For these youngsters, reading-readiness activities may appropriately extend throughout the first years of school. The early years of schooling for the disadvantaged child should stress vocabulary and oral language development; encoding and decoding written language may not be relevant until the middle school years.

> It would seem obvious . . . that particularly in the primary years children should be given every opportunity to overcome their language deficiencies and to learn to use standard American English with ease and agility. It is not enough for them to acquire an enriched vocabulary in a socially unmarked dialect alone. They must learn to manipulate language in meaningful and efficient ways. . . . Language skills should be established before the reading program commences.[24]

After language skills have been developed several approaches for teaching reading to the disadvantaged seem worthy of consideration. The *language-experience* approach can be effective because it builds on the unique experiences of each child as he learns to read by decoding what he has dictated.[25] The *initial teaching alphabet* (ITA) can also be effective with disadvantaged youngsters.[26] The initial teaching alphabet consists of forty-four symbols each of which represents only one sound. Children who know the twenty-six letters of the alphabet may be slightly confused by ITA, but most disadvantaged children will not

---

[23] Other helpful suggestions are given by Irwin Teigenbaum, "Developing Fluency in Standard Oral English," *Elementary English* LXVII (December 1970): 1053–59.

[24] Jean York and Dorothy Ebert, "Primary Level: Grades 1–3," in *Reading for the Disadvantaged: Problems of Linguistically Different Learners*, ed. Thomas D. Horn (New York: Harcourt Brace Jovanovich, 1970), pp. 186, 187.

[25] See Doris M. Lee and R. V. Allen, *Learning to Read through Experience* (New York: Appleton-Century-Crofts, 1963).

[26] John Downing, *The Initial Teaching Alphabet Explained and Illustrated* (New York: The Macmillan Co., 1964).

know the alphabet when they enter school. The regularities of sound-symbol relationship can be stressed with ITA, reducing the confusion resulting from the inconsistencies of the English language.

It is important to note that regardless of the approach used in teaching reading, the teacher's attitude is paramount. The method that seems best to the teacher will likely be the one that is most effective for him.[27]

The specific strategies utilized in reading instruction will vary according to basic approach; therefore, no strategies will be presented here. The following goals are among those which could be incorporated into the reading program, however.

Cognitive	The student should: know generalizations about the symbol-sound relationships of English. be able to apply knowledge of generalizations in attacking new words.
Psychomotor	The student should: have the necessary eye coordination for reading. be able to real aloud smoothly.
Affective	The student should be interested in reading.

Writing.   Writing is an important process for recording language. It makes permanent thoughts and ideas which in oral form have only momentary existence. A thought or a spoken word always preceded the written word. Thus, instruction in writing should be minimal until the student's oral language is fluent.

When instruction in writing does become appropriate, two basic types should be considered: the functional and the creative. Functional writing is the presentation of expository material. It should be clear and concise. Generally, formal English is used in functional writing. Knowledge of punctuation is required if the written word is to communicate accurately. Knowledge of sentence and paragraph structure also becomes important as students advance in their writing ability.

Creative writing can take many forms. Free verse, haiku poetry, short stories, fairy tales, and puppet plays are only a few ways in which

---

[27] See *The Reading Teacher* (May 1966). The entire volume is devoted to summaries of the twenty-seven studies of first-grade reading, supported by U.S.O.E. Different problems were handled in different ways; no definitive answer was reached regarding the "best" way to teach reading. All studies concur on the importance of the teacher favoring the method he is using.

children can write creatively. Disadvantaged children may excel in the area of creativity according to Torrance. Among the creative positives he has identified for the disadvantaged are "richness of imagery in informal language and creative writing," and "originality of ideas in problem-solving and brainstorming."[28]

An important facet of writing is spelling. If written words are to communicate they need to be spelled correctly. The use of nonstandard dialects in oral language can cause spelling problems in written language. For example, *l-lessness* in oral language may result in the absence of the final *l* when a word is written. Knowledge of dialects spoken by students is requisite in analyzing such spelling errors. If students spell words as they pronounce them, they are making the transition from the spoken to the written word with consistency. Their spelling errors will not likely be corrected until they recognize the patterns of variation from standard English in their speech. If disadvantaged students' spelling errors do not follow the patterns of their dialect, the problem could be caused by any of the factors commonly associated with spelling errors.[29]

Another aspect of writing is penmanship. Other than the possible lack of practice with pencils or crayons prior to his entry in school, the disadvantaged student should encounter no special problems in this area.

Goals which can be established for writing include:

Cognitive The student should:
know basic punctuation.
be able to use punctuation appropriately.
be able to write a sentence.
be able to spell appropriate words correctly.
be able to express ideas creatively.

Psychomotor The student should be able to write legibly.

Affective The student should be willing to share his ideas and feelings in writing.

The following suggestions can be used in teaching writing:

Students can write down stories dictated by younger children.

---

[28] Torrance, "Creative Problem-Solving," p. 3.

[29] A more extensive treatment of this problem is included in Richard T. Graham and E. Hugh Rudorf, "Dialect and Spelling," *Elementary English* XLVII (March 1970): 363–73.

Pen pals in another school or even another city can be identified
and letters can be exchanged.

Students can make puppets and write stories for the puppets to tell.

Students can write titles for thought-provoking pictures.

Summary

Characteristics of disadvantaged students can be described and
conditions in which they live can quite accurately be postulated. In doing this, however, it must not be overlooked that the disadvantaged have
far more in common with advantaged groups than there are differences
between them. The differences between advantaged and disadvantaged
youngsters can be meaningful, but they should not become over-
powering. In designing curricula for teaching language skills to the
disadvantaged, characteristics of the disadvantaged should be considered as one of many bits of relevant information. Regardless of how
well researched these characteristics may be, however, the assessment
of *individual* characteristics of *individual* learners remains the essential task.

Suggestions for Further Explorations

1. Choose one of the "creative positives" identified by Torrance. Plan
   a language lesson built upon that strength. If possible, teach the
   lesson to a group of disadvantaged children, to test its effectiveness.

2. Make a tape of yourself having a conversation with a friend. Analyze your language to determine what nonstandard forms you used.
   Is there any difference of opinion regarding this? If several different
   people analyzed the tape, would the tally of nonstandard forms
   agree?

3. Make a collection of pictures that you feel would be thought-provoking for disadvantaged children. Can you justify your choice of
   pictures as appropriate for the target group of children? Identify
   the language-motivation uses to which the pictures could be put.

4. Visit an inner-city school and a rural school that have many disadvantaged students. Compare and contrast the student bodies, the
   facilities, the learning problems presented, and the environments.

5. Search census reports, newspaper files, and school records to determine how many and what types of disadvantaged people live in

your community. Is there some way you could determine what these different groups have in common, and how they differ?

Bibliography

Ashton-Warner, Sylvia. *Teacher*. New York: Bantam Books, 1963.

> This warm, sensitive account of teaching Maori and white children in New Zealand details the language-experience approach to teaching reading. Although loaded with information, it is not presented in "typical textbook" fashion.

Bordie, John G. "Language Tests and Linguistically Different Learners: The Sad State of the Art." *Elementary English* XLVII (October 1970): 814–28.

> Teachers in disadvantaged schools are plagued as are all teachers with annual administrations of standardized tests. For many disadvantaged children these tests are unfair at best. The author analyzes such tests pointing out weaknesses. The conclusion reached is that few accurately assess disadvantaged children's language ability.

Cheyney, Arnold B. *Teaching Culturally Disadvantaged in the Elementary School*. Columbus, Ohio: Charles E. Merrill Publishing Co., 1967.

> This book offers many practical suggestions for teaching language skills to disadvantaged students as well as pertinent information on characteristics of disadvantaged students and the role of teacher attitude.

Clark, Kenneth B. *Dark Ghetto: Dilemmas of Social Power*. New York: Harper and Row, Publishers, 1965.

> Clark speaks frankly of the problems facing both blacks and whites in American society. It is a well-written, informative, gutsy book.

Coleman, James S. *Equality of Educational Opportunity*. Washington, D.C.: U.S. Government Printing Office, 1966.

> The Coleman Report focuses on educational opportunities for the disadvantaged. Data regarding school environments, school enrollment, pupil achievement and motivation, and school integration are presented.

Imhoff, M. I. "Preparation of Language Arts Teachers for Ghetto Schools." *Viewpoints* 47 (March 1971): 125–35.

> The author prescribes what he feels is the most successful way to prepare teachers of the culturally disadvantaged. Read this for some contrasts it offers to the suggestions made in this chapter.

Kozol, Jonathan. *Death at an Early Age*. New York: Bantam Books, 1967.

> The subtitle of the book describes it as dealing with "The destruction of the hearts and minds of Negro children in the Boston public schools."

This destruction is detailed in a heart-rending account which should be read by teachers of advantaged as well as disadvantaged learners.

Report of the National Advisory Commission on Civil Disorders. New York: Bantam Books, 1968.

This report by the Kerner Commission, established by the federal government, provides data on conditions of the disadvantaged that Americans in general and educators in particular cannot afford to ignore.

Skeel, Dorothy J. *Children of the Street: Teaching in the Inner-City.* Pacific Palisades, California: Goodyear Publishing Company, 1971.

Conditions of the classroom and qualifications for teachers are discussed prior to suggestions for teaching language arts and other areas.

Teague, Bob. *Letters to a Black Boy.* New York: Lancer Books, 1968.

Teague, a black newscaster, had fewer obstacles to overcome in rising to the top of his profession than many others, yet he is fearful of the hurt ahead for his young son. In a series of sensitive letters, sometimes moving, sometimes comical, he tries to prepare his son for what lies ahead. Fast but worthwhile reading.

Uhl, Norman P. et al. "Receptive and Expressive Vocabularies of Upper-Middle and Low SEL Children." *Elementary English* XLIX (May 1972): 725–29.

The authors identify some important vocabulary differences and similarities between the two groups being studied. Suggestions for vocabulary-teaching techniques are included.

Webster, Staten W. *Knowing and Understanding the Socially Disadvantaged: Ethnic Minority Groups.* Scranton: Intext Educational Publishers, 1972.

This book of readings is particularly useful because it includes articles not only on black Americans but also Mexican Americans, Puerto Ricans, Indians, Chinese, and Japanese.

Index

accountability, 254
acquisition of language, 8, 119
   bibliography, 23
Aesop's Fables, 162
Affective Taxonomy, 42
affixes, 365
Allport, Gordon W., 421
alphabet books:
   bibliography of, 311
alphabet system, 262, 333
Always Room for One More, 345
American Institute of Graphic Arts
      Awards, 198
Anderson, Paul S., 93, 106
Applegate, Maurie, 161, 219
Arbuthnot, May H., 141
artifacts:
   use of, 66
Ashton-Warner, Sylvia, 435
Asimov, Isaac, 340, 372
attitudes:
   of teachers toward disadvantaged,
      420, 422
   toward handwriting, 245

babbling, 12
Bat Poet, The, 106
Bellugi, Ursula, 9, 17
Bereiter, C., 14, 21
Berko, Jean, 14, 21
Birdwhistell Ray, 334
black English, 424
Bloom, Benjamin S., 40, 63, 105, 125
Bloomfield, Leonard, 399
books:
   unit on, 74
   wordless, 138
borrowed words, 284
Borten, Helen, 115, 208

Bostain, James, 356, 395
boustrophedon writing, 267
Boyd, Gertrude A., 276, 308
Britton, James, 11
Brooke, L. Leslie, 341
Brown, Roger, 9
Burrows, A. T., 199, 213, 220

Caldecott Award, 198
Caldecott, R. R., 341
Carroll, Lewis, 341
Cat, The, 101
Cat and Chanticleer, The, 133
Cazden, C., 23
C D B, 309
characterization:
   questions about, 206
Charlotte's Web, 198
Chomsky, C., 119
Chomsky, N., 23, 401
choral speaking, 141
cinquain, 209, 223–24
Classroom Questions: What Kinds?,
      52
code systems, 73–74, 263
Cognitive Taxonomy, 40
Community Resource Question-
      naire, 84
conference telephone:
   language uses of, 67
connotation, 367
conversation, 71–72, 123–26
Corcoran, Gertrude B., 290
creative dramatics, 160
creative writing conferences, 207
creative writing:
   definition of, 193
   editing in, 203
   evaluation of, 205–8

Crosby, Muriel, 391
cultural differences in listening, 97
curriculum:
    approaches to in kindergarten, 65
    levels of responsibility in develop-
        ing, 30
    typing in the, 260–62
cursive writing, 241
    difficult letters in, 248, 256

Dale, Edgar, 355, 374, 379
Dale, Phillip S., 393
Davis, A. L., 342
Davis, D. C., 62–63, 85, 335
Deighton, Lee C., 360, 365–67
denotation, 367
describing competencies, 126–29
dialect, 286, 331, 369, 391, 422
    nonstandard, 423
dictionaries:
    beginning, 360, 379
    changing role of, 292–94
    specialized, 371
disadvantaged:
    bibliography, 435
    creativity of, 419
    language problems of, 10, 88, 417
discussion, oral, 71
Donoghue, Mildred R., 261, 276, 302,
    375
Do You Hear What I Hear?, 115
drama:
    bibliography, 181
    components of, 157–60
    definition of, 156
    evaluation in, 159
    leader, 161
    movement in, 156, 159, 162, 178–79
    qualities of, 165–69
    sessions, 164
    values of, 169
Duker, Sam, 88, 92, 94

editing, 203
educational goals, 36
egocentric language, 18

electronetic writing, 73
Emig, Janet, 9
Epstein, Sam and Beryl, 342, 380
etymology, 360, 368–69
evaluation:
    of creative writing, 205–8
    of drama sessions, 159–60
    of listening skills, 107–11
    of oral language, 122
expansion, 10

field exploration, 66
Fitzhugh, Louise, 362
foundational treatment, 64, 74
Fox and the Grapes, The, 162
Francis, W. Nelson, 386
From Painted Rock to Printed Page,
    268
Future Shock, 358
Fyleman, Rose, 143

Gag, Wanda, 313
George, Jean, 329
gestures, 73
    in story telling, 136
Gingerbread Boy, The, 339
Glubok, Shirley, 105
goals, educational, 36
Goblin, The, 143
Grahame, Kenneth, 362
grammar:
    classroom applications of, 404
    components of, 387
    definitions of, 15, 385
    pivot and open stage, 16
    research studies about, 403–4
    stratificational, 403
    traditional, 398
    transformational, 401
grapheme, 283
Green, Harry A., 277, 354, 403
Greenaway, Kate, 313

haiku, 209, 221, 224
Hale, Lucretia, 362

handwriting:
  approaches to teaching, 241
  attitudes toward, 245
  bibliography, 271–75
  developing legibility in, 255–59
  individualization in, 248
  regularization of, 256–59
  time allotments for, 244
  transition in, 253
  variability in standards, 259–60
Hanna, Paul R., 287, 308
haptics, 334
Harriet The Spy, 362
Harrington, Michael, 416
Hawaii Handwriting Program, 250
hearing:
  definition of, 88
  impairment, 89–90
Herrick, Virgil, 244–45
Holling, H. C., 329
holophrases, 13
Holt, John, 269
Homer Price, 362
Horn, Ernest, 357

ideographic systems, 263
idiolect, 331, 369
impressional treatment, 64, 74
improvising, 163
imitation and reduction, 9
interpreting, 162
individualized handwriting
    programs, 248–51
ITA, 431
It's Like This, Cat, 359

Jabberwocky, 145
Journey Cake, Ho!, 73
juncture, 174, 389

keystones of language, 63, 80
kernel sentences, 401
kindergarten, reading in the, 61
kinesics, 174–76, 334

Labanotation, 264, 266
Labov, William, 424

Lamb, Pose M., 247, 410
language:
  acquisition of, 3, 336
  attitude of teacher toward disad-
    vantaged, 420
  bibliography of books about, 340
  change in, 337
  child's knowledge about, 4
  competency in using, 4, 119
  developmental stages in, 6, 18
  egocentric and socialized, 18
  films about, 349
  forms of, 331
  functions of, 58
  history of, 336
  improvisation among young chil-
    dren, 11
  nature of, 336
  nonverbal, 334
  norms in, 337
  observing and describing, 128
  problems of the disadvantaged,
    417
  written, 332
language-experience approach, 431
Leaf, Munroe, 407
Lear, Edward, 313, 344
learning environments, 68, 80
Lefevre, Carl A., 376, 400, 403, 411
left-handed child, 276–77
legibility, 255–59
Lenneberg, Eric H., 6, 8, 17
Lenski, Lois, 344
letter writing, 213–14, 372
Lewis Carroll Shelf Awards, 198
linguistics:
  structural, 399
  teaching materials about, 358
Lionni, Leo, 104, 359
*Lion, the Witch and the Wardrobe,
    The*, 227
listening:
  activities, 427
  amount required, 91

listening (Cont.)
  bibliography of children's books about, 11
  conditions for effective, 95
  critical, 104
  cultural differences in evidences of, 97
  definition of, 88
  evaluation of, 107–11
  goals for, 427
  sequence of skills in, 98
  sex differences in, 90
  speed in, 93
Listening Walk, The, 116
literature:
  functions of, 325
  presentation of, 329
Little House in the Big Woods, 331
Little Red Riding Hood, 166
Loban, Walter, 122, 406, 417, 423, 425
Lore and Language of School Children, The, 376
Loudest Noise in the World, 115
Lundsteen, Sara W., 90, 111, 114

Mager, Robert F., 38
manuscript writing, 243
  difficult letters in, 247
  reasons for teaching, 253
Marckwardt, Albert H., 370, 404
Mary Poppins, 362
masks, uses of in drama, 189
Mayer, Mercer, 345
McCaslin, Nellie, 183
McCloskey, Robert, 362, 363
meaning, determined by listening, 103
Mearns, Hughes, 199, 221
mechanics in writing, 199, 210–13
metaphor, 209
Midas Touch, The, 163
miniature play, language stimulated by, 69
Moffett, James, 202
Montessori, Maria, 112, 272

morpheme, 390
morphology, 6, 14, 129, 390
Mother Goose, 37, 141
movement in drama, 156, 159, 162, 178–79
music in storytelling, 136
My Side of theMountain, 329
Mysterious Cat, The, 102

names, study of, 371
Nebraska Curriculum, 204, 407
Neville, Emily, 359
Newbery Award, 198
NicLeodhas, Sorche, 345
nonstandard English, 392, 423
nonverbal communication, 10, 175–76
notation systems, 264–67
nouns, 400

objectives:
  evaluation of, 49
  instructional, 38–48
obbligatos, verbal, 144
Ogg, Oscar, 272, 346
Old Mother Hubbard, 177–78
O'Neill, Mary, 116, 382
Opie, Iona and Peter, 376
oral language:
  activities, 71, 430
  bibliography, 149
  goals for, 429
  lack of curriculum in, 120
oral reading, 130–33

Pagoo, 329
Pancake, The, 73
paralanguage, 173, 335
Parent Letter, sample of, 82
patterns in spelling, 288–90
Peabody Language Development Kit, 60
Pei, Mario, 120, 291
Perrault, Charles, 74
The Peterkin Papers, 362
Petty Walter T., 150, 172, 222, 304, 354, 358, 403
phoneme, 283, 388

phonology, 6, 129, 388, 424
  acquisition of, 12
Piaget, Jean, 18
Pitch, 99, 173, 388, 391
pivot and open class, 16
planning speech, 20
play, types of, 69
plot, questions about, 206
poetry, 145, 148, 209, 220–25, 228
Pooley, Robert, 408
practical writing, 210–16
prejudice, feelings of toward the
  disadvantaged, 421
Psychomotor Domain, 44
punctuation, 262
Push Back the Desks, 172
Pyle, Howard, 346

qualities of drama, 165–69
questioning, 105–7, 125–26, 215–16
questions about editing, 204

Rand, Paul and Ann, 347
Raths, Louis E., 35
reading:
  and the disadvantaged, 431
  goals for instruction in, 61, 432
  importance of, for creative writ-
    ing, 197–99
  oral, 130–33
*Reflections on a Gift of Watermelon
  Pickle*, 142
Reid, Alastair, 347, 382
reports:
  oral, 71
  written, 214
resource persons, 66
Roberts, Paul, 284, 369, 400, 402, 408
Russell, David, 422

Sanders, Norris, 52, 150
Sandhill Crane, The, 187
Sawyer, Ruth, 150, 194
Schiller, Andrew, 387, 390
schwa, 286
Secret Codes and Ciphers, 309

sentence:
  expansion of, 405
  kernel and transformed, 401, 405
  moveables in, 407
  patterns, 399
sequence in listening, 100
Sequential Tests of Educational
  Progress, 110
setting, questions related to, 207
Shane, Harold G., 301
Sherwin, J. Stephen, 280, 302, 309, 398
Shuy, Roger W., 370, 422
*Signs and Symbols Around the
  World*, 343, 381
Siks, Geraldine B., 170
similes, 208–9
skill groups, 210–13, 396
skill treatment, 63
slang, 370
slot and filler technique, 400, 404
Snakes and Snails, 167
socialized language, 18
sound, duration variability in, 99
Spache, George and Evelyn, 303
speaking (see oral language)
spelling:
  analyzing a series, 309
  and the disadvantaged, 433
  approaches to teaching, 294
  attitudes toward, 300
  basic list in, 296
  bibliography, 305
  correctness in, 361
  games, 302
  grouping, 296
  individualized, 317
  multi-level approach, 298
  patterns in, 288–90
  problems, causes of, 281–83
Stageberg, Norman C., 387
stenotype writing, 265, 267
Steptoe, John, 347–48
Story of Ferdinand, 407
Story of Language, The, 120
storytelling, 133–41

stress, 173, 389
Strickland, Ruth G., 170, 299, 354
suprasegmentals, 13, 388
Swimmy, 359
syntax, 4, 129, 390

tagmemics, 403
Taba, Hilda, 421
Talking Without Words, 342
taxonomies, 105, 427
Taxonomy of Educational Objectives, 40–46, 105
telegraphic stage in language, 13
Theodore and the Talking Mushroom, 104
Thomas, Owen, 412
Tiedt, Iris and Sidney, 374
timbre, 99
Toffler, Alvin, 358
Torrance, E. Paul, 59, 139, 180, 419, 433
Travers P. L., 362
treatment:
    foundational, 64, 74
    impressional, 64, 74
    skill, 63
Twain, Mark, 348
typing instruction, 260–62

units of action, 133
unit topics, 73
usage, 391
    diagnosis of errors in, 396
    problems in changing, 393
    realistic approach, 394, 396
    skill groups in, 396

values, 33
    of drama, 169
verbal obbligatos, 144
vocabulary:
    acquisition of, 353
    bibliography, 379
    changes in, 284

vocabulary (Cont.)
    developing describing words, 99, 126–29
    direct experience in, 363
    encouraging growth in, 171–73, 359
    games, 375
    precision in, 372
    reading affects, 362
    research studies on size of, 355
    types of, 356
    word families in, 290

Ward, Winifred, 172, 176
Weir, Ruth H., 354
What-if . . . ? Questions, 139, 148
Whitehead, Robert, 362
Wht's Yr Nm?, 309
Wilder, Laura I., 331
Wilt, Miriam E., 91, 210, 249
Wind in the Willows, The, 137, 198, 362
Wisconsin English Language Arts Curriculum Project, 408
Wolfe, Don M., 405
word families, 290
word list studies, 295
wordless books, 138
Words and Caligraphy for Children, 271
Words from the Myths, 337, 340, 372
writing:
    bibliography, 219–25
    creative, 432
    definition of creative, 193
    editing and correcting, 203
    electronetic, 73
    goals in, 433
    idea, 333
    mechanical, 335
    practical, 210–16
    sequential development in creative, 200
    stenotype, 265, 267
writing systems, studying, 262